ReFocus: The Films of William Wyler

ReFocus: The American Directors Series

Series Editors: Robert Singer, Frances Smith, and Gary D. Rhodes

Editorial board: Kelly Basilio, Donna Campbell, Claire Perkins, Christopher Sharrett, and Yannis Tzioumakis

ReFocus is a series of contemporary methodological and theoretical approaches to the interdisciplinary analyses and interpretations of neglected American directors, from the once-famous to the ignored, in direct relationship to American culture—its myths, values, and historical precepts.

Titles in the series include:

Preston Sturges Edited by Jeff Jaeckle and Sarah Kozloff

Delmer Daves Edited by Matthew Carter and Andrew Nelson

Amy Heckerling Edited by Frances Smith and Timothy Shary

Budd Boetticher Edited by Gary D. Rhodes and Robert Singer

Kelly Reichardt E. Dawn Hall

William Castle Edited by Murray Leeder

Barbara Kopple Edited by Jeff Jaeckle and Susan Ryan

Elaine May Edited by Alexandra Heller-Nicholas and Dean Brandum

Spike Jonze Edited by Kim Wilkins and Wyatt Moss-Wellington

Paul Schrader Edited by Michelle E. Moore and Brian Brems

John Hughes Edited by Timothy Shary and Frances Smith

Doris Wishman Edited by Alicia Kozma and Finley Freibert

Albert Brooks Edited by Christian B. Long

William Friedkin Steve Choe

Robert Altman Edited by Lisa Dombrowski and Justin Wyatt

Mary Harron Edited by Kyle Barrett

Wallace Fox Edited by Gary D. Rhodes and Joanna Hearne

Richard Linklater Edited by Kim Wilkins and Timotheus Vermeulen

Roberta Findlay Edited by Peter Alilunas and Whitney Strub

Richard Brooks Edited by R. Barton Palmer and Homer B. Pettey

William Wyler Edited by John M. Price

edinburghuniversitypress.com/series/refoc

ReFocus
The Films of William Wyler

Edited by John M. Price

EDINBURGH
University Press

Edinburgh University Press is one of the leading university presses in the UK. We publish academic books and journals in our selected subject areas across the humanities and social sciences, combining cutting-edge scholarship with high editorial and production values to produce academic works of lasting importance. For more information visit our website: edinburghuniversitypress.com

© editorial matter and organization John M. Price, 2023, 2024
© the chapters their several authors, 2023, 2024

Edinburgh University Press Ltd
13 Infirmary Street
Edinburgh EH1 1LT

First published in hardback by Edinburgh University Press 2023

Typeset in 11/13 Ehrhardt MT by
IDSUK (DataConnection) Ltd

A CIP record for this book is available from the British Library

ISBN 978 1 4744 1046 2 (hardback)
ISBN 978 1 3995 1047 9 (paperback)
ISBN 978 1 4744 1048 6 (webready PDF)
ISBN 978 1 4744 1049 3 (epub)

The right of John M. Price to be identified as editor of this work has been asserted in accordance with the Copyright, Designs and Patent Act 1988, and the Copyright and Related Rights Regulations 2003 (SI No. 2498).

Contents

List of Figures	vii
Acknowledgments	x
Notes on Contributors	xi

    Introduction: William Wyler—Chariot Races and Flower Shows   1
    John M. Price

Part I   Style

1 Wyler's Early Films: Evolution of the "Styleless Style"   25
    John M. Price
2 More than Meets the Eye: Perspectives on William Wyler and the Auteur Theory   54
    Kyle Barrowman
3 Traumatic History and the Prosthesis of Myth in Wyler's *The Best Years of Our Lives*   68
    Carol Donelan
4 Persistent Presence: Space and Time in the Films of William Wyler   88
    Francis Mickus

Part II   Collaboration, Genre, and Adaptation

5 Clash of the Titans: The Hidden Collaboration of William Wyler and David O. Selznick on *Carrie* (1952)   109
    Milan Hain
6 Narratives of Failure: *Dead End* (1937), *The Desperate Hours* (1955), and Gangsters in Distress   127
    Terrance H. McDonald

7 Wyler's *Wuthering Heights* (1939): Genre, Transnationalism, and the Adaptation of the Victorian Novel   143
Gabrielle Stecher

Part III Gender and Sexuality

8 William Wyler's *The Heiress* (1949) and the Unknown Woman   161
Agustin Zarzosa

9 *These Three*: Wyler and his Two Adaptations of *The Children's Hour*   176
Matthias Smith

Part IV War and Peace

10 A War of the People: Destruction, Community, and Hope in William Wyler's Wartime Films   191
Robert Ribera

11 Turning the Other Cheek: Wyler's Pacifism Trilogy—*Friendly Persuasion* (1956), *The Big Country* (1958), and *Ben-Hur* (1959)   208
John M. Price

Part V Global Wyler

12 William Wyler's Voyage to Italy: *Roman Holiday* (1953), Progressive Hollywood, and the Cold War   227
Anthony Smith

13 "Down Eros, Up Mars!": Post-Colonialism, Imperial Violence, and the Corrupting Influence of Hate in William Wyler's *Ben-Hur* (1959)   244
Kaitlin Pontzer

14 "Life Isn't Always What One Likes": The Unbearable Lightness of Royalty, and Other Stereotypes in *Roman Holiday* (1953)   258
Etienne Boumans

Filmography   278
Academy Awards for Acting under Wyler   281
Index   284

Figures

I.1	Early Wyler staging-in-depth (*The Shakedown*, 1929)	8
I.2	Deep focus dialogue (*Wuthering Heights*, 1939)	8
I.3	Deep focus dialogue (*The Little Foxes*, 1941)	9
I.4	Deep focus dialogue (*The Children's Hour*, 1961)	9
I.5	Deep focus demonstrating character's reaction to significant object (*The Little Foxes*, 1941)	10
I.6	Staging-in-depth without deep focus as to direct attention to one part of frame over another (*The Little Foxes*, 1941)	13
1.1	Staging-in-depth (*The Shakedown*, 1929)	28
1.2	Staging-in-depth with character movement within a static shot (*The Shakedown*, 1929)	29
1.3	Extreme staging-in-depth with static characters in the foreground and moving characters middle- and background (*The Shakedown*, 1929)	31
1.4	Fairly shallow staging-in-depth but with character arrangement allowing for single shot dialogue (*The Shakedown*, 1929)	31
1.5	Shot composition that allows action–reaction in one shot (*The Love Trap*, 1929)	33
1.6	Long take which allows actors to play the scene longer (*The Love Trap*, 1929)	33
1.7	Composition and shot length preventing the interruptions of edit points (*The Love Trap*, 1929)	34
1.8	Staging-in-depth and frame within a frame composition (*The Love Trap*, 1929)	35
1.9	Staging-in-depth without deep focus, but with rack focus between planes to shift attention (*The Love Trap*, 1929)	36

1.10	Staging-in-depth without deep focus, both characters in frame but the emotion of only one is important (*The Love Trap*, 1929)	37
1.11	Staging-in-depth and frame within a frame (*Hell's Heroes*, 1929)	39
1.12	Use of stairs (*These Three*, 1936)	41
1.13	Use of stairs (*The Heiress*, 1949)	41
1.14	Use of stairs (*Ben-Hur*, 1959)	42
1.15	The dynamic and confined nature of office activity displayed by the crossing movement of characters (*Counsellor at Law*, 1933)	43
1.16	Spatial dimension created by movement toward and away from camera and past other characters (*Counsellor at Law*, 1933)	44
1.17.1	The hectic nature of office activity demonstrated by movement in and out of doors (*Counsellor at Law*, 1933)	45
1.17.2	The hectic nature of office activity demonstrated by movement in and out of doors (*Counsellor at Law*, 1933)	45
1.18	Creating deep spatial reality without deep focus (*Counsellor at Law*, 1933)	46–7
1.19	Use of proto-film noir lighting to express character's dark emotions (*Counsellor at Law*, 1933)	48
1.20	Use of staging and lighting to express characters' emotional separation (*Counsellor at Law*, 1933)	48
1.21	The mirror limbo from *Citizen Kane* (1941) antedates . . .	50
1.22	. . . Wyler's use of the same effect in *The Good Fairy* (1935)	50
1.23	Staging-in-depth for humorous effect (*The Good Fairy*, 1935)	51
3.1	Character relations expose a postwar social reality premised in hierarchies of class, gender, and race difference (*The Best Years of Our Lives*, 1946)	75
3.2	Wyler maintains a relation between interiors and exteriors (*The Best Years of Our Lives*, 1946)	76
3.3	Viewers see the protagonists as well as what the protagonists see, simultaneously (*The Best Years of Our Lives*, 1946)	76
3.4	Wyler composes in depth, splitting viewer attention (*The Best Years of Our Lives*, 1946)	78
3.5	Wyler invites viewers to construct meaning from character relations, blocked and staged in deep space (*The Best Years of Our Lives*, 1946)	79
3.6	Acting style and lighting contributes to the creation of an expressionist reality, or inwardness, outwardly expressed (*The Best Years of Our Lives*, 1946)	83
3.7	Wyler uses style to achieve a verisimilar appearance of inner subjective reality (*The Best Years of Our Lives*, 1946)	84
4.1	The loneliness between the end of one life and the beginning of another (*Dodsworth*, 1936)	91
4.2	The ominous nature of an extremely low angle (*Dead End*, 1937)	91

4.3	Multiple planes and multiple frames (*Dead End*, 1937)	92
4.4	Hemming in the characters (*Detective Story*, 1951)	95
4.5	Hemming in the suspect (*Detective Story*, 1951)	96
11.1	Staging-in-depth to demonstrate dissimilar views toward violence simultaneously (*Friendly Persuasion*, 1956)	215
11.2	Fight scene shot with extremely long lens to express the futility of violence (*The Big Country*, 1958)	218
11.3	God's-eye expressing detachment from or disapproval of human violence (*The Big Country*, 1958)	219
11.4	Staging-in-depth and deep focus expressing the futility of kindness when faced with extreme violence . . . or perhaps the exploitation of violence for good (*Ben-Hur*, 1959)	222
14.1	Life isn't always what one likes (*Roman Holiday*, 1953)	263
14.2	Duty comes before pleasure (*Roman Holiday*, 1953)	266
14.3	*Flâneurs* are invisible to others (*Roman Holiday*, 1953)	269
14.4	"Positive" stereotypes of Italian locals (*Roman Holiday*, 1953)	270
14.5	The iconic Vespa ride from *Roman Holiday* (1953) lives on	271

Acknowledgments

I would like to thank the *ReFocus* series editors, especially Robert Singer whose support and assistance was indispensable to me. I would also like to express gratitude to everyone at Edinburgh University Press, especially Sam Johnson and Eddie Clark. A special thanks goes to Carol Donelan for her help in collecting and preparing still images, as well as all the contributing authors, not only for their efforts but also their enthusiasm for the works of William Wyler and for the desire which they shared with me to make this "greatest film director you've never heard of" better known to all. Lastly, I wish to acknowledge the debt this volume owes to my late wife, Theresa, whose enormous love continues to inspire and guide me.

Notes on Contributors

Kyle Barrowman has a Ph.D. from the Cardiff University School of Journalism, Media, and Culture, an M.A. from the University of Chicago in Cinema and Media Studies, and a B.A. from Columbia College in Film & Video. Dr. Barrowman has taught World Cinema, and Film and Cultural Theory at Cardiff University, Cinema Analysis and Criticism at Columbia College, and History of Cinema at DePaul University. He has been published in *Mise-en-scène: The Journal of Film & Visual Narration* 5.2 (2020), *Media Res* (2020), *The Journal of Ayn Rand Studies* 18.2 (2018), and *Offscreen* 22.7 (2018).

Etienne Boumans is an independent scholar, researching popular culture and the arts and their relationship to human rights, and is the chair of the evaluation committee on the Arts Flemish Parliament Act, as well as the former head of the European Parliament's committee secretariat on culture and education (2004–7). Boumans has published on European policies, human rights, film history and cultural heritage issues in *Limina: A Journal of Historical and Cultural Studies* 25.1 (2020), *The Quint: An Interdisciplinary Quarterly from the North*, 12.2 (2020), *The Apollonian – A Journal of Interdisciplinary Studies* 5 (2018), and was a contributing author to *The Encyclopedia of Racism in American Films* (2018).

Carol Donelan received her Ph.D. from the University of Massachusetts-Amherst in Comparative Literature (Film Studies), and her M.A. is in Film Studies and Comparative Literature from the University of Iowa. She has taught in the Department of Cinema & Media Studies at Carleton College since 1999. She has been published in *A Critical Companion to Stanley Kubrick* (2020), *A Critical Companion to James Cameron* (2019), *Film Criticism* 42.1 (2018), and *Quarterly Review of Film & Video* 35.1 (2018).

Milan Hain is an Assistant Professor and Area Head of Film Studies at the Department of Theater and Film Studies at Palacký University in Olomouc, Czech Republic. A former Fulbright visiting researcher at University of California, Santa Barbara, Dr. Hain is the author of *Hugo Haas a jeho (americké) filmy* [Hugo Haas and His (American) Films] and editor and co-author of three other books on cinema. His most recent articles have been published by *Jewish Film and New Media* 7.1 (2019) and *Journal of Adaptation in Film and Performance* 13.3 (2020).

Terrance H. McDonald has a Ph.D. from Brock University (St. Catherines), with a dissertation entitled "Mediated Masculinities: The Forms of Masculinity in American Genre Film." Dr. McDonald has taught Cinema Studies at the University of Toronto Mississauga and he has been published in *Men and Masculinities*, 21.1 (2018), and *From Deleuze to Posthumanism: Philosophies of Immanence* (2022). Dr. McDonald also currently has a chapter accepted by Edinburgh University Press for inclusion in *Refocus: The Films of Denis Villeneuve*.

Francis Mickus works at the Musée d'Orsay in Paris and is a current Doctoral Candidate in History at the University of Paris I, Pantheon-Sorbonne. Mickus holds a Masters in Art History from the Sorbonne's Institut National d'Histoire de l'Art (University of Paris IV) and a Maîtrise in Modern Letters from the Sorbonne Nouvelle (University Paris III). Mickus has written on American filmmakers such as Capra, Hitchcock, Welles, and Zemeckis, as well as on King Henry V and the relationship between history and images. He has been published in *The Quint* 13.2 (2021), *A Critical Companion to Robert Zemeckis* (2020), and *La revue du Cinéma* 4 (2006). Mickus affords this collection an integral international frame of reference toward an American filmmaker. Unlike the contributors who approach Wyler from a strictly cinematic expertise, Mickus brings great credentials in Art History and therefore a unique frame of reference on Wyler's visual style.

Kaitlin Pontzer received her Ph.D. from Cornell University in 2021. Before pursuing doctoral studies at Cornell, she studied the history of early modern England at Loyola University Chicago and Humanistic Studies at Saint Mary's College, Notre Dame. Dr. Pontzer works on political culture in early modern England and the British Empire. Her research interests include partisan politics, rhetoric, empire, history of emotions, and gender. She was a contributing writer for *Synapsis, A Health Humanities Journal* and has taught courses on the early modern death penalty at Cornell University. Her academic background in European History brings a unique perspective to Film Studies.

John M. Price has both a professional and an academic background in Film and Literature. He has a Ph.D. in Film and Literature from Northern Illinois University and a B.A. in English and Communications from the University of Notre Dame. Dr. Price has taught English at both Northern Illinois University and the University of Wisconsin-Eau Claire. He also has over twenty years of professional film and television production experience as a producer, director, scriptwriter, and lighting director. He has been published in *The Performativity of Villainy and Evil in Anglophone Literature and Media* (2021), *Literature/Film Quarterly*, 47:1 (2019), *Critical Insights: Alfred Hitchcock* (2017), *Jonathan Swift and Philosophy* (2017), and *Poli-Femo: Letteratura e Arti* (2016).

Robert Ribera received his Ph.D. from Boston University, focusing on Film Studies, Twentieth Century American History, and Twentieth Century American Art History. Dr. Ribera teaches Race & Class in Contemporary American Film, Animation History, Contemporary Female Directors, Film History, Documentary Film Production, Documentary History, The Cinema of Walt Disney, Contemporary and Classical Film Theory, Film Analysis, Advanced Film Analysis, Narrative Film Production, and Documentary Film of the 60s and 70s at Portland State University. He is the editor of *Martin Scorsese: Interviews (Revised and Updated)* (2017) and has a chapter in *ReFocus: The Films of Paul Schrader* (2020).

Anthony Smith received his Ph.D. from the University of Minnesota in American Studies and a B.A. from Boston College. He has been an Associate Professor at the University of Dayton since 2010. Dr. Smith has been published in *Roman Catholicism in America: A Thematic History* (2019), *Rivista luci e ombre*, 3.4 (2016), and *Catholics in the Movies* (2008).

Matthias Smith currently works at the Eye Filmmuseum in Amsterdam. He has also worked at the UCLA Rare Book School and performed film restoration for Columbus State University. He has taught Introduction to World Cinema, the Woman's Film genre, and Queer Cinema at the University of North Carolina, from which he received his master's in Art in Film Studies. Smith has also studied Film and Art History at the University of Oxford and spoken at the 2018 Stars and Screen Conference at Rowan University. His current research project concerns the surprisingly ahead-of-its-time *Anna und Elizabeth* (German, 1933), a lesbian drama, which has immersed Smith in several European film archives. Smith's academic interest include pre-Stonewall queer cinema, Golden Age Hollywood, and the Women's Film genre.

Gabrielle Stecher's areas of academic expertise are eighteenth- and nineteenth-century British literature and visual culture, museum studies, feminist literary criticism and art historiography, history, theory of the novel, and Victorian literature on film. She has presented at the American Society for Eighteenth-Century Literature, the Dickens' Universe Conference, and the British Women Writers Conference. Her current manuscript in progress is *Vanity Fair on Film*. Stecher received her Ph.D. in English in 2022 from the University of Georgia, and is now part of the faculty at Indiana University Bloomington. Stecher's expertise is essential to this collection as a chapter dealing specifically with Wyler's skills in adapting literature to the screen.

Agustin Zarzosa has a Ph.D. from the University of California, Los Angeles, Department of Film, Television and Digital Media, an M.A. from New York University in Cinema Studies, and is currently an Associate Professor and the Chair of Cinema Studies, School of Film and Media Studies at Purchase College. Dr. Zarzosa is the author of *Refiguring Melodrama in Film and Television: Captive Affects, Elastic Sufferings, Vicarious Objects* (2012), and he has also been published in *Cinema: Journal of Philosophy and the Moving Image* 2 (2011), *New Review of Film and Television Studies* 8.4 (2010), and *Colloquy: text theory critique* 13 (2007).

Introduction: William Wyler—Chariot Races and Flower Shows

John M. Price

He was an ace professional, a perfectionist. Were he alive in full spade today, we'd have rather better films than we actually have now.[1]

Every aspect of his films, he took great care over, probably at the expense of promoting his own name. It's extraordinary that his films are so famous, and so celebrated, more so than William Wyler, the name.[2]

A broad range of experience and the skills to handle diverse situations is usually thought to be an asset. However, it seems that William Wyler's mastery of a wide variety of film genres is precisely what caused him to be devalued by many film scholars. Indeed, the current status of and the problem with Wyler is summed up by Jan Herman, "Today, despite his extraordinary accomplishments, Wyler is hidden from view."[3] A similar assessment would lead columnist David B. Green, in 2015, to christen Wyler, "the most famous director you never heard of."[4] Wyler often proclaimed his desire to attempt every type of film. When asked why he accepted the project of the 1959 version of *Ben-Hur*, he replied: "I said it would be intriguing to see if I could make a Cecil B. DeMille picture."[5] The venue was not important to Wyler. The challenge for him was to tell a story in the clearest and most understandable way for the audience, regardless of the material. This diversity, however, worked against recognition as an auteur, for when he did agree to helm *Ben-Hur*, the auteurists declared it a blatantly crass attempt at simply making money.[6] Wyler did nothing to assuage them; he stated quite openly, "I thought this picture gonna make a lots of money, and maybe I'll get some of it."[7] A more serious reason for Wyler shepherding this project was given by producer Sam Zimbalist who "wanted Wyler to give . . . the picture what it needed—body, depth, intimacy—the sophisticated treatment for which

Wyler's work was prized."[8] So, despite those who may see Wyler as only a gifted craftsman and not a true artist, Zimbalist's desire for Wyler's hand was the recognition of the director's most valued skill—breathing life into characters and examining the complexities of human relationships.

In terms of Wyler's diversity, André Bazin admits that "there is no consistent motif in the work of Wyler."[9] However, Bazin does not see this as a stumbling block to Wyler appreciation: "I do not think that it is more difficult to recognize the signature of Wyler in just a few shots than it is to recognize the signatures of Ford, Fritz Lang, or Hitchcock."[10] Undoubtedly, Wyler detractors will point out that, unlike the cinematic auteurs previously mentioned, Wyler did not focus upon a certain theme and explore it over and over to examine all its possibilities (e.g. suspense and Hitchcock). Bazin sees the Wyler signature as something different than specific genres in specific settings exploring specific themes. "There is an evident fondness," Bazin says of Wyler, "for psychological scenarios set against social backgrounds . . . his work as a whole leaves us with the piercing and rigorous impression of a psychological analysis."[11] Wyler's talents as a filmmaker fall into three distinct capabilities: the ability to adapt material from the stage or literature to the screen and do so with cinematic vitality, the use of camera movement and staging-in-depth to create a type of screen "realism," and last, but perhaps most important, the gift of collaboration. Such collaborations were often contentious, but these amalgams generated some of the most awarded films of all time. Further analysis reveals that Wyler's collaborations also have three distinct strains: with producers, namely Samuel Goldwyn; with technological artists, like Gregg Toland; and with a wide range of performers.

Wyler felt that the genre should dictate the style. Therefore, in Wyler's opinion, a style of direction must be malleable in the face of each specific film.[12] The result is that those who have denied Wyler status among an elevated echelon of filmmakers have described his style as "styleless." If such an epithet is meant to suggest that Wyler's style is not intrusive, then Wyler would agree:

> The camera is a marvelous instrument [but] you have to use it with discipline . . . A director should not try to attract attention to himself [and] away from the actors and away from the story. He should attract attention to himself by making great films, great performances . . . Don't detract from the story or the actors. That's what the people have come to see. They did not come to see what you can do with a camera.[13]

This declaration should not be seen, however, as just Wyler's cinematic ethos. It is, in fact, the very definition of classic Hollywood's so-called "invisible style." This artistic propensity for self-effacement is of course a misnomer. Any film technique is only "invisible" by comparison with other techniques and by the smoothness of its execution. A camera movement may be less intrusive than a violent edit point, but both are highly manipulative. While Wyler's style emphasizes *mise en scène* over montage, the former and the latter are both constructs. The classic Hollywood style is not "invisible" nor is Wyler's style "styleless." Due to his beginnings in action-packed Westerns, Wyler developed early on a fondness for moving the camera, but this proclivity would also become wedded to an affinity for staging-in-depth and later deep focus. This volume of the *ReFocus* series intends to explore the many facets of the Wyler canon which comprise this style.

Whatever opinion one holds of the Wyler style, there is no denying that his formula for filmmaking yielded phenomenal success, not only at the box office but also in accumulated awards. Wyler's three Academy Awards for Best Director[14]—*Mrs. Miniver* (1942), *The Best Years of Our Lives* (1946), and *Ben-Hur* (1959)—are second only to John Ford's four wins for director. Wyler was also nominated for Best Director an additional nine times and three times as a producer.[15] He was also nominated for Best Director by the Directors Guild of America seven times and winning once for *Ben-Hur*.[16] Perhaps even more telling than his own awards are the myriad of acting Oscars that Wyler had helped his stars to achieve. No other film director has ever shepherded more actors and actress to Oscar-winning performances than Wyler—thirty-six nominations and fourteen wins, both in leading and supporting roles. Life-long friend, writer–director–actor John Huston[17] said that Wyler had "a genius for getting the truth out of an actor."[18] The list of his award-winning performers[19] bears witness not only to the wide range of genres that he mastered, but also to a proficiency with woman's stories and characters' psychology that few of his contemporaries possessed, and perhaps most significantly a dedication to collaborative craftsmanship and a belief that cinematic technique is there to forefront performance and enhance the story.

Of the all the influences on Wyler's style, no doubt one of the most formative was his immigrant experience. William Wyler was born Willy Wyler (the William would be added later in America) on July 1, 1902, in the province of Alsace-Lorraine, today part of France but then, and since France's defeat in the Franco-Prussian War, part of the recently unified Germany. Thus, at the time of Wyler's birth, his hometown was not known as Mulhouse, but Mülhausen. His mother, Melanie, was German, born in Stuttgart, and his father, Leopold, Swiss, and although his family and their town spoke German, Wyler's mother insisted that her family all spoke French as well. The family was Jewish and Wyler's mother, even before the advent of National-Socialism, felt that Germany had a long-standing history of antisemitism. Alsace found itself contested for and changing hands several times early in the First World War and young Willy was a first-hand witness to the ravages of war. Indeed, the Wylers had to take refuge in the cellar several times. Young Wyler was never a strong student, and showed little talent or desire to succeed at the family haberdashery business. Even when he was later sent to work in Paris, his strengths remained hidden and his mother did not know what to do with him. Fate took a hand, however, in the person of Wyler's uncle, Carl Laemmle. Laemmle was one of the founding owners of Universal Pictures, and he suggested that the family allow the young William, now eighteen, to immigrate to the United States and work for him in the movies. So Wyler moved to America in 1920 and began a career in the film industry, and after one year in New York with Universal's publicity office, he moved on to Hollywood, at age nineteen.

As his uncle's life would attest, Wyler was not unique as an immigrant filmmaker. The influx of European filmmakers had a decided influence on early Hollywood and the classic era. Yet, Wyler's specific experience may explain at least one thematic continuity in his films. While Wyler certainly valued his new homeland—he became a US citizen in 1928—his films are not full of the overly optimistic Americanism and belief in the individual and community to overcome oppression of big government and big business that characterized the films of another immigrant director, Frank Capra. Wyler's films were not visually demonstrative like German Expressionism nor concerned with exoticism like Josef von Sternberg. His films were not as dark as Erich von Stroheim nor as cynically humorous as Billy Wilder (a director whose name is often confused with Wyler). The territorial turmoil that Wyler saw, in the First World War, seems to have fostered films that deal with the individual struggling in circumstances that seem beyond their ability to handle. In addition, Wyler's "fascination with America and things American" but seen through "European sophistication and temperament," and executed with a visual style which appears at times detached, "suggest[s] the point of view of an interested, sympathetic outsider."[20] For Wyler, his insight into his adopted country bestows a viewpoint very different from a native-born perspective. Gregory Peck would describe Wyler as having European sensibilities but also a hundred percent American.[21] Wyler's characters are almost exclusively Americans, and, while his explorations of the human condition surely have universal application, they are uniquely set in and derived from American society. Even *Dodsworth* (1936), set largely outside of the United States, views European culture and society through the eyes of an American.

Wyler's early days in Hollywood, and the very nature of the business at that time, would serve to create the craftsmanship that is at the core of his style. Starting at the lowest level of moviemaking acquainted him with all aspects of production, helping him to develop a variety of skills, and he quickly became a third assistant director and then second assistant director. In fact, in a career harbinger, Wyler served as an assistant on the 1925 silent version of *Ben-Hur*. It was also in 1925, at the age of twenty-three, that Wyler got his first chance to direct. It was a two-reeler, running approximately twenty-four minutes, entitled *The Crook Buster* and was part of a group of Westerns called the Mustang series. He would go on to direct twenty-one such "shorts" for Universal in this series. Wyler himself would later describe this filmmaking situation as "a training school for directors . . . even girls . . . or any young fellow who showed he was eager, ambitious, and wanted to get . . . to direct."²² Wyler would direct one of these Westerns every week, each with a total budget of $2,000. The rate at which Hollywood "cranked out" these two-reelers—hundreds of them each year—as well as their rudimentary narratives, fostered an emphasis on developing techniques that were subservient to and enhancing of the story.

In 1926, six months after *The Crook Buster*, Wyler graduated to directing his first five-reeler, *Lazy Lightning*. As a five-reeler, *Lazy Lightning* is considered Wyler's first feature-length movie. He would do six of these as part of Universal's Blue Streak series of Westerns. After the Blue Streak series, Wyler did not wait long to expand his type of movies. His next three projects, all now considered to be lost films, did include two more Westerns, *Desert Dust* (1927) and *Thunder Riders* (1928), but the third, *Anybody Here Seen Kelly?* (1928), was his first non-Western, his first comedy, and his first film with a running length greater than an hour. It was also a film for which he was allowed to shoot largely on location in New York City. This gave the film an almost documentary appearance, and no doubt gave birth to the characterization of "Wyler realism."

Wyler's next film, *The Shakedown* (1929), was a "part-talkie," in that it was produced in both silent and sound versions. *The Shakedown* was once considered lost, but was found and restored in 1998. Wyler would then return to comedy with *The Love Trap* (1929), a film which also straddled the silent and sound eras in that it was silent except for the last few scenes. In the opinion of Michael Anderegg, it is *The Love Trap* that demonstrates Wyler's "growing maturity and self-confidence," as the young director "transition[s] from outdoor adventure to domestic intrigue with remarkable ease."²³ In *The Love Trap*, Wyler presents us with a female lead character who is more than a match for the male characters, "exposes sexual hypocrisy, [and] takes control of her life."²⁴ The deft handling of such a strong heroine would prove great practice for his later collaborations with Bette Davis and the development of her screen characters.

It would be the advent of sound, however, that would allow Wyler to further develop his style and advance his sense of realism. *Hell's Heroes* (1929) was not only Wyler's first "all-talkie," but was also Universal's first all-sound film. The film was shot outdoors on location—clearly an opportunity for Wyler to enhance realism. Furthermore, the story was told through the eyes of the "bad guys," which made it an unorthodox Western. This was an early and portending example of what would become one of Wyler's defining characteristics—the ability to take a familiar situation and look at it from a different, and often unique, perspective. As *Sunday Times* film critic, Stephen Armstrong, would put it, "Wyler would take standard tropes, and give them a subtle twist, to make them unusual."²⁵

In 1933, Wyler made *Counsellor at Law*, his first adaptation of a play to the screen, a talent that he would come to perfect throughout his career, and challenge him to find various ways to "open up" a stage presentation.²⁶ Wyler felt that "opening up" a play too much could destroy the vitality of the original story, but just recording a stage production was not the answer either. Wyler's solution was to hold a high regard for the source material without the restrictive yardstick of pure textual fidelity. This approach, whether adapting a novel or play, prevented his films from becoming static or monotonous. Anderegg, in praising Wyler's handling of theatrical material, opined, "that an unmoving camera focused on an actor's face can be as 'cinematic' as a cavalry charge."[27]

The entirety of *Counsellor at Law* takes place, as the title suggests, solely in the offices of a law firm. The cramped shooting space no doubt appealed to Wyler's love of realism, but also required that he develop more innovative ways to work in camera movement, and to continue to exploit long takes, which allow the actors to perform longer without cuts. Wyler's masterful control of the rapid-fire dialogue also adds to the film's verisimilitude. This film was also the first time that Wyler worked with a major Hollywood star, John Barrymore, and the accompanying ego. Often seen as one of Barrymore's better screen performances, Wyler extracts from him that character complexity which became Wyler's signature. Despite great difficulties (Barrymore's drinking), this would lay the groundwork for his later collaborations with some of the biggest name performers in Hollywood. Collaborations that, as stated previously, were more successful than any other director–actor relationships.

Although Wyler's teamwork with performers is the most famous aspect of his style, troublesome work relationships were not isolated to actors. One of the stormiest professional relationships of Wyler's career was with one of his bosses, the independent movie mogul Samuel Goldwyn. Wyler, despite having been given his first opportunity at Universal, had gone about as far as he could with the studio. Wyler's uncle had handed most of the decision-making responsibilities to his son Carl Jr., a producer who was incredibly tight with a dollar. In 1935, Wyler would make his last film for Universal, *The Good Fairy*, and it would be followed by *The Gay Deception* (1935), his only film for Fox. Then Wyler would embark on a new contract with Goldwyn. Despite their many disputes, their collaboration would unarguably produce some the finest films in both men's canons: *These Three* (1936), *Dodsworth* (1936), *Dead End* (1937), *Wuthering Heights* (1939), *The Westerner* (1940), *The Little Foxes* (1941), and *The Best Years of Our Lives* (1946). Goldwyn would also bring in Wyler to replace Howard Hawks on *Come and Get It* (1936)—a film that Wyler would disavow authorship of, saying that it was another director's film. When Goldwyn told Wyler that he was taking over for Hawks, Wyler initially refused. Goldwyn became enraged and threatened that he would see that Wyler never worked in Hollywood again. Wyler would relent and finish the picture, mostly because he knew that Goldwyn had the power to do just that.[28]

One of the many disagreements between Wyler and Goldwyn was the subject of realism. *Dead End*,[29] another stage adaptation,[30] is a story that contrasts wealthy city-dwellers with the slum life around them. Wyler had wanted to film this story on location for maximum reality. Goldwyn said "no" and built an elaborate set on a sound stage. When Wyler would "dirty up" the set to add more realism, Goldwyn would come in and demand it be cleaned up. It was clear that the difficulties between Wyler and Goldwyn stemmed from the fact that they were too much alike—both perfectionists who were certain that their way was the right way. Throughout their relationship, the debate among filmgoers was whether the quality of their motion pictures was due to the "Goldwyn touch" or the "Wyler touch." Goldwyn seemed to answer this when he once uttered to a reporter, "I made *Wuthering Heights*. Wyler only directed it."[31] There certainly is no denying that Goldwyn offered Wyler the chance to get away from Universal that he had sought, and the ability to tackle more prestigious projects, all with a producer who, unlike Laemmle Jr., was not afraid to spend money, if he were convinced it would equal high quality. However, it should also be pointed out that Wyler was the only director to ever win Goldwyn an Oscar for Best Picture.[32]

Wyler's first film for Goldwyn, *These Three*, would also be his first collaboration with cinematographer Gregg Toland, a working relationship that would codify the visual look of a Wyler film. Toland shot six of the seven films Wyler directed for Goldwyn (seven of eight if you include *Come and Get It*), and one of them, *Wuthering Heights*, resulted in Toland's only Academy Award. Needless to say, Toland is best known for his work on *Citizen Kane* (Orson Welles, 1941), but it should be noted that five of Wyler–Toland's collaborations (six including *Come and Get It*) occurred before Toland worked on *Kane*. Furthermore, *Kane* is often credited with techniques that Wyler and Toland had already exploited. Moreover, Wyler had displayed his love for staging-in-depth and expressive camera angles long before teaming up with Toland. This is evidenced by this shot from *The Shakedown* (Figure I.1), which shows Wyler staging deep shots even in his silent film days. What Toland added to Wyler's concept of shot composition was the ability to employ deep focus which, by keeping all planes within the frame in focus, allowed Wyler to "have action and reaction in the same shot, without having to cut back and forth from individual cuts of the characters,"[33] as superbly demonstrated by these shots from *Wuthering Heights* (Figure I.2), *The Little Foxes* (Figure I.3), and from *The Children's Hour* (1961)[34] (Figure I.4). While most often employed by Wyler to see two characters' emotions at the same time, it could also be used to show a character's reaction to the introduction of a significant object without cutting to each in turn (Figure I.5). The sense in which Wyler and Toland's technique is an example of realism is that, by having different action take place on the screen simultaneously, the spectator, making their own choices as to what to look at, becomes the editor of the scene.[35] This vision selection, of course, mimics the way in which we view the world. This visual realism would support the wide range of Wyler stories, which Ian Nathan, contributing editor for Empire magazine, describes as, "Real people in real kinds of worlds."[36]

Figure I.1 Early Wyler staging-in-depth (*The Shakedown*, 1929)

Figure I.2 Deep focus dialogue (*Wuthering Heights*, 1939)

Figure I.3 Deep focus dialogue (*The Little Foxes*, 1941)

Figure I.4 Deep focus dialogue (*The Children's Hour*, 1961)

Figure I.5 Deep focus demonstrating character's reaction to significant object (*The Little Foxes*, 1941)

Much less tranquil than Wyler's collaboration with Toland, and more famous as well, was his highly successful teamwork with performers. During Wyler's contract with Goldwyn, he was loaned out to Warner Bros. for *Jezebel* (1938). This would be the first of three times that he would work with Bette Davis. Their relationship would generate three great performances, one Academy Award for Best Actress, and an equally as tempestuous personal love affair. When Davis won her second Oscar for *Jezebel* (1938), she said, "He made my performance … It was all Wyler."[37] Even forty years later, at the American Film Institute's ceremony for Davis's lifetime achievement award, she still credited Wyler's direction of her performance in that film as not only making her a better actress, but also catapulting her to the status of superstar.[38]

However, Davis also acknowledged that Wyler was "an amazingly inarticulate man."[39] This characterization would be backed up by Charlton Heston, who said that during the filming of *Ben-Hur*, Wyler's direction amounted to, "You gotta be better."[40] Barbara Streisand would observe that "he couldn't tell you how to do it differently; he would just tell you to do it again."[41] He may not have been able to convey to his stars what he wanted from them, but Wyler always said, "I'll know it when I see it."[42] The confrontations between performers and Wyler was due to his unrelenting perfectionism and his inability to express what he wanted from an actor. Despite this inarticulation, his on-set repetitions would always yield outstanding results, but it also led to his reputation as "forty-take Willy." Davis related that once after endless takes, which she felt had no distinctions, she decided to look at the dailies, and not only was there clear, but subtle differences between the takes, but that the take Wyler had proclaimed the best was in fact the best.[43] The perfectionist that was Wyler was the result of a strong eye for detail—nothing escaped his scrutiny. His style was stern and uncompromising, taciturn and reluctant to praise.[44] Davis would describe Wyler's style as "charming and treacherous,"[45] a "combination of sympathy and strength."[46]

Davis recalls that Wyler was always saying that he was not running an acting school. Laurence Olivier, whose strong stage background would lead him to, in response to Wyler's criticism during the filming of *Wuthering Heights*, describe cinema as an "anemic little medium."[47] Years later, however, Olivier would credit Wyler with making him into a screen actor, and he would even work with Wyler again on *Carrie* (1952). Perhaps, Wyler had indeed been running a school for actors. In addition to Wyler's berating of Olivier, he once made Audrey Hepburn cry during her first film performance. Greer Garson, because of Wyler's reputation, did not want at first to do *Mrs. Miniver*. The story is that she sent Wyler a velvet glove and a note that said, "to use on Miss Garson."[48] Despite her hesitations at working with Wyler, she would win an Oscar under his direction. The strangest relationship, however, was the warlike conditions on the set of *The Good Fairy* (1935) between Wyler and leading lady Margaret Sullavan. Such was their on-set animosity that all were shocked when Wyler and Sullavan married. Unfortunately, but perhaps predictably, the marriage would last only two years.

Wyler once said, "Mediocrity in films is the direct result of playing it safe ... A picture without an idea is a picture without vitality."[49] Fittingly, as Wyler's career progressed, there is an increasingly clearer "message" in his works. With *Dead End*, for example, Wyler was thrilled to learn that his gritty realism had instigated serious legislation for urban renewal. However, in a Wyler film, social significance is not always tied to a social issue. Many times, the social statement is simple observation of the human condition, and, more specifically, how the individual struggles against what seems to be overwhelming conditions. Wyler's aim was to present these relationships with considerable compassion. Wyler was certainly able to achieve this with *These Three*.

These Three was based on Lillian Hellman's play *The Children's Hour*. This play dealt with the story of a rich, brattish schoolgirl who ruins the lives of her two schoolmistresses by accusing them of being lesbians. Both Goldwyn and Wyler knew that such a topic would not make it past the censors of that day, so the title was changed to *These Three* and the rumor the child starts is a more conventional, heterosexual, triangular love affair between the two ladies and the fiancé of one of them. Surprisingly, Hellman had no problem with this change, as her work on the screenplay attests, because she felt the play had never been about prejudice against homosexuals, but the destructive, wildfire-like force that a malicious lie can be. Wyler would have a chance to revisit Hellman's original narrative when, twenty-five years later, he directed his own remake, this time keeping the original title, *The Children's Hour*. The restoration of the lesbian aspect may well be simply the result of an increasing societal acceptance of the topic and not an increasing boldness on the part of Wyler toward difficult issues, but whichever it was, as Herman would say of Wyler, he "managed to combine poetic truthfulness with social awareness," and do so with mass appeal.[50] In fact, by 1939, it was said of Wyler that

> His films steadily grow in stature: his content becomes deeper, his execution more thoughtful, his problems more vital and relevant. Purposefulness lifts his films higher and higher out of the ordinary ... [and] reveal[s] his increasing social awareness, sharper sensitivity and penetration into character, and conscious effort at organic unity.[51]

Wyler had definitely achieved his major goal in leaving Universal: he was now making prestigious pictures.

In addition to mastering successful adaptations of plays, Wyler would tackle an adaptation of the Sinclair Lewis novel, *Dodsworth*. As a performer's director, Wyler would be reunited on this film with Walter Huston, whom he had directed back in one of his earliest sound efforts, *A House Divided* (1931). In both films, Huston's performance is multi-layered, and for *Dodsworth*, he would be nominated for an Oscar for Best Actor. This was also Wyler's first nomination for Best Director. *Dodsworth* was a serious, and at the time, uniquely penetrating examination of marital struggles, and in an example of art reflecting real life, during this film, Wyler would begin to divorce his first wife Margaret Sullavan. Two years later, he would marry his second wife Margaret Tallichet. He would have five children with "Talli" and remain married to her until his death.

After again successfully bringing page to screen, this time with Emily Brontë's *Wuthering Heights*, Wyler returned to his origins with his first Western since *Hell's Heroes*, *The Westerner*. Wyler would again utilize gritty realism, only now to give his old genre a new perspective—a deglamorized West. An example of this is seen in one of the most realistic fight scenes in any Western. *The Westerner* was also the first time Wyler worked with Gary Cooper, but it was the supporting performance by Walter Brennan that took home the Oscar for this film. This film also features another example of a reoccurring theme for Wyler, the troublesome nature of male friendships.

In 1940, Wyler would also work again with Davis in *The Letter* (an adaptation of a Somerset Maugham novel), and the following year, work with her for the third and last time in *The Little Foxes* (another adaptation of a Hellman play). During these films, Wyler's reputation was continually enhanced: "not only is [he] a proficient filmmaker but . . . [he] has an eye for characterization and human relationships."[52] It is interesting, for example, that in *The Good Fairy*, Wyler "was roundly chastised for overindulging in closeups . . . but his prodigal use of the same device in *Wuthering Heights* four years later was accepted without a murmur."[53] Despite Toland's augmentation of deep focus to Wyler's *mise en scène*, Wyler knew when and when not to make use of it. Case in point is the famous scene (Figure I.6) in *The Little Foxes* where Davis's character sits unassisting her husband, whose heart is failing. He crawls up the stairs in the background, out of focus. Davis, in the foreground, is in sharp focus. Wyler, through Toland, could have had both actions in focus, but he knew that the essence of the scene was in Davis's face.

The Little Foxes can be seen as a great dividing point between two distinct halves of Wyler's career. As war in Europe raged on, many felt that Wyler's next film, *Mrs. Miniver*, was his attempt to inch the United States from its isolationism. Wyler himself considered the film to be a call-to-arms. The story of a supposedly average British family and their struggles to survive

Figure I.6 Staging-in-depth without deep focus as to direct attention to one part of frame over another (*The Little Foxes*, 1941)

the Nazi blitz, which must have reminded Wyler of his own wartime experiences as a child in Alsace, was more fortunate than such films as *Sergeant York* (Howard Hawks, 1941).[54] Unlike other films accused of war-mongering propaganda, *Mrs. Miniver* was released in the summer of 1942, well after Pearl Harbor. However, during the pre-production of *Mrs. Miniver*, there certainly were concerns as to whether or not it would be seen as pushing the United States into the war and therefore a violation of the Neutrality Act. Being Jewish, Wyler was naturally concerned with Nazi aggression, but he, like many studio executives, had to be careful not to be seen as advancing a strictly Jewish cause. Despite these fears, *Mrs. Miniver*, as Neil Norman characterizes it, "etched its way into the hearts of the public."[55]

Mrs. Miniver was to win Wyler his first Academy Award for Best Director. However, he would not be present to accept it; he had joined the US Army Air Corps. During the war, he would fly on bombers, including during combat, and make two documentary films for the military to show the public, *The Memphis Belle* and *Thunderbolt*. Four other directors, Ford, Capra, John Huston, and George Stevens would also leave Hollywood to lend their filmmaking skills to the war effort. While all these men were greatly affected by their close interaction with combat and its aftermath, and certainly their work after the war was significantly altered, Wyler was also physically injured. The noise in the aircrafts had caused him to go deaf. Wyler was certain this would end his career. How could he direct if he could not hear? Toland came to the rescue and rigged up for Wyler a special sound device that would allow him to hear dialogue. Wyler did eventually regain partial hearing in one ear, but this experience as a wounded war veteran was to prompt what many would consider his greatest film ever, *The Best Years of Our Lives* (1946). This powerful story of the struggles of returning veterans to assimilate back into their homelives would be Wyler's last film with both Goldwyn and Toland and would win Wyler his second Oscar for directing.[56] In 1945, fellow director, Frank Capra, had started a production company for independent directors and producers called Liberty Films and Wyler signed on. While Liberty would prove unsuccessful, only producing two films, independent production was the inevitable wave of the future, and on Wyler's next seven films, beginning with *The Heiress*, he would be producer as well as director.[57]

Despite the triumph of the human spirit which *The Best Years of Our Lives* displays, there is no mistaking the fact that, after the war, Wyler's films were darker, not necessarily more pessimistic, but certainly his characters were enduring ever greater seemingly insurmountable situations. In addition, an element of ambiguity had been introduced to his films. In 1949, Olivia de Havilland won an Academy Award for Best Actress in *The Heiress* (yet another stage to screen adaptation), but her character leaves the audience, at the end of the film, with some doubt as to whether she has triumphed or not. Increasingly dark, some have described *Detective Story* (1951) and *The Desperate Hours* (1955) as Wyler's foray into the genre of film noir, but this label is extremely debatable. They do both deal with crime, but so does *Dead End*. In terms of characters, Kirk Douglas in *Detective Story* possesses some of the attributes of the film noir "hero," but neither film has what could be called a femme fatale. In the end, these two films may again demonstrate Wyler's propensity for altering recognizable scenarios, or, as Norman puts it, Wyler was "being an innovator in a genre that is already established."[58]

This period of his career, however, was not without its lighter and brighter moments as well. Wyler's exceedingly popular romantic comedy, *Roman Holiday* (1953), was not only the screen debut of Audrey Hepburn, but her performance was also the fourth time that Wyler directed his leading lady to an Oscar for Best Actress. In 1956, Wyler would make his first color film, *Friendly Persuasion*. In 1958, he would make his first widescreen effort, *The Big Country*. The adjustment to the 2.35:1 screen aspect ratio was not a small hindrance to Wyler's trademark composition.

> Accustomed as he was to employing the screen as an area of three dimensional space, with height, depth, and width, he found himself in the late 1950s trying to deal with a screen image that seemed to eliminate everything except width.[59]

Wyler's typically tight narratives and tight shot composition would need to be adapted, or even jettisoned, in the realm of a widescreen epic. How successfully he did this in *The Big Country* is debatable, but there would be no questioning the success of his next colossal production. *Ben-Hur* generated, among its many awards, Wyler's third statue for directing and would hold the record for most Academy Awards until 1997 and then it was only tied. Furthermore, the box-office success of this unfamiliar genre for Wyler would also help MGM to avoid bankruptcy.

In his last five motion pictures, Wyler would end one with a suicide, *The Children's Hour*; deal with a man so obsessed with a woman that he abducts her in *The Collector* (1965); and attempt to combine suspense with racial comment in his last film *The Liberation of L.B. Jones* (1970). *The Collector*, the most anomalous and darkest of all his films, was a return to the more confined visuality of early films like *The Storm* and *Counsellor at Law*, especially after the wide-openness of *The Big Country* and *Ben-Hur*. Despite these rather heavy ventures, Wyler still mixed in, among these darker films, a heist comedy, *How to Steal a Million* (1966), his first comedy since *The Gay Deception* in 1935, and a musical *Funny Girl* (1968). Wyler, up to the very end of his career, was obviously still trying to make as many different types of movies as he could.

One would think that Wyler's military service would have proved his dedication to his country beyond any question, but he would, as would many members of Hollywood, experience strong challenges to his patriotism after the war. Wyler's history with blacklisting seems paradoxical. On one hand, he, John Huston, and other Hollywood personages formed the Committee for the First Amendment, which went to testify before Congress, but when suggestions of "guilt by association" began to attach themselves to Wyler, he wrote a memo making it clear that he was not a Communist nor would he work with any. This proclamation, and the fact that his brother Robert worked on the rewrite of *Friendly Persuasion*, tainted his efforts to not give screen credit to the original, and blacklisted, screenwriter. Still, it must be pointed out that Wyler did make an open declaration that, in his opinion, the House Un-American Activities Committee (HUAC) was not only destroying creativity in Hollywood but inflicting their concept of Americanism on others.[60] As for Wyler's concept of Americanism, Herman observes that Wyler's films combined "a compassionate honesty and a dramatic intensity in their vision of American life."[61] Wyler's Americanness, however, goes far beyond just his topics, settings, and themes. Bazin states,

> Wyler wants only to allow him [the viewer] . . . to see everything [and] . . . make choices . . . This is an act of loyalty toward the viewer, a pledge of dramatic honesty . . . Wyler aims at being liberal and democratic, like the consciences both of American viewers and of characters.[62]

Bazin's comment asserts that the Wyler style of filmmaking is the very embodiment of what it means to be an American.

During his retirement, Wyler was given the Life Achievement Award by the American Film Institute in 1976. Upon accepting this honor, he told the audience that he had not stopped making films—his wife, Talli, and he travelled greatly and he always took his home camera with him. He took that bit of information as an opportunity to address the issue that had always dogged him and still does to this day. "By no longer being burdened with great and famous cinematographers . . . by doing everything myself, I have at last become the complete and genuine auteur," and while acknowledging that during his career, he had not been an auteur, nonetheless, he was "one of the few directors who can pronounce the word correctly."[63] William Wyler died in 1981 at the age of seventy-nine; his legacy, a career in cinema that spanned over forty-five years and included, depending on whose list you look at, thirty-seven feature films.

In identifying Wyler's legacy, Stephen Armstrong would describe him as quite simply a pioneer in storytelling.[64] Herman says: "His pictures not only resonate with poetry and humor, they offer psychological maturity and sophisticated treatment of character more typical of literature than movies."[65]

Beyond these observations, the Wyler style contains something undefinable. Fellow director, Billy Wilder, said that "there was an instinct in him that told him when it was right, when it felt true."⁶⁶ Streisand may well have identified the secret to Wyler's film instinct: "He was wonderful because he was the audience."⁶⁷

In addition to providing an in-depth analysis of Wyler and his works, this volume of the *ReFocus* series attempts to augment American views on an American director with international perspectives as well. In the first part, entitled "Style," Chapter One, "Wyler's Early Films: Evolution of the 'Styleless Style,'" looks at Wyler's late silent and early sound films and points out how the development of an embryonic style can be detected even at this stage. Chapter Two defends not only the legitimacy of the auteur theory, but Wyler's rightful place among filmmakers who have achieved the moniker "auteur." It is entitled "More than Meets the Eye: Perspectives on William Wyler and the Auteur Theory." Chapter Three of this part is "Traumatic History and the Prosthesis of Myth in Wyler's *The Best Years of Our Lives*." This chapter, through a close study of Wyler's first postwar film, will argue that Wyler rehabilitates classical Hollywood cinema through the use of, what Bazin termed, "reborn realism." The last chapter in this part is entitled "Persistent Presence: Space and Time in the Films of William Wyler," which argues that the past looms large in the films of William Wyler, that is, that many of Wyler's works, including *Wuthering Heights*, *Mrs. Miniver*, *The Heiress*, and *Ben Hur*, are structured around an inescapable past.

"Collaboration, Genre, and Adaptation" is the second part and contains Chapter Five, "Clash of the Titans: The Hidden Collaboration of William Wyler and David O. Selznick on *Carrie* (1952)." This chapter suggests that one of the reasons for the film *Carrie*'s critical and financial failure was the interference of producer David O. Selznick, and that this relationship exemplifies the problematic nature of collaboration. Also in this part is Chapter Six which is entitled "Narratives of Failure: *Dead End* (1937), *The Desperate Hours* (1955), and Gangsters in Distress." This chapter evaluates William Wyler's so-called gangster films in relation to existing discourses on the genre and characterizes both films as narratives of distress, through which Wyler reflects socio-cultural issues involving masculinity. Also in this part is Chapter Seven, "Wyler's *Wuthering Heights*: Genre, Transnationalism, and the Adaptation of the Victorian Novel." This chapter argues that Wyler's film adaptation of Emily Brontë's classic serves as a fresh case study for the Victorian novel-as-film relationship and through a transnational lens reveals the influence of Wyler, a foreign-born director, on the adaptation of a quintessential Victorian novel and yet within the Hollywood tradition.

Part III, "Gender and Sexuality," contains Chapter Eight, "William Wyler's *The Heiress* (1949) and the Unknown Woman," which asserts that *The Heiress* caps Wyler's significant role in women's films during the 1930s and 1940s. This chapter, in referring to a small subgenre, which Stanley Cavell calls, "the melodrama of the unknown woman," suggests that *The Heiress* and this genre are not concerned with the questions we associate with melodrama (the recognition of virtue) but rather with stoicism (self-reliance, independence of mind, and freedom from the world). Chapter Nine, "*These Three*: Wyler and His Two Adaptations of *The Children's Hour*" delves into the differences in each of Wyler's versions of Lillian Hellman's play and his approach to queer representation in a somewhat more liberated censorship of the early 1960s.

Part IV is entitled "War and Peace." In it, Chapter Ten, by examining *Mrs. Miniver* (1942), and *The Best Years of Our Lives* (1946), as well as Wyler's wartime documentary films, *The Memphis Belle: A Story of a Flying Fortress* (1944), *The Fighting Lady* (1944), and *Thunderbolt* (1945, released 1947), argues that, rather than producing a muddled political message, the overall feeling of Wyler's wartime films, both his fictional narratives and his documentaries, is a clear call to action—something must be done—and a call to a community—it must be done *together*. This chapter is entitled "A War of the People: Destruction, Community, and Hope in William Wyler's Wartime Films," and asserts that these films combine a sense of duty with the breaking down of social barriers, and by finding the common ground of self-sacrifice, and the healing of wounds both seen and unseen. Chapter Eleven, "Turning the Other Cheek: Wyler's Pacifism Trilogy—*Friendly Persuasion* (1956), *The Big Country* (1958), and *Ben-Hur* (1959)," contends that Wyler's "pacifism trilogy" presents audiences with an insight into Wyler's complex sentiments on non-violence, and that over the course of these three films, there is an evolutionary trajectory in the director's depiction of pacifism and its efficacy.

This Introduction has stressed the influence of the European immigrant experience on Wyler's concept of Americanism. As stated previously, the vast majority of his films deal with American characters in American situations, but in his later career, Wyler would adventure back to Europe in terms of not only shooting on location, but also expanding to more international themes. In addition to *Roman Holiday*, Wyler would also make *The Collector* set in the UK and *How to Steal a Million* set in Paris. The final part of this volume examines this adjusted perspective and is entitled "Global Wyler." In it, Chapter Twelve, "William Wyler's Voyage to Italy: *Roman Holiday*, Progressive Hollywood, and the Cold War," explores the complex history of Hollywood, politics, and transnationalism in Wyler's *Roman Holiday*, and argues for Wyler's significance at the intersection of the central developments of postwar cinema, the rise of Hollywood on the Tiber, the eclipse of neorealism, and the Red Scare in America. Chapter Thirteen provides a post-colonial examination of Wyler's *Ben-Hur* (1959). It demonstrates how this widescreen epic presents commentary on Empire, both as a critique of imperial power and a warning against post-colonial cycles of violence. This chapter applies scholarship in the academic field of History to Film Studies. This chapter is entitled, "Down Eros, Up Mars!": Post-Colonialism, Imperial Violence, and the Corrupting Influence of Hate in William Wyler's *Ben-Hur* (1959)." The final chapter also examines *Roman Holiday*, but focuses on the film's pervasive stereotypical representations of, inter alia, royalty and nobility, rich folk, servants, women, American gentlemen, and Italian locals and locales. This chapter will also contextualize such stereotypes through other films, such as *The Bicycle Thieves* (De Sica, 1948), *Journey in Italy* (Rossellini, 1954), and, a recent remake of *Roman Holiday*, *Rome in Love* (Bross, 2019). This chapter is entitled "'Life Isn't Always What One Likes': The Unbearable Lightness of Royalty, and Other Stereotypes in *Roman Holiday* (1953)."

The arguably best observance of Wyler is in a 2020 article written by Kenneth Lonergan for the Criterion Collection. The article describes the sentimental, yet effective, presentation of a local flower contest in *Mrs. Miniver*. Lonergan points out, as this introduction has, that Wyler was downgraded by many for "lacking a personal stamp," but that perhaps that was "to be expected when you can make a flower show as exciting as a chariot race," and that there certainly is "genius in a director who can breathe life into either one."[68]

NOTES

1. Derek Malcolm, film critic, in *The Directors: William Wyler*, directed by Lyndy Saville (3DD Entertainment, 2018).
2. Neil Norman, film critic, in ibid.
3. Jan Herman, *A Talent for Trouble: The Life of Hollywood's Most Acclaimed Director, William Wyler* (New York: G. P. Putnam's Sons, 1995), 4.
4. David B. Green, "This Day in Jewish History, 1981: The Most Famous Director You Never Heard of Dies," *Haaretz* (July 27, 2015), <https://www.haaretz.com/jewish/1981-a-directing-great-dies-1.5379346> (last accessed July 28, 2022).
5. *Directed by William Wyler*, directed by Aviva Slesin. (Topgallant Prod., 1986).
6. Wyler said "All of the artistes, they will never forgive me for *Ben-Hur*. For me to have made one of the most successful commercial pictures in the history of the business is an unforgivable sin" (see Curtis Hanson, "William Wyler, Pt. 1. An Interview," *Cinema* 3, no. 5 (Summer 1967): 23).
7. *Directed by William Wyler*.
8. Herman, 395.
9. André Bazin, "William Wyler, or the Jansenist of Directing," in *Bazin at Work: Major Essays and Reviews from the Forties and Fifties*, trans. Alain Piette and Bert Cardullo, ed. Bert Cardullo (New York: Routledge, 1997), 1. (Originally published as "William Wyler ou le janséniste de la mise en scene," in *Revue du Cinéma* no. 10 (February. 1948)).
10. Bazin, 2
11. Bazin, 1.

12. Hanson, 23.
13. Hanson, 28.
14. Wyler might well have won a fourth Best Director Oscar as he was originally slated to direct *The Sound of Music*, but backed out. The film did go on to win Best Director for Robert Wise.
15. For a complete list of Wyler's films and his Academy Award wins and nominations, see "Filmography" and "Academy Awards for Acting under Wyler" at the back of the book.
16. Wyler's other Directors Guild of America (DGA) nominations, in addition to his win for *Ben-Hur*, were for *Detective Story*, *Roman Holiday*, *Friendly Persuasion*, *The Big Country*, *The Children's Hour*, and *Funny Girl*. Wyler might have received additional nominations for his earlier films, but the DGA only made their first award for directing in 1948.
17. John Huston would work as co-writer for three Wyler films: *The Storm* (1930), *A House Divided* (1931), and *Jezebel* (1938).
18. *Directed by William Wyler*.
19. For a complete list of performers who won acting Oscars under Wyler's direction, see "Academy Awards for Acting under Wyler" at the end of the book.
20. Michael A. Anderegg, *William Wyler* (Boston: Twayne, 1979), 21.
21. *Directed by William Wyler*.
22. Hanson, 25.
23. Anderegg, 26.
24. Anderegg, 27.
25. *The Directors: William Wyler*.
26. "Opening up" a play means moving the story out of the confines of its stage-limited locations.
27. Anderegg, 106.
28. Arthur Marx, *Goldwyn: A Biography of the Man Behind the Myth* (New York: W.W. Norton & Co., 1976), 225.
29. *Dead End* would star Humphrey Bogart, at a time in his career when he was still playing "bad guys," and Bogie's screen persona fit well this play about impoverished street gangs and other criminals.
30. *Dead End* was another chance for Wyler to work with Lillian Hellman. This time she would be the screenwriter for someone else's play. The highly successful play *Dead End* was written by Sidney Kingsley.
31. Roger Ebert, "The Directors," *Roger Ebert* (January 21, 1968), <https://www.rogerebert.com/roger-ebert/the-directors> (last accessed July 28, 2022).
32. Of the myriads of films that Goldwyn produced, only eight were nominated for Best Picture, and of that eight, five were directed by Wyler.
33. William Wyler, "No Magic Wand," *The Screen Writer* 2, no. 9 (February 1947): 10, <https://archive.org/details/screenwriterjun102scre/page/n457/mode/2up> (last accessed July 28, 2022).
34. Toland was not the Director of Photography for *The Children's Hour*, which shows how the effect of deep focus, by 1961, was within the purview of most cinematographers.
35. Wyler, 10.
36. *The Directors: William Wyler*.
37. Bette Davis, *The Lonely Life: An Autobiography* (New York: G. Putnam's Sons, 1962), 177.
38. "Bette Davis Accepts the AFI Life Achievement Award in 1977," *American Film Industry*, <https://www.youtube.com/watch?v=UHiaRq3fpEc> (last accessed August 1, 2022).
39. *Directed by William Wyler*.
40. *Directed by William Wyler*.
41. *Directed by William Wyler*.

42. James Spada, *More Than a Woman: The Intimate Biography of Bette Davis* (New York: Bantam Books, 1993), 131.
43. Spada, 131–2.
44. Spada, 139.
45. Spada, 135
46. Gary Carey, "The Lady and the Director: Bette Davis and William Wyler," *Film Comment* 6, no. 3 (Fall 1970): 19.
47. Scott A. Berg, "*Wuthering Heights*," *The New York Times*, February 19, 1989, 86.
48. Carey ("The Lady and the Director," 19) considers this story to be apocryphal and indeed different authors have related the story with slight variations in the details. Herman (*A Talent for Trouble*, 231) says that the message was on a card that read, "For the iron hand of William Wyler." Axel Madsen (*William Wyler: the Authorized Biography*, New York: Crowell, 1973, 215) related the same message Herman does, but says that the words were actually engraved on the buttons of the gloves.
49. "Don't Play 'Safe' on Pix-Wyler," *Variety* 176, no. 5 (October 12, 1949): 20.
50. Herman, 85.
51. Jacob Lewis, *The Rise of the American Film: A Critical History* (New York: Harcourt, Brace and Co., 1939), 490–1.
52. Lewis, 490.
53. Hermine Rich Isaacs, "William Wyler: Director with a Passion and a Craft," *Theatre Arts* 31, no. 2 (February 1947): 21.
54. In 1941, the Nye-Clark Senate Committee accused Hollywood (*Sergeant York* and seven other films) of violating the Neutrality Act by making propaganda films that promoted US intervention in Europe. *Sergeant York* was initially released in the summer of 1941 and because of the Committee was forced to pull the film from release. It would subsequently be re-released to tremendous success in 1942.
55. *The Directors: William Wyler*.
56. *The Best Years of Our Lives* would also win Harold Russell an Oscar for Best Supporting Actor. Russell was not an actor. He was a real-life war veteran who had lost both hands in the war.
57. The selling of Liberty Films to Paramount would lead to a deal between Paramount and Wyler to produce and direct five films: *The Heiress, Detective Story, Carrie, Roman Holiday,* and *The Desperate Hours*.
58. *The Directors: William Wyler*
59. Anderegg, 200.
60. Gordon Kahn, *Hollywood on Trial: The Story of the Ten Who Were Indicted* (New York: Boni and Gaer, 1948), 221.
61. Herman, 85.
62. Bazin, 9.
63. "William Wyler Accepts the AFI Life Achievement Award in 1976," *American Film Industry*. <https://www.youtube.com/watch?v=oxwf_ZNl3PY> (last accessed July 28, 2022).
64. *The Directors: William Wyler*.
65. Herman, 2.
66. *Directed by William Wyler*.
67. *Directed by William Wyler*.
68. Kenneth Lonergan, "Depth of Vision: The Grounded Cinema of William Wyler," *The Criterion Collection* (January 3, 2020), <https://www.criterion.com/current/posts/6745-depth-of-vision-the-grounded-cinema-of-william-wyler> (last accessed July 28, 2022).

PART I
Style

CHAPTER I

Wyler's Early Films: Evolution of the "Styleless Style"

John M. Price

> I think that the story dictates its own style rather than the director's style dictating the story.[1]

Classic Hollywood, a period that helped to define cinematic grammar, sought to help the audience forget that they were watching a movie. Cinematic techniques were only supposed to serve the narrative, not draw attention to themselves, and certainly not to the director's "brushstrokes." This approach to filmmaking, of course, stands in stark contrast to the Soviet school of montage, which said that the essence of cinema was to "crash" one image with another, and only then, when you have noticeably manipulated the form, do you achieve the level of "art." Such "formalism" conflicts with attempted "realism." In the case of the latter, André Bazin thought editing should be limited and preferred reliance on *mise en scène* (composition of the shot) as the primary cinematic tool for capturing the real world. This definition of *realism* fostered what is called the "invisible style" of filmmaking which was meant to hide the "brushstroke," and achieve a verisimilitude. Editing was to be masked by techniques such as cutting on motion. Staging-in-depth, which allowed for action and reaction in a single shot, and therefore, presumably more closely resembled reality, allowed individuals to choose what to view. "Wyler particularly likes to build his *mise en scène* on the tension created in a shot by the coexistence of two actions of unequal significance."[2] This is the essence of William Wyler's style, which this chapter argues is not the signature of a mere journeyman technician.

Bazin states that "the realism of the cinema follows directly from its photographic nature,"[3] and that "artificiality . . . is totally incompatible with the realism which is the essence of cinema."[4] Bazin says of Wyler that he "tried to find aesthetic equivalents for psychological and social truth in the *mise en scène*."[5] In so acknowledging, Bazin believes that Wyler "deprives himself . . . of certain technical means . . . [and] tends . . . [toward] neutrality. This *mise en scène* seems to define itself through its absence."[6] Bazin praises this "absence" as the realistic benefit of the Wyler style. "The depth of field of Wyler is . . . the perfect neutrality and transparency of style, which must not interpose any filter, any refractive index, between the . . . [audience's] mind and the story."[7] Wyler said, however, that "a picture of reality alone is nothing . . . Only when reality has been molded into a dramatic pattern can it hold an audience."[8] This is a different kind of realism, one that is not just camouflage for the mechanics of filmmaking nor simply the absence of intrusive cinematic techniques.

It would be the cinematography of Gregg Toland, and their seven film collaborations, that would perfect Wyler's desire for meaningful staging by adding deep focus to deep composition. A distinction should be made between staging-in-depth which refers to shot composition, specifically placing performers (or objects) in various distances from the camera in order to convey a sense of three dimensions within the two dimensions of the movie screen, and deep focus, which, through the addition of increased lighting allows the cinematography to stop down the iris and thus increase the range of objects that are in focus. Despite the credit that is often given to *Citizen Kane* (1941), it should be noted that deep focus had been experimented with before Toland and Orson Welles. One of the most striking examples of this is Erich von Stroheim's *Greed* (1924). It should also be stated that deep focus was always possible in bright daylight.

Unfortunately, this realism, or lack of artistic intrusion into the narrative, led many film scholars to see classic Hollywood directors not as auteurs but as mere technicians. This is the fate that befell Wyler. However, when serious consideration is given to the immensely diverse genres in which Wyler worked, certain visual and thematic tropes become apparent. Wyler may not have ever referred to his filmmaking technique as the "invisible style," but he certainly espoused the philosophy that "the set and the camera are there only to permit the actor to focus upon himself the maximum dramatic intensity; they are not there to create a meaning unto themselves."[9] Despite his rejection of a director directing attention to himself, Wyler's camera movement, especially tracking, and his staging-in-depth are all intrusions into the narrative. These not so transparent techniques helped to create a sense of realism and delivered many of his early films from mawkish melodrama. The evolution of Wyler's so-called "styleless style" is clearly on display, beginning in his earliest works.

The characters in Wyler's early Westerns would "all behave according to a pattern . . . The stories were elementary. They were all formula."[10] It was up to the individual director to be visually creative in some way if he wanted any originality. Wyler would say, "I used to sit up nights trying to think of a new way to get on a horse."¹¹ The significance of this early work to his later style cannot be underestimated:

> For a long time, Wyler labored on obscure Westerns whose titles nobody remembers. It is through this work on Westerns, work not as an aesthetician but as craftsman, that he has become the recognized artist . . . [whose] only concern is to make the viewer understand the action as precisely and fully as possible. Wyler's immense talent lies in this 'science of clarity' obtained through the austerity of form as well as through equal humility toward his subject matter and his audience . . . [in so doing] he invented one of the most personal styles in contemporary cinema.[12]

It was in these extremely basic formulas that Wyler would develop his fondness for camera movement. As he would later describe it, the more elementary the story, the more it had to move. "One could learn a great deal doing Westerns because it was an action film and you were dealing basically in movement, which is the fundamental ingredient of motion pictures."[13] Such dedication to pacing would earn him recognition from critics as having a "brisk style,"[14] even within the constraints of the Mustang series (two-reel Westerns). Furthermore, in one of his five-reelers (feature length) for the Blue Streak series, he makes *Blazing Days* (1927), which is worthy of note in that, amid the conventions of an otherwise formulaic Western, Wyler chooses to focus on the relationship between the two heroes. This focus on friendships, and the tensions within such relationships, would time and again (*The Westerner* and *Ben-Hur* being two major examples) be a major part of Wyler's psychological examinations of human relationships.

Wyler's first two films, after the Blue Streak series, were still Westerns, but in 1928, Wyler would take his first step away from his incubating genre. Wyler's first foray into comedy was entitled *Anybody Here Seen Kelly?* While this is unfortunately lost to us today, this film was noticed, at the time, for having a Wyler style; a Universal memo opined that Wyler's work "shows a sense of realism and pace that endows . . . it with charm."[15] There was on the horizon, however, a development that was to play, as it would for many careers, a major role in the evolution of the Wyler style. Wyler's next two films were, what has been termed, part-talkies: *The Shakedown* (1929) was made with two versions, silent and sound, and *The Love Trap* (1929) is silent except for the last few scenes.

The very first shot of *The Shakedown* is a rather unusual, only slightly motivated, and very awkwardly executed camera move. It begins with a racked set of pool balls at the end of the pool table closest to the camera, then tilts up and over, with a substantial jerk, to two men, one of whom is about to break. When the man, Dave Roberts (James Murray), shoots, the camera follows the cue ball back to the break, and then back again up to Dave and the other man who is now paying Dave; obviously, they had a bet on the break. Despite the near home-movie quality of this move, it demonstrates Wyler's love of camera movement, and his favoring of it over cuts.

Early in the film, Wyler shows his affinity for staging-in-depth, but he also infuses it with more movement, in this case, movement of the performers not the camera. This shot (Figure 1.1) is an interior of a bar, including beer taps in the foreground. Two men, Dave and Roff (George Kotsonaros), are making a wager in the middle ground of the shot, and the onlookers behind them are in the background. While the camera may be static, there is considerable character movement within the shot. Dave and Roff have moved into their positions, and more than one onlooker crosses through the shot, at various depths within the frame, and in opposite directions. This movement helps to shape a three-dimensional representation. While this shot is certainly not yet deep focus, it is, nonetheless, a rudimentary example of multiple planes within a shot. In fact, the depth of field, in this particular shot, becomes even more pronounced after the wager, when the loser, Roff, returns to sit at the bar in the foreground, and we can now even see street activity outside (Figure 1.2). Throughout this scene, Wyler uses close-ups only when absolutely necessary.

Figure 1.1 Staging-in-depth (*The Shakedown*, 1929)

Figure 1.2 Staging-in-depth with character movement within a static shot (*The Shakedown*, 1929)

Two noticeable tracking shots follow. The first one is a "side" tracking shot, the camera moving parallel to the moving characters, as a young lady outside the bar, after asking directions of Dave, walks away and up the street, across the square, to sit on a park bench. She is being followed by Roff, who ends the tracking shot by accosting her on the bench. A side tracking shot like this allows us to observe every moment of a particular character(s), but not really be a part of it. We are not with them, just observing them. Such a lengthy move creates a realistic sense of time. Unabridged by cutaways, screen time equals real time. There is no temporal manipulation as with montage. The temporal unity of this first tracking shot, however, is broken once when we cut to a close-up reaction shot of Dave while he watches, with distain, Roff's pursuit of the young lady. This is followed by a "lead" tracking shot of Dave, with no close-ups to break up the camera move, as he follows in order to come to the aid of the lady. With such a tracking shot, we are out in front of the moving character and backing up. We travel the same path; we are with the character. Obviously, we are to identify with Dave more than Roff. The intrusive nature of the close-up reaction shot in the first tracking move is why Wyler, throughout his career, would try to keep close-ups to a bare minimum. Wyler believed that the close-up "functions as cinematic punctuation, an exclamation mark which contributes to the syntax of the whole scene,"[16] and not in some perfunctory breaking up of a scene. "I don't believe in overworking the close-up," Wyler would say, "and only use it when I want to make a point by excluding everything else from the audience's view."[17] In other words, in a Wyler film close-ups are few and therefore more poignant.

The story moves to an oil boomtown where a gang of conmen intend to perpetrate their next scam. Both Roff and Dave are part of this gang. The previous animosity between them was a prevarication intended to get the men in the bar to bet more heavily. While ingratiating himself with the people of this boomtown, Dave falls in love with a local woman, Marjorie (Barbara Kent), and becomes a father figure to an orphan boy, Clem (Jack Hanlon). The latter relationship leads the narrative into the stilted realm of melodrama, such as when Clem prays, "God please make me a good guy like Dave," but the gritty reality of the oil derricks, the dingy bar, and other images of earthiness, in other words, Wyler's form of realism, serve to make the melodrama more palatable.

In addition to the realism of deep composition, Wyler also begins to use humor to offset melodrama. Marjorie begins to admire Dave for taking in Clem and making the boy better. Wyler cuts from Dave telling Marjorie that under his care Clem will soon sprout wings to a tracking shot of Clem being chased by the corrections officer. The irony of the edit point is followed by a staging-in-depth shot which blends Wyler's visual realism with Wyler's sense of humor. In a single shot, we see Dave and Marjorie seated on a swing in the foreground, while Clem is hurtling the fence in the middle ground, and his pursuer, the corrections officer, is in the background, still chasing Clem (Figure 1.3). Even when the composition is not possessing of great depth, Wyler still prefers to keep all the principles in one shot (Figure 1.4) so that their performances are simultaneously viewable.[18]

There is another example of Wyler realism that occurs when Dave is at his lowest point. Marjorie has learned Dave's real purpose, to swindle the people of this town by ingratiating himself with them, get them to bet on him, and then throw a staged fight against Roff. She runs from the room and Dave runs after her, leaving the camera statically staring at an empty room for what, in screen time, seems like an eternity. After nine seconds of absolutely no action, Dave finally and slowly comes back into the room unsuccessful in catching her. While this realism runs the risk of alienating (boring) the audience, it definitely demonstrates a young director who is dedicated to the creation of temporal reality.

Wyler's next film, *The Love Trap*, is also a "transition" movie for the industry, in that it is mostly silent, but has sound at the very end. It is also a transition for Wyler from visual humor to comical dialogue. *The Love Trap* would also give Wyler the opportunity to increase "his control over film syntax."[19] As with *The Shakedown*, Wyler employs, early in this film, a marriage of actor's movement and camera movement.[20] The film opens with Evelyn (Laura La Plante) fired from a chorus line. As she enters the dressing room to collect her things, we dolly with

Figure 1.3 Extreme staging-in-depth with static characters in the foreground and moving characters middle- and background (*The Shakedown*, 1929)

Figure 1.4 Fairly shallow staging-in-depth but with character arrangement allowing for single shot dialogue (*The Shakedown*, 1929)

her as she crosses the room and sits at the makeup table. The camera then tilts down from her face to her feet. The music from the rehearsal is still going on (we must presume since the scene is silent) and her feet begin to tap in rhythm with it; music and the theater are obviously a significant part of her. The camera then tilts back up and she lays her head down in her arms to cry. All this is in one shot.

That night, in an effort to cheer her up, Evelyn's wild friend Bunny (Jocelyn Lee) takes Evelyn to a "wild party." At this gathering, a Casanova-like Guy Emory (Robert Ellis) shows particular interest in Evelyn. He takes her by the hand and leads her through the crowded dance floor, weaving their way around the dancing couples. The accompanying tracking shot, along with their winding path, lend a stronger perception of depth to the room for the audience. Guy is able to maneuver Evelyn upstairs. Upstairs and downstairs and the thematic differences they represent through divided physical distance would become a reoccurring motif in many Wyler films. Evelyn manages to thwart the advances of Guy, but when she returns home, she has been evicted and all her possessions are out on the street. It also begins to rain.

The first appearance of Paul (Neil Hamilton), Evelyn's eventual love interest, is an unusual reveal. We see, in the background of the shot, the rear of a taxicab, which has just come to a stop, having been moving away from the camera. The taxi hesitates for a moment, then begins to back up toward the camera until it fills the frame. It is then that we first see Paul, a close-up through the rear window of the cab. Presumably, he has told the taxi to stop because of the pitiful sight of Evelyn. In this character reveal, Wyler mixes movement within the frame and a final shot composition of framing within the frame.

In the following shot, we see Wyler's fondness for having the audience see two characters' reactions in the same shot. Paul is helping Evelyn to wash away mud from her face as she sits amid all her possessions. The Wyler vision of realism counters the melodramatic tone of this scene as does his use of humor. She has just invited him to sit down, as if he were in her home (and in a way he is) (Figure 1.5). This is followed by Paul asking, "Have you been living here long?" We see that Wyler has a touch for humorous dialogue even before the movies could talk. They share a laugh together in this one shot (Figure 1.6). Then her mood shifts back to her reality, she begins to cry (Figure 1.7), and he reacts accordingly, all still in the same shot. Even though Paul and Evelyn are not far apart in this shot, and many would suggest therefore that this composition is hardly staging-in-depth at all, it still allows for two reactions in one shot. This relates more about their relationship, even at this early stage of the story, than cutting back and forth would, or that a two shot, side by side in profiles, would. The total running time of this one shot is two minutes, which does not sound very long, but in the classic Hollywood style of cutting on exchanging of dialogue (action, cut, reaction), this is an incredibly long shot. In this shot, we see that Wyler's realism works for humor as well as drama.

Figure 1.5 Shot composition that allows action–reaction in one shot (*The Love Trap*, 1929)

Figure 1.6 Long take which allows actors to play the scene longer (*The Love Trap*, 1929)

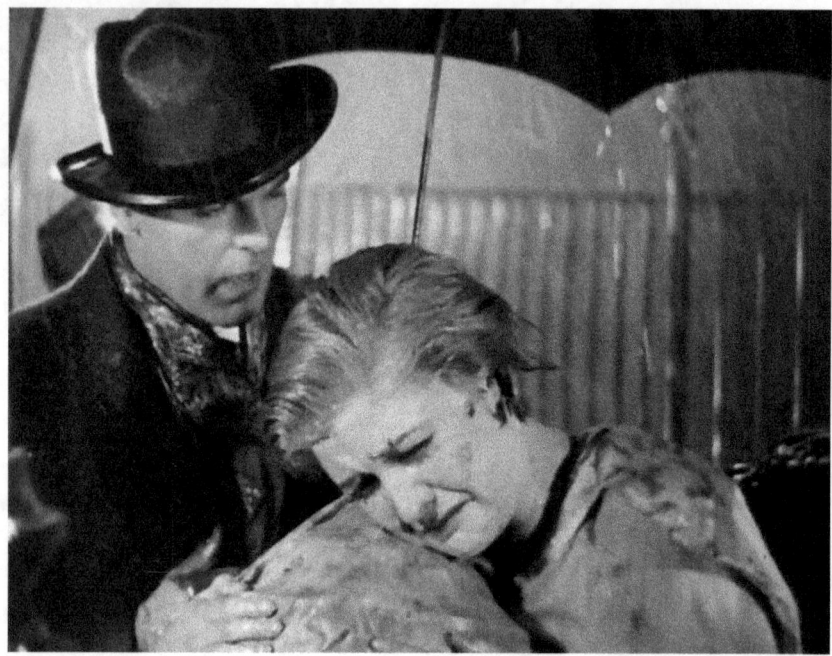

Figure 1.7 Composition and shot length preventing the interruptions of edit points (*The Love Trap*, 1929)

The earliest of silent films would often hold on a shot for much longer than even two minutes, because the scenes so often took place in wide, theater-like, tableaux. However, holding on a single medium close-up of two faces for two minutes was unusually long in 1929, as it is now. The only interruption to the temporal continuity of this shot comes, not from cutting between close-ups, but from four intrusions of intertitles, supplying the written dialogue. This explains why, once sound arrived, classic Hollywood adopted the practice of cutting back and forth in dialogue scenes, since such a practice was already standard for the industry. However, for Wyler, the intrusion of intertitles also explains why his sense of realism accepted wholeheartedly the advent of sound.

Wyler also uses staging-in-depth for humorous effect after Paul hires several taxis to help convey all of Evelyn's belongings. When the string of cabs finally stops, in the middle of nowhere, the driver shows Paul the fare meter and wants some payment. Paul gives the driver what he has and says he will wire for the rest at the next town. The driver is incredulous. The next shot is from inside the cab, with Paul and Evelyn in the foreground, and out the back window, we see the line of cabbies covering middle and background, creating a great depth of field, as the drivers of each cab begin unloading Evelyn's furniture (Figures 1.8.1 and 1.8.2).

WYLER'S "STYLELESS STYLE" 35

Figures 1.8.1 and 1.8.2 Staging-in-depth and frame within a frame composition (*The Love Trap*, 1929)

Such staging-in-depth was not in need of Toland's techniques since deep focus was achieved by sunlight. Beyond that, however, there are times when, even if Wyler had had deep focus at his disposal, it would not have been desirable. After Evelyn is married, and has her first fight with Paul, she calls her old friend Bunny and asks her to come over. Bunny is at another party, not unlike the one at the beginning of the film. After saying yes to Evelyn, Bunny invites everyone at the party to go over to Evelyn's place with her (Figure 1.9). When she does this, we see Bunny out of focus in the background inviting everyone to go, while in the foreground, in sharp focus, with two other guests, is Guy. When Guy hears whose house they are going to, it is important that he be in focus, but when he decides to join the others, to go to Evelyn's, Wyler racks focus to bring Bunny and the entire party group into our focus. In such a situation, since the audience's attention is supposed to shift, a rack focus is preferable to deep focus.

It might have seemed strange, when sound takes over with twenty-three minutes left in the film, were it not for Wyler's efforts to integrate it as smoothly as possible. In the first sound exchange of dialogue, Paul and his uncle, Judge Harrington (Norman Trevor), are arguing. The Judge reveals everything he

Figure 1.9 Staging-in-depth without deep focus, but with rack focus between planes to shift attention (*The Love Trap*, 1929)

knows about Evelyn's past, being an unemployed chorus girl, and specifically, the wild party where she went upstairs with Guy. The Judge is convinced that Evelyn is only a gold digger. Naturally, Paul reacts angrily. Wyler's use of shot composition which contains both speakers, rather than cutting between close-ups, is one which he also uses in the previous silent scenes, thus fostering continuity and creating a sense that we had heard these characters talking all along. At first it seems that the addition of sound to *The Love Trap* has forced Wyler to regress into more tableau-like composition. However, when Evelyn is trying to get back at her malicious Uncle-in-law, the Judge (Figure 1.10), we get a return to Wyler's staging-in-depth. Evelyn, sharp in the foreground, is crying, while the Judge, extremely out of focus in the background, tells her she must divorce Paul. Here again, depth of field without deep focus instructs us that Evelyn's emotions are the crux of this scene, while the Judge, even though he is the one speaking, becomes the formless specter of accusation. This foreshadows later compositions such as the famous shot from *The Little Foxes* (1941), where Bette Davis sits in the foreground in sharp focus not aiding her dying husband, out of focus, in the background.

Wyler's fondness for experimentation would also serve him well once sound fully arrived. While more established directors were leery of this new

Figure 1.10 Staging-in-depth without deep focus, both characters in frame but the emotion of only one is important (*The Love Trap*, 1929)

development, Wyler embraced it: "I was just beginning to make pictures," Wyler would remember, "so to me it [sound] didn't mean a great big upheaval, although some of the older directors at that time, they were very worried about something new coming in."[21] Wyler was determined that sound add to his realism, not detract from it. This required dialogue to be as natural as possible. Wyler wanted dialogue that would avoid both the artifice of montage,[22] and the intrusion of intertitles.

Wyler's love of camera movement, however, would prove problematic for some in early sound filmmaking. Wyler was told, during the shooting of his first "all-talkie," *Hell's Heroes* (1929), that with sound it was impossible to move the camera during the scene, because of the noise it would make. "I'd say, 'I want to move the camera during this shot,' and he'd [the sound engineer] say, 'Oh, you can't do that. That's crazy.'"[23] Wyler's response to the sound engineer was that he would simply move the camera in a way that would not make any noise. *Hell's Heroes* was about three bank robbers on the run, and so Wyler insisted that the audience move with them. Wyler has us track with them as they slowly attempt to make their escape through the desert.

One of the most remembered camera moves in this film is not of any people but just of the tracks that the last remaining bank robber has left in the sand. This thirty-second shot shows us that Bob (Charles Bickford), the last surviving bank robber, slowly dying of thirst, is shedding items as he drudges along. First, we see his rifle laying in the tracks and we can tell he has been dragging it. A little further lies his hat and a little further still a piece of clothing. This shot is followed by what starts as a "God shot," high above the staggering Bob. It is, however, the beginning of a crane move, married to a zoom, which brings us down to Bob's level by the time the camera gets close to him. After the crane shot, we return to a tracking shot. Now we move along with struggling Bob as he sheds another item. This time, it is the gold from the bank robbery. This sequence is meant to symbolize a cleansing of his sins, first the means of his sinful ways, the gun, and ending with the ill-gotten gains from his most recent crime.

This is not to say that, with all the camera movement in this film, Wyler has forsaken staging-in-depth. When the bank robbers come upon a stranded wagon with a dying pregnant woman inside, the camera movements cease for some time. Their escape, like the camera, has been stifled by their difficult situation. Indeed, one of the most famous shots in this film is from inside the wagon with one of the three badmen standing in the foreground at the opening of the wagon cover, and the other two men in the background on a ridge (Figure 1.11). This again combines two of Wyler's favorite techniques: staging-in-depth and framing within the frame.

On *Hell's Heroes*, Wyler not only fought with his sound engineer about merging camera movement with sound, but also with his cameraman over

Figure 1.11 Staging-in-depth and frame within a frame (*Hell's Heroes*, 1929)

Wyler's desire to not "prettify" the cinematography. He was told that flat landscapes and skies without clouds looked horrible and Wyler was supposed to have told him—"good"—that was what he wanted. Being shot on location only enhanced Wyler's ability to foster realism, and he enhanced the gritty, unglamourous nature of the story with no non-diegetic music (except for the opening credits). *Hell's Heroes* was the story of outlaws who find themselves in the doomed position of trying to do good. They promise the dying woman, in the abandoned wagon, to save her newborn child, but through Wyler's near documentary look, he is able to avoid the sentimentality of other versions of this story.[24]

Wyler's propensity for pushing the limits of cinema's early grammar continued, with varying degrees of success, throughout his early sound films: *The Storm* (1930), *A House Divided* (1931), *Tom Brown of Culver* (1932), and *Her First Mate* (1933). *The Storm* is the story of two friends trapped in a mountain cabin during a blizzard with a woman, with whom they both fall in love, thus straining their friendship to the breaking point and, perhaps, beyond. As that claustrophobic description suggests, this was an early test of Wyler's ability to sustain dramatic interest in an extremely confined location. It is also another example of Wyler exploring tension within friendships. In addition, it was Wyler's first collaboration with screenwriter John Huston. He would also work with Huston on his next film, *A House Divided*, which would star John's father, Walter Huston. Wyler would again team up with the older Huston in *Dodsworth* (1936), a collaboration which would result in a Best Actor Oscar nomination for Walter Huston. *A House Divided* concerns a love triangle between a widower, his mail-order bride, and his grown son. Under Wyler's guidance, Walter Huston creates a brutish character, yet one who is also able to elicit some degree of audience sympathy. This film also allows Wyler to experiment with rough and realistic dialogue. Unfortunately, the primitive technology of early sound also produced a lack of realism, in that scenes without dialogue were often shot without any sound. *A House Divided* actually opens with a funeral procession on the beach, but there are no sounds of waves at all.

Wyler's shot composition and camera work in *A House Divided* is at its most striking when a crippled Seth (Walter Huston) dragging himself on his hands, on the floor and in the foreground, bursts into his son Matt's (Kent Douglass) room, where in the background, Matt, and Seth's mail-order bride, Ruth (Helen Chandler), are sitting together on the bed. Seth flies into a rage and what ensues is a masterful use of close-ups, wide shots, and camera moves that capture the ugly clumsiness of this highly realistic fight scene (more accurately described as an attempted fight). This scuffle also involves both upstairs and downstairs action, and, as stated previously, this would become a frequent visual motif for Wyler.

Stairs figure prominently as a visual representation of narrative and thematic characteristics in several Wyler films. Wyler often employs the staircase as a central construct between people, their actions, their personalities, and their social positions. There is the renowned staircase scene in *The Little Foxes* (1941) (see Introduction, Figure I.6) and the moment of truth scene from *Friendly Persuasion* (1956) (see Chapter Eleven, Figure 11.1), but other examples can be found in *These Three* (1936) (Figure 1.12), *The Heiress* (1949) (Figure 1.13), and even *Ben-Hur* (1959) (Figure 1.14). All these Wyler moments, and many others, make use of the staircase to separate people who are at very different places psychologically and/or morally.

In *A House Divided*, we also see Wyler handling ever deeper psychological examinations of the human condition. In this case, the narrative wrestles with the theme of dysfunctional families. Wyler vividly displays the antagonism of father–son rivalries, and the destructive force of marrying the wrong person. It is Wyler's continuing exploitation of realism, both visual and thematic, that allows his films to overcome their often melodramatic content. This is decidedly the case with *A House Divided*.

Wyler's next two films, *Tom Brown of Culver* and *Her First Mate*, were less remarkable in the extending of his artistic technique, and in box-office success. However, with *Counsellor at Law* (1933), Wyler would greatly improve control of his technique and become even more daring in its application. *Counsellor at*

Figure 1.12 Use of stairs (*These Three*, 1936)

Figure 1.13 Use of stairs (*The Heiress*, 1949)

Figure 1.14 Use of stairs (*Ben-Hur*, 1959)

Law was based on an Elmer Rice[25] play of the same title and marks the beginning of a career-long association with, and a recognized talent for, screen adaptation on the part of Wyler. Wyler's style would need to serve two purposes: to "open up" the play to the screen and make dynamic the confined space of an urban office setting. Wyler employs extensive, sometimes subtle, sometimes very conspicuous (which flies in the face of Wyler's ethos that techniques should not exist to draw attention to themselves) camera moves and quick cuts (also something not often associated with Wyler).

Adding to the dimensional realism that Wyler creates via camera movement, he again has characters move extensively through the shots—crossing paths with each other (Figures 1.15.1 and 1.15.2), moving in and out of the frame, walking toward the camera while weaving their way between other characters in the shot (Figure 1.16), people going in doors while others are coming out (Figures 1.17.1 and 1.17.2), and even having opaque doors close "in the camera's face." In addition to all this movement, Wyler continues to show that deep spatial reality can be created without the use of deep focus (Figures 1.18.1, 1.18.2, and 1.18.3). Wyler conveys the clutter of the office world despite his clear visual separation of those that inhabit that world. It is in *Counsellor at Law* that critic Neil Norman believes Wyler starts "to experiment with camera angles ... He makes the screen alive by the simple way he actually shoots people. He doesn't shoot straight on. He shoots over the people's shoulders when they're having dialogue."[26]

In the climax of the film, the main character is beyond despondent and is ready to jump out his office window. Here, Wyler adds lighting, which, if the film were a decade later, we would be tempted to characterize as film noir, to convey the darkness that has enveloped the character (Figure 1.19). When his secretary enters and interrupts his suicide, Wyler adds his staging-in-depth to this expressionistic lighting, filling the frame left to right, as well as front

WYLER'S "STYLELESS STYLE" 43

Figures 1.15.1 and 1.15.2 The dynamic and confined nature of office activity displayed by the crossing movement of characters (*Counsellor at Law*, 1933)

Figure 1.16 Spatial dimension created by movement toward and away from camera and past other characters (*Counsellor at Law*, 1933)

to back, to illustrate that these two people are truly both lost souls, yet, at this moment, there is an emotional abyss between them (Figure 1.20).

Perhaps even more significant, Wyler would later view *Counsellor at Law* as his first film that dealt with a social issue, albeit cursory. In this case, the issue was antisemitism. The main character, portrayed effectively by John Barrymore, is a Jewish lawyer who has lifted himself from a poor background and, despite his great success, feels ostracized by the "boys who came over on the Mayflower." Although this subject is only vaguely touched on, Wyler's appreciation of such content demonstrates his growing belief, manifested ever-increasingly throughout his career, that a film should "say something."

In his last film for Universal, Wyler's visual style was concretized. With regard to *The Good Fairy* (1935), Norman feels that no one had ever done some of its techniques before.[27] Indeed, Wyler's innovations led Ian Nathan to proclaim, "It's one thing to say, Welles was this great pioneer, but actually, Wyler did all the hard work beforehand."[28] If one protests the statement that *Citizen Kane* owed much to Wyler and believes it to be, at the very least, a gross exaggeration, they should compare two shots which employ mirrors to create a limbo effect. Figure 1.21 is from *Kane* and Figure 1.22 is from Wyler's *The Good*

Figures 1.17.1 and 1.17.2 The hectic nature of office activity demonstrated by movement in and out of doors (*Counsellor at Law*, 1933)

Figures 1.18.1, 1.18.2 and 1.18.3 Creating deep spatial reality without deep focus (*Counsellor at Law*, 1933)

Fairy. The hall of mirrors scene in *The Good Fairy*, as the heroine daydreams her way through an expensive department store, predates *Kane*'s scene by six years and is even a year before the first time Wyler would work with Toland. *The Good Fairy* is the story of a grown-up orphan, Luisa (Margaret Sullavan), totally unprepared for the outside world, who leaves the orphanage to take a job as an usherette in a local movie theater, armed only with her patroness's charge to strive to "do a good deed every day." In this adaptation of what was originally a French play, Wyler puts all his honed visual techniques into the service of Preston Sturges's witty script.

While working in the movie theater, Luisa becomes engrossed in an extremely melodramatic film that is playing. Luisa situates herself next to a member of the audience, a gentleman, who is listed in the credits only as "the Waiter" (Reginald Owen). This scene is a great bit of self-parody, as if Wyler realizes some of the melodramatic aspects of his previous films. The movie, that Luisa and the Waiter are watching, is extremely maudlin, with weepy music, overacting, insipid dialogue, and unrealistic and repetitive gestures, yet they are both emotionally drawn into it. The scene mocks our tendency, as filmgoers, to deride melodrama, and yet swallow it as well, and in this case, not

Figure 1.19 Use of proto-film noir lighting to express character's dark emotions (*Counsellor at Law*, 1933)

Figure 1.20 Use of staging and lighting to express characters' emotional separation (*Counsellor at Law*, 1933)

just the naïve Luisa, but the cynical and more worldly Waiter too. It has been said that this scene is the brainchild of Sturges; however, the visual construction, juxtaposing the screen action with both individual shots of Luisa and the Waiter, as well as two shots of them both in frame, is all Wyler and shows his maturing style and the further adapting of his screen techniques to comedy. Wyler, whose realist tendencies depend heavily on camera moves and staging-in-depth, realizes in this scene that comedy is often best communicated through editing.

However, the contribution of Sturges's dialogue should not be underemphasized. In the previously mentioned movie theater scene, a family of three is viewing the same movie and the father gets up to leave right after the male character on-screen has uttered, for the umpteenth time, to the female he is kicking out of his life, "Go!" The father, as if responding to the command from the screen, says, "Let's go." His son replies, "But this isn't where we came in, Poppa." The father responds, "This is where we go out, just the same." The quippy dialogue is not far above vaudevillian at times, such as, "Oh yeah sure. I didn't recognize you without your pants." Another example is when the Waiter arranges to get Luisa into a fancy affair, at which he is working, and she is greeted upon arrival by the maître d' who says to her, "Your cloak, madam?" She responds, "Why certainly it's my cloak." This was already an old joke in 1935, but most of the dialogue is more original, and overly honest. For example, the Sturges's sardonicism is fully on display when Luisa, in an attempt to resist a masher, tells him, in regard to his pressing "invitation" that she hates music, and beer, and sandwiches. Later, however, when the less threatening and much older Waiter makes the same offer, she replies, "Oh yes, with a face like yours." When Luisa mistakes a rich importer/exporter, named Konrad (Frank Morgan), because of his formal attire, for another waiter like her friend, Konrad protests, "Well, I'll have you know, madam, that far from being a waiter, I'm not a waiter. I'm anything but a waiter." This is unmistakably Sturges's dialogue.

To praise Sturges's wit is not to say that Wyler's staging is not a significant element in the humor of *The Good Fairy*. Despite turning more to cuts for comic effect, Wyler has not abandoned his proclivity for staging-in-depth, such as when Konrad and Luisa are sitting at the table, while the Waiter stands in the background (Figure 1.23). As the Waiter is leaving the room, he is wagging his finger at Luisa, warning her to avoid Konrad. The humor of his warning is actually increased by the fact that, without Toland's deep focus, the Waiter is out of focus, visually suggesting that Luisa is not getting his message.

A perfect melding of Sturges's writing and Wyler's staging is when Konrad steps up his attempts to seduce Luisa. Konrad tells her how rich he is and how he can give her anything. Framing it around a hypothetical meeting with a wizard, one with a checkbook instead of a wand, he asks her if there is anything

Figure 1.21 The mirror limbo from *Citizen Kane* (1941) antedates . . .

Figure 1.22 . . . Wyler's use of the same effect in *The Good Fairy* (1935)

she *likes*. He should have worded it—is there anything you *want*—which is more to his purpose. She begins to rattle off a long list of everything she likes: pretty dresses, lobsters, diamond bracelets, fur coats, automobiles. During this seemingly endless list, the smile on Konrad's face slowly fades, and thanks to Wyler's affinity for showing both actors, we simultaneously see her naïve expression and his rapidly sobering face. Sturges underlines the moment by having Konrad observe, "I see you've given the matter some thought . . . poor wizard has gotten himself into something." In hindsight, the line becomes even more humorous as Frank Morgan would go on to play the title character in *The Wizard of Oz* (1939).

The Good Fairy would, in addition to its witty script and deft directorial handling, be noteworthy for two reasons outside of its content or form. First was the surprising wedding of the battling director and his leading lady. Secondly, it was Wyler's last film for Universal. Wyler's next film, *The Gay Deception* (1935) is the only film Wyler made for Fox (which would become 20th Century-Fox), but more significantly it was the last comedy Wyler would make for thirty-one years. In the years to come, Wyler would continue to craft a style that James Agee describes as "purity, directness, and warmth."[29] It is unarguable that Wyler grew at Universal, and there is no denying the evolution of his style during that

Figure 1.23 Staging-in-depth for humorous effect (*The Good Fairy*, 1935)

period, but it is also clear that it was time for Wyler to move on—moving on to a producer who matched his desire for excellence, Samuel Goldwyn, and to a cameraman who would fulfill his visual style, Toland, and to an actress, Bette Davis, whose collaboration would cast both him and her forever as superstars of the industry.

NOTES

1. Wyler in Bernard R. Kantor, Irwin R. Blacker, and Anne Kramer, eds. *Directors at Work: Interviews with American Film-makers* (New York: Funk & Wagnalls, 1970), 412.
2. André Bazin, "William Wyler, or the Jansenist of Directing," in *Bazin at Work: Major Essays and Reviews from the Forties and Fifties*, trans. Alain Piette and Bert Cardullo, ed. Bert Cardullo (New York: Routledge, 1997), 16.
3. André Bazin, "Theatre and Cinema-Part Two," in *What is Cinema?*, vol. 1, trans. Hugh Gray (Berkeley: University of California Press, 1967), 1:108.
4. André Bazin. "Theatre and Cinema-Part One," in *What is Cinema?*, vol. 1, trans. Hugh Gray (Berkeley: University of California Press, 1967), 1:86.
5. Bazin, *Bazin at Work*, 6.
6. Ibid. 10.
7. Ibid. 9–10.
8. Hermine Rich Isaacs, "William Wyler: Director with a Passion and a Craft," *Theatre Arts* 31, no. 2 (February 1947): 22–3.
9. Bazin, *Bazin at Work*, 18.
10. Curtis Hanson, "William Wyler, Pt. 1. An Interview," *Cinema* 3, no. 5 (Summer 1967): 25.
11. Hanson, 25.
12. Bazin, *Bazin at Work*, 17.
13. William Wyler, interview by Gene D. Phillips, *Focus on Film*, no. 24 (Spring 1976): 6.
14. *Moving Picture World* 85, no. 9 (May 2, 1927): 3.
15. Universal report on picture (November 17, 1928), quoted in Jan Herman, *A Talent for Trouble* (New York: G. P. Putnam's Sons, 1995), 85.
16. Michael A. Anderegg, *William Wyler* (Boston: Twayne, 1979), 54.
17. Thomas M. Pryor, "William Wyler and His Screen Philosophy," *The New York Times*, November 17, 1946.
18. Some detractors might argue that this is not cinematic realism as it mimics stage composition. If we are to accept the notion that staging-in-depth, which allows the audience choice of what to look at, is a sign of realism in film, and is also more theatrical than cinematic, as some would say, that would lead to the conclusion that a play is more realistic than a film. This is quite a conundrum.
19. Anderegg, 27.
20. Eventually, Wyler would also add limited editing to his combination of character movement and camera movement to achieve one of his most forceful scenes in all his films. The Olympus Ball sequence from *Jezebel* (1938) integrates all three effects to capture the isolation and humiliation of both Julie (Bette Davis) and her irate fiancé (Henry Fonda).
21. Kantor, et al., 411.
22. André Bazin, "Virtues and Limitations of Montage," in *What is Cinema?*, vol. 1, trans. Hugh Gray (Berkeley: University of California Press, 1967), 1:41–52.
23. Kantor, et al., 411.

24. *Hell's Heroes* was based on a novel by Peter B. Kyne entitled *The Three Godfathers*, the title by which the story would be re-filmed, with a much more optimistic tone, by John Ford in 1948. This story was filmed at least six other times beside Wyler's and Ford's versions.
25. Rice also wrote the screenplay for *Counsellor at Law*.
26. *The Directors: William Wyler*, directed by Lyndy Saville (3DD Entertainment, 2018).
27. Ibid.
28. Ibid.
29. James Agee, *Nation* (December 14, 1946), quoted by Jan Herman. *A Talent for Trouble*, 85.

CHAPTER 2

More than Meets the Eye: Perspectives on William Wyler and the Auteur Theory

Kyle Barrowman

In the course of recounting his "autobiography" of moviegoing in *The World Viewed*, Stanley Cavell describes the "clarifying shock" that accompanied his realization of the fact "that films were directed, that some human being had undertaken to mean, or was at any rate responsible for, all the angles of a movie." Not only does Cavell attest to feeling "rebuked for [his] backwardness in having grown to fatherhood without really knowing where movies came from," but he examines his "former backwardness" and asks: "How could anyone not have known what the auteur theory forces us to know?"¹ It is a significant historical fact that these words were first published in 1971. At that time, a paradigm shift had occurred. The auteur theory, which at that time had only recently made its way from France to the English-speaking world, provided a new piece of knowledge about film; it allowed for the articulation of something about films that was previously only intuited or spoken about in imprecise terms. The auteur theory forced people like Cavell to rethink how films were made, what films could do, indeed *what films are*, hence the ease with which Cavell could speak about "what the auteur theory forces us to know." It also provided a rationale for the reevaluation of classical Hollywood cinema, as a result of which such figures as John Ford, Alfred Hitchcock, Howard Hawks, Otto Preminger, and Nicholas Ray were recognized as unique and skilled artists who worked within the confines of the Hollywood studio system yet who crafted original and personal works of art. In short, the auteur theory marked the dawning of a new age in film criticism.

Today, the state of affairs has curiously been reversed. Where once someone like Cavell could point to his ignorance regarding film authorship as evidence of his backwardness, now scholars would point to Cavell's endorsement of the auteur theory as evidence of his backwardness. Rather than speaking of what the auteur theory *forces us to know*, it is more common now to speak of what it *deludes us into believing*, hence it is more common now to ask: How could anyone not have known that the auteur theory was wrong? This shift from belief in the rightness of the auteur theory to certainty in its wrongness was part and parcel of the shift from film criticism to film theory, which shift gave birth to the academic discipline of film studies. To justify its academic status, so the first generation of film scholars believed, film criticism had to become more theoretically rigorous. To this end, the top priority became interrogating the auteur theory and challenging the validity of author-based criticism. Looking back on this disciplinary history from our contemporary perspective—the jettisoning of author-based criticism in favor first of structuralist and then of poststructuralist methods of criticism, the reliance on psychoanalysis and confused conceptions of the unconscious to further vitiate the notion of authorship, and so on—it is clear that this shift produced a decidedly schizophrenic discipline. Today, scholars accept and deny in the same breath "what the auteur theory forces us to know"—namely, that filmmakers undertake to mean and are responsible for the films that they make—endlessly vacillating on the issue of authorship and producing hopelessly confused and often self-refuting criticism.[2]

If we *know* that films are intentional objects, why do we so often *refuse to acknowledge* filmmakers in our criticism? Why do we so often try to avoid such epistemological and ethical issues as intention and responsibility in our scholarly quests for meaning and value? Enlightening though answers to such questions would undoubtedly be, "curing" the discipline of its schizophrenia is not my purpose here. Admittedly, the quixotic is always appealing, but my aim in what follows is decidedly more modest than trying to eradicate the anti-author animus that is endemic to film studies. In what follows, I will conduct a metacritical investigation of one particular auteur, William Wyler, in an effort to restore the reputations of both Wyler and of the auteur theory itself. In the disciplinary history of film studies, there has not emerged a critical consensus on Wyler comparable to the consensus that has been established with respect to such renowned Hollywood auteurs as Ford or Hawks, to say nothing of such international auteurs as Akira Kurosawa or Ingmar Bergman. Initially, Wyler was championed by French critics like André Bazin and Roger Leenhardt, who marveled at Wyler's deep focus compositions, which Bazin argued were exemplary of a new form of realist aesthetics in the cinema.[3] Shortly thereafter, American and British critics like Andrew Sarris and V. F. Perkins rejected the French assessment of Wyler. To Sarris's mind, there is "less than meets the eye"[4] when it comes to Wyler's films, an assessment which Perkins considered kinder even than the "fifth-rate"[5] artist deserved.[6]

Given the precarious and contested place that Wyler occupies in the classical Hollywood canon, my goal in what follows is two-pronged: To establish a clear sense of Wyler's artistry—its originality, consistency, and excellence—which I hope will equally showcase the validity and utility of author-based criticism. To accomplish this, I will work through some of the claims of Wyler's greatest champion, Bazin, and his fiercest critic, Perkins. It is my contention that there is actually more than meets the eye in Wyler's films, and that in the history of film criticism, both fans and detractors alike have missed or mischaracterized crucial aspects of Wyler's artistry. As a result, I maintain that we have yet to fully comprehend or adequately appreciate the richness and complexity of Wyler's themes and aesthetics.

To my mind, Wyler's narrative and aesthetic touchstone, the theme that subtended his stories and inspired his visual strategies, was the concept of perspective, and it is only by analyzing his films with reference to the concept of perspective that we can understand and appreciate the depth and nuance of his films. To be sure, the reduction of a filmmaker's career to a one-word "essence" is by definition reductive and essentialist. Is guilt really *the* Hitchcock theme, or is it just one theme among many others, including love, betrayal, trauma, forgiveness, and so on? Is death really *the* Bergman theme, or is it just one theme among many others, including faith, art, family, communication, and so on? I readily concede that filmmakers are—and should be—more complicated than any one-word definition of their art could ever hope to convey. In Wyler's case, themes such as justice, community, pride, and redemption are certainly prominent throughout his career. Is it possible to understand either *Counsellor at Law* (1933) or *The Children's Hour* (1961) without reference to the concept of justice? Can we comprehend either the scope of the problems in *Dead End* (1937) or the root of the difficulties in *The Best Years of Our Lives* (1946) without reference to the concept of community? Are the tragic flaws that cause so much trouble for the protagonists of *The Letter* (1940) and *Detective Story* (1951) even intelligible without reference to the concept of pride? Is there any power to the endings of either *The Shakedown* (1929) or *Jezebel* (1938) without reference to the concept of redemption? I submit that the answer to every one of these questions is: No.

To be clear, then, in choosing to emphasize the theme of perspective, I do not mean to say or imply that this is the *only* theme about which Wyler was concerned or to which he returned in his films. Rather, emphasizing the theme of perspective draws attention to the significance in Wyler's films of characters seeing (or failing to see) things certain ways and then acting (morally or immorally, to their benefit or their detriment) based on their (accurate or mistaken) perspectives. In Wyler's films, the different ways that his characters see (or fail to see) each other and see (or fail to see) the worlds in which they live—the way that Julie Marsden (Bette Davis) sees her place in society and the consequences of her actions based on that perspective in *Jezebel*, the way that Homer Parrish (Harold Russell) sees his disability and how his shame negatively affects his relationship with his family in *The Best Years of Our Lives*, the way that Detective Jim McLeod (Kirk Douglas) sees criminals and how his sense of moral purity makes it difficult for him to forgive his wife Mary (Eleanor Parker) for the life that she lived before he met her in *Detective Story*, the way that Judah Ben-Hur (Charlton Heston) sees the occupation of Judea by the Romans and how his commitment to his own and his people's freedom, while just, nevertheless causes him unjust psychological and physical suffering in *Ben-Hur* (1959), and so on—not only fuels the plots of his films: It serves quite literally as the *raison d'être* for his rigorous *mise en scène*.

The key to reconsidering Wyler along these auteurist lines is found between the two poles of Bazin and Perkins. For his part, Bazin focused his critical energy on Wyler's realist aesthetic, which he believed was predicated on fidelity to human perception. Bazin characterized Wyler's *mise en scène* as defined by an "ethical reverence for reality,"[7] and he most appreciated Wyler's meticulous compositions for the way that they allegedly achieved a "perfect neutrality and transparency of style," a style which Bazin labeled "the styleless style" and which he claimed refuses to "interpose any filter" and which instead "rigorously conforms to reality" so that "action [would] never be an *abstraction*."[8] For Perkins, meanwhile, Wyler's aesthetic was neither realistic nor organically integrated, but was rather insufferably "bombastic" and redolent of "overcalculation" with respect to its "all-out assault on our responses." In no uncertain terms, Perkins denied that Wyler cared at all about, in Bazin's language, rigorously conforming to the reality of events depicted or eliminating authorial filters and stylistic flourishes. Quite the contrary, Perkins found that "atmosphere and 'point' customarily take precedence [in Wyler's films] over what is important, the action." In sum, Perkins dismissed Wyler as a contrived expressionist for whom the narratives and the aesthetics of his films were "calculated in order to impose" artificial thoughts and feelings on viewers rather than in order to facilitate genuine thoughts and feelings in viewers.[9]

To begin with Bazin's assessment of Wyler, I think that we ought to reject the claim that Wyler's artistry is predicated on a reverence for reality, at least in the sense that Bazin seems to imply: He seems to be under the impression that Wyler's goal as a filmmaker—which goal Bazin seems to think that Wyler achieved, and in spectacular fashion—was to preserve the objective reality in which his characters exist and to present that reality in such a way that characters within his films and viewers of his films could equally if not identically perceive that reality. Although this picture captures an important piece of the Wyler puzzle—namely, Wyler's tremendous geometric sense of framing and the extraordinary richness of his imagery, where in each and every shot Wyler makes brilliant use of every millimeter of frame space—it ultimately obscures more than it reveals. First, Wyler's "style" seems the antithesis of "styleless." Is the geometrical precision of his frame not evidence of meticulous planning and calculation, that is, of an unmistakable style of filmmaking? Though it provides the ground for a negative value judgment, Perkins is surely correct when he describes Wyler as wanting "to make everything 'effective.'"[10] Bazin even seems to admit as much himself when he says that Wyler's method aims "at a maximum of clarity and, through this clarity, at a maximum of dramatic efficiency."[11] Second, the action in Wyler's films is almost always an abstraction, at least if we define "abstract" as communicating ideas beyond that which is immediately discernible in what transpires on the screen. Once again, though it provides the ground for a negative value judgment, Perkins is surely correct also in observing that abstract themes customarily take precedence in Wyler's films over concrete action. And once again, Bazin seems to admit as much himself insofar as he appreciates the complex construction of the scene in *The Little Foxes* in which Regina (Bette Davis), shot in clear focus in the foreground, sits immobile while her husband Horace (Herbert Marshall), shot out of focus in the background, suffers a heart attack.[12] To the extent that the concrete action of Horace dying from a heart attack is the most significant action in the scene, Wyler's choice to place Regina in the foreground and to relegate the dying Horace not just to the background, but to the out of focus background, should go a long way toward indicating that the abstract and the ambiguous interested Wyler far more both thematically and aesthetically than the simple and the concrete. For Perkins's part, he cites as evidence of Wyler's preference for the abstract over the concrete the gunfight at the end of *The Big Country* (1958) between the warring patriarchs Maj. Henry Terrill (Charles Bickford) and Rufus Hannassey (Burl Ives), for which Wyler's camera is so far removed that, rather than two larger-than-life gunslingers shooting it out for supremacy, which is what we would expect the grand finale of a three-hour color and widescreen Western epic to build to, they are reduced to two indistinguishable, virtually imperceptible, and ultimately insignificant specks having a silly fight in country much bigger than their petty war of egos.[13]

Interestingly, these two scenes from *The Little Foxes* and *The Big Country* highlight the single most important aspect of Wyler's artistry, which aspect neither Bazin nor Perkins seemed to register in their criticism. Discernible in Wyler's preference for abstraction—which preference is clearly on display in the (not-grand) finale in *The Big Country* cited by Perkins and the half-seen heart attack suffered by Horace in *The Little Foxes* cited by Bazin, as well as in Fred's (Dana Andrews) inaudible breakup with Peggy (Teresa Wright) at her father and his friend Al's (Fredric March) request in *The Best Year of Our Lives* and Mary's (Karen Balkin) inaudible whisper of a malicious lie of lesbianism in her grandmother Amelia's (Fay Bainter) ear in *The Children's Hour*—is his primary intention and guiding aesthetic principle as a filmmaker. Against not only Bazin's assertion that action is never an abstraction in Wyler's films, but also against his assertion that "there is no consistent motif in the work of Wyler,"[14] we must recognize not only that action in Wyler's films is always if not abstract then certainly complex and ambiguous, but also that *this* is the consistent motif in Wyler's films: His films are designed to challenge both characters and viewers to reconsider what is truly important, obvious, just, contemptuous, and so on, based on the perspective from which a given character or event is seen and interpreted. Countless themes are explored in a wide variety of narrative contexts across all of his films, but the cinema of William Wyler is defined not by the absence of an authorial perspective, but rather by a commitment on Wyler's part to give expression to a wide range of character perspectives, which range Wyler presents carefully and powerfully in his *mise en scène* and which range we as viewers must grapple with if we are to do justice to the richness and the complexity of his films.

Along these lines, we can reconsider the famous scene in *The Best Years of Our Lives* in which Fred acquiesces to his friend Al's request to stop seeing his daughter Peggy. For different reasons, aspects of this scene are unacceptable to both Bazin and Perkins. For Bazin, believing as he did that Wyler had an ethical reverence for reality such that his films were constructed with the intention of being isomorphic to reality, the cuts from the long deep focus shot with Homer playing piano in the foreground, Al leaning on the piano in the middleground, and Fred in the phone booth in the background, to the two-shot with Al in the foreground in close-up and Fred in the phone booth in the background, have the effect of "interrupt[ing] . . . the scene." Interpreting the long deep focus shot as the scene "proper" and the cuts to Al in close-up as "improper" shots interrupting the action of the scene and destroying the perceptual isomorphism, Bazin dismisses these shots as "safety shots": He infers from Wyler's decision to edit the scene in this fashion that he "probably feared that the viewer might become too absorbed in the piano playing and gradually forget the action in the background."[15] Counter to Bazin's interpretation, rather than fearing that we would "forget" that Fred was in the background on the phone with Peggy, would it not make more sense to infer that Wyler wanted us, at the precise moments that he cut to those close-up shots of Al, to shift—with Al—from focusing on Homer to focusing on Fred? This would require that we deny Bazin's position on Wyler, as wanting above all else to establish in his *mise en scène* an objective field of vision which his viewers would be free to perceive in their own way for their own reasons, and to conceive of his intention instead as wanting to establish a subjectively encoded field of vision, a *mise en scène* shot through with dramatic and thematic import. In the interest of accurately assessing Wyler's artistry, I submit that deny Bazin's position we must.

In this scene from *The Best Years of Our Lives*, when Wyler cuts to the close-up shots of Al in which we are no longer able to see Homer playing the piano, Al is at those exact moments turning away from Homer himself and is also no longer able to see him playing the piano. In effect, Wyler's *découpage* is attuned to, and designed to attune us with, Al: We *can* shift our perspective and look first at Homer, then at Fred, then back at Homer, then over at the bar, and so on, but we are *meant* to look at Homer and Fred *with Al*, and when Wyler cuts to the close-ups of Al, those are the moments when we (are meant to) feel the closest to Al and (meant to) share the most profoundly in his conflicting emotions of joy (in response to Homer's apparent improvements in both body and spirit) and sorrow (in response to Fred's life being made more difficult than it already is for Peggy's sake).[16] If Wyler were to have shot the entire scene in that one long shot, with no cuts to Al, then if in those moments when Al turned away from Homer to look at Fred we happened to be focusing on Homer and smiling to ourselves in response to his carefree piano playing, the problem would not be that we had "forgotten" about Fred; it would be that we would not be on the same wavelength of feeling with Al. This was Wyler's abiding concern, to ensure that we viewed the goings-on in this scene from Al's perspective and felt the warring emotions in ourselves that Al was feeling in that moment in time, hence his choice to construct the scene the way that he did.[17]

Undoubtedly, Perkins would also have objected to this scene, but for different reasons than Bazin. For Perkins, if there is anything objectionable in this scene, it is that Wyler chose not to allow us to hear the content of Fred and Peggy's phone conversation, not even Fred's end of it. If, in Bazin's criticism, the dialectic of art and reality is the fundamental issue which informs—and at times distorts—his criticism, in Perkins's criticism, the most intractable issue is his antipathy toward abstraction. As Perkins has stated in no uncertain terms, and specifically in opposition to Wyler's artistry, "it's almost inevitably wrong to use the camera, as Wyler does, in order to *conceal*," for, in Perkins's estimation, "film is the art of *showing*,"[18] hence his assertion that if something is "important enough to be in" a film then "it's important enough to be shown" in that film.[19] For starters, the number of examples which could demonstrate the extraordinary depth of Perkins's wrongness with respect to the entirely valid and often extremely effective choice *not* to show something in a film is so astronomical that I trust that readers will have no shortage of examples that they know and cherish which they can call to mind to counter Perkins's dubious claim.[20] More pertinently given the present context, I want to stress that the concept of "showing" something in a film is by no means straightforward.

Even if we were to accept Perkins's argument that if something is important enough to be in a film then it is important enough to be shown in that film, there are no laws dictating *how* something must be shown in a film. If Perkins wanted to object to Wyler's decision not to allow us to hear what was being said by Fred or between Fred and Peggy in *The Best Year of Our Lives*—for similar reasons as he objected to Wyler's decision not to allow us to hear what was being said by

Mary to her grandmother in *The Children's Hour*—in neither case could Perkins object that Wyler did not show what happened. He did not show it *completely*, or *separately*, but he most certainly *did* show it: We *do* "see" Fred break up with Peggy and we *do* "see" Mary whisper to her grandmother. In a rather telling admission, Perkins himself acknowledges that, in the scene from *The Children's Hour*, "there is no need for us to hear the actual words spoken since we are well enough aware that the accusation is of homosexuality."[21] Likewise, in the scene from *The Best Years of Our Lives*, there is no need for us to hear the actual words spoken by Fred or between Fred and Peggy since we are well enough aware that the conversation is a breakup. The reason for this, which is equally the justification for Wyler's choices in both scenes, should be obvious: In neither case is the content of what is said the point.

In both *The Best Years of Our Lives* and *The Children's Hour*, Wyler's reason for allowing us to see but not hear Fred break up with Peggy and see but not hear Mary whisper to her grandmother is to keep our focus on the characters' reactions. In the former, what exactly Fred says to Peggy to end their relationship is not the point of the scene. The point, rather, is how Fred reacts. We see him slowly hang up the phone and remain in the phone booth for several moments after the call has ended, and then once he has collected himself, he leaves the bar without even acknowledging Al or Homer. Fred's isolation is now complete. In the latter, meanwhile, it is significantly the grandmother Amelia to whom we are attuned, at least by the end of the scene if not for its entirety. If at the beginning of the scene it is Mary's sense of increasing panic that Wyler amplifies by virtue of his editing and sound design—desperate for a way to avoid going back to school, as she gets closer and closer to the school, Mary's desperation increases, and so too does the outrageousness of what she has to say—by the end of the scene, once Mary has gotten her grandmother believing in the possible truth of what she has said, Wyler has subtly shifted our perspective away from Mary and has now attuned us to Amelia. Upon hearing what her granddaughter had to say, Amelia is now in the difficult position of having to decide what to do about it. It is her reaction—first of screaming for her chauffeur to stop the car, which is amplified coming as it does after she slides open the partition which kept us from hearing Mary's whisper, and then of determination to find out if the seemingly too-lurid-for-a-child-to-invent claim is true—that Wyler foregrounds in the scene, not least by the way that, after the chauffeur stops the car and waits outside as instructed, Wyler shoots a rather long and significantly wordless scene in which Amelia, gripping her granddaughter by the shoulders, appears to be scrutinizing Mary's face for any possible sign of deception, only to resign herself to the fact that Mary might just be telling the truth after all. In both films, Wyler does not offer "objective" views of his cinematic worlds. On the contrary, he uses all of the techniques at his disposal in order to put us in the very different shoes of his very different characters, and in so doing he provides a rich tapestry of different and sometimes conflicting thoughts, emotions, motivations, consequences, and so on. In this way, he ensures that the ethical stakes of his films and the affective power of their central conflicts hit his viewers just as hard as they hit his characters.

Though their judgements of Wyler, and cinema in general, are vastly different, and for equally different reasons, I cannot help but wonder if it was Bazin's and Perkins's shared skepticism of the auteur theory that caused them both to miss or minimize the importance and the ubiquity throughout Wyler's films of issues of perspective. Bazin famously loved above all else, above even his favorite auteurs, the "genius of the system,"[22] and he was thus suspicious of the auteur theory insofar as it is geared toward individuals rather than genres, studios, national cinemas, and so on. (Is it a coincidence that Bazin's most famous writings are on such topics as the ontology of the photographic image,[23] the evolution of the language of cinema,[24] and Italian neorealism,[25] vast subjects which transcend individual auteurs?) Perkins, too, had his methodological doubts about the auteur theory, but he was suspicious of it insofar as it was geared toward individual filmmakers rather than individual films. For Bazin's part, he believed that it was possible to maintain a balance in criticism between film and filmmaker, even if he wanted the need for such balance to be stated openly and often lest we forget it. For Perkins's part, however, he believed that the auteur theory was fundamentally flawed, and to this end, he leveled two significant objections, the first pertaining to, for lack of a better term, the ethics of criticism, and the second pertaining to, for lack of a better term, the epistemology of criticism.

With respect to the ethics of criticism, Perkins objected to the way that "concern with the continuities and coherence across the body of a director's work" was allegedly "exaggerated" in the auteur theory insofar as it "does not just observe or welcome continuity from film to film; it insists on continuity."[26] The problem, to Perkins's mind, was that "an observation about authors—that their works often display striking continuities and coherent development—was transformed into a test of authorship, a qualification for author status."[27] I must confess, I do not see how this is a problem. If Perkins's quarrel with the auteur theory on this front is that it opens the door to snobbery—which it does, and which Perkins does object to, as when he decries the way that "the term 'author,' when used of a film director, is almost inevitably a term of acclaim; it is an honorific title—like 'artist'—at least as much as it is description"[28]— then I would say that the problem is not with the auteur theory, but rather with snobby auteurist critics. To designate a filmmaker an auteur—whether that filmmaker is an indisputably great filmmaker, like Stanley Kubrick, or an indisputably bad filmmaker, like Ed Wood—is simply to say that said filmmaker has a unique personality and a distinct set of stories, themes, and/or aesthetic strategies discernible across their films. Whether auteurs or films are good or bad is a separate issue, one which is in no way meaningfully connected to whether a given filmmaker is or is not an auteur. Ted Kotcheff is no less exceptional a filmmaker for not being an auteur and *First Blood* (1982) is no less exceptional a film for not being made by an auteur. If an auteurist critic takes the one to follow from the other, that is an error for which they are responsible. Theoretically speaking, the one does not logically follow from the other the way that Perkins seems to fear.

If that takes care of Perkins's first objection to the auteur theory vis-à-vis the ethics of criticism, his second objection vis-à-vis the epistemology of criticism remains to be answered. To Perkins's mind, the "pattern theory" first promulgated by Sarris,[29] if taken to its logical conclusion, allegedly ends up in the nonsensical position where critics and scholars "cannot understand one of a director's films until [they have] seen them all." The flaw here, in Perkins's estimation, is that

> if perceptions within the single film have no critical value, it is not sensible to aggregate them across films, so you cannot get started. You need some ground for the claim that a feature is pertinent in one film before it becomes interesting that it is repeated . . . [or] varied . . . in another.[30]

The problem here is two-fold. On the one hand, similar to the equivocal notion of "showing" on which Perkins relied in his argument to the effect that if something is important enough to be in a film then it is important enough to be shown in that film, Perkins is here relying on an equivocal notion of "understanding." On the other hand, Perkins is overstating the case vis-à-vis "critical value" in individual versus sets of films.

To the first point vis-à-vis Perkins's equivocal notion of "understanding," a viewer is perfectly capable of understanding *The Best Years of Our Lives* without having ever seen another of Wyler's films. That is to say, a viewer is perfectly capable of registering in *The Best Years of Our Lives* Wyler's ability to shift perspective within scenes, his emphasis on the plight of the individual in society, his profound humanism, and so on. By the same token, a viewer is equally capable of understanding *The Best Years of Our Lives* even *more* if they then watch other films of Wyler's like *Dead End*, *Jezebel*, *Detective Story*, and *The Big Country*. That is to say, a viewer is equally capable of registering Wyler's thematic concern with how individuals internalize and deal with the sense of being an outsider in a community and how this is manifest in many of his films—for example, the way that Julie in *Jezebel* internalizes and deals with her perceived exemplary status with respect to 1850s New Orleans; the way that Homer in *The Best Years of Our Lives* internalizes and deals with his outsider status as a disabled veteran incapable in his mind of leading a normal life with respect to his family in 1940s Boone City, the fictional enclave of quintessential Americana; and the way that James McKay (Gregory Peck) internalizes and deals with his outsider status as a New Englander looking to make a life for himself in 1880s Texas—or his aesthetic preference for placing multiple characters in different regions of the frame all experiencing different emotions in response to what is transpiring—for example, the way that he shoots Birdie (Patricia Collinge) and the Hubbard siblings (Bette Davis, Charles Dingle, and Carl Benton Reid) relative to each other and the content of the conversation in *The Little Foxes*; the way that he shoots Fred on the phone, Homer on the piano, and Al watching them both in *The Best Years of Our Lives*; and the way that he shoots Jess Birdwell (Gary Cooper) riding off to join the fighting in the Civil War as three different members of the Birdwell family react to his departure in three different ways all in one extraordinary shot in *Friendly Persuasion* (1956).

In point of fact, what Perkins raises as an epistemological objection to the auteur theory can be viewed, from a different perspective, as its salutary benefit: The auteur theory allows for if not a complete understanding of a filmmaker and their films then at the very least a more complete understanding than would otherwise be possible.[31] It is one thing to watch and marvel at the construction of such films as *The Little Foxes*, *The Best Years of Our Lives*, and *The Children's Hour* in and of themselves. It is another thing to marvel at the consistent originality and excellence of an individual filmmaker's rich storytelling, complex characterizations, thematic profundity, and aesthetic beauty across films over time. In the first place, the individual film must be well-made; the story must be coherently constructed and compellingly told using all the elements of cinema to facilitate coherent and compelling storytelling. Bazin and Perkins are both certainly correct on this point. But why should we stop here? If upon watching more and more films we begin to notice that a great number of coherently constructed and compellingly told cinematic stories were made by the same filmmakers, and if we then begin to notice the characteristically brilliant ways that individual filmmakers construct and tell their stories, does this not warrant appreciation? And if we notice these characteristic ways that individual filmmakers construct and tell their stories, should this sense of the auteurs "behind" the films not inspire us to return to the individual films and check our previous assumptions and apprehensions against our newfound senses of their auteurs? In his effort to encourage the striking of a balance in criticism between film and filmmaker, Bazin nevertheless tilted the scales from filmmaker to film, asking, "*Auteur*, without doubt, but *of* what?"[32] To my mind, in appreciation of the filmmakers who have given us such an embarrassment of riches in the form of their wonderful films, including not least William Wyler, we ought to put the question differently: *Films*, without doubt, but *whose* films?

NOTES

1. Stanley Cavell, *The World Viewed: Reflections on the Ontology of Film* (Cambridge, MA: Harvard University Press, [1971] 1979), 7.
2. To be clear, my invocation of schizophrenia is more than mere rhetorical bluster. The frequency with which scholars go on record with theoretical rejections of author-based criticism only to proceed thereafter to conduct author-based criticism is absolutely staggering, as if unaware that their criticism contradicts the theory on which it was ostensibly built, indeed as if there exists within every film scholar two distinct scholarly "personalities," one auteurist and one anti-auteurist, vying for control. Since I have already argued this elsewhere, in the interest of time and space, I am not going to reargue this here. However, to the extent that my position on the emergence of this tendency in film criticism—both when it emerged and how it has manifested in criticism past and present—is quite polemical, I want to let readers know that I elaborate my position on the disciplinary history of film studies vis-à-vis authorship in my "Signs and Meaning: Film Studies and the Legacy of Poststructuralism," *Offscreen* 22, no. 7 (2018), <https://offscreen.com/view/signs-and-meaning-film-studies-and-the-legacy-of-poststructuralism> (last accessed August 8, 2022), "A Plea for Intention: Stanley Cavell and Ordinary Aesthetic Philosophy," *Movie: A Journal of Film Criticism* 9 (2021): 65–75, <https://warwick.ac.uk/fac/arts/film/movie/movie_journal_issue_9._a_plea_for_intention.pdf> (last accessed August 8, 2022), "How to Do Things with Camera Movement: *The Lure of the Image: Epistemic Fantasies of the Moving Camera*, by Daniel Morgan," *Senses of Cinema* 101 (2022), <https://www.sensesofcinema.com/2022/book-reviews/how-to-do-things-with-camera-movement-the-lure-of-the-image-epistemic-fantasies-of-the-moving-camera-by-daniel-morgan/> (last accessed August 22, 2022), and "Alfred Hitchcock and the Moving Camera: Authorship, Style, and Declarative Aesthetics," *Offscreen* (forthcoming).
3. See André Bazin, "William Wyler, or the Jansenist of Directing," in *Bazin at Work: Major Essays & Reviews from the Forties & Fifties*, trans. Cardullo and Alain Piette, ed. Bert Cardullo (London: Routledge, [1948] 1997), 1–22. See also Bazin, "The Evolution of the Language of Cinema," in *What is Cinema? Volume 1*, ed. and trans. Hugh Gray (Berkeley: University of California Press, [1955] 2005), 9–16, and "An Aesthetic of Reality: Cinematic Realism and the Italian School of the Liberation," in *What is Cinema? Volume 2*, ed. and trans. Hugh Gray (Berkeley: University of California Press, [1948] 2005), 16–40.
4. Andrew Sarris, *The American Cinema: Directors and Directions 1929-1968* (Cambridge, MA: Da Capo Press, [1968] 1996), 167–8.
5. V. F. Perkins, "An Important Re-Release: George Stevens' *Giant*," in *V.F. Perkins on Movies*, ed. Douglas Pye (Detroit, MI: Wayne State University Press, [1962] 2020), 126–7.
6. Interestingly, Bazin himself commented on Wyler's fall from critical grace. In a note added in 1958 to the end of his original 1948 analysis of Wyler's artistry—which in my estimation still stands as the most insightful analysis of Wyler's filmmaking, though Neil Sinyard and Gabriel Miller also deserve acknowledgment for their excellent work in, respectively, *A Wonderful Heart: The Films of William Wyler* (Jefferson, NC: McFarland, 2013) and *William Wyler: The Life and Films of Hollywood's Most Celebrated Director* (Lexington: University of Kentucky Press, 2013)—Bazin observed with palpable sadness that the initial French championing of Wyler occurred during "a time when Roger Leenhardt was shouting 'Down with Ford! Long live Wyler!'" but that "history did not echo that war cry." See Bazin, "William Wyler, or the Jansenist of Directing," 22, n. 19.
7. Ibid., 5.

8. Ibid., 9–10.
9. Perkins, "An Important Re-Release," 126–7.
10. Perkins, "An Important Re-Release," 126.
11. Bazin, "William Wyler, or the Jansenist of Directing," 12.
12. Ibid., 3–4.
13. I owe a debt of gratitude to Ron Falzone for his insightful comments on Wyler's filmmaking strategies in general and his construction of this final gunfight in *The Big Country* in particular.
14. Ibid., 1. Curiously, not only was Sarris also confounded by Wyler's artistry, concluding his vicious critique of Wyler with the defeated admission that "Wyler's career is a cipher as far as personal direction is concerned" (Sarris, *The American Cinema*, 166), even Perkins seemed unable to track anything resembling a consistent style or thematic thread in Wyler's films. After denouncing Wyler's filmmaking, he moves on to a consideration of George Stevens, and he gives Stevens the following backhanded compliment: "Even [in Stevens's] most crudely calculated pictures [there are] sequences which suggest a sympathetic personality striving to emerge from the welter of effects" (Perkins, "An Important Re-Release," 127). I confess to being unsure as to whether what distinguishes Stevens from Wyler in Perkins's estimation is that he finds in Stevens's films *a* personality striving to emerge (as opposed to Wyler's films, in which he finds no personality) or a *sympathetic* personality striving to emerge (as opposed to Wyler's films, in which he finds an unsympathetic personality). In any case, all three of these critics—Bazin, Sarris, and Perkins—were in different ways and for different reasons stumped by Wyler's filmmaking, and given the argument that I am advancing in this chapter, I submit that what all three of them missed was the centrality of issues of perspective and how the concept of perspective informed not only the construction of Wyler's stories but also the composition of his visuals.
15. Bazin, "William Wyler, or the Jansenist of Directing," 16.
16. I am indebted to Daniel Morgan's work on camera movement for the way that he articulates the notion of filmmakers using aesthetic devices to attune us to characters. See his "Max Ophuls and the Limits of Virtuosity: On the Aesthetics and Ethics of Camera Movement," *Critical Inquiry* 38, no. 1 (2011): 127–63 and *The Lure of the Image: Epistemic Fantasies of the Moving Camera* (Berkeley: University of California Press, 2021), as well as my "Otto Preminger and the Moving Camera: Feminist Attunement in *Whirlpool*," *Mise-en-scène: The Journal of Film & Visual Narration* 5, no. 2 (2020): 1–13. Interestingly, Morgan has even provided a brilliant analysis of a shot in Wyler's *Wuthering Heights* (1939), in which he argues, rightly in my estimation and in corroboration of my larger argument here vis-à-vis the centrality of perspective in Wyler's narratives and aesthetics, that the camera is expressive of the perspective of the young outsiders Cathy (Merle Oberon) and Heathcliff (Laurence Olivier) as they spy through a window on a high society ball. See Morgan, *The Lure of the Image*, 77–8.
17. To corroborate this account of Wyler's artistry, we can compare Wyler's visual strategies in *The Best Years of Our Lives* to his visual strategies in *The Little Foxes*. In one of the many spectacularly shot and edited sequences from this film, the character Birdie (Patricia Collinge)—dejected while the rest of the family is elated following the departure of the rich William Marshall (Russell Hicks), with whom they plan to make a great deal of money—goes off and sits in a chair by herself while her husband and in-laws scheme in the living room. For nearly the entire scene, regardless of the particular composition of this or that shot, Wyler invariably constructs his shots so that Birdie is visible in the background, small and in shadow. But early in the sequence, he cuts to a single of Birdie sitting alone, dejected, while her family talks audibly but off-screen. By virtue of this choice to insert a single of Birdie—in much the same way that Wyler inserted the close-up shots of Al in *The Best Years*

of Our Lives—Wyler attunes us to Birdie. Not only that, but by the end of the scene, when Regina is forced to consider marrying off her daughter Alexandra (Teresa Wright) to her nephew—Birdie's son—Leo (Dan Duryea), Wyler trusts that we have not forgotten about Birdie: Obscured now from the camera's—and our—line of sight for the first and only time in the sequence, when the conversation turns to Alexandra and Leo potentially getting married, we hear Birdie's voice before we see her get up and reenter the frame. However, when she does reenter the frame, her presence is not accompanied by shock upon seeing this forgotten character suddenly reemerge on the screen; rather, because Wyler used his camera at the beginning of the scene to attune us to Birdie and in effect emotionally tether us to her, we are all but waiting for her to try at this point in the scene, even if futilely, to protect the innocent Alexandra from the same fate as befell her. Furthermore, at the end of the scene, when the family has dispersed and Birdie stays behind to talk to Alexandra one-on-one and to implore her never to marry Leo, Wyler does not cut at all: He trusts that during this dialogue exchange between Birdie and Alexandra in the foreground we will notice Birdie's husband Oscar (Carl Benton Reid) come into view and stand at the entrance to the living room in the background, obscured by a curtain so that only his torso is visible but clearly close enough to have heard Birdie tell Alexandra not to marry Leo. And once Alexandra leaves and Wyler finally does cut, he significantly cuts not to Oscar's angry expression, but to Birdie's expression: First, she is happy when she hears Alexandra's bedroom door close, relieved by a sense, however illusory, that Alexandra is safe now from the evil machinations of this awful family, but this brief happiness is replaced by a heartbreaking look of resignation to her fate when she turns to look at her husband and walks to him like a prisoner about to be escorted back to their cell. To reiterate, Wyler's sensitive attunement to characters and his management within scenes of character perspective are the major takeaways from his films and ought to be the way that we interpret his visual strategies in his films.

18. V. F. Perkins et al., "*MOVIE* Differences," in *The MOVIE Reader*, ed. Ian Cameron (London: November Books, [1963] 1972), 22.
19. Ibid., 20.
20. For my part, I have previously analyzed one such example—an example which, given his fondness for Hitchcock, I suspect that even Perkins would agree was a valid and effective example—from Hitchcock's *Frenzy* (1972). See my "Alfred Hitchcock and the Moving Camera."
21. V. F. Perkins, *Film as Film* (New York: Da Capo Press, [1972] 1993), 125.
22. André Bazin, "On the *Politiques des Auteurs*," *Cahiers du Cinéma in English* 1 ([1957] 1966), 18.
23. André Bazin, "The Ontology of the Photographic Image," in *What is Cinema? Volume* 1 (1945), 9–16.
24. Bazin, "The Evolution of the Language of Cinema."
25. Bazin, "An Aesthetic of Reality."
26. V. F. Perkins, "Film Authorship: The Premature Burial," in *V.F. Perkins on Movies* (1990), 220–1.
27. Ibid., 222.
28. Ibid., 227.
29. Cf. Sarris, *The American Cinema*, 19–37.
30. Perkins, "Film Authorship," 224.
31. For a remarkably coherent and argumentatively persuasive case to this effect, see the essays that comprise William Cadbury and Leland Poague's *Film Criticism: A Counter Theory* (Ames: Iowa State University Press, 1982).
32. Bazin, "On the *Politiques des Auteurs*," 18.

CHAPTER 3

Traumatic History and the Prosthesis of Myth in Wyler's *The Best Years of Our Lives*

Carol Donelan

The Best Years of Our Lives (William Wyler, Samuel Goldwyn Productions, 1946) follows three World War II servicemen, Army sergeant Al Stephenson (Fredric March), Army Air Corps captain and bombardier Fred Derry (Dana Andrews), and Navy seaman Homer Parrish (Harold Russell), returning home after the war, returning to "civilization, after being in the jungle, with savages." During the flight home, as Homer sleeps, Al and Fred have a quiet exchange regarding their fears of returning home, "nervous out of the service," and what it means to be "rehabilitated." Both agree that rehabilitation depends on a successful marriage, which means not only finding love with a woman but also achieving economic stability through work. The rehabilitation that seems possible for middle-class Al and working-class Fred, both of whom are able-bodied, seems less possible for Homer, who lost both hands during the war and has been outfitted with prosthetic hooks. In contrast with Homer's physical disability, explicitly cued in the film, available for viewer comprehension, the mental trauma experienced by Homer and Fred is implicitly cued, unspoken but expressed through style, available for viewer interpretation.[1] Comprehending and interpreting the cues reveals that the film functions to demythologize white male veterans by removing the prosthesis of myth—the myth of the invincible American warrior—to expose the historical truth of their physical disability and mental trauma, explicitly and implicitly.[2]

With the theme of rehabilitation in mind, this chapter argues that Wyler rehabilitates the narrative structure and style of *The Best Years of Our Lives* in the interest of prioritizing the truth of traumatic history over the compensatory prosthesis of myth by committing to the verisimilitude of "reborn realism" identified by French critic André Bazin. Reborn realism aims to achieve in the appearances onscreen the ambiguity and irresolution of meaning associated with reality, rather than the melodramatic clarity and mythical resolution of meaning conventional of classical Hollywood cinema.[3]

In terms of rehabilitating narrative structure, Wyler engages a multiple-focus character following-pattern that has Homer's single-focus presence disrupting the dual-focus paralleling and contrasting of middle-class Al and working-class Fred, thwarting the mythical resolution of binary contradictions conventional of classical Hollywood cinema. The rehabilitation of all three protagonists remains ambiguous and open to interpretation, with contradictions of meaning evolving dialectically in history rather than resolving in Hollywood's melodramatic myth.

In terms of rehabilitating style, Wyler enhances the spatial dimensionality and temporal duration of shots by composing in depth and maintaining a verisimilar approximation of real time through long takes. These techniques allow him to block and stage characters in relation to each other and their surroundings in the same shot. He leaves it to viewers to construct meaning from the ambiguity in the appearances onscreen, rather than predetermining the meaning through selective focus and analytical editing, as is conventional of classical Hollywood style.

Ultimately Wyler's rehabilitation of narrative structure and style through reborn realism has implications for how we comprehend and interpret the characters in *The Best Years of Our Lives*. In the classical Hollywood film, the physically disabled or mentally traumatized character is often perceived through the lens of sentimental melodrama, as an embodiment of difference to be pitied or feared. The contradictions posed by embodied difference in relation to normative identity are typically resolved in Hollywood's melodramatic myth. The physically disabled or mentally traumatized character is mythologized, transformed into a static symbol of something abstract and ahistorical. By committing to the verisimilitude of reborn realism, Wyler ensures that physically disabled or mentally traumatized veterans are recognized as part of the collective social identity evolving in time, constituted as selves in relation with other selves in history rather than transformed into ahistorical symbols in Hollywood's melodramatic myth.

WYLER'S NARRATIVE PATH TO REBORN REALISM

The aim of this section and the next is to deepen the understanding of Wyler's narrative and stylistic path to reborn realism in *The Best Years of Our Lives*. Bazin defines narrative as "the ordering in time of fragments of reality" or "image facts," and style as "the inner dynamic principle of narrative, somewhat like the relation of energy to matter," or a magnet that "polarizes the filings" of the image facts "without changing their chemical composition."[4] For

Bazin, there is no single narrative or stylistic path to reborn realism. Directors may choose different paths, but the goal is the same: to achieve in the verisimilar appearances onscreen the ambiguity of reality rather than the timeless certainty of Hollywood's melodramatic myth.

With respect to achieving ambiguity in the narrative, Bazin points to the example of an Italian neorealist film, Roberto Rossellini's *Paisà* (1946). The ordering of "fragments of reality" or "image facts" in the film do not "mesh like a chain with the sprockets of a wheel" in predetermining the meaning, as in classical Hollywood narrative. Meaning only emerges afterward, in the mind of the viewer, which "leap[s] from one event to the other as one leaps from stone to stone in crossing a river." The presentation of events is simultaneously "elliptic and synthetic."[5] By keeping the linkages of image facts loose, indeterminate, not only between but also within shots, Rossellini achieves the ambiguity and irresolution of meaning that is consistent with reborn realism and analogous to the experience of reality itself.

Like Rossellini, Wyler wants to achieve narrative ambiguity for viewers of *The Best Years of Our Lives*, such that meaning remains open, indeterminate, evolving in time. Conventional of classical Hollywood cinema, the "image facts" in Wyler's film are largely character centered. Wyler's narrative path to reborn realism involves putting characters in relation to each other and their surroundings in a verisimilar appearance of postwar social reality onscreen and leaving it to viewers to construct meaning.

To draw out the implications of Wyler's character-centered narrative path, Rick Altman's character-centered theory of narrative proves useful.[6] Altman proposes to segment narratives based not on plot events, as is conventional, but by following characters. Altman identifies three major following-patterns in film and literature: dual-focus, single-focus, and multiple-focus. A dual-focus pattern follows two characters who occupy the same space but embody differing values, paralleling and contrasting them. A single-focus pattern follows one exceptional character's birth of desire and journey into the unknown. A multiple-focus pattern follows several characters making up a collective whole. The dual-focus following-pattern is prevalent in the popular genre-oriented Hollywood cinema while the single-focus following-pattern is prevalent in international art cinemas.[7]

Wyler rehabilitates the narrative in *The Best Years of Our Lives* by combining dual-focus and single-focus following-patterns. The result is a multiple-focus following-pattern that stretches a classical Hollywood melodrama toward the art cinema horizon of reborn realism. In effect, Homer's single-focus presence in the narrative functions to thwart the dialectical synthesis and resolution of opposing values anticipated by the dual-focus contrasting of middle-class Al and working-class Fred with respect to their experiences of rehabilitation. The multiple-focus following-pattern functions to keep the rehabilitation experiences of all three protagonists open, still in play, evolving dialectically in history rather than resolving in melodramatic myth.

Throughout *The Best Years of Our Lives*, strategically placed multiple-focus following-units depicting all three characters in the same space allow viewers to recognize the whole of the film as oriented toward collective experience. These units include a shared plane flight and taxi ride home, a reunion that night at a bar, Butch's Place, a second round of encounters at Butch's Place, and Homer's wedding. The placement of these units reveals the scaffolding of a three-act plot structure, with multiple-focus units beginning and ending the film and framing act two. Act one, approximately thirty minutes, is divided into two fifteen-minute segments. Act two, approximately seventy minutes, is divided into two twenty-minute segments and one thirty-minute segment. Act three, approximately thirty minutes, is divided into two fifteen-minute segments, mirroring act one.

Conventional of classical Hollywood cinema, dual-focus following-units branch into single-focus following-units that function to parallel and contrast the class-determined rehabilitation experiences of Al and Fred in acts one and two, and the disrupting effects of physical disability and mental trauma on the rehabilitation experiences of Fred and Homer in act three. For example, in the second segment of act one, following a dual-focus unit depicting Al and Fred sharing a taxi ride home, in parallel single-focus units, middle-class Al is delivered to a swanky apartment and working-class Fred, to a shack across the tracks. Al is greeted by his loving wife Milly (Myrna Loy), to whom he has been married for "twenty years," while Fred is unable to locate his wife Marie (Virginia Mayo), whom he barely knows, having been married for only "twenty days" before leaving for the war. In the first segment of act two, after the multiple-focus reunion of all three characters at Butch's Place, a dual-focus unit depicting Al's daughter Peggy (Teresa Wright) and wife Milly driving Fred and Al home branches into parallel single-focus units of Milly putting Al to bed and Peggy putting Fred to bed. The visual contrasting of drunk Al's inert hand versus drunk Fred's grabby hand cues the construction of implicit meaning regarding each man's sexual desire and ability.[8] The next day, in the second and third segments of act two, alternating single-focus units continue to follow and parallel Al and Fred as they wake up, get dressed, have breakfast, reconnect with their wives, and return to work, Fred to a drugstore, where he formerly worked as a soda jerk, and Al to a bank, to resume his career as a loan officer.

The dual-focus paralleling and contrasting of Al and Fred is disrupted by Homer while each man is at work, however. Homer, physically disabled, ambiguously unable or unwilling to work, greets Al at the bank in act two and Fred at the drugstore lunch counter in act three. These encounters prompt both men to advocate on behalf of a disadvantaged fellow veteran, putting his own job at risk and endangering his own rehabilitation. Al gives a loan to Novak (Dean White), a veteran without sufficient collateral. Fred slugs a right-wing customer on Homer's behalf after the customer tells Homer he fought on the wrong side. Fred gets fired, but Al's risk appears to pay off. Al is provisionally rehabilitated in act two, having achieved success in love and work, if ambiguously so. It is implied that Al and his wife Milly make love at the end of the second segment, and in a speech delivered at a company dinner in the third segment, Al manages to split the difference between advocating for veterans without sufficient collateral and the bank president's concern to protect the bank's assets. Still, uncertainty remains regarding the success of Al's rehabilitation into the future, not only given his liberal philosophy of loan management, but also his alcoholism. The ambiguity and irresolution of meaning is consistent with reborn realism.

In the third and final segment of act two, the dual-focus pattern of alternation between Al and Fred is further disrupted with the introduction of single-focus units of Homer for which there are no obvious structural parallels to this point, momentarily underscoring Homer's difference as exceptional, not fully integrated into the collective social self. While engaging in target practice, Homer implicitly contemplates suicide. Lacking hands, he requires the assistance of his father in getting ready for bed. These orphaned units will find structural parallels in act three, however, integrating Homer's exceptional difference into the collective social self as the focus shifts to paralleling Homer and Fred, with dual-focus units branching into single-focus units depicting their experiences of rehabilitation, of love and work, given the consequences of physical disability and mental trauma. For example, in the dual-focus unit depicting Fred's encounter with Homer at work, Fred slugs the right-wing customer on Homer's behalf, making use of his hand, after which, walking home together, Fred encourages Homer to marry Wilma (Cathy O'Donnell), despite lacking hands. This dual-focus unit branches into single-focus units of Homer exposing the truth of his physical disability to Wilma, sans prostheses, while Fred packs his bags to leave town after getting fired from work and leaving Marie.[9] The marriage theme is thus provisionally resolved for Homer in the first segment of act three, as Wilma accepts him as he is, physically disabled, lacking hands, while the marriage theme for able-bodied Fred remains unresolved.

Returning to the airfield, waiting for his flight, Fred climbs into the nose of a junked plane, and in subjective reflection, recalls his war trauma. This single-focus unit, which aims to achieve the subjective verisimilitude of an inner reality, expressed through camera movement and sound effects, has a displaced structural parallel in a single-focus unit orphaned in the third segment of act two, depicting Homer engaging in target practice while contemplating suicide. Both segments function to express a verisimilar inner reality, not explicitly, in so many words, but implicitly, through style. Whether able-bodied or disabled, with hands or without hands, both men are mentally traumatized from their war experiences. When Fred, the "junked" veteran, emerges from the junked plane, he lands a job with a crew that disassembles the planes and repurposes the materials for building prefabricated houses. The work theme is thus provisionally resolved for able-bodied Fred—the wartime pilot will be repurposed as a peacetime worker at an airfield—but remains unspoken and unresolved for physically disabled Homer. Moreover, uncertainty remains regarding whether the symptoms of mental trauma will continue to affect the rehabilitation of each character into the future. The ambiguity and irresolution of meaning is consistent with reborn realism.

In the final segment of the film, Homer marries Wilma and Fred reunites with Peggy. However, the film's conclusion is an "unhappy happy ending" more in keeping with the ambiguity and irresolution of reborn realism than the melodramatic clarity and mythical resolution of classical Hollywood cinema. Both couples find love but remain economically precarious. Homer and Wilma will subsist on government benefits. Fred and Peggy will "have no money, no decent place to live." Rehabilitation depends on the success of these marriages, which in turn depend on Homer and Fred not only finding love but also work. But what if the men are unable or unwilling to work due to war disability or trauma? The possibility of Wilma and Peggy contributing to the economic stability of the household is left open, unacknowledged and unthought. For more reasons than one, both visible and invisible, explicit and implicit, the ability of Homer and Fred to achieve economic stability through work remains ambiguous and unresolved, as does their rehabilitation, consistent with reborn realism and analogous to the experience of reality itself.

WYLER'S STYLISTIC PATH TO REBORN REALISM

In classical Hollywood cinema, style functions to endow the appearances onscreen with the continuum of reality, spatially and temporally, despite the fragmentation of the shots. Classical style aims for invisibility, effacing itself while transmitting the narrative unambiguously. In *The Best Years of Our Lives,* Wyler achieves invisible style—"styleless style," in Bazin's words[10]—but he does so in the service of achieving rather than eradicating ambiguity for viewers, consistent with reborn realism.

Wyler's stylistic path toward reborn realism involves enhancing the spatial dimensionality and temporal duration of shots, contributing to their verisimilitude. In classical style, space is shallow, with everything blocked and staged on one plane, in the foreground of the image, in selective focus. Wyler composes in depth, on multiple planes, in deep focus. Rather than cutting to direct the attention of viewers, isolating image facts in separate shots, as in analytical or continuity editing, he blocks and stages actors and actions relationally in the same shot, in the foreground, middle-ground, and background of a realistically detailed *mise en scène*. Wyler enhances temporal duration by favoring long takes, holding shots longer than is conventional of classical style, before cutting. He uses invisible cuts and dissolves to maintain the illusion of flow between shots. He avoids close-ups, preferring to capture the actions and reactions of actors in the same shot, relationally. The camera tends to be fixed rather than reframing with figure movement, as in classical style. Wyler is ultimately more interested in the performances of actors than in "showing off" with the camera.[11] His approach to scenes is not unlike that of Italian neorealism with respect to reality: centripetal rather than centrifugal. In other words, rather than hurrying from one scene to the next, on a quest for spectacular illusions and heightened emotions, as in classical cinema, Wyler lingers inside scenes, seeking to discover through analysis what is revealing about the scene itself. The attitude toward the scene is analytic, rather than that of boredom and impatience.[12] This attitude, along with his penchant for adapting plays, has prompted critics to describe Wyler's films as "theatrical." And yet, beyond the theatrical surfaces of Wyler's films lies "pure cinema," argues Bazin, which is another way of saying "no cinema," or the verisimilar appearance of reality itself.[13]

Wyler's stylistic path to reborn realism is immediately apparent in *The Best Years of Our Lives*. The film opens in a busy airport terminal, with Fred at a ticket counter, attempting to book a flight home to Boone City, his fictional hometown. By positioning Fred, a white working-class veteran, at the center of a triangular composition that includes a white upper-class businessman, a white working woman, and a Black porter, all in the same shot, a long take, Wyler gives viewers a verisimilar appearance of postwar reality, leaving it to viewers to comprehend and interpret the cues. Everyone is just going about their business. And yet, the character relations expose a postwar social reality premised in hierarchies of class, gender, and race difference. White upper-class businessmen expect to be served—and are. White working-class returning veterans such as Fred deserve to be served—but are not. White women and Black men are in the workforce, in service positions, there to serve (Figure 3.1).

When Fred eventually joins fellow veterans Al and Homer in boarding a military transport plane for the flight home to Boone City, Wyler favors multiple-focus following-units, blocking and staging all three protagonists in the same shot, bunched together collectively in the nose of the plane and subsequently in the back seat of a shared taxi, leaving it to viewers to comprehend and interpret the cues and construct the meaning, based on the differential relations of the characters to each other and their surroundings. The men differ in age, rank, appearance and attitude, but their experiences of rehabilitation will be determined primarily by class and physical ability on the explicit

Figure 3.1 Character relations expose a postwar social reality premised in hierarchies of class, gender, and race difference (*The Best Years of Our Lives*, 1946)

level of meaning—and by whiteness, masculinity, and mental trauma on the implicit level of meaning. From within the cramped interiors of the plane and taxi, Wyler achieves expansive exterior views through window frames, composing in depth, maintaining a relation between interiors and exteriors. We often see the men seeing and what they are seeing simultaneously in the same shot. For example, in one shot, the taxi driver is positioned in the foreground of the image, in the front seat, the three protagonists are positioned in the middleground, in the back seat, while a taxi window in the background reveals the exterior social reality in deep focus (Figure 3.2). In another shot, we see all three protagonists in the rear-view mirror of the taxi and simultaneously see what they see through the windshield, ordinary people going about their lives in everyday postwar America (Figure 3.3). Throughout the film, Wyler uses windows and mirrors as frames within frames to achieve a deep-focus relation between characters and the surrounding social reality.

Multiple-focus following-units beginning and ending act two, depicting all three protagonists convening at Butch's Place, are composed in depth, in long takes, with actions occurring simultaneously on multiple planes, with everything in sharp focus. Much has been written about the contributions of

Figure 3.2 Wyler maintains a relation between interiors and exteriors (*The Best Years of Our Lives*, 1946)

Figure 3.3 Viewers see the protagonists as well as what the protagonists see, simultaneously (*The Best Years of Our Lives*, 1946)

Gregg Toland's deep focus cinematography to Wyler's visual style.[14] Wyler challenged Toland to achieve deep focus in *The Best Years of Our Lives*, to "carry focus" to the extreme background of each set while maintaining the verisimilar appearance of normal vision.[15] Wyler did not want lens optics to be visible in the film. This meant Toland could not rely on the short focal-length lenses typically used to achieve deep focus, as he did in *Citizen Kane* (Orson Welles, RKO, 1941).[16] Short focal-length or wide-angle lenses introduce noticeable distortion in the image, suitable for Welles' expressionistic style in *Citizen Kane* but not for Wyler's neutral style in *The Best Years of Our Lives*. Toland used near-normal and normal focal-length lenses in *The Best Years of Our Lives*, but increased the light levels and stopped down apertures to increase the depth of field, approximating normal vision as best he could in the service of Wyler's neutral style.[17] Wyler attributes Toland's "remarkable facility for handling background and foreground action" for enabling him to "develop a better technique of staging my scenes," in that he could include "action and reaction in the same shot, without having to cut back and forth" between the characters, letting viewers "look from one to the other character of their own will, do their own cutting."[18]

In the multiple-focus unit at the beginning of act two, the three protagonists meet at Butch's Place, along with Al's wife Milly and daughter Peggy. The characters enter the bar from the deep focus background and are seated in the foreground of the image. Single-focus units then follow each protagonist individually as he interacts with another character in a two-shot. Homer watches his uncle Butch (Hoagy Carmichael) play piano. Al dances with his wife Milly. Fred talks with Al's daughter Peggy. It is up to viewers to comprehend and interpret the cues and construct the meaning, registering the contradictions in the ambiguous and evolving relations of each man to the other characters, to each other, and to their social surroundings. A limited amount of cross-cutting between parallel lines of action is sufficient to maintain a sense of the collective whole. Notably, among the two-shots of Al and Milly dancing, several are close-ups with shallow focus, an instance of Wyler's use of classical style for emphasis, for directing viewer attention, for prioritizing Al's storyline and his experience of rehabilitation at this point in the film. Drunk and confused, Al does not recognize Milly as his wife. By the end of act two, he is sobered up and provisionally rehabilitated, if ambiguously so.

Throughout the film, Wyler creates dramatic tension by blocking and staging simultaneous actions in deep focus, often in the same shot, typically in a long take—what Bazin refers to as "simultaneous *mise-en-scène*."[19] This technique is evident when the three protagonists convene for a second time at Butch's Place (Figure 3.4). A multiple-focus following-unit has Homer in the foreground playing a duet on the piano with Butch, Al in the middle-ground, standing next to the piano, watching Homer play, but distracted by Fred, who is in a phone booth in the background, calling Peggy because Al has asked that Fred stop seeing his daughter. Viewer attention is split, along with Al's, between simultaneous foreground and background actions. Bazin identifies an inverse relation between the dramatic importance of the simultaneous actions and their spatial positioning, with the primary action in the background and the secondary action in the foreground, but given the ambiguity of the image, one could interpret the foregrounding of Homer's piano playing as a turning point for his character that is no less dramatically significant than Fred's breakup with Peggy is for his character—although the meaning in Homer's case is implicit whereas the meaning in Fred's case is explicit.[20] Wyler also creates dramatic tension through simultaneous *mise en scène* in a multiple-focus unit at Homer's wedding. Viewer attention is split between Homer and Wilma joining hands in the middle-ground and Fred and Peggy gazing across the room at each other from the foreground and background respectively. Al and Milly are positioned in the background, between the other two couples, balancing the composition, symbolizing the possibility of rehabilitation through a successful marriage, if ambiguously so (Figure 3.5).

Figure 3.4 Wyler composes in depth, splitting viewer attention (*The Best Years of Our Lives*, 1946)

Figure 3.5 Wyler invites viewers to construct meaning from character relations, blocked and staged in deep space (*The Best Years of Our Lives*, 1946)

EXPOSING THE HISTORICAL TRUTH OF PHYSICAL AND MENTAL DISABILITY

Wyler's purpose in rehabilitating the narrative structure and style in *The Best Years of Our Lives* is to demythologize white male veterans in the postwar era, to expose the historical truth of their physical disability and mental trauma rather than uphold the myth of the invisible American warrior. Wyler was inspired in part by his own experience of war disability. He served four years in the United States Army Air Forces, filming bombing raids over Germany and Italy. His morale-boosting 16mm color feature documentary *Memphis Belle: A Story of a Flying Fortress* (US Army Air Forces First Motion Picture Unit, 1944) was commercially released to great acclaim. While shooting B-roll footage for his second documentary, *Thunderbolt* (US Army Air Forces First Motion Picture Unit, 1945), during a routine flight in a noisy, unpressurized B-25 bomber, Wyler sustained nerve damage in his ears and lost his hearing. Assuming he would never direct again, he became depressed. He was sent home to a military hospital, where he submitted to psychiatric therapy with sodium pentothal treatments, or "truth serum," hoping to discover whether his deafness had a psychosomatic component.[21] He eventually recovered some hearing in his left ear and resumed his directing career in Hollywood by engaging the use of a prosthesis. On set, sitting near the camera, a headset and amplifier was patched directly into the sound equipment, allowing him to hear what the microphones heard with no distractions, a practice that ultimately proved advantageous for coaching actors on their line deliveries.[22]

When Wyler returned to work in Hollywood, producer Samuel Goldwyn offered him scripts for a film about Eisenhower and for *The Bishop's Wife* (Henry Koster, Samuel Goldwyn Productions, 1947), but Wyler turned them down. After his war experience, he was not interested in making a film about a famous general or sentimental entertainment. He was looking for something "honest," less implicated in Hollywood's melodramatic myth.[23] He chose a manuscript called *Glory for Me* (1945), developed by novelist and war correspondent MacKinlay Kantor from a *Time* magazine article about Marines on furlough.[24] The manuscript was written in blank verse—metrical but unrhymed lines of poetry. Goldwyn found the manuscript unreadable and tried to talk Wyler out of it, but Wyler insisted. Pulitzer Prize-winning playwright Robert Sherwood was hired to write the script, eventually renamed *The Best Years of Our Lives*. Sherwood and Wyler, working together, kept many of the essentials of Kantor's manuscript but were concerned about whether an actor could successfully play the role of Homer, spastic due to a brain injury incurred during the war. They considered cutting the character until Wyler attended a war bond rally to raise funds for disabled veterans and saw a documentary, *Diary of a Sergeant* (US Army Pictorial Service Signal Corps, 1945), featuring Harold Russell, who lost both hands in a training accident and was adept in the use of prosthetic hooks. Wyler cast Russell, a non-actor, in the role of Homer, incorporating details of Russell's real-life experience into *The Best Years of Our Lives*.

Diary of a Sergeant documents Russell's rehabilitation at Walter Reed Army Medical Center in the District of Columbia. Russell undergoes an operation to remove what is left of his damaged hands, followed by recovery and occupational therapy. Throughout the film, a narrator (Alfred Drake) assumes the voice-over narration on Russell's behalf as a nurse inscribes Russell's words in his diary, both functioning prosthetically, in place of Russell's actual voice. Russell's main concern, post-operation, is not wanting to go through life dependent on others for everyday tasks, a concern shared by Homer in *The Best Years of Our Lives*. Fitted with prosthetic hooks for the first time, Russell returns to his ward proudly smoking a cigarette without help, only to experience frustration and embarrassment when he spills a drink—a detail Wyler incorporates into *The Best Years of Our Lives*. In *Diary of a Sergeant*, an inspirational documentary is shown to the men in the ward, prompting Russell to set for himself the goal of learning to "live normally," like he did before the accident. The film within the film, *Meet McGonegal* (US Army Pictorial Service Signal Corps, 1944), is about a man who lost his hands in the first World War. Charlie McGonegal is fitted with prosthetic hooks, learns to use them proficiently in three months, and goes on to live a "normal life," which includes a career, marriage, and children. Inspired by McGonegal, Russell in *Diary of a Sergeant* masters the use of prosthetic hooks in three months, beating his doctor's prediction of six months. Released on furlough, Russell enrolls in college, something he could not afford without the government support he receives for his war service. Overcoming self-consciousness about his hooks, Russell asks a woman out on a date, the proverbial "girl next door," recalling Wilma in *The Best Years of Our Lives*. In the conclusion of *Diary of a Sergeant*, Russell inscribes the final entry in his diary, holding the pen himself, "more interested in looking to the future than remembering the past." *The Best Years of Our Lives* ends similarly with Homer holding a wedding ring and placing it on Wilma's finger himself, more interested in looking to the future than remembering the past.

With each successive film, from *Meet McGonegal* (1944) to *Diary of a Sergeant* (1945) to *The Best Years of Our Lives* (1946), the prognosis for the rehabilitation of the physically disabled protagonist becomes increasingly uncertain, countering the expectation that the documentaries will express the ambiguity and irresolution of real life whereas the Hollywood film will offer melodramatic clarity and mythical resolution. In all three films, the protagonist's rehabilitation depends on finding love with a woman and economic stability through work while adjusting to life with a physical disability. In *Meet McGonegal*, Charlie McGonegal is unambiguously successful on both fronts. He works in an office, where he is shown typing, making phone calls, signing paperwork, using his prosthetic hooks to do "everyday things with everyday ease." At the end of the film, he reports that he is married and has two boys. In *Diary of a Sergeant*, Harold Russell enrolls in college and goes on a date with a woman. Although it will take him four years to complete the degree before he can land a job, he is optimistic because the timeline is clear, not open-ended, as were timelines during his military service. With respect to the woman, despite losing his hands, he expresses certainty about "not having lost his touch." This statement is backed up with a shot of the woman taking his arm as they walk home from their date. In *The Best Years of Our Lives*, Homer Parrish marries Wilma, the girl next door, but how he intends to support himself and his wife, beyond living on government benefits, remains ambiguous, unresolved. Is it that Homer cannot work, or is it that he is unwilling to work? Without having viewed the two documentaries, one might be inclined to assume that Homer cannot work due to his physical disability. Viewing the two documentaries shifts the meaning: Homer now seems unwilling to work, for reasons that remain unspoken, implicit. Homer may be more angry and bitter about his disability than his affable persona suggests.[25]

David Gerber makes a compelling case for the dualism of Homer's character and why this goes underrecognized by viewers.[26] Disabled characters in popular film evoke competing emotions of pity and fear in viewers. Whereas pitying the disabled person is a socially condoned emotion, fearing the disabled person is a socially condemned emotion. Viewers are therefore more inclined to pity Homer; he is greatly impaired and deserves our sympathy. And yet, there is another side to Homer's character that viewers are reluctant to acknowledge, as is Homer himself. Homer is suppressing a violent temper, as evidenced in the target shooting scene in the garage, when he uses his hooks to break through a window, scaring the kids, and in the lunch counter scene at the pharmacy, when he confronts the intrusive right-wing customer. Homer's hooks are potentially menacing. There are undertones of menace in the scene with Wilma in the bedroom, expressed stylistically. According to Gerber, Homer's potential for violence (and implicit suicidality) can be traced to the unspoken shame and embarrassment he feels about his hooks and the public attention they evoke. Being the object of the gaze is culturally feminizing. Homer is humiliated and emasculated by public attention, more than he lets on. His repressed anger and bitterness run counter to the affable showmanship he displays whenever others notice or comment on his hooks. Gerber cites research about how confronting the daily oppression of unwanted public attention can be psychologically debilitating for people with disabilities. In response, they develop "strategic behaviors" for "preserving their self-respect and maximizing their self-confidence."[27] Homer has learned to put people at ease by adopting an affable, performative, non-threatening persona. In effect, Harold Russell was already acting before Wyler cast him in a Hollywood film.

In addition to the implicit dimensions of Homer's character identified by Gerber, we might also note there are implicit dimensions to Fred's character, having to do with his unspoken mental trauma. Fred, like Homer, is a melodramatic mute, unable or unwilling to say what he is thinking and feeling. The melodramatic mute is a familiar character type in classical Hollywood cinema, given the prevalence of melodrama as a narrative mode.[28] In melodrama, that which is unspoken is still expressed, not in words but in the elements of film style, especially in the visuals and music.[29] Although the mute character eventually names that which is unspoken and unknown, Wyler resists the clarity and resolution of meaning conventional of Hollywood's melodramatic myth in favor of achieving the ambiguity and irresolution of reborn realism. Fred's mental trauma remains implicit, unspoken but expressed through style.

In representing Fred's mental trauma, Wyler shifts from a neutral, transparent style to an overtly expressionistic style to signal the shift from objective to subjective verisimilitude. This occurs in two scenes, both of which involve Fred revisiting his war trauma in his mind. In the first scene, which takes place at night, Fred has a nightmare. Wyler uses camera movement and combined music and sound effects to outwardly express the verisimilar appearance of Fred's inner subjective reality. Chiaroscuro lighting and Dana Andrew's expressionistic acting style also contribute to the verisimilar appearance of inwardness, outwardly expressed, recalling film noir, a Hollywood narrative mode known for stylistic hybridity, for combining realism and expressionism (Figure 3.6). In a second scene, which takes place in daylight, Fred revisits his war trauma while seated in the nose of a junked plane. Once again, Wyler uses expressionistic style, including dramatic camera movements and framings, close-ups, quick cuts, and sound effects combined with louder music, to express the verisimilar appearance of Fred's inner subjective reality (Figure 3.7).[30] That the historical truth of Fred's mental trauma is implicitly cued through expressionistic film style rather than explicitly expressed in dialogue can be interpreted as a symptom of repression, of an inability or unwillingness to confront mental trauma in returning veterans.

Figure 3.6 Acting style and lighting contributes to the creation of an expressionist reality, or inwardness, outwardly expressed (*The Best Years of Our Lives*, 1946)

Figure 3.7 Wyler uses style to achieve a verisimilar appearance of inner subjective reality (*The Best Years of Our Lives*, 1946)

In the postwar myth of the invincible warrior, physical disability could be explicitly acknowledged but mental disability was disavowed. This theory is bolstered by the example of *Let There Be Light* (John Huston, US Army Pictorial Service Signal Corps, 1946). The documentary depicts veterans undergoing treatment for mental trauma at Mason General Hospital in Long Island, New York. Huston, a close friend of Wyler's, completed the film as Wyler and Robert Sherwood were working on the script for *The Best Years of Our Lives*. Although Huston's documentary was exhibited in nontheatrical settings, mostly military but also civilian,[31] the War Department banned the film from exhibition to non-military commercial audiences on the grounds that it invaded the privacy of patients depicted in the film. A statement from the War Department claimed that the patients had participated "in furtherance of the war effort," but that once the war was over, "it was difficult to see how distribution of this film to the public at large or to groups other than military would be permissible."[32] Huston argued otherwise, that the patients were proud of the film, that participating in the making of it helped with their rehabilitation, and that it disclosed nothing of which they were ashamed. When Huston submitted the film to a documentary festival at the Museum of Modern Art in 1946, it was confiscated by military police. Ultimately the film was banned from commercial exhibition until 1981. Huston locates the reason for the ban in the War Department's need to prioritize myth over history:

> It boils down to the fact that [the War Department] wanted to maintain the "warrior" myth, which said that our American soldiers went to war and came back all the stronger for the experience. [. . .] They might die, or they might be wounded, but their spirits remain unbroken.[33]

WYLER'S CLASSICAL HOLLYWOOD MODERN ART CINEMA

David Bordwell remarks that "certain classical filmmakers have something of the art cinema about them."[34] Wyler is one of those filmmakers. According to Bordwell, art cinema explicitly defines itself against classical Hollywood cinema in subscribing to an expanded notion of reality, encompassing the outer reality of the world as well as the inner reality of perception and the imagination, and strives to depict these realities as realistically as possible, by means of a correspondingly expanded notion of realism, encompassing both "documentary factuality" and "intensive psychological subjectivity."[35] Wyler's contribution to the postwar American cinema is to expand Hollywood's art cinema aesthetic beyond film noir to other genres, including the World War II rehabilitation drama. *The Best Years of Our Lives* fits the profile of 1940s cinema that Bordwell identifies as the "first New Hollywood," in that Wyler "adheres to the basic norms" of classical Hollywood cinema, but "stretch[es] the horizons of cinema for those who followed."[36] Ultimately, *The Best Years of Our Lives* is a transitional text, a classical Hollywood film that stretches narratively and stylistically through the Bazinian reborn realism of the 1940s toward the art cinemas yet to come, including the European and Latin American art cinemas of the 1950s and 60s and the New Hollywood of the 1970s—cinemas more interested in confronting the truth of history than upholding the compensatory prosthesis of myth.

NOTES

1. On comprehending and interpreting film, see David Bordwell, *Making Meaning: Inference and Rhetoric in the Interpretation of Cinema* (New Haven: Harvard University Press, 1991), 9.
2. On the myth of the invincible American warrior, which figures the male body as a mythical symbol of American national identity, see Susan Jeffords, *Remasculinization of America: Gender and the Vietnam War* (Bloomington: Indiana University Press, 1989); Kaja Silverman, *Male Subjectivity at the Margins* (New York: Routledge, 1992); and Christina

S. Jarvis, *Men at War: American Masculinity during World War II* (Dekalb, IL: Northern Illinois University Press, 2004).
3. Bazin valorized Wyler along with Orson Welles and Italian directors Roberto Rossellini and Vittorio De Sica for "giving back to the cinema a sense of the ambiguity of reality," each via their own distinctive narrative and stylistic paths, constituting the "reborn realism" of the 1940s. André Bazin, "The Evolution of the Language of Cinema," ed. Hugh Gray, *What is Cinema? Volume 1* (Berkeley: University of California Press, 1967/2005), 39.
4. André Bazin, "An Aesthetic of Reality: Neorealism," ed. Hugh Gray, *What is Cinema? Volume 2* (Berkeley: University of California Press, 1971/2005), 31.
5. Ibid., 35.
6. Rick Altman, *A Theory of Narrative* (New York: Columbia University Press, 2008).
7. The Hollywood Western conventionally opposes two male characters as embodiments of competing cultural values while the musical and screwball comedy oppose female and male leads on their way to becoming a romantic couple. The art film, on the other hand, typically follows a socially marginalized protagonist undergoing a secular version of a passion narrative that reveals abstract truths about the human condition.
8. The visual motif of hands proliferates implicit meaning related to masculine identity and sexuality throughout the film.
9. Marie gets involved with Cliff (Steve Cochran), a villainous veteran, someone who takes advantage of others, a lookalike structural counterpart to Novak, a virtuous veteran, who is only asking for his fair share. These secondary characters are clearly delineated as virtuous or villainous, in keeping with melodrama's emphasis on moral identity, whereas the social identities of the main protagonists are ambiguous, in keeping with reborn realism. Sarah Kozloff argues along similar lines that with the female characters, "realistic technique frequently takes a backseat to melodramatic impact." Sarah Kozloff, *The Best Years of Our Lives* (London: BFI, 2011), 97.
10. André Bazin, "William Wyler, or the Jansenist of Directing," ed. R. J. Cardullo, *André Bazin, the Critic as Thinker* (Rotterdam: Sense Publishers, 2017), 211.
11. Curtis Hanson, "William Wyler: An Interview," ed. Gabriel Miller, *William Wyler Interviews* (Jackson: University Press of Mississippi, 2010), 33.
12. Cesare Zavattini, "A Thesis on Neo-Realism," ed. David Overbey, *Springtime in Italy* (Archon Books, 1979), 67–78.
13. Bazin, "William Wyler, or the Jansenist of Directing," 219.
14. Wyler and Toland made seven films together: *These Three* (1936), *Come and Get It* (1936), *Dead End* (1937), *Wuthering Heights* (1939), *The Westerner* (1940), *The Little Foxes* (1941), and *The Best Years of Our Lives* (1946).
15. William Wyler, "No Magic Wand," ed. Richard Koszarski, *Hollywood Directors 1941-1976* (New York: Oxford University Press, 1977), 112.
16. Gregg Toland, "Realism for *Citizen Kane*," *American Cinematographer* (February 1941): 54–5.
17. Barry Salt, "Film Style and Technology in the Forties," *Film Quarterly* 31.1 (Fall 1977): 50.
18. Wyler, "No Magic Wand," 112.
19. Bazin, "William Wyler, or the Jansenist of Directing," 210.
20. Ibid., 216.
21. Jan Herman, *A Talent for Trouble: The Life of Hollywood's Most Acclaimed Director, William Wyler* (New York: Da Capo Press, 1997), 276.
22. Ibid., 287.
23. William Wyler, "Escape to Reality," *Liberty* 24.1 (1947): 16; Herman, *A Talent for Trouble*, 283.

24. Herman, *A Talent for Trouble*, 279. The *Time* magazine article upon which author MacKinlay Kantor developed *Glory for Me* is "The Way Home," *Time* 44.6 (August 7, 1944): 15–16.
25. Sociologist Willard Waller discusses the anger and bitterness of returning and disabled veterans in *The Veteran Comes Back* (New York: Dryden Press, 1944).
26. David Gerber, "Heroes and Misfits: The Troubled Social Reintegration of Disabled Veterans in *The Best Years of Our Lives*," *American Quarterly* 46.4 (December 1994): 552.
27. David Gerber, "Anger and Affability: The Rise and Representation of a Repertory of Self-Presentation Skills in a World War II Disabled Veteran," *Journal of Social History* (Fall 1993): 8.
28. Peter Brooks, *The Melodramatic Imagination: Balzac, Henry James, Melodrama, and the Mode of Excess* (New Haven: Yale University Press, 1995), 56.
29. Geoffrey Nowell-Smith, "Minnelli and Melodrama," ed. Christine Gledhill, *Home is Where the Heart Is: Studies in Melodrama and the Woman's Film* (London: BFI, 1987), 73.
30. A pitiful scene in *Till the End of Time* (Edward Dmytryk, RKO, 1946), a film with which *Best Years* is often compared, depicts an unnamed veteran seated at a lunch counter, shaking uncontrollably from war trauma, embarrassed about being seen. In contrast with Wyler, who uses expressionistic style to represent the symptoms of war trauma subjectively, from the inside, as experienced mentally by Fred, Dmytryk uses classical style—even lighting, symmetrical framing, shallow focus, and analytical editing—to represent the unnamed veteran's symptoms of war trauma objectively, from the outside, as viewed by others.
31. Noah Tsika, *Traumatic Imprints: Cinema, Military Psychiatry, and the Aftermath of War* (Berkeley: University of California Press, 2018), 170.
32. Mark Harris, *Five Came Back: A Story of Hollywood and the Second World War* (Edinburgh: Canongate Books, 2015), 410.
33. John Huston, *An Open Book* (New York: Alfred A. Knopf, 1980), 125; Harris, *Five Came Back*, 413; Scott Simmon, "Film Notes, *Let There Be Light*," National Film Preservation Foundation, <https://www.filmpreservation.org/preserved-films/screening-room/let-there-be-light-1946> (last accessed August 8, 2022).
34. David Bordwell, "Art Cinema as Mode of Film Practice," eds. Leo Braudy and Marshall Cohen, *Film Theory & Criticism: Introductory Readings*, eighth edition (Oxford: Oxford University Press, 2016), 588.
35. Ibid., 583.
36. David Bordwell, *Reinventing Hollywood: How 1940s Filmmakers Changed Movie Storytelling* (Chicago: University of Chicago Press, 2018), 478–9.

CHAPTER 4

Persistent Presence: Space and Time in the Films of William Wyler

Francis Mickus

A sense of cohesion in Wyler's films is not immediately apparent. Filmmakers like Frank Capra, Preston Sturges, and Alfred Hitchcock were closely associated with specific genres. This in turn allows critics to easily study these filmmakers simply by disregarding the narrative wrapping. Thus, a critic can focus on a given filmmaker's preoccupations, by cataloguing recurrent narrative tropes and themes. Wyler, on the other hand, switches from one genre to another with ease; his diversity of subjects complicates critical analysis and the narrative cannot simply be dismissed. One cannot study Wyler for variations in a single story. To capture the binding thread of his *œuvre*, one studies instead *how* he tells each story. Critics often explore his use of deep focus, but Wyler has a particular method of manipulating space in his films that is not limited to a single technique. How characters interact with one another, how they inhabit the space of the film, even how they are framed tell us more of the story and the characters than the specifics of dialogue and action.

Wyler learned his craft by shooting a string of two-reel Westerns, which taught him how to show his stories rather than tell them. How many different ways can a man get on a horse? Once he graduated to longer formats, to avoid being typecast as a "Western director," he kept his distance from the genre, shooting only three Westerns between 1930 and his retirement in 1970. Be it a Western (*Hell's Heroes* 1929), a comedy (*The Good Fairy* 1935), a domestic drama (*Mrs. Miniver* 1942), a film noir (*Detective Story* 1951), a spectacle (*Ben-Hur* 1959), or a musical (*Funny Girl* 1968), the stories themselves are told so originally that they are difficult to define by traditional genre categories. Is *Roman Holiday* (1953), for example, a comedy or a drama? When watching his films, one discovers that Wyler uses aspects of personal, social, and at times meta-filmic history to convey a sense of inescapability. The past clearly plays a significant role in his films.

Many of Wyler's films are based on novels (*Wuthering Heights* 1939, *Dodsworth* 1936) or plays (*Dead End* 1937, *The Children's Hour* 1961). One would expect such literate source material to be dominated by literate aspects of storytelling, such as dialogue and dramaturgy, but Wyler is noted for his ability to make adaptations that are visual and cinematic.[1] Indeed, Wyler's films are filled with such powerfully cinematic images that few are willing to accept that he could be solely responsible for having created them; many critics and scholars are quick to point out that he made several of his greatest films with cinematographer Gregg Toland.

Toland is best remembered for his collaboration with Orson Welles on *Citizen Kane* in 1941. Wyler's collaboration with Toland consisted of only six out of the forty-odd films in Wyler's filmography. Toland also worked with many other directors, visual stylists like Frank Borzage, William Dieterle and Rouben Mamoulian, as well as more classically oriented filmmakers like Howard Hawks and John Ford. While Wyler admired and respected Toland, a good way to start an appreciation of Wyler's work is by noting both the extent of as well as the limits to the scope of their collaboration. Toland and Wyler had similar philosophies in approaching a film: both men saw how vital it was to show the story through images. While Toland indeed brought many rich ideas to Wyler's images, Wyler had a very specific visual sense of his own. Indeed, it is his sense of film space that gives form to the narrative structure of Wyler's films. Furthermore, Wyler's exploitation of space is closely linked to his manipulation of time. These aspects of Wyler's work—Toland, space, and time—help us to appreciate how the past shapes Wyler's characters and give his films their emotional as well as narrative thrust. This collaboration of style would find its fullest expression in Wyler's last film for Samuel Goldwyn, and his last time working with Toland, *The Best Years of Our Lives* (1946).

WYLER AND TOLAND

Gregg Toland's creative partnership with Wyler lasted as long as both men worked with Samuel Goldwyn. Toland's famed deep-focus photography, so closely associated with Welles's film *Citizen Kane*, was developed at Goldwyn's studios, particularly in his six collaborations with William Wyler. What made Toland different from other cinematographers was his desire to maintain creative freedom, which Wyler appreciated. In his early days at Universal, Wyler would tell the cinematographer what the desired set-up and angle would be, going as far as to explicitly request the required lens.

> Making Westerns at Universal . . . I directed the camera work. I considered it part of my job. Well, Gregg Toland, you don't do that with a man like Gregg Toland. So we had an understanding, and I showed him the

> scene, and then I showed him how I thought it should be photographed, and maybe he had some changes, some improvement.[2]

However, Toland had carefully developed over the first decade of his career, a reputation that Wyler could depend on. His status was indeed enviable, as George Turner explains it:

> At Goldwyn, Toland had a situation that was the envy of other cinematographers. Generally, cinematographers were—and still are—forced to work on most pictures with little or no preparation. Goldwyn put Toland onto the pre-planning team with the director and designers as much as six weeks in advance. Between pictures he was able to work in Goldwyn's experimental lab, devising new lenses, filters and camera gadgets. He was aware of the advantages of his situation and often expressed a wish that his colleagues could work under similar conditions.[3]

Such was Toland's reputation and Welles's admiration that he shared the same screen card with the director in the credits for *Citizen Kane* in 1941, and for *The Long Voyage Home* the previous year with John Ford. Wyler was always generous with credit.[4] He would refrain from explaining the mechanics of Toland's camerawork, but he understood many of these techniques. His years at Universal taught him camerawork. He knew what lens and f/stop were needed to achieve the desired effect. He achieved similar imagery in films like *Dodsworth* (1936) which was shot by Rudolph Maté (Figure 4.1). Wyler also carried over Toland's techniques to other cinematographers, such as Joseph Ruttenberg at MGM for *Mrs. Miniver* (1942) and Leo Tover for *The Heiress* (1949), which uses many of Wyler's previous expressionistic strategies for developing a heightened sense of confinement.

The results of the Toland–Wyler collaboration are visually stunning. Barry Salt states that in the thirties, "There is no sign of any deep focus in the *Citizen Kane* sense, nor is there much sign of the 'Tolandesque' compositions that typify his work in the forties."[5] However, such an observation must be modified when viewing a film such as the 1937 *Dead End* which already explores the exaggerated angles (Figure 4.2), multiple-plane and multiple-frame compositions (Figure 4.3), which point directly towards *Kane*. Toland even returned from his venture with Welles to bring Wyler visual solutions for his staging-in-depth, most notably a deep focus to Wyler's multiple-plane structure, and through lighting, fuse them in a single shot.

Despite Salt's observation, it is not inaccurate to say that Wyler's influence on Toland was as significant as Toland's influence on Wyler. Film historians are quick to point out Toland's impact on Wyler's work, but much less is made of Charlie Chaplin's collaboration with Rolland Totheroh, who

Figure 4.1 The loneliness between the end of one life and the beginning of another (*Dodsworth*, 1936)

Figure 4.2 The ominous nature of an extremely low angle (*Dead End*, 1937)

Figure 4.3 Multiple planes and multiple frames (*Dead End*, 1937)

worked as cinematographer on every Chaplin film from 1916 to 1947 (he even started on *Limelight* in 1951), or Joseph Walker who shot Frank Capra's entire Columbia output from 1930 to 1939, as well as *It's a Wonderful Life* (1946). The practice continues with contemporary filmmakers: Steven Spielberg has worked for years with Janus Kaminski, and Clint Eastwood worked with Jack Green until the latter's retirement. Wyler's "dependency" on his cameraman was not a unique relationship in Hollywood.

What makes the collaboration between the two men of particular interest is that both worked with the objective of telling the film's story as the primary concern. Toland would tell young cameramen to

> Forget the camera. The nature of the story determines the photographic style. Understand the story and make the most out of it. If the audience is conscious of tricks and effects, the cameraman's genius, no matter how great it is, is wasted.[6]

Wyler's attitude was similar: "A director should not attract attention to himself away from the actors and away from the story."[7] For both men the story was to be told visually, in a way that explored the image in the frame and the space that characters occupied. Wyler's interest in the space characters occupy predates Toland. The importance of space permeates Wyler's filmography, as he would get many of his cinematographers to actively explore the images they made.

A SENSE OF SPACE

There are three types of space in film: the space of the screen, the space of the set, and the space of the action, which Éric Rohmer designates as Pictorial Space (*espace picturale*), Architectural Space (*espace architecturale*), and Filmic Space (*espace filmique*).[8] Making a film consists of manipulating the interplay between these three spaces. Even in his early films for Universal, Wyler would explore the psychological significance of framing, depth of field, and spatial distance between characters. For instance, in the 1929 film *The Love Trap*, as historian Neil Sinyard describes,

> The shot of [the young married couple] as they stare across at each other from either side of the room conveys mutual social embarrassment at its most acute, with camera position behind Evelyn emphasizing the space between them, which now looks vast—physically, emotionally, and socially.[9]

When discussing space in film, one must keep in mind the diverse nature of the concept. "Capra and Wyler," notes Barbara Bowman, "use space in an overt manner, making emotional and intellectual confrontations apparent in that space."[10] Where analyses of other directors will focus on the lighting (Josef von Sternberg), the pacing (Sturges), or even effective visual flourishes (Hitchcock and Welles), Wyler's films are often explored specifically through his staging and directing of actors—that is, his manipulation of *architectural* space. Bowman's general thesis follows this trend by focusing only on the second of Rohmer's three film spaces. She disregards the spatial aspects of the 1950s films such as *Roman Holiday* which "just sprawls in a travel log sort of laxness as the couple wanders through it,"[11] or *Detective Story*, which in her eyes is little more than well-filmed theater.[12] Bowman finds the spatial dynamics in these films more conventional. Few filmmakers are as acutely aware as Wyler of the plasticity of *space* in a film, which is an expressive thread throughout his career. It is a plasticity which goes beyond the business staging of actors and the use of props. Jean Housen's evaluation of the nature of filmic space aptly describes Wyler's philosophy.

> The way the frame is filled, measured, occupied, abandoned determines an internal spatiality which reinforces or contradicts the visual spatiality, that of the lens' perspective (with its effect on focal length, the width of framing) and that of the set, the "real" space where the action takes place.[13]

The sophistication in Wyler's approach to images increases over time. Much of this may be a result of the technological possibilities available to him. Earlier films develop characters' relationship through the staging: essentially, their relationship with the set. In *Jezebel* (1938), Julie Marsden's (Bette Davis) downfall is most effectively marked by the tremendous space all the other dancers create when abandoning the floor. Preston Dillard (Henry Fonda), her suitor, to press the impropriety of her gesture (she had insisted on coming to the ball in a red dress instead of the customary white), first demands that they dance despite Julie's public humiliation, only to put an end to their relationship when he brings her home.

One should not disregard Wyler's use of the other filmic spaces. The 1958 Western *The Big Country* is "big" precisely because Wyler shoots it in such a way that the characters are dwarfed by the surrounding space. Not only is the VistaVision frame itself vast, but Wyler augments the vastness by pushing characters away from the camera. The fight between McKay (Gregory Peck) and Leech (Charlton Heston) is reduced to insignificance by the fact that Wyler insists on shooting in an extremely long shot. Close-ups in the film become all the more violent, such as Buck's (Chuck Connors) attempt to rape Julie (Jean Simmons), which is interrupted by his father Rufus's (Burl Ives) intervention. The entire sequence is shot in a closed and cluttered space, with Julie's bed in the foreground, only to cut into the two men's confrontation with a double close-up. Throughout the film, Rufus's entries are shot in close-up, giving them a sense of overpowering invasiveness in scenes otherwise shot in more social scales of the half and three-quarter shot, often grouping two or more characters. *The Big Country* explores our own engagement in the film through the distances Wyler maintains. (The French translated the film title as *Les Grands Espaces*, which literally means *The Vast Spaces*.)

When Rohmer suggested that the frame itself was a space to be filled (*l'éspace picturale*), he reminds us of the physical reality of a film. To watch a film is to see a screen filled with visual information, shape, shade, and color, that in our minds are converted into objects, action, and events which we as an audience react to emotionally and intellectually. The screen itself remains a fixed surface that receives this information. What is often discussed as "framing" is the study of the proxemics established between characters (as in the case of Buck's attempted rape), and the proxemics with the audience through the evolution of camera placements. To state that the space of the frame is a real space, which must be dealt with, is to remind us that it is, in fact, the only reality to which we are privy. Welles's *Othello* (1953) is a stark reminder of the fact that a reverse angle can be shot a thousand miles away. The only reality of space is the shot itself.

Welles's Kuleshovian reinvention of architectural space through editing finds a curious confirmation a year later with the invention of the crab dolly that allowed Wyler to design the film *Detective Story* the way he did. The crab dolly is a multi-wheeled tripod that can move the camera in any direction. By choosing to place the entire film in virtually a single set, he effectively neutralizes the set as a dramatically evolving element of the film. Its cramped nature is there to "set the stage" for the even more cramped psychological realities that exist within the space of the frame. The film is an exploration of pictorial space. In the film, Wyler makes the actors move within the frame as if they were stuck in a very tight box. When Detective McLeod (Kirk Douglas) rises to taunt his suspect, he must bend over to remain visible within the frame (Figure 4.4).

Wyler constantly makes the tight spaces even tighter through framing. Interrogations are regularly carried out with the detective crowding the space of their suspects and the camera following suit. In one shot, three policemen and the criminal, who they manage to "turn" informant, are bunched into a single frame (Figure 4.5). The suspect is surrounded by the cops, within both the set and the frame. He is seated on the bench against a wall with a policeman siting on either side. The third cop is standing in front of him blocking the possibility of his bursting from his seat. The camera itself closes any visual breathing space (or escape route) as the four people can barely stay within the

Figure 4.4 Hemming in the characters (*Detective Story*, 1951)

Figure 4.5 Hemming in the suspect (*Detective Story*, 1951)

shot. The standing policeman has to bend forward, pushing even further into the suspect's space. When the suspect does turn, the camera suddenly pulls back to show the room. The characters of this sequence then leave the precinct, allowing the camera to close in on another case. Throughout the film, the camera remains at eye level, placing audience and characters on an equal footing. That is until James McLeod finds out about his wife's (Eleanor Parker) past. Then the image vacillates between high and low angles. McLeod's life and certainties visually lose balance.

Rohmer's architectural and pictorial spaces, as applied by Wyler, naturally inform the third, filmic space. The first two show us where and how characters live, but, as we have just seen, they also point to the world they live in. The cops in *Detective Story* are hardly any better than the robbers they arrest (they are often worse). However, in the sense that McLeod feels his moral superiority through a sense of moral certainty, we see his tragic flaw. McLeod's world view is one of binary oppositions. There are cops and there are robbers; women are either virtuous or they are tramps. There are no in-betweens and redemption is impossible, which is a particularly curious trait in McLeod's character, for what is the value of arresting criminals if they cannot thereafter redeem themselves and follow honest pursuits? The revelation of his wife's past destroys McLeod, as he cannot accept the redemptive value of her life with him. McLeod's world is the neutral grey of the film stock. It is not even the black and white of good versus evil (though McLeod would like to believe so); but he cannot see the shades of color—the moral variety of life. These are just some examples of Wyler's deft handling of space.

A MATTER OF TIME

Space becomes the external landscape that illustrates internal turmoil, a turmoil which for Wyler is anchored in time. Wyler's films show how time in film can be explored along lines that approximate those that Rohmer established when discussing space. There is screen time (the time to watch the movie), narrative time (the arc from the beginning of events to their conclusion), and filmic time (the time that frames the characters' lives). Films often explore the tensions between screen time and narrative time. Hitchcock's *Rope* (1948) pushed such tensions to their limits, by binding the very ribbon of film to the sense of time. The Fox television series *24* (2001–10) tells a story that runs through twenty-four hours and is segmented into twenty-four-hour long episodes in the season.[14]

It is a truism to say that all that is needed to understand a film is stated in the film. However, what that usually implies is that the audience registers the characters' natures and personalities by analyzing how they react to the present situations that occur over the course of the film. Everything we need to know about the characters in *It Happened One Night* (Frank Capra, 1934) can be derived by what they do in the space and timespan of the plot. We know surprisingly little about their past, besides the few bits of information that establish the basic situation. Similarly, a Hawks film is often concerned with the idea of existential redemption, but what needs redemption can be summarized in a few sentences of dialogue.

In most cases, filmic time is relegated to backstory. While this can be an important element in characterization and narrative structure, giving psychological depth to the crisis, it is the present problems that maintain the film's thrust. Backstory moreover tends to partition the characters. Each has a past that is independent from the other characters' histories. The film becomes the crossroads where these various trajectories meet. Fred Zinnemann's *High Noon* (1952) is structured around Frank Miller's (Ian MacDonald) desire to avenge himself against the town, and it is the marshal, Will Kane (Gary Cooper), who sent him to prison. Past events are vital to understanding the film's present situation, but it is the present situation that matters.

What Wyler does is something more unusual and more intricate. He explores the relationships between narrative time and filmic time. A Wyler film carries the weight of all that is outside the narrative. The "travel log" atmosphere Bowman sees in *Roman Holiday* stands in direct contrast to the weight of the realities that life has erected for these characters, realities which are illustrated by Joe Bradley's (Gregory Peck) noisy, crowded newsroom and Ann's (Audrey Hepburn's) ornate royal gilded cage. "Were I not completely aware of my duty to my family and my country," Ann explains to the servants who previously dictated the movements in her life, "I would not have returned tonight—or ever." Ann's holiday allows her to assume the initiative in her life, but her assessment of the situation underscores the emptiness at the core of the future that awaits her. The weight of generations of tradition dictates her entire life. Consequently, Ann and Joe's final meeting is with a gap of stately protocol separating them.

Space bears the scars of time. The evolving reuse of space in Wyler's films becomes the dramatic expression of the film's core emotional thrust. "[I]n his [Wyler's] *Mrs. Miniver*," notes Barbara Bowman,

> space does not simply function as location. It does not simply provide a stage. Instead, it is an intimate carrier of the thematic implications of the scene, not just by controlling the movement of the characters but by implying their presence even in their absence. A number of crises in the film converge in the space of the front hall . . . The severe control of feeling in this space especially when Carol [Teresa Wright] dies, informs all the returns to it.[15]

The changes in the structure of the church in *Mrs. Miniver* offer another image which has filmic and even meta-filmic temporal value. It becomes a metaphor for the hardships that the English lived through during the Blitz. At the outset of the film, it is a magnificent gothic structure that underlines the permanence of the community and the coherence of it denizens. At the end of the film, the church is a shattered hulk reflecting the now-shattered world around it. The family, as well as the entire village, is as devasted as the church's collapsed roof, and yet family, village, and church all remain resilient. It is among the rubble of the gutted church that the vicar makes his famous speech,[16] and in the broken nave, the two families join in solidarity around Carol's (Teresa Wright) spirit, as her widower goes to join her grandmother who is alone in her pew. The church embodies the centuries of English heritage, now standing against the Nazi onslaught.

The film that most feels the weight of time is *The Heiress*, as the story revolves around the relationship between Catherine Sloper (Olivia de Haviland) and her father (Ralph Richardson). He constantly belittles his daughter through unfavorable comparisons with her mother who died bringing Catherine into the world. One after the other, rooms close down in the film. Though never stated, one can imagine that the late Mrs. Sloper's room has been closed off since her death. When Dr. Sloper finds that he will never return to his study, he takes the picture of his wife and closes off that room. When Catherine finally realizes to what extent her father despises her, she mentally shuts him out, to the point of refusing even to see him on his deathbed. That room is subsequently shut off. Catherine finally shuts out the world when she refuses to let in her erstwhile lover who is left pounding ineffectually at the door. Catherine's pyrrhic victory reduces her life to the parlor, the staircase, and her room.

Wyler's characters, such as those in *Detective Story* or *The Heiress*, have shared pasts that make the film one of many events in their lives. Rediscovery of past information becomes central to the plot. *Wuthering Heights* stresses the importance of such an intricate past relationship by setting up a preliminary scene that introduces the young Heathcliff into Cathy's life. *Ben-Hur* is predicated on the long-standing friendship between Messala (Stephen Boyd) and not only Ben-Hur (Charlton Heston), but his family as well. *Dodsworth* opens at the end of twenty years of the main character building and running a car company. The sense of finality is offset by the hopeful idea that Dodsworth and his wife will be able to have time together and start a new life. There is a meta-filmic irony in *Dodsworth* as it follows Capra's *American Madness* by a few years, and in both films, Walter Huston plays the leading character, a successful businessman. Capra's film ends with the hero taking a long-awaited vacation with his wife. Wyler's film begins with the vacation, and is structured around its tragic consequences. Despite the name changes, Wyler's film is, in many ways, the cinematic sequel to Capra's film. The careers of Capra and Wyler would intersect many times as would their personal lives when both directors would enlist in the military for World War II.

THE BEST YEARS OF OUR LIVES

Upon returning from the war, both Wyler and Capra would embark on what would be their most personal works. The first two films that each man created after the War, echo one another, beginning with the bitter irony in their titles. Barbara Bowman notes that,

> *It's a Wonderful Life* can be seen historically as the inverted version of *The Best Years of our Lives* made in the same year, 1946. Whereas *Best Years* dramatizes the anxieties of returning soldiers, *Wonderful Life* dramatizes the anxieties and irrational guilt felt by the men and women who stayed home: the guilt of survivors. If *Best Years* is a film about coming home, *Wonderful Life* is a film about staying home under duress and watching a younger brother get all the glory and return home a hero.[17]

The comparisons continue. What can be said of the one film can be said of the other. "After several years of patriotic war films, in which the forces of good (i.e., the United States) inevitably triumphed over evil, *Best Years* came as sharp and not unwelcome corrective with its sombre tone and lack of overt propaganda."[18] The degree to which the "corrective" that Martin Jackson alludes to was desired can be questioned, as the opposite fates of the two films[19] also underline that audiences were not ready to deal with *every* aspect of the war and its effects. Scholars and historians single out both films as the best representations of that curious twilight between the war years and the Red Scare. Wyler poured his soul into *Best Years*, as the film's subject matter so closely reflected his own wartime experiences. Most importantly, these films are rightly presented as the epitome of both filmmakers' work. Indeed, *The Best Years of Our Lives* synthesizes many of the aspects of Wyler's work and career we have already discussed. It is Wyler's last collaboration with Toland before the cinematographer's untimely death, and stands as a monument to both men's achievements.

The story of three veterans returning from World War II who must readjust to civilian life is built upon layers of past experiences which in turn develop several ironies. Not only do the returning troops have to readjust to civilian life, they have to adjust to the fact that they cannot retrieve the civilian life they left behind. The first of many ironies in the film is the social relationship between the three service men. In military life, Fred Derry (Dana Andrews) is the officer and superior to infantry sergeant Al Stephenson (Frederick Marsh). The situation is inverted in civilian life where the former is a working-class soda jerker and the latter a well-respected banker. The inversion comes to a head when Fred and Al's daughter Peggy (Teresa Wright) fall for one another. Al makes it clear to Fred that he does not approve of Fred's attentions. While the ostensible reason is that Fred is married, one cannot help but feel that the pre-war class distinctions are also a factor in Al's reaction to Fred's interest in his daughter.

The significance of the war is not the same for all Wyler's characters. These divergences are given several disturbing scenes. Fred's wife (Virginia Mayo) is appalled when she sees him in civilian clothes, as it signals the end of their episodic (and essentially irresponsible) relationship. Al shows his war trophies to his son who is less than enthusiastic. The son sees them as reminders of the enemy's final destruction. Rather than explore the objects in his hands, Al's son asks his father about the "Bomb" (implicitly equating his father's action in the war with the dropping of the atomic bomb). A similar scene involves the third veteran, Homer Parrish (Harold Russell), and points to a very unpleasant American future. A Red-baiting, "America Firster" (deliciously portrayed by Ray Teal) openly questions the value of Homer's sacrifice, maliciously suggesting that they fought the wrong enemy. The scene is particularly cruel as Homer has lost both hands in the war, as did real-life, double amputee Russell.

Wyler has Fred Derry do what Wyler himself did in a similar situation—punch out the "creep." In the film, Fred quits his job before his boss can fire him. In real life Wyler nearly faced a court-martial and a dishonorable discharge.[20]

Wyler's sense of overarching filmic time gives audiences an acute sense of what life outside the movies was like at the time—and what was going to happen in the near future. In real life, returning servicemen certainly faced visible and invisible anxieties at home, and, within the framework of the plot, Wyler also leaves the audience with the uneasy sense that these men's problems are far from solved. We are, for example, left with Al's increasing reliance on alcohol, like a slowly ticking time-bomb that has yet to go off. The Red-baiting scene could have been just a personal touch, but it unexpectedly foreshadowed the stark political realities that were to plague the U.S. over the next decade. Merely a year later, Wyler stated "I wouldn't be allowed to make The *Best Years of Our Lives* today."[21]

This film is a monument to Wyler's sophistication as a filmmaker and a catalogue of his various narrative strategies—the most important aspects of the film's problems are *shown* to us rather than related through dialogue. Al's alcoholism, which appears throughout the film as a minor piece of business, is brought to the fore when his wife (Myrna Loy) counts the number of drinks he has had by etching bars on the tablecloth with her fork. Fred's difficulties and Peggy's emotional concern are related through a shot in which Peggy comes into their bedroom where Fred is having a nightmare. Toland applies deep focus with Fred lying on the bed in the foreground and Peggy's entrance in the background, both in focus. Their respective problems are both underscored by keeping multiple planes of action equally in focus. Similarly, in his uncle Butch's bar, Homer, in the foreground, demonstrates his mastery of his infirmity by playing "Chopsticks" with his hooks. He is juxtaposed with Fred's telephone call to Peggy, in the background, in which he is ending their budding relationship. Between Homer and Fred stands Al, who is both listening to the piano and watching the phone call in the background. This shot is the quintessential example of deep-focus photography and the technique's ability to display multiple actions and emotions simultaneously.

There is a conflict between domestic life and public life that is illustrated spatially. Al's kitchen is a safe-haven of domesticity, where he can make light of the chasm between the war ("kill Japs") and the peace ("make money"). It is also where Fred can discuss his hopes with Peggy and (implicitly) about Peggy with her mother. Fred's scenes with his wife are much more painful, as they are played out in his apartment; Fred cannot find peace in his own home. Domestic discomfort also causes Homer to yell at the kids on his street, punching his hooks through the window of his workshop. The workplace, on the other hand, is always fraught with tension. Even getting a promotion is harrowing for Al. Worse yet, Fred punches out the Red baiter at the department store where he works. A liminal space is found at uncle Butch's bar, which is troublesome yet ambivalent. It increasingly becomes the scene of testy relationships, but is also often juxtaposed with scenes of hopeful renewal, as epitomized in Homer's piano playing for Al.

The film's very essence, the exploration of the pain as well as the hopes of homecoming, is summarized when the three servicemen fly over their hometown. This journey echoes Wyler's war films in an eerie way. Wyler began his 1944 wartime documentary, *Memphis Belle*, with picturesque views of the English countryside, which are designated a battleground. In *Best Years*, the characters fly over their hometown in the nose gun of a plane that could very well have been the Memphis Belle. The overpass can be read as a map of the three men's past lives, as well as their future, with the view of a warplane graveyard and a football field. Homer's reference to his football exploits reminds the audience and the characters alike that the past will in fact be irretrievable; a new life will have to be created in its place.

Finally, the flyover tells the audience something else: while ostensibly returning to the same hometown, these three men are returning to three very different hometowns. Were it not for the mutual understanding of the shared wartime experience, and the chance meeting on the airplane that brings them home, these three men would never have met, nor would they have seen their lives braid into a shared destiny. In a very real sense, the war has created a united nation, symbolized by the bond that these three men share and that will continue throughout the film and beyond. By the end of the film, Fred is Homer's best man and will soon be Al's son-in-law. The war has united the hometown through the bond of the three servicemen.

LIVING WITH THE PAST

Wyler could be described as the cinema's greatest novelist. His films create worlds in ways that few filmmakers achieve. That world is fashioned by the way time and space are so fully explored. Wyler illustrates how we are shaped by what came before, not only our own personal choices but also by the choices others have made—in short, by the very world we are born into, and how we respond to that world, a response that is often tragically violent. In Wyler's world, what makes the past so powerful is the effect it has on the present.

Even in one of Wyler's last films, and his first comedy since *The Gay Deception* (1935), we see the significance of the past. *How to Steal a Million* (1966) wittily explores our fetishistic obsession with past artifacts. We frown upon an artist who builds a career on reinventing art with the styles and techniques of earlier artists, but what are we angry about? Ostensibly, for having been fooled into thinking that a work recently created is of a great recognized (preferably dead) artist. But one could say that we are more interested in owning the name than the work. It is an idea that in itself Wyler mocks by showing the sincere appreciation the collector has for the (fake) sculpture. Welles will also explore this idea with similar observations and conclusions nearly ten years later in *F for Fake*. Both Wyler and Welles point out that the artistic value of a work is in the work itself, not in who made it. Wyler demonstrates this attitude by mocking the anger associated with fraudulent art. The film ends well because the art collector (Eli Wallach) is kept in blissful ignorance. With the example of art, the film shows how we fetishize the past, imbuing it with a sense of perfection that clearly did not exist. But this is the case in almost all of Wyler's films, be it *Dodsworth* and its desire to retrieve past happiness, *Ben-Hur* and its desire to rekindle an old friendship, or *Best Years* with a soldier's hope to return to a home which has vanished during his absence.

Anger is an emotion that permeates Wyler's films. In *Jezebel*, Julie Marsden's resentment of the social norms and expectations leads not only to her own downfall, but to the destruction of those around her. Messala's anger sends Ben-Hur down a similar path of anger and resentment, and he risks becoming that which he hates. The importance of the past can be felt mostly in its absence. Critics have noted how *Dead End* seems to fall flat after Baby Face Martin's (Humphrey Bogart) death. The truth of the matter is that his story overrides the rest of the film. He returns to his neighborhood in hopes of reconciling himself with his past. Unfortunately, his mother's rejection of him, as well as that of his ailing ex-girlfriend, now a prostitute and ill with syphilis, leads to his destruction. "I didn't get what I came for," Martin angrily concludes, so he plans to commit his final crime, which, to him, is a way to go out with style. Blind anger is his only solution for a past which cannot be reconciled with his present. Meanwhile, the other characters plod along with neither past nor future. The neighborhood, as the film's title points out, is a "dead end."

This then may well be the very essence of the Wyler style. "With a brilliant sense of space and duration," notes Serge Chauvin, "Wyler chronicles [characters'] prolonged reintegration into the world and transcends his recurring motif, by applying it to the immediacy of reality: bodies in search of bounds of the right scale."[22] The relationship between the past and the present is not just the source of dramatic tension for a Wyler film, it is the very meaning of his entire *œuvre*. Wyler's films are resolved by whether or not characters can come to terms with an overwhelming legacy. The past looms large in the films of William Wyler.

NOTES

1. Wyler's talent for adaptation led Laurence Olivier to ask him to direct *Henry V*. Wyler declined. Wyler avoided Shakespeare, but one could imagine his cinematic interpretation of a play like *The Tempest*. Furthermore, and perhaps due to Wyler's influence, Olivier's version of *Henry V* remains one of the most imaginative visualizations of Shakespeare's work.

2. Ronald D. Davis, "Southern Methodist University Oral History Project" (a 1979 interview with Wyler) in Gabriel Miller, ed. *William Wyler: Interviews* (Jackson: The University Press of Mississippi, 2010), 88.
3. George E. Turner, "Gregg Toland—An Enduring Legacy," *American Cinematographer* (June 2017), <https://ascmag.com/articles/gregg-toland-asc-an-enduring-legacy> (last accessed August 9, 2022).
4. It even created problems in the case of the screenwriting credits for *Friendly Persuasions*. The writer for the original version of the script, Michael Wilson, could not be hired due to the blacklist. Wyler turned to the author of the stories the script was based on, Jessamyn West, who with Wyler's brother, Robert, greatly reworked the original screenplay. Wilson baulked at the suggested credits that deleted his name. Wyler tried to suggest a variation that covered all the participants, but it fell through. The credits for the final product created such an entanglement that the film received no screenplay credit. Jan Herman, *A Talent for Trouble* (New York: Putnam & Sons, 1995), 376–8.
5. Barry Salt, "Film Styles and Technology in the Forties" in *Film Quarterly*, Vol. 31, N°1 (Autumn, 1977), 48.
6. As quoted by Turner, "Gregg Toland."
7. Curtis Hanson, "William Wyler: An Interview" (1967) in Miller, *Wyler: Interviews*, 33.
8. Éric Rohmer, *L'Organisation de l'espace dans le Faust de Murnau* (Paris: Union générale d'éditions 10/18, 1977), 9.
9. Neil Sinyard, *A Wonderful Heart: The Films of William Wyler* (Jefferson, NC and London: MacFarlane & Co., 2013), 15.
10. Barbara Bowman, *Master Space: Film Images of Capra, Lubitch, Sternberg and Wyler* (New York: Greeenwood Press, 1992), 10.
11. Bowman, *Master Space*, 135.
12. Ibid., 133.
13. "La façon dont le champ est investi, arpenté, occupé, abandonné détermine une la spatialité propre qui renforce ou contredit la spatialité visuelle, celle de l'objectif perspectif (avec son jeu sur les focales, la largeur de son cadrage . . .) et celle du décor, du lieu 'réel' où se déroule l'action," (my translation). Jean Housen, *Espace plastique et espace filmique*, Revue Belge du Cinéma, N°5 (Automne 1983), 9.
14. An interesting problem the series does not address is concomitance, that is, when two events happen at the same time.
15. Bowman, *Master Space*, 119.
16. Wyler made the film to urge America into war. Churchill thought it "propaganda worth a hundred battleships." Roosevelt liked the vicar's final speech so much that he had it transcribed and translated with the printed leaflets air dropped over occupied Europe. See Sinyard, *A Wonderful Heart*, 15.
17. Bowman, *Master Space*, 25.
18. Martin A Jackson, "The Uncertain Peace: The Best Years of Our Lives (1946)" in John E. O'Connor and Martin A. Jackson, eds. *American History/American Film: Interpreting the Hollywood Image* (New York: Ungar Publishing Co., 1979), 156. One can add the irony of the fact *Mrs. Miniver* was at the beginning of the series of wartime propaganda films.
19. Wyler's film was a critical and commercial success, winning Academy Awards in virtually every major category, except cinematography (where it did not even receive a nomination). It would launch his successful postwar career. Capra's film failed at the box office. It severely strained his financial resources and more importantly shook his self-confidence. *Wonderful Life* was to launch the independent production company, Liberty Films, he had formed with Wyler, George Stevens, and producer Sam Briskin. While the three others wanted to continue with the project, Capra persuaded them to sell the company to

Paramount Pictures. He later regretted the decision, but it made a certain amount of sense. Capra had lost the artistic balance he enjoyed before the war, and the subsequent political atmosphere would make it impossible to try. His "touch" was to make ostensibly political dramas that were in fact moral paradoxes. His own subsequent projects didn't function artistically, and his other projects were more successfully made by others. Wyler's *Roman Holiday* and *Friendly Persuasion* were originally Capra projects for Liberty Films. A third film, *Westward the Women*, would be made by William Wellman in 1951.

20. Herman, *A Talent for Trouble*, 266–8.
21. Herman, *A Talent for Trouble*, 303.
22. "Avec un sens génial de l'espace et de la durée, Wyler chronique leur longue réadaptation au monde, et transcende, en l'appliquant à la réalité immédiate, son motif de toujours : des corps en quête de cadre, à leur juste mesure," (my translation). Serge Chauvin, "William Wyler," introduction to the Retrospective on Wyler at the Cinémathèque Française (April 25 – May 28, 2018), <https://www.cinematheque.fr/cycle/william-wyler-437.html> (last accessed August 9, 2022).

PART II

Collaboration, Genre, and Adaptation

CHAPTER 5

Clash of the Titans: The Hidden Collaboration of William Wyler and David O. Selznick on *Carrie* (1952)

Milan Hain

William Wyler's *Carrie* seemed destined to become another triumph in the director's rich, twenty-five-year-long career. It was adapted from the celebrated literary classic by Theodore Dreiser, boasted a stellar cast headed by Laurence Olivier and Jennifer Jones, and was produced with the same meticulous care typical of the best product coming from Paramount Pictures. The film had many of the same attributes that turned Wyler's previous pictures such as *Wuthering Heights* (1939), *The Little Foxes* (1941), *Mrs. Miniver* (1942), and *The Best Years of Our Lives* (1946) into critical successes as well as big commercial hits. However, *Carrie* did not live up to its potential and ended up a bitter disappointment. The film took in only $1.8 million in rentals and the reviews were mixed at best.

Many critics complained that the adaptation distorted the celebrated original story and "whitewashed [the title protagonist] until she's as pure as the driven snow . . . In Dreiser's novel, the heroine had some grey and black shadings to go with her all-white traits; she was thus a more convincing character," wrote one reviewer.[1] Bosley Crowther in *The New York Times* had no qualms about calling the character of Carrie

> a weak and distorted shadow of the young woman whom Theodore Dreiser drew in his classic novel . . . This arrant distortion of Carrie—and the coy performance Miss Jones gives—reduces the theme of the drama to that of hopeless, deathless love, with most of the human implications and social ironies of the novel removed.[2]

The renowned critic was so disturbed by the film that he revisited the subject a few days later. In an article entitled "Halleluiah, Sister! Carrie Becomes a Good Girl on the Screen," Crowther once again complained about the unwarranted changes from the novel, which removed all social commentary from the material and transformed it into a routine romance. He also offered several possible culprits. According to him, it may have been the still powerful Production Code Administration with its regulations and strict enforcement of traditional morality; Wyler and Paramount Pictures executives seeking commercial success; or the actress Jennifer Jones, who "didn't wish (or wasn't able) to portray a woman for whom the feminine audience might not have overflowing sympathy."[3]

To a certain extent, Crowther was right on all counts, but he had no way of knowing that there was yet another figure behind the scenes who had a big influence on the film, although he wasn't working on it in any official capacity. The legendary producer David O. Selznick came to *Carrie* as Jennifer Jones' husband, employer, and de facto manager. But as the surviving correspondence between him and Wyler shows, his ambitions far exceeded his uncredited function. He consistently entered all phases of the film's execution, and while his intentions were certainly noble, I argue that it was he who was perhaps ultimately most responsible for *Carrie*'s critical and commercial failure. This chapter details the uneasy and hidden collaboration between William Wyler and David O. Selznick during the pre-production, filming, and post-production of *Carrie*, with an emphasis on their creative differences, which I believe caused the film to fail.

HOLLYWOOD MAVERICKS

Selznick and Wyler come from the same generation of Hollywood filmmakers. Both were born in 1902, both were Jewish, and both got into film thanks to family connections. Selznick began working for his father's company as a teenager, but when it had to declare bankruptcy in the mid-1920s, he struck out on his own to California, where he held various, increasingly more prominent, positions at Paramount, MGM, and RKO. Wyler came from a German-speaking family living in Mulhouse, Alsace (now France, then part of the German Empire). When he was eighteen, his mother's cousin Carl Laemmle—then head of Universal Studios—invited him overseas to try his hand at film. Within a few years Wyler was directing two-reel Westerns.

In the early 1930s, Selznick became a leading Hollywood producer. After a series of hits for RKO such as *A Bill of Divorcement* (George Cukor), *Bird of Paradise* (King Vidor) (both 1932), and *King Kong* (Merian C. Cooper, 1933), he returned to MGM, where he oversaw the production of slick, star-studded dramas such as *Dinner at Eight* (Cukor, 1933), *Manhattan Melodrama* (W. S. Van Dyke, 1934), *Anna Karenina* (Clarence Brown), *David Copperfield* (Cukor), and

Tale of Two Cities (Jack Conway) (all three 1935). In the middle of the decade, he founded the independent production company Selznick International Pictures, which soon secured the respect of Hollywood with commercial and artistic triumphs such as *Little Lord Fauntleroy* (John Cromwell, 1936), *Nothing Sacred* (William Wellman), and *A Star Is Born* (Wellman) (both 1937). His crowning achievement was the spectacular adaptation of Margaret Mitchell's bestselling novel *Gone with the Wind* (Victor Fleming, 1939), which became the most expensive and highest-grossing film in Hollywood's history. Selznick followed this extraordinary success with another adaptation, the gothic romance *Rebecca* (Alfred Hitchcock, 1940) based on Daphne du Maurier's novel, which, like *Gone with the Wind* the year before, won the Academy Award for Best Picture.

Wyler established himself among the top Hollywood filmmakers at about the same time and with the same vigor as Selznick. In 1933 he directed John Barrymore in the acclaimed comedy drama *Counsellor at Law*. In the latter half of the decade, he formed a highly productive professional partnership with Selznick's chief competitor among independent producers, Samuel Goldwyn, for whom he directed such prized films as *These Three*, *Dodsworth* (both 1936), *Dead End* (1937), and *The Westerner* (1940). In the years of Selznick's back-to-back Oscar triumphs, Wyler was nominated for the Academy Award on both occasions for directing *Wuthering Heights* and *The Letter* (1940). In the following ten years, he completed only four films—*The Little Foxes, Mrs. Miniver, The Best Years of Our Lives*, and *The Heiress* (1949)—but they were all extraordinary successes. *Mrs. Miniver* grossed $5.4 million, thus topping the list of box-office hits for 1942, and earned Wyler his first Oscar for Best Direction. *The Best Years of Our Lives* even surpassed that success, winning seven Academy Awards and, with rentals of over $11 million, becoming the biggest commercial hit of the decade. The receipts for *The Heiress* were less impressive, but the film still received four Oscars and nominations in the Best Picture and Best Director categories.

The same year Wyler released *The Best Years of Our Lives* about the plight of war veterans returning from combat, Selznick completed his megalomaniac Western *Duel in the Sun* (Vidor, 1946). It would be hard to find two more diverse films: while Wyler's award-winning picture is a thoughtful, highly relevant drama about the lives of ordinary people, Selznick took the path of escapism and over-hyped flamboyance. The film grossed over $10 million but was met with merciless rejection in the press and severely damaged Selznick's reputation based on his refined taste and prestige. Like Wyler, Selznick was less productive in the 1940s than he had been earlier in his career. After *Rebecca*, he took a production hiatus of several years, which he broke only with his home-front female epic *Since You Went Away* (Cromwell, 1944). In lieu of producing films, he devoted himself to developing his star stable, which in time included actresses Ingrid Bergman, Joan Fontaine, Vivien Leigh, Dorothy McGuire, Jennifer Jones, and Shirley Temple, and actors Joseph Cotten and Gregory Peck. He succeeded in transforming these personalities into attractive commodities, which he used mainly as a source of income in loan-outs to other Hollywood studios. In the late 1940s, however, even this part of his business did not work as smoothly as before. In quick succession, the contracts of Selznick's most valuable discoveries—Bergman, Leigh, and Fontaine—expired, and the producer was unable to find adequate replacements. Moreover, his films from the end of the decade, notably *The Paradine Case* (Hitchcock, 1947), the last title to emerge from his collaboration with Alfred Hitchcock, and *Portrait of Jennie* (William Dieterle, 1948), were huge commercial flops.

Thus, in 1949, when Paramount began preparing its adaptation of Dreiser's *Sister Carrie*, Wyler and Selznick could not have been in more different positions. The former had an impeccable reputation as a respected and reliable director, brimming with instinctive taste and a flair for selecting material and guiding actors; the latter was seen more as a has-been, the man who brought the world *Gone with the Wind* and other hits, but who had recently lost his touch and understanding of the needs of postwar audiences.

A TALE OF TWO EGOS

To understand the dynamics between the two filmmakers, it might be helpful to note that *Carrie* was not the first occasion on which Wyler and Selznick met, and clashed, professionally. In 1938 Wyler directed the antebellum-set drama *Jezebel* (1938) for Warner Bros. starring Bette Davis and Henry Fonda. It was widely considered as a competitor to the thematically similar *Gone with the Wind*, which had been in the works since mid-1936 and had been closely watched by the industry and the public ever since. Selznick attacked *Jezebel* for plagiarizing his production, calling particular attention to a dinner scene where men discuss the imminent war between the South and the North, but it was no use.[4] The film, based on a 1933 play by Owen Davis, won two Academy Awards and grossed approximately $1.5 million on a budget of over a million, thus making "a tidy profit."[5]

Selznick was also angered because he thought that *Jezebel* parasitized on the publicity that surrounded *Gone with the Wind*, especially in conjunction with the search for a suitable female lead for the role of the Southern belle Scarlett O'Hara. One of the many candidates for the part was a promising young actress named Margaret Tallichet, born in Dallas in 1914. She came to Selznick's attention thanks to the actress Carole Lombard who met her when she worked as a typist at Paramount. Selznick had his talent scout Kay Brown arrange for acting lessons for Tallichet and, after signing an exclusive, seven-year contract with her in December 1936, he cast her in uncredited roles in his productions of *A Star Is Born* and *The Prisoner of Zenda* (Cromwell, 1937). In 1938 she continued to undergo intensive acting training, was loaned out to Republic and Columbia for two minor B-movies, and repeatedly tested for the role of Scarlett for which she received an inordinate amount of publicity. Her acting inexperience proved to be a hindrance, but the studio still believed in her star potential. Kay Brown described her as

> one of the nicest, most cooperative young actresses I have seen in many a day. She is enormously hard working, wastes no time, and makes the most pleasant impression both personally and on behalf of the company any place she appears.[6]

However, her employment at Selznick's studio did not last long. On October 23, 1938, after a short acquaintance, the actress married William Wyler and decided to withdraw from the film industry. Selznick was infuriated by the whole situation but could do nothing about it. The contract was terminated, and the actress had to pay a sum of $1,000 to the studio in settlement of her obligations.[7]

The Wyler–Tallichet wedding took place only a few months before another incident with Selznick that forms perhaps the most significant and telling prelude to what would happen with *Carrie* ten years later. In the first half of 1939, Selznick began preparing the romantic drama, *Intermezzo: A Love Story* (Gregory Ratoff), which was to introduce his new acquisition, the young Swedish actress Ingrid Bergman, to American audiences. The film was a remake of one of her Swedish films that had made her a star in her homeland. Wyler, who had just completed *Wuthering Heights* for Goldwyn, was brought in as director. Selznick seemingly made a safe bet with his choice, but soon there was a rift between the two and after several weeks Wyler left the production. As he later admitted,

> he [Selznick] said I walked out, and I say he fired me. The truth is somewhere in between. Our contracts weren't signed. We got into an argument. Anyway, I left. I don't remember the reason. He made things difficult for me and I said, "To hell with this." I worked about six weeks on the picture—story conferences, tests, that sort of thing—and I never got a penny. That I do remember.[8]

Unfortunately, Wyler's recollection is rather vague (perhaps deliberately so) and it is not possible to trace the exact reasons for his departure from archival documents either. We can speculate, however, that it was primarily a creative disagreement related to the way Ingrid Bergman was photographed which was, according to Selznick's instructions, an aspect to which the entire production was to be subordinated. This is also suggested by the fact that not long after Wyler, the cinematographer Harry Stradling also left the set because he failed to adequately capture the actress's charm and beauty. The replacements for Wyler and Stradling—director Gregory Ratoff and cinematographer Gregg Toland—were tasked with proceeding in agreement with Selznick's directions so that the resulting film would most effectively sell Bergman to audiences as a rising Hollywood star.

The *Intermezzo* incident must have offended Wyler. When he saw the finished film in November 1939, he wrote a letter in which he called it a "butchery:"

> I was shocked beyond description. I was prepared for a certain amount of disappointment, but how it was possible to miss every point and every value in every scene is beyond my comprehension ... The original Swedish picture was a masterpiece compared to yours because at least it told its story ... You may have received satisfaction out of some good reviews that I've read in the local trade papers. But ... those reviews [are] nothing short of perjury. One of the purposes of this letter is to correct any impression they may have made on your mind. It is all right to make a bad picture—if not too often, but it is important that we know it when it is done.[9]

In the end, however, Wyler apparently recognized that sending such a strongly worded letter would do more harm than good and so he decided to shelve it. It may have been at least partially satisfying for him that *Wuthering Heights* beat Selznick's *Intermezzo* for the Academy Award for Cinematography in a black and white picture (*Intermezzo* didn't make it to the final nomination but was shortlisted with ten other titles).

It is unclear if any bad blood due to their clash on *Intermezzo* remained between Wyler and Selznick in the long run but their reunion on *Carrie* may have revived some sentiments from a decade ago. However, their professional relationship now had very different parameters. Selznick was no longer Wyler's employer; rather, it was Wyler—the director and producer of *Carrie*—who was, at least on paper, calling the shots. But as we shall see below, Selznick was not used to such a subordinate position and consistently claimed a say in the film's development.

CASTING AND WRITING *CARRIE*

Paramount was preparing the adaptation of Theodore Dreiser's turn-of-the-century novel, *Sister Carrie*, as one of its most prestigious and classiest postwar projects. Selznick immediately sensed in it a great opportunity for his contract actress and, since July 13, 1949, wife Jennifer Jones. She had become one of the greatest acting discoveries in Hollywood in the mid-1940s. She won an Oscar for her first major role in the spiritual drama, *The Song of Bernadette* (Henry King, 1943), and was nominated for the award in three consecutive years for her roles in *Since You Went Away*, *Love Letters* (Dieterle, 1945), and *Duel in the Sun*. By the end of the decade, however, her professional status was in jeopardy: Selznick's *Portrait of Jennie* ended up a major flop, and the two films for which Jones was loaned out, *We Were Strangers* (John Huston) and *Madame Bovary* (Vincente Minnelli) (both 1949), were also commercial and artistic failures. *Carrie* promised to break this unflattering record of recent years and restore the actress's industry standing and rapport with audiences.

That Selznick was highly interested in the role for Jones is evidenced by the fact that he significantly reduced the price for the actress's services: instead of the $200,000 he had received from Columbia and MGM for *We Were Strangers* and *Madame Bovary*, respectively, he settled for $125,000.[10] Both Paramount and Wyler seemed intrigued by the offer, but before they were willing to accept the terms, they wanted to explore other options, including the possibility that one of their contract actresses would get the title role.

Selznick, however, took the negotiations almost as a done deal, and as early as November 1949—ostensibly at Wyler's request—provided detailed feedback on an early version of the screenplay from author and husband-and-wife duo Ruth and Augustus Goetz, who had already successfully adapted Henry James's novel *Washington Square* for Wyler under the title *The Heiress* (based on their 1947 stage version). Selznick's main suggestion was to make "this thing into a love story . . . The whole thing has to be re-examined from the standpoint of the girl in love." He strongly criticized "inconsistency in the writing of Carrie" and demanded "gradual change in her characterization" instead of sudden and unexplained changes in her attitudes and moods.

According to Selznick, what the script lacked was establishing Carrie as a "full, three-dimensional" character:

> what she is, what she thinks and feels, what she wants—and all of these changing as her life changes . . . I don't think any of you have decided just what it is you do want to tell about Carrie, and herein is the root of all your problems.

To prevent the film from becoming a sequence of disjointed scenes, Selznick recommended a dramatic strengthening of the third act based on the previous plot, citing his own production of *A Star Is Born* as an inspiration. On thirteen pages he then listed a total of twenty-nine points (often further subdivided) concerning characterizations and motivations of characters and individual plot moments.

Selznick claimed that his intention was to put himself in the position of the mainstream audience and, through his criticism, help the film become the commercial and artistic triumph that everyone involved surely aspired to. In reality, however, most of his remarks were directed at the character of Carrie, with the aim of strengthening her centrality in the story:

> I hope you'll come up with a role that will be a really great challenge to Jennifer, who, I agree, is perfect for the role . . . But there's no point in having her attempt to play a character whom even you couldn't describe to me when I challenged you; and whose story isn't worth telling because we know nothing about her, because it has no beginning, no middle, and no end . . . so soon after "Bovary," neither of us wants her to play another shallow character . . . without a thought in her head except marriage and pretty clothes, without motivations or purpose, without objectives or either progression or retrogression, without viewpoint, without understandable dramatic climaxes or conclusion, without change or variety—merely a creature of circumstance who goes all the way up the ladder from the bottom to the first rung.[11]

Selznick was also very interested in who would play the male lead of George Hurstwood, manager of an upscale Chicago restaurant who falls head over heels in love with the much younger Carrie and ruins his personal and professional life because of her. Selznick's preferred candidates included John Wayne (despite being not "entirely developed enough as an actor"), Ronald Colman, William Powell (both probably "too old" for the part), Charles Boyer ("too much the aged ex-exotic lover"), Spencer Tracy, Vittorio De Sica and, as a "wild idea," Humphrey Bogart, "if you don't think he's too much the mug for the elegance the man should have."[12] But the safest bet was Laurence Olivier, who "has every single thing the part requires" and "the whole enterprise would gain enormously in stature, in prestige, in commercial possibilities, not only in this country, but the world over."[13]

It seems that Wyler disagreed with his colleague. He didn't share his enthusiasm for Olivier at first, and the casting of the female lead was not a done deal for him either. Quite possibly, it was not so much working with Jones that frightened him, but rather the prospect of endless interference from Selznick of which he got a good sampling at this early stage already, long before actual filming began. After a short hiatus in the early part of 1950, Wyler returned to *Carrie* and started considering other options for the title role, including 20th Century-Fox's Jeanne Crain, fresh from the success of *Pinky* (Elia Kazan, 1949) for which she was nominated for the Academy Award. Selznick lived under the belief that he and Wyler made an agreement whereby Wyler would not fill the role with another actress before advising him, and likewise Selznick would not cast Jennifer in another part before informing Wyler. When he learned about Wyler's behind-the-scenes dealings, he considered it a betrayal, and his response was worded accordingly. In a telegram from June 14, 1950, he fired:

> I must now ask you to . . . consider that Jennifer is not available . . . I do not wish further to demean [her] or her great standing as a star by what I am forced to regard as the type of double dealing which has made me so fed up with Hollywood . . . either you or your associates had the consummate bad taste and ingratitude to use my willingness to let Jennifer play the role and Jennifer's willingness to play the role with Olivier to attempt to get another star . . . or you or your people . . . were dishonest enough to state that Jennifer was dying to play the role but that you did not want her.[14]

As it turned out, Wyler, despite initial resistance, agreed to Selznick's original proposal to cast Laurence Olivier as Hurstwood but then felt that the thirty-one-year-old Jennifer Jones was too old to play Carrie and began looking for younger actresses—in addition to Crain (age twenty-six at the time), the candidates included Elizabeth Taylor (nineteen) and Ava Gardner (twenty-eight). He did not inform Selznick of this move, so as not to lose the opportunity to cast Jones if all negotiations failed. In the end, however, all alternatives did fall through, and Wyler had no choice but to return to Selznick with an apology.[15]

The looming crisis was therefore averted. On July 10, a contract was signed between Selznick and Paramount for the loan-out of Jennifer Jones for $125,000. If the film grossed double its budget, Selznick was to receive an additional $25,000. Olivier's salary was higher, around $200,000.[16] The contract also specified that Jones would be billed after Olivier, but before the film's title, in the same font size as her male co-star.[17] Despite his usual practice in negotiating the terms of his contract players' loan-outs, Selznick did not have approval rights regarding Jones's stand-in, stylist, make-up artist, costume designer, and cinematographer, for which he heavily criticized his inexperienced studio lawyer Robert Dann.[18]

As the start of filming approached, attention had to be paid to the script once again. Under Wyler's supervision, the Goetzes prepared a new draft which reached Selznick in late July. When the producer became familiar with it, he sent Wyler a twenty-nine-page letter, ironically prefaced with the sentence, "As you know, I promised myself that I would venture no more comments on SISTER CARRIE."[19] Some sources suggest that Wyler stopped reading Selznick's messages right from the start,[20] but this seems unlikely. For one thing, Wyler's copies of the memos contain the director's marks and notes, which show that he read and engaged with them. Secondly, Selznick could not simply be ignored: he was a major influence on Jones, on whom the entire film depended, and moreover, despite his recent setbacks, he could still draw on his reputation as a renowned filmmaker and a skilled adapter of literary material. It would therefore be unwise of Wyler to flatly dismiss his input.

In his most recent and longest letter,[21] Selznick expressed satisfaction that many of his earlier comments had been accepted and incorporated by the screenwriters: the script was, in his view, more dramatically convincing as a result. However, the producer was still dissatisfied with the characterization and motivations of the central character (although this is where, he admitted, the script made the most progress). For example, he wanted Carrie's interest in the theatre to be established at the very beginning of the story, and the bigamy motif to be retained, because Carrie would not, in his view, live with Hurstwood outside of marriage. Wyler clearly liked the suggestion of including scenes of Carrie and Hurstwood's two contrasting wedding ceremonies (one made-up and one real), for he made a note here, "I LIKE THIS. SHOULD BE EXPLORED." Selznick repeatedly urged Wyler to think about Carrie's motivations, as some scenes (particularly in her interactions with men) made her character come off as a naïve "idiot" (a word that comes up repeatedly in the letter). At the same time, he pleaded for the audience's sympathies to be more clearly on her side: she should not be so harsh with Hurstwood, and instead should accept the information about the loss of his position with understanding and reassure him that their relationship, not their social status, is what matters most. Similarly, Selznick wanted to curb her materialism and desire to live in luxury, even though these very traits play a central role in Dreiser's novel.[22]

In addition to the construction of Carrie's character, Selznick was concerned with the film's ending. He urged Wyler to have Carrie leave Hurstwood only for his sake—she is supposed to be convinced (and the viewers with her) that it will be for his benefit. Overall, he thought the film should end on a high note and while he did not advocate a classic happy ending, which he knew was inappropriate, he insisted that it was in Wyler's commercial interest to conceive of the film as a tragic love story, which was only possible if Carrie was not portrayed as a cold-hearted monster, and instead was greatly humanized in comparison to Dreiser's novel: "I beg you to understand [that] you need for the audience to watch not only intellectually, but with understanding and heartbreak and with sympathy and without frustration." Selznick argued that such a shift could mean a million-dollar difference in sales.[23]

Even though Selznick claimed that the letter was his "valedictory to the script," the ending was still on his mind almost three months later when the picture was nearing completion. He even sent Wyler three versions of the last few pages of the script (with dialogues, director's notes, and all) in which Carrie acknowledges her feelings for Hurstwood, making her character more sympathetic and urging the audience not to leave the cinema so depressed. Although Wyler accepted many of Selznick's suggestions—probably to the detriment of the final work, as it took the film away from the well-established qualities of Dreiser's celebrated literary classic, the ending remained rather downbeat: while Carrie does show some generosity after all, the last shots belong to Hurstwood, who first fumbles with the gas burners in a hint of suicide and then, without saying goodbye, walks away towards an uncertain future.

SHOOTING AND CUTTING *CARRIE*

During the pre-production of *Carrie*, Selznick styled himself as an experienced script expert who, as his frequent argument went, wanted to benefit the quality of the whole film. But once the actual filming began, his interest turned to the only point that really mattered to him, and that was Jennifer Jones. It was not uncommon for him to send terrified telegrams to Wyler, either directly or through his staff, saying, for instance, "PLEASE PLEASE CABLE IMMEDIATELY CONCERNING SITUATION JENNIFER'S PHOTOGRAPHY (AND) MAKEUP."[24] It was the visual presentation of his wife and contract actress that soon became a source of tension.

The principal photography commenced on August 14, 1950 but even before that Selznick closely monitored Jones's camera and make-up tests, sent detailed suggestions, and voiced numerous concerns. His main criticism was the choice of cinematographer George Barnes, who, while having done brilliant work for Selznick on *Rebecca* (for which he won his only Oscar), was also, according to the producer, "the only cameraman who has not been able to 'get' Jennifer" when given the opportunity to do so in *Since You Went Away*. Selznick therefore encouraged scrutiny of Barnes' work and warned against jumping to conclusions based solely on screen tests: as he advised Wyler, only the film itself could properly bring Jennifer to life.[25]

Another important topic was the actress's make-up. Selznick was very harsh in his criticism of the outdated practices of Paramount's make-up department headed by Wally Westmore and urged a move away from full-face "warpaint" to a more subtle application of make-up around the eyes and under the chin.[26] Among other things, he also kept an eye on Jones's time commitments, and whenever he thought she was overworked (as was the case when she reportedly worked sixteen hours straight), he didn't hesitate to speak up. The producer sent many of these recommendations (insisting that they were not demands or requirements) secretly behind his wife's back and repeatedly asked Wyler not to mention the contents of these letters and telegrams to her. Persistent pressure and criticism eventually led to the removal of cinematographer George Barnes—according to Selznick the main culprit for the unsatisfactory visual quality of the material shot with Jones—and his replacement by another experienced matador, Victor Milner, famous for his collaboration with Cecil B. DeMille. Wally Westmore remained in his position, but his work continued to be closely monitored by Selznick and his staff.

Another serious complication was caused by Selznick and Jones themselves. In early August, Selznick wanted Wyler to promise "that Jennifer should not work on one day each month—the one day on which she simply cannot be photographed."[27] However, during September, it became clear that such a guarantee was not necessary, as the actress found out she was pregnant. Even before this information was confirmed, Selznick had already urged Wyler and his crew to let his wife, who was complaining of fatigue and excessive sweating, to loosen her corsets during breaks.[28] When the true reason for these conditions was revealed, Wyler had to devise a way to photograph the actress so that her pregnant belly would not be visible. He and Milner therefore opted for more tight framings. Later, some critics complained about the uncharacteristically static feel of the film when compared to other Wyler's works.[29]

Filming ended on November 2 and was immediately followed by retakes. Selznick was outraged when Wyler requested that Jones come "unofficially," and asked whether Olivier, too, was not getting paid for his work. The producer also wondered when he would be able to see a rough cut of the film so that he could make comments. His main concern was still the ending of the film and the motivations of the main character and her relationship with Hurstwood:

> Perhaps the miracle has been accomplished and these key questions will not be asked because of the quality of the film—but if the miracle has not been accomplished, then you may be very sure that millions of people are going to ask the same questions, and if they can't answer them to their satisfaction, you may have another great critical success, but Lord help you the next time you try to make a high-budget film at Paramount.[30]

In early December, Selznick saw a very rough assembly of *Carrie*, which provoked him to write nine pages of notes. In addition to the obligatory critique of the ending, he commented on everything from Jennifer's odd-looking eyebrows in some scenes to poorly handled transitions between sequences to unintelligible lines. Most of the remarks do show an effort to benefit the film as a whole, though Selznick was sometimes blinded by his over-concern for his wife (for example, when he blamed the camera when she looked unbecoming in a hat). The producer also became interested in the film's release strategy. Through Wyler he pushed for Paramount to put the film in art theatres first "to give the picture word of mouth and reputation and the kind of 'must see' appeal" before taking it into wide distribution. The title didn't escape his attention, either: according to Selznick, *Carrie* was "all right," but, as an alternative, he suggested *The Loved and the Unloved*, which aptly communicates the producer's interest in turning the film into a tragic romance.

The finishing of the film was affected by an unfortunate event in mid-December when Jennifer Jones suffered a miscarriage. Some saw the cause in the too-tight corsets the actress reportedly insisted on during shooting.[31] In January, she was still recuperating, but at the same time, she was already able to resume work taking part in retakes and dubbing.

If Wyler felt that this was the end of Selznick's involvement, he was wrong. In March 1951, the producer sent a fifteen-page letter in which, while calling the film "outstanding," he added that it had been severely damaged by being cut to under two hours:

> I don't say, mind you, that what is left isn't magnificent; but I do say, and most emphatically, that you have thrown away moments that would belong in any anthology of the great scenes of motion picture history. And for what? WHY?

According to Selznick, numerous emotionally powerful moments and scenes that deepened the characters' motivations had disappeared, and Jones's and Olivier's performances suffered as a result. The current version sat on two chairs, so to speak—it was neither an art film nor a sure-fire box-office hit:

> Its great chance ... was that it would build such tremendous prestige out of this additional and highly lucrative audience [in art theatres] as to make it a "must" with the more conventionally minded, average moviegoer. When you tamper with the appeal of the picture to this selective audience, you therefore damage its commercial value.[32]

Selznick was probably unaware of the contradiction in his claims. On the one hand, he wanted the film to be a masterpiece along the lines of Olivier's *Hamlet* or Michael Powell and Emeric Pressburger's *The Red Shoes* (both 1948), but on the other hand, his remarks pushed it away from a faithful rendition of Dreiser's naturalistic original towards a run-of-the-mill love story that did not stand a chance with critics or more sophisticated patrons of art theatres.

SELLING *CARRIE*

As if Selznick's constant interference and inconsistent demands weren't enough, Paramount itself dealt another blow to *Carrie*. The studio apparently sensed that the depressing film, based on a novel by the liberal-minded Dreiser, who had even joined the Communist Party shortly before his death in 1945,[33] was not suited to the Cold War atmosphere when Hollywood was rocked by another wave of House Un-American Activities Committee interrogations, and a number of artists were blacklisted. Vice president in charge of studio operations, Frank Freeman, and studio president, Barney Balaban, therefore decided to shelve the film for a while and not release it until the second half of 1952. Selznick repeatedly urged Paramount's officials to put *Carrie* in at least a small number of theatres because of its chances at the Oscars and the positive buzz that was expected to help the film the moment it reached wide distribution.[34] In a letter addressed directly to Freeman, he stated in an urgent tone ("Please, Frank, give *Carrie* its chance") that the film must be treated as a prestige title aimed at sophisticated big-city audiences. He also mentioned that *Carrie* had a good chance of catching on in Europe and that a special version with longer running time could be made for that purpose. According to Selznick,

> here is a film made-to-order for prestige . . . These are days when it is desperately necessary to the future of the business that that rare superb film gets its every chance to prove that a large portion of the public would patronise better things.[35]

The producer noted with concern the changes in the film industry and feared that serious films derived from classic literary sources would find it difficult to gain support in the face of television. This fear was confirmed: Paramount decided to prioritize the Technicolor, star-studded, high-budget *The Greatest Show on Earth* (1952) directed by Cecil B. DeMille, which seemed better suited to the postwar climate.

Wyler welcomed Selznick's initiative and thanked him for it. Eventually, however, he also came to believe that it would be better if *Carrie* gave way to DeMille's spectacle, as Paramount was simply not equipped to promote two important films at the same time. In this context, he recalled the situation from 1949, when the box-office result of *The Heiress* was hurt by direct competition with DeMille's previous film, *Samson and Delilah* (1949).[36] *Carrie* was eventually released in August 1952, almost a year and a half after its completion. In the meantime, Wyler had managed to finish the drama *Detective Story* (1951) with Kirk Douglas and started shooting *Roman Holiday* (1953) at Rome's Cinecittà Studios.

The postponement, however, did not help any, as the picture became a flop in theatres. It made only half as much as the adaptation of another Dreiser's novel, *An American Tragedy*, produced and directed by George Stevens (also for Paramount) under the title *A Place in the Sun* (1951). Boasting an attractive, young cast led by Montgomery Clift and Elizabeth Taylor (one of the candidates for Carrie), the film made it into the top ten of highest-grossing films of 1951, while *Carrie* a year later finished at the fifty-fourth position, with the top occupied by high-budget spectacles *The Greatest Show on Earth*, *Quo Vadis* (Mervyn LeRoy, 1951) and *Ivanhoe* (Richard Thorpe, 1952).[37] DeMille's film also succeeded at the Oscars, taking home the Best Picture award, while Wyler had to settle for only two nominations for Best Art Direction and Best Costume Design in a Black and White Film.

Most critics agreed that the material was too old-fashioned and bleak to appeal to mainstream audiences. Murray Horowitz in *Motion Picture Daily* stated that "some customers may find the virtually unrelieved undertone of sadness, which builds to various pitches, too much for their taste,"[38] a sentiment which seems to resonate with Selznick's warnings. Others, on the other hand, blamed the filmmakers for dulling the edges of a sociologically biting subject matter and turning the novel into a "sentimental display of emotional ecstasies and despairs."[39] Promotion used slogans such as "A seething, passionate love story every girl will understand!" to target a predominantly female audience, but judging by low box-office figures, this strategy did not work. In Europe, at least, there were voices that hailed the film as an artistic success. The British magazine *Picturegoer* awarded it the "Seal of Merit" and called it Wyler's creative triumph.[40]

While not the only culprit, Selznick seems to have contributed significantly to this mixed reception, especially by incessantly pushing the film in the direction of a tragic romance that was inconsistent with the literary source. On a more general level, his unrelenting interference certainly did not help, either, as it put constant pressure on Wyler and his collaborators and contributed to the less than cheerful atmosphere during the shoot.

CONCLUSION

During the finishing of *Carrie*—long before the 1952 premiere—Selznick asked Wyler about other possibilities for collaboration. When Wyler evasively responded that none of his upcoming projects were a good fit for Jennifer Jones, Selznick offered his own options, including adaptations of the 1918 short story *Private Pettigrew's Girl* (already filmed twice under the title *The Shopworn Angel*) and the novel *The Rain-Girl*. Wyler rejected all of these proposals without much thought.[41] It is quite possible that the prospect of further collaboration with Selznick, despite its occasional productive aspects, discouraged him.

In the years that followed, their careers went in markedly different directions. Despite the failure of *Carrie*, Wyler remained a leading Hollywood director. Throughout the rest of the 1950s, he managed to succeed in a wide range of genres, from the romantic comedy *Roman Holiday* and the thriller *The Desperate Hours* (1955), to the Western *The Big Country* (1958) and the historical epic *Ben-Hur* (1959), which became the highest-grossing film of the decade. Thus, Selznick's fear that, in the event of *Carrie*'s commercial failure, Wyler would have difficulty getting Paramount to let him direct another prestige, high-budget film was proved wrong.

If *Carrie* served as a warning for Wyler about what to avoid in the future, Selznick failed to learn from the experience. On most other projects, he had serious creative disputes with directors, whether they were films he was preparing in his own production or projects for which he was lending out Jennifer Jones. His collaborations with renowned directors Vittorio De Sica, John Huston, King Vidor, and the duo of Michael Powell and Emeric Pressburger often ended in rifts and creative breakups. Selznick was less and less able to trust the judgment of others, but just as vehemently he refused to acknowledge that in the postwar era, he no longer understood the needs and desires of the public. While Wyler rebounded easily after *Carrie* and went on to strengthen his reputation as "Hollywood's most acclaimed director,"[42] Selznick lived only on the successes of the distant past.

NOTES

1. Lowell E. Redelings, Carrie, *Hollywood Citizen-News*, August 20, 1952. The excerpt is part of the file Carrie, The Core Collection, Margaret Herrick Library, Academy of Motion Picture Arts and Sciences (further abbreviated as AMPAS).
2. Bosley Crowther, "The Screen in Review; Carrie, With Laurence Olivier and Jennifer Jones, Is New Feature at the Capitol," *The New York Times*, July 17, 1952, 20:2.
3. Bosley Crowther, "Halleluiah, Sister! Carrie Becomes a Good Girl on the Screen," *The New York Times*, July 20, 1952, 2:1.
4. Gabriel Miller, *William Wyler: The Life and Films of Hollywood's Most Celebrated Director* (Lexington: University Press of Kentucky, 2013), 139.
5. Jan Herman, *A Talent for Trouble: The Life of Hollywood's Most Acclaimed Director* (Boston: Da Capo Press, 1997), 182.
6. Memo from Kay Brown, August 3, 1937, Margaret Tallichet—correspondence, b. 985, f. 13, Selznick Collection, Harry Ransom Center (further abbreviated as HRC).
7. See various documents in Margaret Tallichet—correspondence, b. 985, f. 13, HRC. A description of Tallichet's short career can be found in Steve Wilson, *The Making of Gone with the Wind* (Austin: University of Texas Press, 2014), 52.
8. Qtd. in Herman, *A Talent for Trouble*, 203.
9. Letter from William Wyler (not sent), November 10, 1939, 17.f-232 Intermezzo—general 1939, William Wyler Papers, Special Collections, AMPAS.
10. See Comparative Synopsis, Jennifer Jones Loanouts for "We Were Strangers" (Columbia), "Madame Bovary" (Metro) and "Victoria Grandolet" (Warner Bros.), June 30, 1950, Jennifer Jones Loanouts, b. 555, f. 5, HRC.
11. Letter from David O. Selznick, November 11, 1949, 1.f-19 Carrie—correspondence, William Wyler Papers, AMPAS.

12. See Selznick's letters from November 11 and 14, 1949, and the telegram from January 5, 1950, 1.f-19 Carrie—correspondence, William Wyler Papers, AMPAS.
13. Letters from David O. Selznick, November 11 and 14, 1949, 1.f-19 Carrie—correspondence, William Wyler Papers, AMPAS.
14. Telegram from David O. Selznick, June 14, 1950, 1.f-19 Carrie—correspondence, William Wyler Papers, AMPAS.
15. Letter from William Wyler, June 19, 1950, 1.f-19 Carrie—correspondence, William Wyler Papers, AMPAS. See also the letter from David O. Selznick, June 22, 1950, 1.f-19 Carrie—correspondence, William Wyler Papers, AMPAS.
16. See Herman, *A Talent for Trouble*, 323.
17. See the contract from July 10, 1950, Jennifer Jones—loanouts, b. 908, f. 24, HRC.
18. See memo from David O. Selznick, July 24, 1950, Jennifer Jones—Liberty Loanout, b. 555, f. 3, HRC.
19. Letter from David O. Selznick, July 29, 1950, 1.f-19 Carrie—correspondence, William Wyler Papers, AMPAS.
20. See, for instance, Neil Sinyard, *A Wonderful Heart: The Films of William Wyler* (Jefferson, NC, and London: McFarland, 2013), 138.
21. Letter from David O. Selznick, July 29, 1950, 1.f-19 Carrie—correspondence, William Wyler Papers, AMPAS.
22. Early in the novel, we learn that "self-interest . . . was . . . her guiding characteristic" and that "her craving for pleasure was so strong that it was the one stay of her nature." Theodore Dreiser, *Sister Carrie* (Mineola, NY: Dover Publications, 2004), 2 and 22.
23. Letter from David O. Selznick, July 29, 1950, 1.f-19 Carrie—correspondence, William Wyler Papers, AMPAS.
24. Telegram from David O. Selznick, September 9, 1950, Jennifer Jones—Liberty Loanout, b. 555, f. 3, HRC.
25. Letter from David O. Selznick, August 11, 1950, 1.f-19 Carrie—correspondence, William Wyler Papers, AMPAS.
26. Letter from David O. Selznick, August 24, 1950, 1.f-19 Carrie—correspondence, William Wyler Papers, AMPAS.
27. Letter from David O. Selznick, August 11, 1950, 1.f-19 Carrie—correspondence, William Wyler Papers, AMPAS.
28. See the letter from David O. Selznick, August 26, 1950, 1.f-19 Carrie—correspondence, William Wyler Papers, AMPAS.
29. See Herman, *A Talent for Trouble*, 328.
30. Letter from David O. Selznick, November 15, 1950, 1.f-19 Carrie—correspondence, William Wyler Papers, AMPAS.
31. See Herman, *A Talent for Trouble*, 328.
32. Letter from David O. Selznick, March 10, 1951, 1.f-19 Carrie—correspondence, William Wyler Papers, AMPAS.
33. Thomas P. Riggio, Biography of Theodore Dreiser, 2000, available from: <http://sceti.library.upenn.edu/dreiser/tdbio.cfm> (last accessed February 16, 2022).
34. See for example letter from David O. Selznick, June 11, 1951, 1.f-19 Carrie—correspondence, William Wyler Papers, AMPAS.
35. Letter from David O. Selznick, November 20, 1951, 1.f-19 Carrie—correspondence, William Wyler Papers, AMPAS.
36. Letter from William Wyler, November 29, 1951, 1.f-19 Carrie—correspondence, William Wyler Papers, AMPAS.
37. See Top Grossers of 1951, *Variety*, January 2, 1952, 70; Top Grossers of 1952, *Variety*, January 7, 1953, 61.

38. Murray Horowitz, Review: "Carrie," *Motion Picture Daily*, June 9, 1952, 4.
39. Crowther, "The Screen in Review; Carrie," 20:2. For other reviews, see the Carrie clippings file, Core Collection, AMPAS.
40. Carrie, *Picturegoer*, July 5, 1952, 16.
41. See telegrams from William Wyler, April 23, 1951, and January 2, 1952, and letter from William Wyler, March 3, 1952, 1.f-19 Carrie—correspondence, William Wyler Papers, AMPAS.
42. See the title of Jan Herman's biography.

CHAPTER 6

Narratives of Failure: *Dead End* (1937), *The Desperate Hours* (1955), and Gangsters in Distress

Terrance H. McDonald

William Wyler, as this edited collection demonstrates, worked within a wide range of genres and modes throughout his career in Hollywood, but his contributions to the gangster film are some of his least discussed pictures. In Wyler's *Dead End* (1937) and *The Desperate Hours* (1955), a distinct narrative structure can be mapped which reveals the gangster film to have undergone a much more complex development with diverse plot types than initial discussions surmise.[1] Through a critique of Thomas Schatz's focus on the "classical" gangster cycle, Amanda Ann Klein argues that "his privileging of the classical cycle does damage to genre history; clearly, the genre's narrative formulas sprang from somewhere."[2] Moreover, as Klein demonstrates, this privileging of "the classic cycle ignores variations and anomalies in order to create continuity and stability in a genre's definition."[3] Wyler's gangster films illuminate a divergent narrative structure that becomes more prevalent in the late-1930s with the enforcement of the Production Code that would bring an end to the classical cycle. While I agree with Klein's critique of an evolutionary model for understanding the genre, Schatz does acknowledge that the gangster films' "evolution was severely disrupted by external forces, and its narrative formula was splintered into various derivative strains."[4] A derivative strain may be a useful framing of Wyler's gangster films because neither film relies on a "gangster-hero"[5] in the same way that *Little Caesar* (Mervyn LeRoy, 1931) or *Scarface* (Howard Hawks, 1932) do. The presence of dual protagonists in each film—the hero is an average civilian as opposed to a gangster—can be attributed to the influence of the Production Code which sought to avoid the glorification of the gangster-hero. However, Wyler's films also rely on an immensely short timeline—each film takes place over only a few days—which cannot be explicitly attributed to the influence of the Production Code.

Over a few days, a gangster film cannot possibly show audiences the notorious ascension that most gangster-heroes make within the world of crime—such as Tony in *Scarface* or Rico in *Little Caesar*. Therefore, Wyler's gangster films are unique because the condensed timeframe of the narrative, in conjunction with the presence of dual protagonists, intensifies the length of time that the plot teases out the distress of the gangster. Specifically, Wyler's gangsters do not undergo the same "precipitous rise and fall"[6] as gangster-heroes of the classical cycle do. Instead, we find "Baby Face" Martin in *Dead End* and Glenn Griffin in *The Desperate Hours* to be mid-fall and, perhaps, never having risen high within the hierarchy of the gangster world.

WYLER'S GANGSTER FILMS AND THE GENRE

While the gangster-hero usually has humble beginnings, throughout the course of the narrative, they typically accumulate monetary wealth and social status. From Tony in *Scarface* to Vito in *The Godfather: Part II* (Francis Ford Coppola, 1974) to Henry in *Goodfellas* (Martin Scorsese, 1990), the main character starts in a lower socio-economic environment, then transitions to the upper-class through their participation in criminal activities. "The gangster's milieu is the modern city," states Schatz, "generally seen at night, with its enclosing walls of concrete and shadow, its rain-soaked streets, and its careening black automobiles."[7] The short timelines and singular locations of *Dead End* and *The Desperate Hours* restrict the gangster's milieu in a manner that contrasts with the modern cityscapes to be found in most gangster films, especially the classical cycle. The outside of a condo building on the riverfront within a tenement neighbor in New York City and a family home within the suburban streets of Indianapolis are certainly part of the modern city, but such isolated locations exaggerate the confinement—physically and psychologically—that most gangsters experience during their fall. Schatz notes that "the city represents a complex, alienating, and overwhelming community that initially creates the gangster and eventually destroys him."[8] These locations form microcosms of the gangster's social praxis that create and destroy gangster-heroes. In *Dead End*, the tenement neighborhood expresses the sociocultural concerns of the Depression era which stripped many Americans of the opportunity to earn decent livings and brought about feelings of emasculation in working-class American men (visible in the character Dave). In *The Desperate Hours*, the family home in the middle of suburbia reflects the sociocultural concerns of the Cold War with a destabilized patriarchal authority which leaves American fathers feeling emasculated amidst the many modern comforts of the 1950s (visible in the character Daniel). Moreover, Martin's, as well as Glenn's, eagerness to use violence and crime to grasp material pleasures become intensified by the sharp contrasts that are sustained within these restricted spaces.

Baby Face Martin and Glenn Griffin, while gangsters of some type (be it racketeers or outlaws), are not typical gangster-heroes who rise to the heights of wealth and social status, at least within the narrative of the films. We do not meet these gangsters on the way up; rather, we meet them on the way down or, perhaps in the case of Glenn, when they have almost completed their fall. Besides his expensive suits and bankroll, we never witness Baby Face's wealth through the iconography of material success. Instead, he becomes quite literally overshadowed by the towering wealth of the upper-class condo building on the river's edge. Similarly, Glenn may have lived a lavish lifestyle before imprisonment, but this possibility can only be speculative because he remains grubby and disheveled throughout the film. The plots of Wyler's films only occupy a few days, which makes it impossible to start with the gangster in humble beginnings, have them rise to the heights of gangster power, and then transition to the gangster's death or incarceration. While Wyler was not the screenwriter for either film, it remains of note that his only two gangster films feature such short timelines. Moreover, Wyler's *Detective Story* (1951)—perhaps better characterized as a crime film or even a film noir—also features a plot that takes place over a brief period of time, in this case one day. We can point to other examples of narratives with short timelines and isolated locations, such as *Key Largo* (John Huston, 1948) and *Reservoir Dogs* (Quentin Tarantino, 1992), which also contain sharp contrasts between gangsters and civilians. However, the particularities of these narratives within the gangster film genre have been underdiscussed.

As mentioned, the enforcement of the Production Code had an impact on Studio Era films which caused gangster narratives to change. Due to the Production Code Administration in the mid-1930s, the gangster film sought new plot types that did not rely as heavily on the gangster-hero. One such plot type replaced the gangster-hero with a law enforcement hero, or 'G' man, who embodied many of the same characteristics as the gangster-hero but on the "right-side" of the law. "It's important to note in this regard that the depiction of Cagney as gangster in *The Public Enemy*," states Schatz, "is basically indistinguishable from that of Cagney as government agent in *G-Men* and other mid-'30s crime films."[9] *'G' Men* (William Keighley, 1935) showcases a standard Cagney gangster-hero from the classical cycle now turned 'G' man-hero. Cagney's 'G' man protagonist hunts down gangsters with, perhaps, more violence than gangster-heroes of the classical cycle in order to get revenge for a murdered friend. Another narrative formation that arose in the wake of the Production Code enforcement was "the social gangster"[10] film, or what Schatz labels "the Cain-and-Abel variation."[11] Wyler's two gangster films rely on this plot type. In this variation, there is no longer a gangster-hero because he has been replaced by a dual protagonist structure, where a civilian-hero pushes the gangster into a more villainous role.

With a dual protagonist structure, the conflict between individualistic pleasure and conservative morality shifts from the internal struggle endured by the gangster-hero to an external struggle between the gangster and the civilian-hero. "The ultimate conflict of the gangster film is not between the gangster and his environment nor is it between the gangster and the police; rather," states Schatz, "it involves the contradictory impulses within the gangster himself."[12] This ultimate conflict becomes more pronounced through visible contrasts between gangster and civilian. While this narrative development—as well as the 'G' Men plot type—can be traced back, at least in part, to the influence of the Production Code, it nevertheless demonstrates that the gangster film displayed the capacity to transform and permeate other genres too.[13] This splintering of narratives away from the classical cycle supports Klein's overall critique of Schatz. "In retrospect," states Schatz, "the gangster genre is one of the few Hollywood formulas that did not grow old gracefully, that did not become richer and more complex with age."[14] However, examining the examples Schatz provides in his chapter on the gangster film, it would appear that the genre did become richer and more complex with age. Looking more intently, as Klein does, at gangster films that pre-date the classical cycle only further establishes this point. Wyler's gangster films are key contributions to this complexity because of the integration of two divergent trends in the genre: the Cain-and-Abel variation in combination with a narrative composed of a short timeline.

Klein's understanding of the genre as a series of cycles appears to align with the splintering of plot types that occurs in connection with the enforcement of the Production Code. "Rather than a series of discrete developmental stages moving along a linear track," states Klein,

> the gangster genre is more accurately described as a series of cycles, that is, as smaller groupings of films that appear at particular historical moments, thrive for a period of time, and then cease to be produced when interest in a subject wanes.[15]

This perspective opposes an evolutionary model in order to better understand the influence of gangster films that pre-date the classical cycle, such as *The Doorway to Hell* (Archie Mayo, 1930). Klein's work demonstrates the importance of melodramatic elements within the gangster film from the classical cycle, specifically *The Public Enemy* (William Wellman, 1931). However, Klein's reading of *The Public Enemy* as a melodramatic gangster film might overlook another possible element within gangster narratives: the gangster failure. Whether an outright failure to succeed in the gangster world or the inability to reach the peak of power and success, the failure and, by extension, the fall become much more pronounced within this narrative type. Rico in *Little Caesar* and Tony in *Scarface* are two gangster-heroes who reach the peak of power and then quickly die from a barrage of gunfire.

In *The Public Enemy*, Tom never quite rises to the heights that Rico and Tony do as he never becomes a boss. He does hold an important position in the gang, and he does enjoy a considerable level of success, but he remains at a rather low-level. Klein proposes that *The Public Enemy* should be classified as a melodramatic gangster film which pushes audiences to identify with the circumstances of the protagonist as opposed to keeping audiences at a distance to enjoy the spectacle. *The Public Enemy*, for Klein, employs one of two melodramatic-redemption plot types. "The gangster film's melodramatic-redemption narrative," according to Klein, "plays out in two basic ways: through the love-triangle narrative and the reforming-mentor narrative."[16] *The Public Enemy*, for Klein, employs the melodramatic trope of the reforming-mentor as Tom repents in the hospital before his murder. "Yet making this choice almost always proves to be a case of too late," states Klein, "since the gangster either dies or loses someone close to him as a result of his past misdeeds."[17] Unfortunately, Tom has already lost his friend to gang violence and now he loses his own life. We can see similarities in *Dead End* and *The Desperate Hours* where Martin has lost his relationship with his mother as well as a future with Francey and where Glenn loses his brother after a police shootout. The reforming-mentor narrative, however, does not quite fit these two films because neither Martin or Glenn ever repent and, in fact, they reaffirm their commitment to a life of crime.

Both Martin and Glenn are much more reminiscent of the classical gangsters from *Little Caesar* and *Scarface* because they never express any regret. Moreover, the two gangsters remain steadfast in their desire for wealth. Once Martin realizes that his mother has rejected him and Francey has become ill from sex work, he does not seek to reform his criminal ways and, instead, devises a plan to kidnap a child from the upper-class condo building on the edge of the river. Hal tries to convince Glenn to take Daniel's money rather than waiting for Helen to arrive with their stashed money, but Glenn rejects the idea and remains unwavering in his greed. In this sense, Martin and Glenn share the qualities of

> the classical gangster hero [who] is marked by his self-serving desires for monetary and social success (hence his ability to murder and steal without regret), and his lack of penance at the film's conclusion makes it difficult to empathize with his demise.[18]

Conversely, Tom displays regret for actions when confronted by his family. "Unlike the hero of the 'classical' gangster film," states Klein, "the melodramatic gangster displays the ability, if only at the last minute, to reflect on the needs and desires of others."[19] Even though Martin and Glenn differ from Tom when it comes to repentance, they do share with Tom a stunted evolution within the gangster world.

This realization that Tom and other gangsters—including those within Wyler's films—never reach the height of power further demonstrates the diversity of the genre. Not only do gangster films have the possibility of employing melodramatic elements but they also can incorporate a wide variety of other elements that can alter a film beyond the rigid conception of the classical cycle. "Outside the classic gangster narrative," states Fran Mason, "the gangster film tended to re-iterate the melodramatic form and ideology of the silent gangster film."[20] However, as Klein demonstrates, even the three canonical films associated with the classical cycle rely on melodrama. In the wake of Schatz's work, misconceptions of the genre are repeated. The classical cycle is often taken "as a defining moment which created the rules, conventions, and iconography of the genre as a whole."[21] Yet, the melodramatic mode of the silent gangster film, as demonstrated by Klein and acknowledged by Mason, does have a major influence on the genre. Furthermore, the gangster-hero and other gangster characters do not always have the "precipitous rise and fall"[22] that Schatz outlines. Sometimes, gangsters fail before they rise and sometimes the narrative of a gangster film ignores the rise altogether.

By assuming Schatz's evolutionary model for the gangster film—which moves from a classical period into periods of subversion and parody—the subtleties and nuances of the period can be overlooked. The ways in which the gangster-hero has been defined in relation to the classical cycle create an artificial idea about the genre. "The effect of presenting a taxonomy of the gangster genre based on the early classic films," states Mason, "has thus had the effect of reducing it to a reified ahistorical system of conventions rather than a mutable and flexible form capable of changing in response to shifts in ideologies and social and cultural practices."[23] The gangster failure becomes one component of a mutable and flexible form that gets overlooked. Neither of Wyler's gangster films align with the limited, evolutionary understanding of the gangster film because of the dual protagonists, the lack of a clearly defined rise, and the focus on a singular location that does not foreground the glitz and glamour of the modern city. Yet, Wyler's films do share a lot of key generic elements, including a non-repenting gangster. "Narratively, therefore," states Mason, "the classic gangster film is located at the interface between traditional systems of restraint, discipline and hierarchy and the chaos and excess of modernity."[24] This location between tradition and modernity appears to be where Martin and Glenn find themselves. Wyler's gangsters both desire the wealth and the power that come from the chaotic, violent, and excessive lifestyles connected to gangster activities.

Wyler's gangster films demonstrate that the iconography of the classical cycle and an expansive rise to power do not need to accompany other elements of the classic gangster film. Indeed, the genre can be understood in a manner that becomes much more divergent. "Ultimately, although the gangster experiences freedom in his mobility around the cultural spaces of modernity he is also subjected to its controls," states Mason, "whether this is within the gang system or in his punishment by another gang or the police (usually resulting in his death) for the excessive freedom his uncontrolled desires have engendered."[25] As a result of the Production Code, the punishment of the gangster pre-dates the classical cycle—such as the death of Louie in *The Doorway to Hell*—and remains a part of many gangster films. The gangster outlaws meet death with a barrage of bullets at the end of *Bonnie and Clyde* (Arthur Penn, 1967), death and law enforcement continually confront the Corleones in Coppola's *Godfather* trilogy, and Henry spirals into paranoia due to fears of death and law enforcement in *Goodfellas*, among countless other examples. In addition, there are other gangster films that do not focus on the rise of the gangster, including *The Petrified Forest* (Mayo, 1936) and *Key Largo* (Huston, 1948). These two examples are similar to Wyler's films because they have a singular location (for the most part), take place within a short timeframe, and contrast the gangster with a civilian with conservative morals. That said, both Duke (*The Petrified Forest*) and Johnny (*Key Largo*) appear to have a considerable amount of wealth as well as a significant group of underlings who do their bidding. In Wyler's films, Martin does have a sidekick who obeys his commands and a substantial bankroll. Glenn has two partners in crime that he orders around, but he certainly lacks visible wealth. However, we do know Helen is on the way to meet Glenn with a large amount of cash. Despite the variations of status, these narratives present gangsters through narratives that focus on their failure. We do not see Duke, Johnny, Martin, or Glenn rise from humble beginnings to possess the power of Rico or Tony. The focus of these narratives becomes much more about loss.

Mason coins the term "gangster-loser"[26] to describe characters from a post-classical cycle that include *The Friends of Eddie Coyle* (Peter Yates, 1973), *The Outfit* (John Flynn, 1973), *Charley Varrick* (Don Siegel, 1973), *The Killing of a Chinese Bookie* (John Cassavetes, 1976), and *Gloria* (Cassavetes, 1980)—I would add *The Nickel Ride* (Robert Mulligan, 1974) and *Mikey and Nicky* (Elaine May, 1976) to this list. Within these narratives the focus is "on the marginalised gangster outside the system of Mafia organized crime."[27] Predominantly, gangster-losers are "small-time gangsters" that find themselves in "a marginal culture where survival is the most important concern, but which is constantly threatened because of the pervasive hostility that is found in this world."[28] The fall of the gangster becomes much more of a focus within these narratives and the plot contains little of the gangster's rise. Moreover, the gangster-loser is often introduced in the midst of escalating trouble where their survival is already threatened. Mason claims that these films "re-use the classic cycle's articulation of the American Dream to show that even in gangster form it is an impossibility."[29] Despite Wyler's films being made within distinct periods of the Studio Era—as opposed to New Hollywood—Martin and Glenn appear to be early examples of the gangster-loser. By mapping the narratives of *Dead End* and *The Desperate Hours* in terms of failures—which reflects the situations of the gangsters as well as the working-class—Wyler's films can be read as reflecting socio-cultural issues in relation to masculinity and they reveal a narrative structure with a linear connection to New Hollywood gangster films.

DEAD END AND A PROLONGED FALL

Viewers do not witness the rise of Baby Face Martin in *Dead End*. The film does not even introduce Martin at the beginning. Early gangster films, according to Ron Wilson, focus on the outcomes of "tenement life" which eventually shifts to "neon-lighted" locations and urban spaces of modern cities in the late 1920s.[30] *Dead End* makes a visible return to outcomes of tenement life with Martin's return to his old neighborhood. He is perhaps recently removed from neon-lighted streets, but he now finds himself surrounded by the realities of the life he left behind. "The romanticization of the gangster-hero and the stylization of his 'underworld' milieu," argues Schatz, "render the genre's connections with reality rather tenuous and complex."[31] *Dead End* does not romanticize the gangster-hero—who is better classified as a gangster-villain—and the reality of the tenement life saturates the narrative. In this sense, *Dead End* can be distinguished from the classical cycle where the gangster-hero will meet their demise because they abandoned their humble upbringing in the pursuit of individualistic greed. Martin has pursued greed, but the narrative begins at a point in his downfall. He no longer possesses the unfettered mobility of a gangster that has reached the peak of power. Instead, Martin is wanted by police as the narrative skips over any sort of rise.

Where a gangster-hero's fall might span the final minutes in a classical gangster film, Martin's fall is much more prolonged as the film begins with him hiding from police. In contrast, much of *Little Caesar* and *Scarface* show Rico and Tony thwarting the efforts of the law. A similarity can be discerned in the conflict that ultimately consumes Martin and the classical gangster-hero. "The ultimate conflict of the gangster film is not between the gangster and his environment nor is it between the gangster and the police;" states Schatz, "rather, it involves the contradictory impulses within the gangster himself."[32] Like the demise of Rico and Tony, Martin's downfall accelerates due to the disloyalty of a friend or family member. Also, like Rico and Tony, Martin intensifies his gangster persona in response to the disloyalty rather than seeking redemption. In *Dead End*, notes Gene D. Phillips, "this gangster's tough exterior hides a sensitivity that yearns for the love both of his mother and of his old flame. Unfortunately, he finds neither of these love objects still waiting for him when he returns home."[33] Where Tom, in *The Public Enemy*, eventually succumbs to the guilt of family members, Martin only momentarily grimaces in response to his mother and Francey. Specifically, despite the looks of disappointment on Martin's face, he never openly expresses these feelings and attempts to compensate with a tougher exterior. In that sense, *Dead End* is the inverse of a melodramatic redemption plot because Martin never repents.

The dual protagonist is a key feature within *Dead End* because Dave provides a counterpoint who demonstrates overcoming the obstacles of the tenement neighborhood through hard work and honesty. Gangster films usually have two tendencies: the gangster is a product of the society that creates them, or the gangster chooses a life of crime due to individualistic greed. The tragic flaw of the gangster-hero, according to Schatz, is "his inability to channel his considerable individual energies in a viable direction."[34] This flaw appears to be present in most gangster characters who are either heroes or important characters within the film. Gangsters demonstrate intelligence through the schemes they design and through the ways in which they thwart law enforcement (at least temporarily). The gangster projects a vibrant personality that attracts followers and romantic interests which is also related to their status. Martin also becomes haunted by this tragic flaw, but whatever power he once possessed from criminal activities has begun to wane by the start of *Dead End*. Nevertheless, he tries to flaunt his wealth and lawlessness as a demonstration of a masculine superiority. People who accept the terms and conditions of the system are often "suckers" from the perspective of a gangster.

The gangster often inhabits a fantasy space which materializes in a manner that is fleeting. Thus, Schatz, as quoted above, notes the romanticization of the gangster-hero complicates a relationship with reality. "The underworld serves up male fantasies," according to David E. Ruth, "where masculine prowess brought awesome power."[35] Martin, like the gangster-hero, is enthralled by the power he possesses, but, also like the gangster-hero, he is unable to discern, or at least accept, that this power is tenuous. A recognition that a gangster's power is temporary becomes a key component of the redemption narrative. To repent and seek transformation, the gangster character must first come to the realization that their power cannot be sustained. Martin refuses this reality. In Wyler's gangster films, the melodramatic elements do not mix with the character of the gangster, unlike *The Public Enemy* which is an example of melodramatic redemption. "In this way," states Klein, "*The Public Enemy* violates the tough 'masculine' tone so often associated with the gangster film, by injecting the comparatively soft, 'feminine' mode of melodrama."[36] Tom may express feelings of weakness and he may repent, but Martin does not. In comparison,

Dave does recognize his limitations, perhaps too much so, and he needs to take a risk that pushes him beyond his conservative morality. By splitting the gangster-hero into a gangster-villain and a civilian-hero, the melodramatic mode is detached from the gangster character.

This splitting of the gangster-hero into a gangster-villain and a civilian-hero is obviously a change that has a fair amount to do with the influence of the Production Code. While gangster-heroes were popular with audiences, a backlash from conservative groups sought censorship of gangster-heroes. Even though the gangster is inevitably punished by death or imprisonment within the classical cycle, a concern remained about the attractiveness of these characters. "Gangsters continued to appear in pictures," explains Richard Maltby, "but as increasingly marginal characters in other people's plots."[37] After all, *Dead End* is really Dave's story and *The Desperate Hours* is really Daniel's story. Martin and Glenn remain stubbornly committed to their gangster persona throughout the narrative. Conversely, Dave and Daniel develop throughout the narrative and rise to the occasion at the climax. In this manner, the civilian-hero reverses the rise and fall of the gangster-hero: fallen or emasculated within a sociocultural milieu, the civilian-hero defeats the gangster and establishes a successful image of themselves.

Dead End introduces us to Martin as he is already falling. He may have used his wealth to receive plastic surgery that alters his appearance, but his wealth fails to secure for him the affection he wants from his mother and the relationship with Francey that he desires. He cannot buy away his reputation and he cannot buy the ability to travel back in time and not abandon his loved ones. "The image of Martin's ignominious fall from the top of the fire escape to the ground below," states Phillips, "symbolizes that he has been knocked off the pedestal on which Tommy and the other boys had placed him."[38] While the ending may be the completion of Martin's fall, he was already shown to be somewhat powerless in previous encounters with his mother and Francey. In comparison, Dave is steadily on the rise in the second half of the narrative when he begins confronting Martin. At first, Martin's masculine prowess is acknowledged by Dave who cautions that he will not go to the police. However, with Martin's bravado fading, Dave seizes the opportunity to demonstrate his superiority. After all, unlike Martin who laments that he is tired of getting only what he can pay for, Dave earns his reputation and success in spite of his inability to pay for much at all.

There are a lot of opportunities to read the film as reflecting a conversative ideology in the wake of the Depression. Dave demonstrates that hard work and strong morals will eventually overcome the obstacles that the tenement neighborhood presents. However, it is not entirely hard work alone that allows Dave to succeed. "*Dead End* sees the failure of the official ideology of success through work," states Mason, "but also sees only cynicism and futility in the knowledge that the gangster has of the world."[39] While Martin is certainly framed as a failure through his prolonged fall, Dave also struggles to rise and, for the most part, remains emasculated due to an inability to overcome poverty. Furthermore, the upper-class residents living in the condo building on the edge of the riverfront illuminate the inequalities experienced by the tenement community. "Both the rich and the gangster represent easy money," states Mason, "and both threaten to destroy society through their idleness and excess."[40] The separation between Martin and Griswald, the rich brother of a judge, is only a matter of degree in *Dead End*. Both characters threaten the lives of the tenement community by using their power to manipulate systems to their advantage. Martin uses the threat of physical violence and Griswald uses his connections to threaten police officers, a gang of tenement youths, and other members of the tenement community.

Because Martin is situated as a villain, *Dead End* more thoroughly undermines the glamorous image of the gangster-hero. Moreover, with the narrative beginning mid-fall, the majority of actions taken by Martin tend towards pathetic and desperate. In contrast, early in the classical cycle films, gangster-heroes take calculated risks that propel them into power. Their rise is much lengthier than their quick falls. A key difference that surrounds the narrative of Martin hinges on the elongation of the time dedicated to his failure. "The film," states Mason, "ends by showing how unattractive the gangster life is by drawing attention to the fact that although it may involve pleasure and easy money it is also brutish."[41] However, the pleasure and easy money that Martin possesses is never romanticized as it is when Rico first reaches the peak of power or when Tony ascends the top of the gangster hierarchy or even when Tom gains more power and respect within the gang. Throughout Martin's fall, his money fails to buy him what he wants as he finds less and less pleasure. "Work and honesty triumph over idleness, excess, and crime," states Mason, "but the film fails to resolve itself ideologically."[42] In a sense, Mason does make an important observation because Dave does not simply triumph in spite of Martin. Rather, Dave succeeds because he, momentarily, succumbs to the pressure to be more like the gangster. Dave cannot overcome Martin by the rules governing society alone and, instead, he must resort to gangster-like violence. Furthermore, Dave is unable to obstruct Griswald's power afforded by wealth and privilege on even ground. It is only the reward Dave receives for murdering Martin—granted for gangster-like actions—that allows Dave to foil Griswald's manipulation of justice and to get Tommy out on bail. In the end, Dave rises to possess success and a relationship with Drina because he displays some of the masculine prowess that sparks the precipitous rise of the gangster-hero. Just as in *The Desperate Hours*, where this need for a heightened "masculinity" is aroused in Daniel by Glenn, here too Martin is the instigator of the change in Dave.

THE DESPERATE HOURS AND AN AMPLIFIED FAILURE

Almost twenty years later, Wyler returned to the gangster film but in a very different socio-cultural milieu. If Martin experiences a prolonged fall in *Dead End*, Glenn experiences an amplified failure in *The Desperate Hours* because he has already fallen by going to prison. When the film opens, Glenn along with his brother and a fellow convict have escaped from prison. Hiding out from the police, the trio of gangsters takes a family hostage while they wait for Glenn's partner to bring them money that they have stashed away. "Bogart plays Glenn Griffin as an older version of Baby Face Martin from *Dead End*;" states Phillips, "it is as if Martin had lived to see middle age."[43] Where Martin had his failure take place over several days before his death, Glenn has been stewing in prison for some time where he has plotted revenge against Jesse Bard who broke his jaw during the arrest. "Because Glenn has reached middle life," states Phillips, "he is presented as a counterpart of Dan Hilliard: Glenn, as a hunted criminal, is a failure, shunned by the society of which Dan is a respectable member. Hence, Glenn is bitterly jealous of Dan."[44] A dual protagonist structure, with men of a similar age, is also reminiscent of *Dead End*, but now the gangster-villain Glenn has reached middle age which is something gangster-heroes rarely achieve. However, because he has lived longer, his failure as a gangster has been amplified. Where the gangster-hero, and even Martin, only live with their failures for a short period of time (a few days at most), Glenn has had to sit with these failures and contemplate them in jail. Furthermore, as Phillips outlines, Daniel intensifies that image of failure through the reflection of his middle-class lifestyle.

Including his role in *Dead End*, Bogart has played a lot of supporting and minor gangster-villains. From *The Petrified Forest* to *Bullets or Ballots* (Keighley, 1936) to *The Amazing Dr. Clitterhouse* (Anatole Litvak, 1938), Bogart's early gangsters are often secondary characters. This character type is a sharp contrast to the flawed heroes that Bogart plays as a star in the 1940s, but he never loses that tough-guy edge in many of his film noir roles. Steven Cohan notes that the character Glenn is "appearing to draw upon the star's previous roles as a gangster."[45] The major difference between Glenn and Bogart's other gangster roles is his age. Bogart's previous gangster-villains meet a quick death at a relatively young age. Conversely, Glenn dwells in his failure as a gangster which may be offset by some financial success—he does have money stashed away—but he has little else to show for his years as a criminal. The effectiveness of the narrative, according to Cohan, arises "from the way that the hardened criminal's personification of those dangers, positioned in opposition to the norm of the homeowner's hegemonic masculinity, externalizes them as psychological deviancy."[46] Where the start of *Dead End* introduces Martin as someone with much more opportunity and success than Dave, *The Desperate Hours* blurs the superiority of Glenn's status which is most expressed by the fact that he is currently an escaped convict. Daniel, in comparison, may not have amassed a significant amount of wealth but he can freely access it through the bank, and he has achieved other personal desires that money alone cannot buy. That said, like Dave, Daniel uses some of the masculine prowess of the gangster, but not until he is forced as a last resort. Only when it is sanctioned by the law, do Dave and Daniel mobilize a little of the gangster's violence and the accompanying threat of violence. Much like the opening of *Dead End*, Daniel's authority is undermined by the socio-cultural conditions of his environment. "In *The Desperate Hours*, when the convicts first take his family hostage, the middle-aged father, Dan Hilliard (Fredric March)," states Cohan, "appears emasculated, unable to defend his home against this invasion, especially as personified by the menacing figure of Glenn Griffin."[47] Dave and Daniel may be emasculated in the opening of Wyler's films, but the two socio-cultural milieus that generate this weakened image are quite distinct. Where *Dead End* frames a Depression era feeling of helplessness due to a lack of gainful employment, *The Desperate Hours* frames a postwar erosion of the authority held by the patriarchal figure within the nuclear, middle-class family.

Another key difference in *The Desperate Hours* is the manner in which the disloyalty of a loved one arises. Martin's mother rejects him because his reputation is too sullied and Francey is perceived to be disloyal because he has come too late. There is a clear difference in *The Desperate Hours* because Glenn's brother Hal only starts to waver in support of Glenn once he becomes familiar with a middle-class lifestyle. "The attraction of middle-class life thus drives a wedge between the two brothers," states Cohan, "rupturing the only relation that moves the older man to show any affect other than anger."[48] Much like Martin, who thinks Dave is a "sucker" for following the law and socio-cultural conventions, Glenn sees Daniel as less masculine because he refuses to pursue individualistic desires and upholds a strong moral standing. Hal, in stark contrast, begins to wish more and more that he could be like Daniel. Hal spurns Glenn by admitting he taught him everything: "Except how to live in a house like this." The fantasy associated with the gangster-hero becomes inverted by the dual protagonist structure of the gangster-villain and the civilian-hero which frames a middle-class life as the superior fantasy to that of the gangster's potential wealth and status. Perhaps, like the gangster fantasy, the connections that this middle-class fantasy has with reality are also as tenuous and complex. "What Glenn Griffin does not understand, because he keeps falling back on a tough-guy working-class mentality," argues Cohan, "is that Hilliard intimidates Hal precisely because the superiority of the middle-class father's social position manifests itself in less tangible form than a clenched fist or cocked trigger."[49] In the end, *The Desperate Hours*, like *Dead End*, reveals another civilian-hero who rises above emasculation in order to demonstrate the superiority of hard work and conservative morality.

However, also like *Dead End*, Daniel can only be successful in thwarting the gangsters and reclaiming his patriarchal authority when he becomes a little bit like the gangster. The threat of gangster violence that Daniel enacts against Glenn, and Kobish retroactively, reveals him to be anything but an emasculated, middle-class father. Instead, Daniel asserts himself as a man capable of displaying unwavering authority and power, but only when absolutely necessary. "While *The Desperate Hours* opposes the masculinities of Griffin and Hilliard in this manner," states Cohan, "the domesticated breadwinner also has to recognize his likeness to the brutish convict."[50] It is possible to read Dave's murder of Martin as signifying the end of the social justification of gangsters. A justification which involves recognizing the conditions that produce criminal behavior and the inequalities within a specific socio-cultural milieu, such as the tenement neighbor. In contrast, Glenn's amplified failure may be read as signifying a lack of justification for the existence of gangsters due to the prosperity available to so many in postwar America. While this ideological message could be visibly undermined by the experiences of many minorities, immigrants, and other people living in lower socio-economic communities during this period, Hollywood's projection of a white, middle-class conservativism would align with such a flawed set of beliefs. Bogart's character in *The Desperate Hours* reflects this perspective because his character is "one which contrasts to his earlier criminal roles in the 1930s at Warners, because," states Sklar,

> there is little effort to situate Griffin's criminality in a social context—he is an antisocial deviant whose resentment of the bourgeois father is a sign only of his personal weakness and envy, not of any failures of the social order.[51]

The inflated sense of superiority and confidence projected through the national image of America following World War II is quite different from the images of Depression era America in the late-1930s.

By the end of *The Desperate Hours*, like *Dead End*, the gangster-villain is dead, and the civilian-hero's success is reflected by a heterosexual union and the solidification of the white, nuclear, American family that perseveres despite the many obstacles encountered within the narrative. The films do not end with a gangster's death, like the classical cycle often does, and, instead, the films end with the rise of a regular, hard-working, American man. "With the tables turned," states Cohan, "Hilliard's moral authority as a domesticated man revitalizes his masculinity in direct proportion to its emasculation of Griffin."[52] While all of the fears and concerns voiced by various conservative groups about the gangster-hero may have stemmed from the dangerous influence of those violent and glamorous images, the fantasy of the patriarchal figure who needs just the right amount of gangster-like behavior to assert their authority within society and the family may be the most dangerous of all. Whether they are gangster-losers or simply gangster-villains, the gangsters in Wyler's *Dead End* and *The Desperate Hours* reveal alternative potentialities that the gangster film spawned in distinct periods of the Studio Era. However, where the gangsters' experience prolonged and amplified distress until their ultimate failure, the average, white, American man is rewarded for being just a little bit like a gangster. In hindsight, this fantasy has likely proved to be far more dangerous and toxic than that associated with any gangster-hero.

NOTES

1. Thomas Schatz, "The Gangster Film," in *Hollywood Genres: Formulas, Filmmaking, and The Studio System* (New York: Random House, 1981), 81–110.
2. Amanda Ann Klein, "Real Gangsters Do Cry: A Cyclical Approach to Film Genres," in *American Film Cycles: Reframing Genres, Screening Social Problems, and Defining Subcultures* (Austin, TX: University of Texas Press, 2011), 36.
3. Ibid.
4. Schatz, 82.
5. Ibid.
6. Schatz, 91.
7. Schatz, 83.
8. Schatz, 84.
9. Ibid.
10. Fran Mason, *American Gangster Cinema: From* Little Caesar *to* Pulp Fiction (New York: Palgrave Macmillan, 2002), 39.
11. Schatz, 99.
12. Schatz, 85.
13. After all, as Janet Staiger and others have demonstrated, film genres during the Studio Era were rarely pure. See Barry Keith Grant, ed., *Film Genre Reader IV* (Austin, TX: University of Texas Press, 2012).
14. Schatz, 110.
15. Klein, 35.
16. Klein, 41.
17. Ibid.
18. Klein, 42.
19. Ibid.
20. Mason, 5.
21. Ibid.
22. Schatz, 91.
23. Mason, 6.
24. Mason, 8.
25. Mason, 15.
26. Mason, 136.
27. Ibid.
28. Ibid.
29. Mason, 138.

30. Ron Wilson, *The Gangster Film: Fatal Success in American Cinema* (London: Wallflower, 2015), 20–4.
31. Schatz, 82.
32. Schatz, 85.
33. Gene D. Phillips, *Exiles in Hollywood: Major European Film Directors in America* (Cranbury, NJ: Lehigh University Press, 1998), 68.
34. Schatz, 88.
35. David E. Ruth, *Inventing the Public Enemy: The Gangster in American Culture, 1918-1934* (Chicago, IL: The University of Chicago Press, 1996), 94.
36. Klein, 27.
37. Richard Maltby, "The Spectacle of Criminality," in *Violence and American Cinema*, ed. J. David Slocum (New York: Routledge, 2001), 143.
38. Phillips, 69.
39. Mason, 40.
40. Mason, 43.
41. Ibid.
42. Mason, 44.
43. Phillips, 87.
44. Ibid.
45. Steven Cohan, *Masked Men: Masculinity and the Movies in the Fifties* (Bloomington, IN: Indiana University Press, 1997), 110.
46. Ibid.
47. Ibid.
48. Cohan, 112.
49. Cohan, 113.
50. Ibid.
51. Quoted in Cohan, 114.
52. Cohan, 114.

CHAPTER 7

Wyler's *Wuthering Heights* (1939): Genre, Transnationalism, and the Adaptation of the Victorian Novel

Gabrielle Stecher

> The Brontës were never noted for gay writing, and the studio here has made a point of adding no touch of humor to the tale of "Wuthering Heights" . . . there is a haunting quality about the picture which will stay with you.[1]

The 1930s bore witness to a multitude of film adaptations of canonical Victorian novels: William Thackeray's *Vanity Fair*, for instance, was adapted in both 1932 and 1935, the Christy Cabanne adaptation of Charlotte Brontë's *Jane Eyre* was released in 1934, and five Charles Dickens novels made their way to the silver screen within the decade. While both literary and film scholars have theorized about and remain invested in the connection between Victorian novels and Hollywood cinema, less attention has been paid to William Wyler's 1939 adaptation of Emily Brontë's 1847 novel *Wuthering Heights*. *Wuthering Heights*—a narrative of both intense passion and visceral hatred, a love story steeped in Gothic horror—has remained a staple in the English literary canon with a, consequently, wide readership. The novel's magnetism has not only attracted a massive body of critics who have attempted for decades to make sense of Catherine Earnshaw and Heathcliff's often violent and terrifying attachment, but it has also become grounds for appropriation and adaptation. In this chapter, I discuss Wyler's approach to adapting the classic Victorian novel, including what drew Wyler to Brontë's fictional realm in the first place, as well as the generic consequences of this transnational film adaptation.

Before discussing the nuances of Wyler's adaptation, it is important to establish a basic, albeit oversimplified, understanding of Brontë's plot—this is a necessary precursor to our understanding of the creative liberties Wyler took with bringing only a select portion of the novel to the screen. Set in the moors of West Yorkshire, *Wuthering Heights* is a novel in essentially two parts. The first is the love story of the wild and devilish Catherine, who defies gendered expectations of the quintessentially Victorian Angel in the House, and Heathcliff, the orphaned Byronic Hero, who enacts his revenge after being rejected by Catherine out of her own self-interest, on the grounds of his low social status. The second part of the novel reveals the extent of the generational trauma and abuse enacted by their chaotic relationship and its effects on the second generation of the novel's characters, including both Catherine's and Heathcliff's children with siblings Edgar and Isabella Linton respectively of neighboring estate Thrushcross Grange. Catherine marries Edgar for stability's sake; Heathcliff seduces and marries Isabella out of revenge after fleeing from Cathy's rejection and returning a wealthy gentleman from abroad. Catherine dies after childbirth as a result of her self-starvation and illness following her inability to cope with Heathcliff's return; in turn, he summons her ghost to haunt him for the rest of his days. Both narratives are intertwined through the storytelling of Ellen (or Nelly) Dean, a servant of the families, who relays these personal histories in a series of flashbacks to Mr. Lockwood, the new tenant of Thrushcross Grange, a property Heathcliff rents to Lockwood just before his death. As we will soon see, Wyler focused solely on the first half of this narrative—the growing up and out of innocence of Cathy and Heathcliff, their unfulfilling separate marriages, and their eventual reunion in death.

The production of *Wuthering Heights* for the screen was part of a larger trend of canonical literary adaptations within the studio system, especially in the 1930s. As Guerric Debona suggests, "redeploying the cultural memory of a Victorian author . . . during the Depression served the strategic advantage of a studio investing itself with the aura of prestige and credibility for the middle class."[2] Canonical literature was marked as possessing both narrative and cultural legitimacy; as such, "in the 1930s, the canonical purchased for the film industry an aura of respectability."[3] This desire for respectability is reflected in Wyler's output: *Wuthering Heights* was one of five films directed by Wyler and produced under Samuel Goldwyn between 1936 and 1939 that was an adaptation of a literary property. Outside of Samuel Goldwyn Productions, it was one of six Victorian literature adaptations released in Hollywood in 1939 alone. While *Wuthering Heights* had previously been adapted by A.V. Bramble and Eliot Stannard for the British Ideal Film Company in 1920, Wyler's version was the first Hollywood, not to mention sound, version. Samuel Goldwyn had previously produced one other adaptation of a Victorian canonical classic, William Thackeray's *Vanity Fair* in 1923 (a silent film directed by Hugo Ballin now considered a lost film), but it was Wyler's direction of *Wuthering Heights* that would earn both producer and director a total of eight Academy Award Nominations, as well as the New York Film Critics Award for Best Film.

Filming began in December 1938, ninety-one years after the novel's original publication. Yet, the process of its adaptation began before Wyler became its director. Wyler was in the process of directing the crime drama *Dead End* (1937), itself an adaptation of a Sidney Kingsley play, when he was approached by starring actress Sylvia Sidney with a copy of the *Wuthering Heights* script. Before Wyler ever signed on to direct *Wuthering Heights* for Goldwyn, the script was in the hands of Walter Wanger, who intended to cast Sidney opposite Charles Boyer; however, Sidney candidly told Wyler that "I'm not going to do it, because I'm not right for it, and neither is [Boyer]."[4] Wyler was intrigued by the script, but Goldwyn was far less interested. According to Wyler,

> I don't think [Goldwyn] read it himself. He had somebody else read it and found out it ended in the death of the two lovers and he said, no, he was not going to make tragedies! So I couldn't get him to buy it.[5]

Additionally, Goldwyn found the "flashback structure" of the narrative's frame tale, in which Lockwood stumbles into the family's history by way of servant narrator Ellen Dean, too confusing and that the lovers' flaws were too tragic and thus too unattractive to have mass audience appeal.[6] Despite this momentary setback, Wyler was eventually able to convince Goldwyn to purchase the script as a vehicle for Merle Oberon after approaching Warner Brothers and their enthusiastic contract star Bette Davis about the film. The competition was too great for Goldwyn; he was finally on board, though as we will soon learn, this was not the end of Goldwyn's dislike of the plot's more tragic, not to mention Gothic, elements.

In a 1970 interview with Bernard Kantor, Irwin Blacker, and Anne Kramer for a volume titled *Directors at Work*, Wyler recounted his own introduction to the worlds of Wuthering Heights and Thrushcross Grange, noting the difficulty of bringing Brontë's moors to life on-screen:

> *Wuthering Heights?* That was very difficult, but it was first done by Ben Hecht and Charlie MacArthur, who had already done the script—more or less, not exactly. I made a few revisions, but I saw the script before I read the book.[7]

Wyler, then, read a screenplay draft before he ever read the original text; he admitted in a 1981 interview that "I read it and I was not familiar with this British literature sort of speak, but it was a wonderful script, I thought, and very unusual kind of story."[8] Unusual as the script was, Brontë's experimentation with the Gothic and the generational trauma of the novel was tampered with by the screenwriters, which later included John Huston, who Wyler brought on to improve the script and serve as a mediator between himself and Goldwyn. Huston recounted the pair would often enter into a "screaming match" during story conferences.[9]

Despite the frequent tension between director and producer, William Wyler was no stranger to the often complex processes of adaptation. While Wyler was particularly drawn to theatrical material, his direction of *Wuthering Heights* testifies to his ability to bring the Victorian novel to the screen in ways that revise yet enliven Brontë's text for a Depression-era American audience.[10] Not all critics, particularly auteurists, believed his knack for adaptation was worthy of an elevated directorial status; however, when we recognize the complexities of adaptation on generic and transnational levels, it becomes easier to understand the extent of Wyler's success at translating the novel into a new medium. Wyler explained that he made a conscious effort to

> avoid wandering very far from the script of a play when adapting it for the screen. But film versions of novels are another matter. I have never felt any obligation to be faithful to every word of authors like Emily Brontë . . . These people didn't write films to be seen but books to be read. So I felt free to add or subtract from the original source in order to best serve my medium. I am sure that this is what they would have wanted me to do: to present their material in a new form in the best possible way for a different medium.[11]

Translating lengthy novels into feature-length films necessitates cuts or exclusions; in this case, the entire second part of the novel that explores the trauma and suffering of the second generation of characters was removed entirely from the script. Cutting the second-generation plot (to the extent that Cathy's pregnancy and both lovers' children are completely absent from the film) allowed the story to become less about generational trauma and domestic abuse, instead capitalizing on what Gabriel Miller describes as "the twisted, passionate love of the two principles."[12] In this way, the text underwent a vast rhetorical shift, one that moved audiences to experience and feel passion rather than horror. The film, then, initiated a different kind of arousal on behalf of the audience—this, I argue, is a consequence of what Judith Mayne calls a "result of a film industry determined to simplify for its mass audience at all costs."[13] Boiling down the plot to a romance affords simplicity and efficiency. For Wyler, he believed the second half of the novel to be too repetitious and that he could still "be faithful to the idea and to the theme of the original author" while telling the story in the most effective, and therefore efficient, manner in his own medium.[14] Additionally, audiences familiar with the complexities of the original plot could be primed to expect an easier to follow, and therefore more enjoyable, narrative; this is reflected in Jack Wade's address to future audiences in an April 1939 *Photoplay* essay that far be it from us to try to condense the masterpiece of Emily Brontë into a couple of sentences, but if you're weak on your English literature, you should know the tale is about a landed English family and how they grew.[15]

Wade's one-liner summary of the novel, so vague that it borders on misleading, attests to how drastic the selective nature of adaptation could be.

In cutting *Wuthering Heights* down to romance, the narrative becomes less of a generic hybrid than it appears in its original novel form. The novel does not necessarily fit cleanly into any one genre: it combines elements of the romance and social novel yet is driven by Gothicism. The British tradition of Gothic fiction was established in the mid-eighteenth century with Horace Walpole's *The Castle of Otranto* and was only furthered in the 1790s with the novels of Ann Radcliffe and later Mary Shelley's *Frankenstein*, first published in 1818. Brontë, then, was operating within an established tradition characterized by the uncanny and the sublime, perverse romantic and sexual desires, not to mention moments of supernatural tension between past and present. This is not to say that there are no moments in Wyler's adaptation that are vaguely terrifying. Viewers have long pointed to the opening scene in which Lockwood, a stranger in the "barren Yorkshire moors," as the intertitle tells us, "dare[s] to knock at the door of Wuthering Heights," as well as the scene where young Cathy is viciously attacked by a guard dog, as the film's scariest moments, however mild they may be.[16] Yet the overall project of the film is not to scare. As such, the manner of its adaptation is a departure from the intentions of the Gothic mode in which, in Ellen Moers' words,

> fantasy predominates over reality, the strange over the commonplace, and the supernatural over the natural, with one definite auctorial intent: to scare. Not, that is, to reach down into the depths of the soul and purge it with pity and terror (as we say tragedy does), but to get to the body itself, its glands, epidermis, muscles, and circulatory system, quickly arousing and quickly allaying the physical reactions to fear.[17]

What *Wuthering Heights* offers the screen is the potential to move the audience, to arouse them into experiencing the range between sadistic terror and romantic sentimentality; yet it is ultimately up to the director in which way the audience will primarily be moved to feel. Wyler himself classified *Wuthering Heights* as "a dark romantic tragedy."[18] Yet, darkness and tragedy do not imply Gothicism; there can be no happy ending and the film can end with the deaths of both Cathy and Heathcliff without inspiring a fear of the supernatural on the behalf of the audience. Through this generic shift, then, the film fails to pass as a "translation of [Brontë's] great original" and becomes little more than, in Fred Inglis's words, a "good enough romantic period-and-wardrobe comed[y]."[19] *Wuthering Heights'* becoming what John Collick calls a sentimental period piece intended to attract a young audience of primarily middle-class women, not unlike films like *Gone with the Wind* and *Casablanca*, I argue, is due to its tempering of the Gothic.[20]

Before articulating how the film becomes a romance, I first must discuss its unbecoming Gothic, or cases in which the novel's famous Gothic elements are censored and/or stripped from the film's final cut. There are two unforgettable moments in the novel that one recalls when thinking about the text as an undeniable work of Gothic fiction: the scene in which Lockwood hallucinates what appears to be a child—or changeling—Cathy clawing her way out of the cold and into her former bridal chamber and the moment in the second volume in which Heathcliff digs up the grave of his beloved in order to gaze upon her face once more. In many ways, these moments in the text are the most cinematic.

In the opening scenes of the novel and after finally being granted permission to spend the night at Wuthering Heights due to the severity of the snowstorm that has halted his ability to get safely back to his residence at Thrushcross Grange, Lockwood falls into a fitful sleep. Led by a housekeeper into a previously forbidden chamber of Wuthering Heights, Lockwood spends his last wakeful moments acquainting himself with the room's former occupant through her material remains. These relics include a small collection of mildewed books inscribed "Catherine Earnshaw," Cathy's diary recounting the childhood abuses enacted against the continually othered Heathcliff by Hindley Earnshaw, Catherine's brother, and an evolving series of names—Catherine Earnshaw, Catherine Linton, and Catherine Heathcliff—scratched by the girl into the paint of a ledge. Lockwood begins to drift off, but his sleep is interrupted by what we may call a promise of the hauntings to come: "my eyes closed; but they had not rested five minutes when a glare of white letters started from the dark, as vivid as spectres—the air swarmed with Catherines; and [I roused] myself to disciple the obtrusive name."[21] Lockwood begins to read Cathy's diary, becoming for a moment a spectator of the past through Cathy's own eyes, before falling into a dreamlike state once again. Except this time, he becomes the temporary victim of Cathy and the estate's past.

Lockwood, in a state somewhere between wakefulness and sleep, makes an attempt to stop the branch of a birch tree from rattling across the windowpane of his chamber and disrupting his rest. He reaches his hand outside when, suddenly, his

> fingers closed on the fingers of a little, ice-cold hand! The intense horror of nightmare came over me; I tried to draw back my arm, but the hand clung to it, and a most melancholy voice sobbed—"Let me in—let me in!"[22]

The ghost child's grip on Lockwood is frightening as it is not immediately clear to Lockwood or the reader if this is a hallucination. It is through his response to Catherine's pining that this moment becomes terrifically Gothic:

> As it spoke, I discerned, obscurely, a child's face looking through the window—Terror made me cruel; and, finding it useless to attempt shaking the creature off, I pulled its wrist on to the broken pane, and rubbed it to and fro till the blood ran down and soaked the bedclothes: still it wailed, "Let me in!" and maintained its tenacious gripe, almost maddening me with fear.[23]

Though Lockwood is able to snatch his hand back to safety and banishes Catherine's ghost back to the moors before a harried Heathcliff rushes to the window in an attempt to reunite with his beloved, this is one of the most, if not *the* most, graphic moments in the entire narrative. Catherine presents herself as a Linton (her married name), yet appears before Lockwood in her child, and therefore her most wild and untamed, form. The scene is Gothic in that Cathy or her apparition and Lockwood are both seemingly in between states of life and death, wake and sleep, past and present. But what is perhaps the most gruesome, and therefore horrifying, is the treatment of Catherine's body; her wrists, her arteries, are purposefully sliced open on broken glass by Lockwood in an effort at self-protection. This moment foreshadows the violence, both physical and psychological, inherent in the rest of the narrative; its shock value makes this moment difficult, if not impossible, for readers to forget, as this is how audiences are initially introduced and conditioned to understand the instability and devilishness of Catherine's character.

Yet, in Wyler's version, this scene plays out much differently. The shutters bang against the window, waking Lockwood; as he reaches out of the window, he hears a woman calling for Heathcliff faintly in the distance. "Let me in—I am lost in the moors. It's Cathy!" the voice calls, calmly and alluringly as if a siren.[24] Lockwood withdraws his cold, shaking hand from outside the window after screaming for Heathcliff's help; however, we never see Cathy's face in the window, nor do we see her and Lockwood's violent entanglement through the glass. Heathcliff banishes Lockwood from the chamber as romantic, dreamlike music plays in the background. Sobbing, Heathcliff calls out "Cathy, come back to me. Oh Cathy, do come. Oh, do once more. Oh, my heart's darling."[25] This dialogue is repeated verbatim from the original text. Yet, what Lockwood describes as "such anguish in the gush of grief that accompanied this raving" is tempered by the scene's soundtrack.[26] Not only does the film drastically alter the terrifying moment of supernatural violence that precedes Heathcliff's monologue, but the scene is framed sonically in such a way that enhances the emotional moment as one of romantic longing.

Nothing about the score, here, in mood or tone evokes even a fraction of the horror present in the original text.

The second famous Gothic snapshot occurs in the half of the novel completely excised from the film, where Heathcliff unburies the corpse of his beloved almost two decades after her death. Heathcliff approaches the sexton as the grave is being dug for Edgar Linton, Catherine's newly deceased widower, bribing him to pull away one side of Catherine's coffin and, upon Heathcliff's own death, slide the side of his out too so that their bodies can decompose and become one in the dust. Nelly chides Heathcliff for his disruption of the dead, but he justifies his actions as "[giving] some ease to myself. I shall be a great deal more comfortable now; and you'll have a better chance of keeping me underground, when I get there."[27] On the one hand, then, Heathcliff threatens to haunt the living members of Wuthering Heights upon his death if he is prevented from reuniting with Cathy in death. On the other hand, he is able to justify any disruption of Cathy's corpse by ruminating on the ways she has continually possessed him:

> Disturbed her? No! She has disturbed me, night and day, through eighteen years—incessantly—remorselessly—till yesternight—and yesternight, I was tranquil. I dreamt I was sleeping the last sleep, by that sleeper, with my heart stopped, and my cheek frozen against hers.[28]

Unity and tranquility can only occur with Heathcliff's death; until then, the moors, and unsuspecting witnesses such as Lockwood, are haunted, if not threatened, by Cathy's ghost.

Catherine's unburial and Heathcliff's mad desire for their corpses to become inseparable in the dirt is entirely removed from the film. That said, part of Heathcliff's narration of Catherine's unburial is the essence of the film's conclusion: "You know, I was wild after she died, and, eternally, from dawn to dawn, praying her to return to me—her spirit—I have strong faith in ghosts; I have a conviction that they can, and do exist, among us!"[29] Catherine and Heathcliff's ghosts are visually realized at the film's conclusion; however, they are done so in a manner that is more angelic than it is haunting. In Wyler's version, Cathy dies in Heathcliff's arms with the promise—her last words—that "I'll wait for you till you come."[30] The camera does not focus on her corpse. We see her take her last ragged breath from behind; once she is laid on the bed, we only are able to see a partial profile of her face. The doctor, Ellen, and Edgar gather around Catherine's body as Heathcliff prays to her spirit:

> Catherine Earnshaw, may you not rest so long as I live on. I killed you. Haunt me, then. Haunt your murderer. I know that ghosts have

wandered on the earth. Be with me always. Take any form. Drive me mad. Only do not leave me in this dark alone where I cannot find you.[31]

This dialogue is adapted from Cathy's death scene in the novel, except the film, once again, removes the violence of the line's original delivery. In the novel, Heathcliff is described as a "savage beast being goaded to death with knives and spears" as he bangs his bleeding head and face against a tree in an unhinged, physical display of grief.[32]

Following Heathcliff's prayer, the film ends with the much calmer conviction that their ghosts not simply exist among the moors, but upon their reunion, are finally able to make the transition from purgatory to heaven. Flashing forward to the present moment, Nelly does not believe that what Lockwood witnessed was Cathy's ghost but rather "Cathy's love stronger than time itself."[33] The entry of Dr. Kenneth, the local doctor who had cared for Cathy, however, is a testament to their ghostly forms existing among the living. Dr. Kenneth tells Lockwood and Nelly that he saw with his own eyes Heathcliff with his arm around a female companion but after following them only finds Heathcliff's body on a ledge of the crag. Heathcliff dies chasing after Cathy's voice, but this is not a tragedy, as in Nelly's words, "they've only just begun to live."[34] The final scene of the film depicts the ghosts walking hand in hand down the path of their beloved Penistone Crag.

The revision of the spiritual reunion between Catherine and Heathcliff was determined, at least in part, by Goldwyn's influence on or support for the film's generic shift from Gothic to romance. As a producer, Goldwyn was certainly preoccupied with beauty and cleanliness:

Goldwyn was always—how should I say—he wanted his pictures to be clean and glamorous, all the women looking beautiful, the hair just in place so you could see the hairdresser's work and the makeup man, the clothes, everything spic and span. Well, not all pictures lend themselves to that.[35]

The narrative's Gothic elements, like the unburial of a corpse, are the antithesis of clean and glamorous. Instead, Goldwyn asked Wyler to transform the final scene into a happy ending, a resurrection of Cathy's and Heathcliff's ghosts walking hand in hand into heaven; Wyler refused. Goldwyn, then, hired director H.C. Potter to film this last scene using doubles seen from behind as they walk along Penistone Crag.[36] Wyler himself believed this to be "an awful shot" but also acknowledged that "I seem to be the only one complaining about it."[37] Wyler instead had envisioned "a sad but very romantic scene" in which Heathcliff dies "as an old man, where he and the girl used to meet" along the crag. Though Wyler wished for audiences at the end of the film to gaze upon

Heathcliff's corpse, he intended to frame this moment as romantic rather than Gothic, departing quite drastically from the unsettling moment of post-mortem spectatorship readers witness thanks to Heathcliff in the novel.

Goldwyn's disinterest in and Wyler's lack of commitment to the nuances of the English Gothic and *Wuthering Heights*' position within this tradition ultimately allowed Wyler to reframe the story as a romance that questions whether true love can ever be fully ruptured by the socioeconomic demands of the marriage market. The film's romantic tension is fueled by Cathy's desire for comfort and respectability. In this way, Wyler was able to give the narrative a new, if not clearer and more realistic purpose, ultimately achieving what a review of the novel in a January 1848 edition of *Douglas Jerrold's Weekly Newspaper* described as "there seems to us great power in this book but a purposeless power, which we feel a great desire to see turned to a better account."[38] The realism of Wyler's *Wuthering Heights*, then, lies in its depiction of domestic tension spurred by socioeconomic pressures. That being said, the film's literary basis—its often over-the-top dramatization of the romantic and sexual tension between characters—affords a degree of melodrama that could command the audience's attention without having to physically shock or terrify them. This is one of the reasons Wyler gravitated towards adapting literary properties "that had been tested and proved successful in other forms, in part because they guaranteed a built-in audience, and in part because they delivered heavy doses of melodrama."[39]

In becoming a melodramatic romance, one of the most famous scenes from the novel retains much of its integrity when brought to the screen. Catherine must choose whether or not to accept Edgar Linton's proposal; doing so would mean prioritizing superficial attraction over a deep love that Nelly prompts Cathy to articulate. Cathy may appreciate Edgar's wealth, cheerful disposition, and beauty, but as she knows all too well "my love for Linton is like the foliage in the woods. Time will change it. I'm well aware, as winter changes the trees."[40] Readers and viewers alike are swept away by Catherine's monologue when she declares Heathcliff is "more myself than I am. Whatever our souls are made of, his and mine are the same," and, soon after, "I *am* Heathcliff—he's always, always in my mind."[41] The film condenses Nelly and Catherine's logistical, and therefore more realistic, discussion of the financial merits of marrying Edgar between these two oft quoted statements, ramping up the pacing to instead frame Oberon's delivery of "I am Heathcliff" as a melodramatic moment of emotional and psychological self-discovery. Thunder claps and lightning flashes outside of the windows that frame Oberon's close-up as she confesses to Nelly, similar to the lightning that illuminates Heathcliff's absence from the hiding place he torturously occupied and rashly abandoned as he eavesdropped on Cathy's making a case for marrying Linton mere minutes earlier.[42] This scene, then, is a prime example of Wyler's ability to compose shots with the "linear effects" of the window in a "dramatically confined interior," a "perfect stage for Wyler to visualize human confrontation."[43] If *Wuthering Heights* is, indeed, a novel "enveloped in an atmosphere of storms and spirits, who speak poetic dialogue as they try to reveal the thoughts and feelings hidden in the depths of their hearts," then Wyler's technical prowess and pairing of the visual and aural indicators of a severe thunderstorm with Alfred Newman's score become a means of tangibly realizing, if not translating, the lyrical nature of Cathy's confession.[44]

What makes Wyler's adaptation of *Wuthering Heights* so provocative is that the generic transformation the narrative undergoes becomes clearer when read as a product of transnationalism. Wyler, the European-born director producing a Hollywood film based on a quintessential British (Victorian) novel, was tasked with re-envisioning an artifact of the previous century for a new audience across the Atlantic. Adaptations of Victorian novels always undergo a degree of transformation; it is impossible to translate text to screen and create a multimodal product without some degree of geographical or temporal metamorphosis. *Wuthering Heights* undergoes a generic shift that is predicated upon the transnational contexts of its adaptation. In the hands of Wyler, *Wuthering Heights* becomes transnational because it reflects Hollywood and, ultimately, American middle-class expectations for romance while downplaying what made the narrative a uniquely important milestone within the tradition of the English Gothic. Speaking of Wyler's adaptation in the context of *Arashi ga oka*, the 1988 Japanese adaptation of *Wuthering Heights* directed by Yoshishige Yoshida, John Collick has asserted that "the question of whether the Japanese or the Americans can do 'justice' to the orthodox Anglo-American literary establishment's assessment of Emily Brontë's book reinforces essentialist beliefs in the purity of the central text."[45] In largely rejecting the Gothic, the Hollywood adaptation made the case that romance, rather than the supernatural, is integral to the text.

Yet transnationalism is reflected in more than just generic concerns. For Collick, if the novel is, indeed, "a novel of landscape," the inability to literally transport the wild moors to Los Angeles is one of the major problems faced by the American production of a British text.[46] Aside from the attempt to recreate a realistic-looking Yorkshire landscape, the film's casting served as a means of creating legitimacy and restoring at least some of the narrative's purity. Jack Wade, writing for *Photoplay* in April 1939, described *Wuthering Heights*' casting as part of a larger "new British invasion hit[ting] Hollywood," as the "entire cast, elite and extras, [are] His Majesty's loyal subjects. The only thing American about the whole place is Sam [Goldwyn]—and he's sporting a Bond Street tailoring job."[47] As a means of adding an air of authenticity to the Hollywood adaptation, the entire cast was outsourced from London, as Wyler "didn't want people speaking English like Americans."[48] Merle Oberon and Laurence Olivier were cast in the main roles of Catherine and Heathcliff; David Niven, Flora Robson, and Geraldine Fitzgerald portrayed Edgar Linton, Ellen Dean, and Isabella Linton respectively.

This is not to say that a British cast had a simpler time bringing to life the novel's characters. A major part of Wyler's philosophy regarding adaptation acknowledged actors' agency. In order to translate "credible" characters from page to screen, the director must, "consider the actor's natural manner and temperament. You've got to mold the character to him, as well as mold him to the character."[49] Wyler illustrated this point with Merle Oberon's performance as Cathy, asserting that the actress lacked the kind of explosive passion and power inherent in Brontë's character. He goes as far to say that to force Oberon to perform in this way

> would have required that she overact in a manner which would have been most unbecoming to her and which would thereby have injured Cathy. So we had to compromise—blend the characters of Cathy and Merle—to get just enough spirit of abandon but not too much.[50]

Though Oberon lacked the kind of devilish passion that makes Cathy so haunting and transgressive in the novel, she made up for this in her delicate beauty and femininity in ways more becoming of a 1930s romance.

Laurence Olivier's performance as Heathcliff was also not immune to criticism. While Gabriel Miller argues that the film's "weaknesses derive [in part] from Merle Oberon's failure to bring alive the earthier aspects of Cathy—much of her performance seems forced," Olivier had difficulty reciting "dialogue that is overly literary and announces its theme too often."[51] Olivier's performance, his attempt to compensate, is hindered by the language itself—the linguistic component of the adaptation. Yet, it is also important to acknowledge the limitations placed on Olivier's performance of a version of Heathcliff that aligned with Oberon's more fragile Cathy. At large, Brontë's novel certainly fit into the rubric for prestige for Depression-era film productions based on literary texts; however, the contents of the novel itself were largely at odds with the Motion Picture Production Code (also known as the Hays Code) of 1930. As a novel, *Wuthering Heights* has no single, clear moral, and the plot is primarily driven by Heathcliff's sadistic pursuit of revenge. One of the first working principles of the Code suggested that "no picture should lower the moral standards of those who see it. This is done . . . when evil is made to appear attractive, and good is made to appear unattractive."[52] In this way, both the script and Olivier's performance were encouraged, if not forced, to downplay Heathcliff's brooding vengeance and, consequently, Catherine's magnetic attraction to it.

Literary critics publishing reviews of the novel soon after its initial publication made it a point to articulate the extent of Heathcliff's villainy. For instance, a review in *The Examiner* published in January 1848 described the man as an "incarnation of evil qualities; implacable hate, ingratitude, cruelty, falsehood, selfishness, and revenge."[53] Additionally, a critic for the *Atlas* suggested he is "the presiding evil genius of the piece, the tyrant father of an imbecile son, a creature in whom every evil passion seems to have reached a gigantic excess."[54] It is through Heathcliff that the novel becomes capable of "present[ing] such shocking pictures of the worst forms of humanity."[55] This is not to say that Olivier's Heathcliff entirely lacks the abusive power and ferocity demonstrated in the novel. Olivier, for example, does slap Oberon's Cathy across the face twice after she chides him for being only a dirty-handed stableboy, but this is an action he immediately regrets.[56] The film, however, excuses itself from ever having to address the greater half of Heathcliff's physical and psychological abuses by excising the portions of the novel that not only depict his horrific treatment of the second generation of characters, including the marital manipulation and "forcible mating" of his own frail son, but also the extent of his mistreatment of his wife Isabella, including his hanging of her dog on their wedding night.[57] American standards for censorship, then, played a part in reframing, if not entirely cutting down, on the aspects of the novel that Victorian critics had originally latched onto.

While the Hays Code supported the adaptation of literary classics on the grounds of their frequent moralizing and cultural significance, a film like *Wuthering Heights* had to undergo a rather drastic set of revisions in order to pass the censors and perform well at the box office. Ultimately, the film's glamorization as a romance was the key to its success. The film was lauded for its beauty and brilliance. For Kate Cameron, the president of the New York Film Critics, *Wuthering Heights* was "a thing of beauty that will remain forever."[58] For A. Scott Berg, writing on the film's fiftieth anniversary, it was "the most brilliant gem in the brightly studded tiara of 1939."[59] Yet, its value lies underneath the makeup and accouterments so valued by Goldwyn. Although Gabriel Miller persuasively suggests we consider *Wuthering Heights* outside of the realm of adaptation in favor of its status as a premier example of "the director's meditations on how the forces of society conspire to destroy the individual," I argue that studying the film's transition from Gothic novel to silver screen romance, including its transnational implications, offers us a new way of examining the importance of genre in within the process of adaptation.[60] In this way, *Wuthering Heights* deserves to be more centrally located in discussions about the adaptation of Victorian novels within the Hollywood studio system and beyond.

NOTES

1. "Wuthering Heights," *Photoplay*, June 1939, 58.
2. Guerric Debona, *Film Adaptation in the Hollywood Studio Era* (Urbana, Chicago, and Springfield: University of Illinois Press, 2010), 9.

3. Ibid., 25.
4. Gabriel Miller, *William Wyler: Interviews* (Jackson: University Press of Mississippi, 2009), 54.
5. Miller, *Interviews*, 124.
6. Gabriel Miller, *William Wyler: The Life and Films of Hollywood's Most Celebrated Director* (Lexington: University Press of Kentucky, 2013), 158.
7. Miller, *Interviews*, 54.
8. Ibid., 124.
9. Jan Herman, *A Talent for Trouble: The Life of Hollywood's Most Acclaimed Director, William Wyler* (Boston: Da Capo Books, 1997), 194.
10. Miller, *William Wyler*, 2.
11. Miller, *Interviews*, 71–2.
12. Miller, *William Wyler*, 157.
13. Judith Mayne, *Private Novels, Public Films* (Athens: University of Georgia Press, 1988), 116.
14. Miller, *Interviews*, 72.
15. Jack Wade, "We Cover the Studios," *Photoplay*, April 1939, 55.
16. *Wuthering Heights*, directed by William Wyler (1939, Samuel Goldwyn Productions; Warner Brothers, 2004), 1:23, <https://www.amazon.com/gp/video/detail/B00BR6MLYO/ref=atv_dp_amz_det_c_UTPsmN_1_2> (last accessed August 9, 2022).
17. Ellen Moers, *Literary Women: The Great Writers* (Oxford: Oxford University Press, 1985), 90.
18. Miller, *Interviews*, 81.
19. Fred Inglis, "*Brideshead Revisited* revisited: Waugh to the Knife," in *The Classic Novel: From Page to Screen*, ed. Robert Giddings and Erica Sheen (Manchester: Manchester University Press, 2000), 179.
20. John Collick, "Dismembering Devils: The Demonology of *Arashi ga oka* (1988) and *Wuthering Heights* (1939)," in *Novel Images: Literature in Performance*, ed. Peter Reynolds (London and New York: Routledge, 1993), 36.
21. Emily Brontë, *Wuthering Heights*, ed. Alexandra Lewis, fifth edition (New York: W. W. Norton & Company, 2019), 16.
22. Ibid., 21.
23. Ibid.
24. *Wuthering Heights*, 6:45 to 6:50.
25. *Wuthering Heights*, 8:02 to 8:08.
26. Brontë, *Wuthering Heights*, 24.
27. Ibid., 218.
28. Ibid.
29. Ibid.
30. *Wuthering Heights*, 1:38:40 to 1:38:42.
31. *Wuthering Heights*, 1:40:24 to 1:40:47.
32. Brontë, *Wuthering Heights*, 130.
33. *Wuthering Heights*, 1:41:41 to 1:41:42.
34. *Wuthering Heights*, 1:43:04 to 1:43:05.
35. Miller, *Interviews*, 125.
36. Herman, *Talent for Trouble*, 198–9.
37. Miller, *Interviews*, 126.
38. Unsigned review of *Wuthering Heights* in *Douglas Jerrold's Weekly Newspaper*, January 1848. Reprinted in Brontë, *Wuthering Heights*, 275–6.
39. Miller, *William Wyler*, 10.
40. Brontë, *Wuthering Heights*, 64.

41. Ibid., 63; 64–5.
42. *Wuthering Heights*, 45:18 to 45:33; 44:54 to 44:57.
43. Miller, *William Wyler*, 7–8.
44. Pamela Mills, "Wyler's Version of Brontë's Storms in 'Wuthering Heights,'" *Literature/Film Quarterly* 24, no. 4 (1996): 414.
45. Collick, "Dismembering Devils," 34.
46. Ibid.
47. Wade, "We Cover the Studios," 54–5.
48. Miller, *Interviews*, 124.
49. Ibid., 4.
50. Ibid.
51. Miller, *William Wyler*, 163
52. Thomas Doherty, *Pre-Code Hollywood: Sex, Immorality, and Insurrection in American Cinema, 1930–1934* (New York: Columbia University Press, 1999), 351.
53. Unsigned review of *Wuthering Heights* in *Examiner*, January 1848. Reprinted in Brontë, *Wuthering Heights*, 277.
54. Unsigned review of *Wuthering Heights* in *Atlas*, January 1848. Reprinted in Brontë, *Wuthering Heights*, 274.
55. *Atlas*, 273.
56. *Wuthering Heights*, 39:46 to 40:00.
57. Juliet McMaster, "The Courtship and Honeymoon of Mr. and Mrs. Linton Heathcliff: Emily Brontë's Sexual Imagery," *Victorian Review* 18, no. 1 (1992): 2.
58. Herman, *Talent for Trouble*, 199.
59. A. Scott Berg, "Wuthering Heights," *The New York Times*, February 19, 1989.
60. Miller, *William Wyler*, 158.

PART III

Gender and Sexuality

CHAPTER 8

William Wyler's *The Heiress* (1949) and the Unknown Woman

Agustin Zarzosa

One of the perplexing aspects of Stanley Cavell's *Contesting Tears* is the exclusion of *The Heiress* (William Wyler, 1949) from what he calls the melodrama of the unknown woman. Derived from the comedies of remarriage, in which conversation becomes a means of mutual recognition between a man and a woman, the melodrama of the unknown woman negates marriage as a route to recognition. Women find their voice and their freedom instead in the transcendence of marriage. As Cavell puts it, in these melodramas, the woman's answer to the "possibility of friendship is an unreserved, No."[1] *The Heiress* certainly concludes with a more unreversed No to marriage than the four films that integrate the genre: *Stella Dallas* (King Vidor, 1937), *Now, Voyager* (Irving Rapper, 1942), *Gaslight* (George Cukor, 1944), and *Letter from an Unknown Woman* (Max Ophüls, 1948).

Dan Shaw has recently speculated that Cavell did not include the film because, unlike the other heroines of the genre, Catherine (Olivia de Havilland), the protagonist in *The Heiress*, has not freed herself from resentment. According to Shaw, Catherine's transformation, tinted by revenge, "does not seem to have led to a satisfying independent life of her own."[2] This explanation remains unconvincing for two reasons: first, Catherine does seem satisfied with her independent life and, second, Cavell does not exclude revenge from the genre. Cavell understands the images of Lisa (Joan Fontaine) assaulting Stephan (Louis Jordan) in *Letter from an Unknown Woman* as a fantasy of revenge.[3] He also characterizes Paula's (Ingrid Bergman's) final spectacle of madness in *Gaslight* as an "aria of revenge" against Gregory (Charles Boyer).[4]

Rather than speculating why Cavell did not include the film, I explain how the inclusion of *The Heiress* reconfigures the genre itself. In his own understanding of genre, Cavell has argued that a genre is not "a form characterized by features, as an object by its properties."[5] Rather than sharing features, members of a genre share a story or a myth. He writes, "The members of a genre will be interpretations of it, ... revisions of it, which will also make them interpretations of one another."[6] In this sense, genre films *"are what they are in view of one another."*[7] What justifies the inclusion of *The Heiress*, then, is its interpretation of the basic myth of the genre: a woman who searches for her own story by transcending marriage. I argue that *The Heiress* makes clear that the melodrama of the unknown woman investigates not the question of skepticism, as Cavell proposes, but rather the stoic strategy of withdrawing from the world. To the extent that the unknown woman judges the world as second-rate, refuses a man's recognition, and seeks interior freedom in the realm of thought (while struggling with her own emotions throughout), she is a stoic and not a skeptic. As the philosopher Epictetus demands of fictions, *The Heiress* teaches us "that things external and outside the sphere of choice are nothing to us," encouraging us to live "in peace of mind and free from perturbation."[8]

A telling sign that these films are informed by stoicism is the centrality of scenes in which the heroine loses her composure. In *Now, Voyager*, Charlotte (Bette Davis) breaks down several times during Dr. Jacquith's (Claude Rains's) first visit to the Vale home. The scene culminates when June (Bonita Grandville), Charlotte's niece, teases Charlotte, suggesting that she is involved in a romantic relationship with Dr. Jacquith. Trembling while she pours tea, Charlotte can no longer take her niece's mocking comments, and frantically rushes upstairs. In *Gaslight*, the scene appears halfway through the film. In his quest to drive Paula mad, Gregory strikes one of his best blows during a soirée organized by Lady Dalroy (Heather Thatcher), a friend of Paula's late aunt. While listening to a piano concert, Gregory pretends that he has lost his watch and "finds" it in Paula's purse. Certain that she is losing her mind, Paula publicly breaks down. In *Stella Dallas*, the scene takes place toward the end of the film. When Laurel (Ann Shirley) refuses to live with her father (John Bowles) and her stepmother (Barbara O'Neal), Stella (Barbara Stanwyck) pretends that she has arranged for Laurel to live with them not for Laurel's sake but rather for her own. Ignoring Laurel's signs of affection, Stella pretends to be expecting Ed (Alan Hale)—her alleged suitor—places his portrait on the chimney, plays loud music, lights a cigarette, and reads *The Love Book*. After making sure that Laurel has left, Stella covers her face with her hands and starts crying. Despite their differences, all these scenes are concerned with controlling overwhelming feelings.

We do not find a similar scene in the film from which Cavell derives the name of the genre—*Letter from an Unknown Woman*. This absence is not surprising to the extent that any similarity between Ophüls's films and the other three members of the genre is merely apparent and not structural. As Cavell himself notes, the outcome of *Letter from an Unknown Woman* is not the transcendence of marriage (as in the other three films) but "the collapse of a fantasy of remarriage."[9] I substitute *The Heiress* for *Letter from an Unknown Woman* as the utmost representative of the genre. Belonging to the period that Cavell investigates, *The Heiress* ties a deliberate refusal of the world of men to the aim of self-reliance.

The film is an adaptation of the homonymous play by Ruth and Augustus Goetz, which is itself based on the Henry James novel, *Washington Square*. Catherine lives with her father, Dr. Sloper (Ralph Richardson), an elegant and sophisticated widower. Perhaps because of Dr. Sloper's constant comparisons between Catherine and her deceased mother, Catherine has grown to be dowdy and socially awkward. Dr. Sloper has invited his sister Lavinia (Miriam Hopkins), an overly romantic widow, to live with them so she might help Catherine develop her social skills. At her cousin's engagement party, Catherine meets Morris Townsend (Montgomery Clift), who quickly proposes to Catherine. Dr. Sloper disapproves of the marriage. For the first time in her life, Catherine opposes her father and promises Morris to marry him. After returning from a trip to Europe that was intended to dissuade Catherine of her marriage plans, Dr. Sloper finally tells Catherine why Morris is marrying her: she has no qualities other than her money. Catherine arranges to elope with Morris, but he deserts her because she will have nothing more to do with her father and, hence, with his fortune. Dr. Sloper dies soon after without Catherine's forgiveness. Years later, Morris returns and Catherine arranges a second elopement. This time, however, she locks Morris outside while she ascends the stairs.

This chapter is divided in four sections, each highlighting a different aspect of stoicism. The first one is dedicated to a primordial scene in which the stoic is humiliated, staging a challenge of self-reliance. The second one explains how, through argumentation, the stoic struggles to determine the meaning of events rather than altering them. The third one focuses on the role of objects in the stoic's transformation. Finally, the fourth one discusses how, through repetition, the stoic turns a forced choice into an act of freedom.

FROM HUMILIATION TO SELF-RELIANCE

I take Hegel's famous dialectics of master and slave as my point of departure. In *Phenomenology of Spirit*, the figure of the stoic immediately follows the result of this struggle; the slave's defeat, which involves not death but obedience, initiates the stoic flight from the world. The primordial scene stresses the condition of oppression, usually showing humiliation as well as the master's absolute knowledge of the slave. The master's assessment of the slave's character triggers the slave's inner movement into unknownnesss. In stoic narratives, the intolerable awareness that one appears revealed before another triggers the desire to become unknown. This primordial scene motivates the narrative, which consists in a struggle for internal freedom. *The Heiress* includes not one, but two primordial scenes halfway through the film. In these two scenes, Catherine finally understands, respectively, how her father and Morris view her.

Dr. Sloper's opinion of Catherine becomes apparent early in the film. At Marian's engagement party, Dr. Sloper tells his sister that Catherine is a "mediocre and defenseless creature with not a shred of poise." On the other hand, the viewer remains unaware of what Morris thinks about Catherine until the failed elopement; his actions do not provide conclusive evidence about his character. As Michael Anderegg observes, Morris, rarely framed by himself, is always interacting with other characters.[10] The first meeting between Morris and Catherine underscores this inscrutability. While Catherine and Lavinia are sitting, framed in a slight high angle, he enters the frame with his back to the viewer. Rather than seeing him, we witness the effect he has on both women.

Dr. Sloper and Catherine struggle over the meaning of Morris's motivation to marry her: while Catherine believes that Morris loves her, Dr. Sloper strongly suspects that he is after her money. Caught between the obedience she owes to her father and her love for Morris, Catherine ultimately decides to marry Morris on the grounds that she believes that her father has misjudged Morris. Once vanquished, Dr. Sloper plays his last card. He explains to Catherine why he believes Morris does not love her: she is plain, witless, and unattractive; her only virtue is her money. Looking over Catherine's embroidery table, he acknowledges she does one thing well. "You embroider neatly," he says as he walks out of the parlor.

Catherine understands that Dr. Sloper opposes the marriage not because he has assessed Morris's character, but rather because he despises her. At first, she refuses to accept her father's interpretation of her character until Morris, in the second primordial scene, confirms it by failing to show up for their planned elopement. This second primordial scene is perhaps more humiliating than the first. She not only learns what she has been for her father and Morris all along, but the ease with which Morris deceived her confirms her father's opinion of Catherine as a naïve fool. However, becoming aware of what she is for both men spawns her metamorphosis.

The primordial scene of humiliation is not concerned with the conflict between virtue and evil. As in the case of *Stella Dallas* and *Gaslight*, the men in *The Heiress* could perhaps be interpreted as villains. However, more than behaving like villains, these characters act on behalf of a hostile world; in the case of Dr. Sloper and Morris, their contempt for Catherine follows from the value they place on sophistication and taste. Critics have noted a similarity between Catherine and Regina (Bette Davis) in Wyler's *The Little Foxes* (1941). Peter Swaab interprets the scene in which Catherine remains impassive while Dr. Sloper announces that he will soon die as a reworking of the famous scene in which the camera focuses on Bette Davis's impassive face while her husband struggles to climb the stairs in the background.[11] The last scene of *The Heiress*, in which Catherine lingers for a few seconds while Morris desperately bangs at the door, reminds George Toles of the same scene in *The Little Foxes*. These two shots from *The Heiress*, which frame Catherine's impassivity, should be understood in relation to another shot during the night of the elopement, in which Catherine collapses after realizing that Morris has deserted her. Despite the resemblance of "the intense focusing of a woman's face," Regina's impassivity indicates her evil nature, whereas Catherine's imperturbability expresses her triumph over her own feelings. In the same manner, the image of Morris pounding at the door like a maimed animal "protesting its pain and captivity" does not express the defeat of evil, but serves to contrast Catherine's self-possession.[12] She has learned to dominate what the stoics called first movements, that is, physical states such as contractions, expansions, appetites, and disinclinations that precede emotions.[13] Her victory, then, is primarily over herself and not over Morris.

The stoic drama is concerned not with the triumph of virtue over evil, but with the creation of a world in which hostile forces are neutralized. Catherine struggles, then, to prove that both men are nothing to her and that she has ridden herself from the worldly attachments that generated her humiliation. Her victory is not defined in terms of virtue, but rather in terms of independence of mind. We could say that the stoic redefines virtue and evil in terms of one's interpretation of impressions. As Epictetus puts it, "both good and evil rest essentially in the proper use of impressions, and . . . things that lie outside the sphere of choice are not by nature either good or evil."[14]

The stoic, then, equates judgment and freedom because only judgment is wholly in one's power.[15] In the beginning of the film, Dr. Sloper exercises his judgment correctly: he judges Catherine as a mediocre creature and Morris as a fortune hunter. This contempt for Catherine is apparent in the ironic way in which he addresses her. For instance, when she dresses up for the engagement party, Dr. Sloper says, "Is it possible that this magnificent person is my child?" The fact that she does not seem to grasp the ulterior meaning of his ironic speech confirms her father's judgment. Catherine is unable to tell appearances apart from reality; she can't see how her father's apparently kind words mask his contempt for her or how Morris's wooing is guided by greed. Catherine learns how to see things and people as they are and not as they appear; in the process, both Dr. Sloper and Morris will appear naked, fully revealed. She, on the other hand, masters the art of appearances to the point that Morris believes that she has forgiven him and that she continues to love him.

The primordial scene shifts the focus of the struggle: it turns a narrative of external oppression into a narrative of self-reliance. In other words, it displaces the conflict, successfully leaving the external master behind but creating its rational substitute: by metamorphosing external obedience into self-imposed discipline, stoicism becomes its own source of oppression.

INTERPRETING EVENTS, NOT CHANGING THEM

The struggle for the recognition of freedom that constitutes the core of the master and slave dialectics does not fully disappear in stoicism. This struggle becomes the stoic's search for the recognition of the act of withdrawal itself, that is, the recognition that the stoic has found freedom in a realm to which the master has no access. Because recognition suffers a change, the site of struggle shifts as well. Whereas the recognition of mastery hinges on a bodily form of obedience, the stoic recognition of withdrawal takes place at the discursive level because stoicism withdraws into the realm of thought. Stoic recognition corresponds to the kind of acknowledgment Stanley Cavell writes in his study of comedies of remarriage, acknowledgment obtained by means of conversation.[16] If these films may appear to rely heavily on dialogue, it is precisely because the stoic struggles over the meaning of things. The stoic finds freedom in interpreting events more than in modifying their course. Because of this emphasis on meaning, we should distinguish between events and narrative commentary.

We should note, however, that events and narrative commentary are not altogether unrelated, as the interpretation of events may influence events. In *The Heiress*, Catherine's freedom to interpret events over which she exerts no control shapes her consequent actions. Just as the film includes two primordial scenes, her passage into unknownness also takes place in two different scenes. The first one takes the shape of what Cavell calls an aria of denunciation, in which the unknown woman names her mother (or lover) a tyrant.[17] For Cavell, the unknown woman's mother "is always present (or her search for or loss of or competition with a mother is always present)."[18] Catherine addresses the aria to her father, thwarting his interpretation of the events; it was not love that made him protect her from Morris, she explains, but contempt. Although the aria is not addressed to her mother, its content is Dr. Sloper's comparison between Catherine and her deceased mother. Accused by him of cruelty, she replies, "This is a field where you will not compare me to my mother."

Specifically, what takes place in the scene is a reversal in terms of their knowledge. Dr. Sloper believes that Catherine has broken her engagement and expresses how proud he is of her. To contradict his version of events, Catherine informs him that Morris deserted her; furthermore, she refuses to promise him that she won't squander his money on Morris after his death. Before their confrontation, Dr. Sloper knew who Catherine was, while she remained ignorant of whom she has been for him. Catherine tells her father who he is for her, while he remains ignorant of whom she has become. Dr. Sloper refuses to change his will on the grounds that he does not know what she will do, recognizing her unknownness.

One of the differences between *The Heiress* and Agnieszka Holland's *Washington Square* (1997), a direct adaptation of Henry James's novel, pinpoints how, in forcing Dr. Sloper to recognize her as unknown, Catherine might still be demanding recognition. In the latter version, Catherine makes every effort to conceal her metamorphosis from her father. After he falls sick, she takes care of him; she simply refuses to promise him that she won't marry Morris after his death or even to explain why she won't promise. Dr. Sloper disinherits Catherine, which proves to her that he has not acknowledged her metamorphosis. Holland's Catherine finds satisfaction not in her father's recognition of her withdrawal but in the fact that she has concealed her transformation from him, proving that she no longer requires his approval. But the solution to the problem of recognition in *Washington Square* is as imperfect as the one in *The Heiress*. Although Catherine does not seek her father's recognition in Holland's version, she insists on preserving her dignity before him. In this version, it is Dr. Sloper who suggests that Morris might have deserted her, and Catherine who insists that she has broken the engagement. Ultimately, in both versions, Catherine's actions seem staged for her father.

These two imperfect solutions point to the fact that the pursuit of recognition contradicts the act of withdrawal. By seeking the master's recognition of one's withdrawal, one acknowledges that one has not fully withdrawn. Stoic freedom depends on a double gesture of recognition by the master, who acknowledges, first, that the slave has achieved independence in a spiritual realm and, second, that the master has become superfluous in this realm. Although the stoic achieves freedom by renouncing to the world, this freedom seems to depend on a gesture of recognition by the master.

Among the other melodramas of the unknown woman, *Gaslight* offers the most interesting articulation of argumentation. The primordial scene appears toward the end of the film, after Paula and Gregory return from Lady Dalroy's soirée: Gregory finally tells her that her absent-mindedness is more than sheer forgetfulness, that she has inherited her late mother's madness. Gregory makes clear what she is for him, and her struggle consists in fleeing away from such an interpretation of herself. The passage into unknownness takes place during their last confrontation, which, like in *The Heiress*, records a change in their positions in relation to knowledge. Whereas throughout the film Gregory "knows" Paula as forgetful and insane, she is always unsure whether he is serious or angry with her. During this confrontation, Paula knows who Gregory is and why he was trying to drive her mad. On the other hand, Gregory does not know if she will help him, if she remains under his influence, or if she has become mad. The film presents a struggle over the meaning of events. Gregory manipulates events to construct a narrative of Paula's insanity and to impose this narrative on her.

Bondage is a state of being in which someone else controls both the meaning of one's actions and the narrative that reveals one's self. To inhabit such an oppressive narrative is the stoic's true form of bondage. Accordingly, stoic freedom consists in liberating oneself from this oppressive narrative and in turning it into a hurdle that must be overcome in a narrative of freedom.

Paula will need Detective Cameron's (Joseph Cotton's) help to construct a different narrative. Why, if she is not insane, can't she figure out by herself what Gregory is doing to her? As Cameron tells her, she already knows that Gregory is trying to drive her mad, and that he is responsible for the noises in the attic and the changes in the gaslight. She herself says that the gaslight dims and the noises appear only when he leaves the house. She can't put this narrative together because Gregory plays a fundamental role in Paula's narrative of loss and fear. According to Paula, her sadness and fear disappeared when she fell in love with Gregory. If she believed that Gregory is trying to drive her mad, she would not only be renouncing her love but also her sense of security. As she says, still resisting the truth, "If that were true, then from the beginning there would have been nothing." It is in such a substitution of narratives that we find both the strongest stoic element of the film and its resemblance to *The Heiress*. Catherine and Paula conceive of romance as the solution to the tyranny of fear. Through different paths, each of them discovers that such a solution cannot be found in someone else, but rather in self-reliance. These films show how the initial solution (romance, love, or marriage) is in fact part of the problem insofar as it merely constitutes an imaginary solution.

FREEDOM AMONG OBJECTS

In *Gaslight*, objects play a fundamental role in the construction of Gregory's narrative of insanity. Gregory hides things, making Paula believe that she loses, misplaces, and even imagines them. Paula is able to oppose a different narrative through objects. First, Cameron legitimizes himself by showing Paula her aunt's glove, which Paula knows her aunt had given to a mysterious admirer. Second, when Cameron witnesses how the gaslight goes down, she realizes that she is not insane. Third, she finds the letter written by Sergis Bauer (Gregory's real name) that he claims she imagined. Afterwards, she finds in the attic the brooch that she thought she had lost. Finally, when Cameron hands her the jewels that she knew nothing about, she understands Gregory's motivations. The stoic relies on these pieces from the empirical world to create a realm of internal freedom.

In his essay dedicated to the role of objects in *The Heiress*, Toles argues that objects begin by reflecting the mental operations of the characters but end up taking over Catherine's minds.[19] Although Toles's careful analysis of objects is exemplary, once we interpret the film as a stoic narrative, Catherine's relationship to objects appears in a different light. Even though, as Toles notes, the film is saturated with things, they are deployed in a subtle manner. Regarding the design of the house, Wyler purportedly told Harry Horner, production designer of the film, that "the structure could not know in advance what its inhabitants would do."[20] This subtlety makes it difficult to determine to what extent the characters are aware of the meaning of objects. This point is crucial for my analysis because I am concerned with the meanings that objects might have not for the viewer, but for the stoic characters themselves.

Catherine would not be able to withdraw from the empirical world without altering the meaning of objects that surround her. In Hegel's famous discussion of self-consciousness, nothing mediates the struggle resulting in the master and slave figures. Nevertheless, the resolution of this struggle demands that the master and slave mediate their relationship by means of objects: the slave expresses obedience by transforming them while the master exercises power by consuming them. In other words, the object's everyday use concretizes a power relationship whose constitutive poles are production and consumption. Hegel explains that the master's relation to things is "a fleeting one," while the slave's desire held in check "forms and shapes the thing."[21] In this process of transforming things, the slave imprints meaning, purpose, and sense on them, abstracting things from their everyday use and situating them in the realm of signification. By means of such an abstraction, the slave creates a parallel, rational realm in which freedom from oppression becomes possible. Objects enable an imaginary space for this realm, signifying freedom itself.

The situation in *The Heiress* differs from this scenario in a crucial aspect. Catherine is not a slave who transforms things through labor (with one exception, as we shall see). Her main problem is inhabiting a world in which others assign objects their meaning. Most of the film takes place in Dr. Sloper's house in Washington Square. Horner explains that, in designing the house, Dr. Sloper's chair in the back parlor should dominate the house, with a direct view to the entrance hall.[22] He also designed the house with three perspectives in mind. As Horner explains, for Dr. Sloper the house bears "the memory of his wife;" for Morris, the house is "a very nearly human temptation;" whereas, for Catherine, the house represents "the enclosure which became torture."[23] The bar-like stair banisters convey this idea of enclosure most prominently in the scene following the failed elopement. Moreover, the house is filled with elegant objects that reflect the taste of both men. Morris himself remarks that it is strange that the two men do not like each other since they share the same taste. Dr. Sloper resents Morris's taste for fine things (his French cologne and his expensive gloves) because it demonstrates that he squandered his own fortune rather than helping his impoverished sister (and that he would squander Catherine's inheritance). A less overt reason might be the fear that Morris is attempting to substitute him as the master of his Washington Square mansion. When Dr. Sloper discovers that Morris has been coming to his home during his absence, he complains that Morris has been treating his home as his club and suggests that Morris might even have been sleeping in his room. Wyler emphasizes this parallelism between the two characters in a scene in which Dr. Sloper arrives to his home while Morris is paying Catherine a visit. With his gloves and hat in hand, he glances at the chest in the foyer, where Morris has left a pair of gloves and a hat very similar to those that Dr. Sloper is holding in his hand.

Both Dr. Sloper and Morris feel at ease in this world filled with elegant objects. In contrast to them, Catherine feels uncomfortable in this environment. At her cousin's engagement party, her clumsy handling of objects is quite apparent. She drops her purse, attempts to dance while holding a cup, handles her dance card undexterously, and flutters her fan too quickly. Her clothes also reveal her lack of grace. When Catherine wears a red cherry dress, Dr. Sloper compliments her, only to say afterwards that, unlike Catherine, her mother "dominated the color." Catherine's clumsiness is also apparent in her lack of "a true musical ear," which her mother possessed. Her awkwardness, then, not only contrasts with the ease with which Dr. Sloper and Morris interact with objects in this world, but also with the poise of her deceased mother.

One aspect of the film clearly echoes the Hegelian scenario of recognition in labor. I am referring to Catherine's embroidery. In his interpretation of the film, Toles claims that "the table has become a rack on which her accustomed pain can be nursed and stretched" and that it "has acquired the joyless efficiency of a factory machine that one must serve daily for a set number of hours."[24] Toles disregards the transformation of the world and the recognition of the self that labor entails, overlooking that embroidery involves a recreation of the world. In her embroidering, Catherine carves out a small part of Dr. Sloper's world of elegant and nostalgic objects to create a world that she both controls and inhabits. This miniature world stands as a blot in an environment surrounded by Dr. Sloper's possessions. This lack of control over an object troubles him. As he enters the back parlor from his office, Dr. Sloper seems bothered by the sight of cloth. "Is she starting another one of these things?" he contemptuously asks Lavinia. We find a similar example of this act of carving out a world in a hostile environment in *Now, Voyager*. Living in a home dominated by her mother's possessions, Charlotte creates miniature boxes out of ivory.

As Mary Ann Doane points out, sewing, weaving, and lacemaking are "signifiers of a specific narrational desire."[25] The opening credit sequence emphasizes this narrational quality of embroidery, displaying a set of embroideries that recreate the world of the film. In the first embroidery, a woman in profile is holding a bunch of flowers in her hand; two pictures of flowers foreground the *mise en abyme* at play in the film; finally, two columns, very similar to the ones in the front parlor, frame her, foreshadowing Catherine's enclosure. At the end of the film, Catherine transposes the flowers from her embroidery to the actual world, as her backyard is full of them. This transposition indicates that she now controls the objects surrounding her. The profile anticipates the framing of Catherine in two key scenes. While Dr. Sloper stands behind Catherine in their first confrontation, she appears in profile, looking off-screen in disbelief and too humiliated to follow her father with her eyes. Wyler frames her again in profile as she sits outside in the middle of the square while her father dies, suggesting no longer humiliation but indifference. She finds herself elsewhere, off-screen.

Catherine's embroidery recalls Penelope's weaving in Homer's *Odyssey*, an act of waiting for the return of one's lover and as a way of controlling events. When Morris arrives for the second elopement, Catherine finishes the embroidery and cuts the last thread. As Doane summarizes the scene, "The narrative is finished, the threads finally tied together, and the man excluded from its discourse, waiting, infinitely, on the doorstep."[26] Catherine informs Lavinia that she won't embroider again, signaling that the narrative has been completed and that she finally has control over the unfolding of events. By giving up embroidery, Catherine also betokens that she no longer needs to recreate a parallel world made of cloth. She is now at ease in the world. Accordingly, when her cousin and aunt ask her why she won't visit them upstate, Catherine simply replies, "I like it here at the Square." The changes in décor indicate that she has transformed the Washington Square mansion into her own. As Horner explains these changes, "the elegance and strictness disappeared, and a feeling of less discriminating taste was noticeable."[27]

Moreover, it is not a matter of which objects surround the stoic as much as the meaning that the stoic confers on them. The changes in signification are most apparent in the meaning of embroidery. It ceases to be a quiet act of resistance that her father resents to signify both her claim to the home and her ability to control the meaning of events. The last object exchanged between Catherine and Morris also indicates this control of meaning. She had brought a set of ruby buttons from Paris as a wedding gift for Morris. During their last encounter, Catherine gives them to Morris. Unbeknown to him, they have ceased to signify her love for him and become a token of her contempt for him.

Finally, we can see how the retreat of the stoic into interiority is not absolute insofar as it ultimately depends on external objects for its success. The control over the meaning of things is never quite a private affair. Even if her father and Morris remain oblivious about the meaning she imparts on things, this signification of internal freedom and self-determination reverberates over the narrative, as both her father and Morris must know what they have become in her eyes.

HOW TO REPEAT LIKE A STOIC

In "On the Tranquility of Mind," Seneca mentions an anecdote about how Diogenes did nothing when his slave Manes ran away. "It would be degrading," Diogenes purportedly said, "if Manes can live without Diogenes and not Diogenes without Manes."[28] Stoic writings abound with examples such as this one, in which sages assent to the fate that befalls them with tranquility. Marcus Aurelius phrases this maxim in the following terms: "To welcome with affection what is sent by fate."[29] This practice of acquiescing to fate should help us understand repetition in stoic narratives. In classical narration, as Raymond Bellour explains, repetition unfolds symmetries to bring out "the dissymmetry without which there would be no narrative."[30] This section discusses the specificity of stoic repetition.

To put it succinctly, stoic repetition turns a forced choice into an act of freedom. In *Enjoy Your Symptom!*, Slavoj Žižek observes how several Hollywood films dramatize this kind of repetition. For Žižek, this scenario involves a primordial scene of a forced choice that marks the hero with guilt, which can only be eradicated through its repetition in a suicidal gesture. Žižek offers the example of Nick (Christopher Walken) in *The Deer Hunter* (Michael Cimino, 1978), who repays his debt by willingly repeating his forced choice of participating in Russian roulette.[31] In stoicism, repetition is spawned by a need not to repay a debt but to free oneself from the humiliation associated with the primal scene.

The Heiress offers an exemplary case of stoic repetition. I am referring to the restaging of the failed elopement, which turns Catherine's forced choice to remain unmarried in her father's home into an act of freedom. Although Catherine's revenge consists in deserting Morris, the fundamental metamorphosis that this repetition spawns takes place within Catherine. In the primal scene, after having waited all night long for Morris to show up for their planned elopement, Catherine, wearing a black dress and carrying her heavy luggage, trudges up the stairs. In the repetition, Catherine, wearing a white dress, carries a light lamp and slowly climbs the stairs. The two scenes are shot from above the stairs to underscore the metamorphosis that has taken place between them.

Of course, in avenging herself against Morris's desertion, Catherine seems to fulfill her father's wishes, that is, that she will remain "rich, respectable and unloved" after his death. Toles suggests that, in a certain sense, Catherine comes to identify with her father. He writes, "She judges him [Morris] with her father's eyes, whose way of measuring value she has internalized and come to appreciate."[32] One should not be mistaken by thinking that, after her father's death, her only choice remains to conform either to her father's or to Morris's wishes. By freely embracing her father's will, Catherine elevates herself above him; she demonstrates her indifference to whatever has occurred or will occur. We could extrapolate Epictetus' argument about Socrates to explain Catherine's situation. He writes, "Socrates was not actually in prison because he was willingly there."[33] By willing the return of what had hurt her in the past, the stoic proves that she remains indifferent to what befalls her.

Gilles Deleuze's theorization of repetition helps us to further understand the underlying mechanisms of stoic repetition. The stoic revisits the primal scene of humiliation not because of a compulsion to repeat or because the repressed must return, but rather because of a need to underscore that both events (the primal scene and its repetition) are simulacra. The following passage underscores how repetition constitutes both the past and the present: "We produce something new only on condition that we repeat—once in the mode which constitutes the past, and once more in the present of metamorphosis."[34] The act of repetition turns the primal scene and its restaging into instances in which the stoic's temperance is tested: retrospectively, the stoic will have failed the test in the primal scene but will succeed in its repetition. By repeating, the stoic transfigures the temporality and significance of the primal scene: it ceases to be the scene that externally triggers the stoic's mode of being to become the first test in which the stoic's unchanging essence will have been tested.

More importantly, the stoic replaces the master in repetition. Deleuze explains how, by means of repetition, the child constructs a virtual mother "that governs and compensates for the progresses of its real activity."[35] In the same fashion, the stoic constructs the figure of the sage, which embodies the possibility of imperturbability and appraises the stoic's own progress. For this reason, the stoic philosophers often evoked the figure of the sage without imagining that they themselves embodied it, acting before the eyes of this theoretical sage. Geoffrey Aggeler argues that the stoic is fundamentally caught between solipsism and self-dramatization.[36] We should specify that his self-dramatization is performed no longer for the master, but for the virtual sage. Because of repetition, there will have never been a father or a suitor, but only a sage who first witnessed Catherine's weakness but now praises her strength.

Cavell contrasts the role of repetition in remarriage comedies, "where repetitiveness is the field of inventiveness, improvisation, of the recurrence of time, open to the second chance," to its role in the melodrama of the unknown woman, where "repetition signals death."[37] Toles' essay abounds with imagery of death: Catherine's brooch, which outlines the profile of a woman, implies not only that Catherine has merged with her mother, but also that she has become "a keeper of the flame at a private altar of the dead;" her embroidery writing evokes "the dead field of the 'uncommitted' alphabet;" her closing the drapes evokes "the Poe-like process of bricking herself in;" and the set of ruby buttons indicate that Catherine now possesses the "ossified gleam of the cold gems."[38] Contrary to Toles, I claim that it is not Catherine who is dead, but the world of men that is dead to her. The fact that she continues to wear the brooch suggests that, despite her dispute with her father, she is at peace with her mother.

Unlike melodrama, which often revels in spectacles of suffering, the stoic drama tackles the problem of oppression by withdrawing from the world. If we find any display of excessive emotion in stoicism, it is precisely to show the failure or the difficulties of the stoic position; excess in melodrama involves an argument against the ideas that bring forth suffering. If melodrama treats virtue and evil as existing categories, the stoic mode internalizes them, identifying virtue with self-possession and evil with intemperance. Franco Moretti has characterized the temporality of melodrama in terms of lateness. He argues that moving literature (for our purposes, melodrama) resorts to death as a means to divorce values from facts. Death reconciles divergent points of view, but it is too late for characters to enjoy this reconciliation.[39] In the stoic drama, as *The Heiress* shows, death only confirms that reconciliation was never possible, that it was already too late.

NOTES

1. Stanley Cavell, *Contesting Tears: The Hollywood Melodrama of the Unknown Woman* (Chicago: The University of Chicago Press, 1996), 11.
2. Dan Shaw, *Stanley Cavell and the Magic of Hollywood Films* (Edinburgh: Edinburgh University Press, 2019), 92.
3. Cavell, *Contesting Tears*, 107.
4. Cavell, *Contesting Tears*, 59.
5. Stanley Cavell, *Pursuits of Happiness: The Hollywood Comedy of Remarriage* (Cambridge, MA: Harvard University Press, 1981), 28.
6. Cavell, *Pursuits of Happiness*, 31.
7. Cavell, *Pursuits of Happiness*, 29.
8. Epictetus, *The Discourses of Epictetus*, trans. Robin Hard (London: J.M. Dent, 1995), 14.
9. Cavell, *Contesting Tears*, 107.
10. Michael A. Anderegg, *William Wyler* (Boston: Twayne Publishers, 1979), 156.
11. Peter Swaab, "The End of Embroidery: From *Washington Square* to *The Heiress*," in *Henry James on Stage and Screen*, ed. John R. Bradley (Basingstoke: Palgrave, 2000), 56–71.
12. George Toles, "Eloquent Objects, Mesmerizing Commodities in William Wyler's *The Heiress*," *Film International* 22, no. 4 (September 2006): 67.
13. See Richard Sorabji, *Emotion and Peace of Mind: From Stoic Agitation to Christian Temptation* (Oxford: Oxford University Press, 2003), 17–143.
14. Epictetus, *The Discourses*, 75.
15. See Epictetus, *The Discourses*, 5–7.
16. Cavell, *Pursuits of Happiness*, 17–18.
17. Cavell, *Contesting Tears*, 146.
18. Cavell, *Contesting Tears*, 5.
19. Toles, "Eloquent Objects," 48.
20. Harry Horner, "Designing *The Heiress*," *Hollywood Quarterly* 5, no. 1 (Autumn 1959), 3.

21. G. W. F. Hegel, *Phenomenology of Spirit*, trans. J.N. Findlay (Oxford: Oxford University Press, 1977), 118.
22. Horner, "Designing *The Heiress*," 5.
23. Horner, "Designing *The Heiress*," 2.
24. Toles, "Eloquent Objects," 64.
25. Mary Ann Doane, *The Desire to Desire: The Woman's Film of the 1940s* (Bloomington: Indiana University Press, 1987), 110.
26. Doane, *The Desire to Desire*, 111.
27. Horner, "Designing *The Heiress*," 5.
28. Seneca, "On Tranquility of Mind," in *On the Shortness of Life*, trans. C. D. N. Costa (New York: Penguin, 1997), 87.
29. Marcus Aurelius, *Meditations*, trans. Gregory Hays (New York: Modern Library, 2002), 34.
30. Raymond Bellour, "To Segment/To Analyze," in *The Analysis of Film*, trans. Maureen Turini, ed. Constance Penley (Bloomington: Indiana University Press, 2001), 193.
31. Slavoj Žižek, *Enjoy your Symptom!: Jacques Lacan in Hollywood and Out* (New York: Routledge, 1992), 105, note 2.
32. Toles, "Eloquent Objects," 64.
33. Epictetus, *The Discourses*, 34.
34. Gilles Deleuze, *Difference and Repetition*, trans. Paul Patton (New York: Columbia University Press, 1994), 90.
35. Deleuze, *Difference and Repetition*, 99.
36. Geoffrey Aggeler, *Nobler in the Mind, The Stoic-Skeptic Dialectic in English Renaissance Tragedy* (Newark: University of Delaware Press, 1998), 29.
37. Cavell, *Contesting Tears*, 108.
38. Toles, "Eloquent Objects," 63–5.
39. Franco Moretti, "Kindergarten," in *Signs Taken for Wonders*, trans. David Forgacs (London: Verso, 1983), 159–62.

CHAPTER 9

These Three: Wyler and his Two Adaptations of *The Children's Hour*

Matthias Smith

In 1935, William Wyler signed a contract with independent producer Samuel Goldwyn and was assigned his first film, an adaptation of Lillian Hellman's *The Children's Hour* (1934). This successful Broadway play, which focused on a rumor of lesbianism between two private school headmistresses, was considered unfilmable by the Motion Picture Association of America (MPAA). In order to appease the MPAA, the resulting film, *These Three* (1936), jettisoned the queer accusation for one of a polyamorous relationship between the two women and one's fiancé. Otherwise, it preserved the story's structure, with an altered happy ending. In 1961, Wyler would remake the film, this time under its original title, with a screenplay much more faithful to Hellman's 1934 play. Drawing on archival research, including the original Hellman script, this chapter will explore not only the differences in Wyler's two treatments of Hellman's story but also his approach to queer representation in the more liberated censorship period of the early 1960s.

Dashiell Hammett had suggested to Hellman that she read the 1930 book *Bad Companions* by William Roughead. A chapter in this book focuses on an 1809 Scottish scandal, in which a "malicious child" accused the school's headmistresses of "an inordinate affection" for each other.[1] Hellman took the basic dynamic, transferred it to a cozy American town, and added her trademark ability to strain the bonds between characters for dramatic effect. The play, Hellman's first, opened on Broadway on November 20, 1935. In the play, two women, Karen Wright and Martha Dobie, operate a private girls boarding school, in which they share teaching duties with Martha's aunt, Lily Mortar. Mrs. Mortar, a former stage actress, who is both critical of her niece and taking advantage of her, notices Martha's cold reaction to Karen's new fiancé, Dr. Joseph Cardin. Cardin makes a sick call on a student, the school terror Mary

Tilford, who is faking illness to spite Karen. Karen has taken away Mary's privileges due to her bad behavior. Naturally, Cardin declares the girl healthy. Meanwhile, Mrs. Mortar and Martha have an argument in the outer room, in which Mrs. Mortar accusingly suggests that Martha has romantic affections for Karen. Unfortunately, this is overheard by two girls who are waiting to hear Mary's diagnosis.

When she has been declared healthy, Mary, a girl of wealthy background, is revealed to be a bully. She believes no rules apply to her, and constantly attempts to emotionally manipulate the adults around her. Additionally, Mary is extremely imaginative, with a psychotic edge, creating narratives of victimhood and harassment by the adults who attempt to contain and admonish her. After being dismissed, Mary goes to her room and overhears the two girls talking and promptly blackmails Rosalie (who had stolen a bracelet from another student), and twists Rosalie's arm to learn what they've overheard. Mary then runs away to her grandmother's mansion with the accusation of lesbianism. Once there, Mary puts on a hysterical act and pretends to have seen evidence of the two women's secret relationship. Mrs. Tilford, an old-money socialite, is properly scandalized and quickly calls the mothers of the other girls enrolled at the school. Soon the rumor spreads to scandal, and Martha and Karen's school is forced to close. When both women confront Mrs. Tilford, Mary corroborates her lie by blackmailing Rosalie into confirming her story.

Both women sue Mrs. Tilford for slander, but when Mrs. Mortar fails to appear as a witness, the case is lost. The reputations of both women are destroyed, and they become social pariahs. The strain of this ends Karen's relationship with Dr. Cardin, as he himself begins to have doubts about Martha's true feelings. All alone, Karen and Martha discuss what has befallen them. Ultimately, the trauma has caused Martha to begin to realize she does have feelings for Karen, which she refers to with shame as "filthy." Karen does not react positively to this development, and Martha, hopeless and shunned by her best friend, kills herself offstage with a gun. In an ironic twist, Mrs. Tilford arrives to make amends having discovered Mary's deception offstage. She pleads for forgiveness and offers, in order to assuage her own guilt, to fund and reopen the school, and to make a public apology. Karen, completely destroyed and numb, rejects Mrs. Tilford's selfish pleas and is left alone as the play closes.[2]

The Children's Hour faced an uphill battle for screen adaptation in the 1930s. The film industry's self-censorship and the play's reputation caused the 1936 screen version to be both whitewashed and carefully presented, domestically and internationally. If a film adaptation of *The Children's Hour* had premiered a few years earlier, it would likely have had fewer troubles from Hollywood, but by 1934 the Motion Picture Production Code, a protective industry self-censorship policy overseen by the Motion Picture Producers and Distributors of America's Production Code Administration (PCA), had taken effect with the goal to "clean up" the violent and moral issues presented in Hollywood films. As part of this process, source material such as books and plays were often pre-screened to avoid lost investment or expensive and divisive censorship at the post-production stage. The PCA sent Vincent G. Hart to the opening night of the play, and he submitted a report to Joseph Breen (head of the PCA) the following day.

In his report, Hart refers to *Mädchen in Uniform* (Leontine Sagan, Germany, 1931), the landmark and internationally successful lesbian drama set at a girls private school in the German Empire period. Hart drew connections between the two based on their theme and setting. He also lays out the objectional portions that would render a film version of Hellman's play in violation of the code:

I. The insinuation that the two girls are degenerates.
II. The sadistic nature of the young student.
III. The confession of the young woman that she has had a mental unnatural affection for her girl friend [*sic*].
IV. All profanity.[3]

In essence, the play's entire plot was in violation of the code, making it unfilmable. This was in line with the PCA's previous disapproval of queer content. Even prior to the new revised code, the PCA had battled David O. Selznick over the lesbian characters in *Thirteen Women* (George Archainbaud, 1932). This resulted in severe cuts that left the film with a fifty-nine-minute running time.[4]

Despite this initial report, there was considerable early interest in the play. In fact, in 1935, there was a rumored adaptation with the Gish sisters, but it was independent producer Samuel Goldwyn who would take on the play, hire Hellman herself to write the screenplay, and have William Wyler direct.[5] Wyler had recently left Universal and had just completed a film for Fox Film Corporation (soon to become 20th Century-Fox), *The Gay Deception*, which had caught the attention of Goldwyn. Wyler's agent introduced Goldwyn as a producer in need of a director for a difficult project. Wyler's response was one of shock, "I thought he had lost his mind. He wanted to make *The Children's Hour*."[6] The PCA's rejection of queer themes in previous films, including *The Thirteen Women*, should have made *The Children's Hour* poisonous, yet controversy seemed to be its primary draw to Goldwyn. Hellman had convinced Goldwyn that the story's main point was "not about lesbians. It's about the power of a lie."[7] Coy and evasive, Hellman clearly knew the shock that homosexuality would be.

In the summer of 1935, meetings between Goldwyn and the PCA took place regarding the film. A new treatment was given, written by Hellman, in which the story was expanded and radically changed. Both lead characters were now

English immigrants, a child dies, and the scandal has been replaced by a supposed love triangle between the two women and Karen's fiancé.[8] Discussions over the film lasted until the end of July, when Breen submitted his approval of the film's development on several conditions.

A) Not to use the title, THE CHILDREN'S HOUR
B) To make no reference, directly or indirectly, in either advertising or exploitation of the picture to be make [sic] under this treatment, to the stage play THE CHILDREN'S HOUR;
C) To remove from your finished production all possible suggestion of lesbianism and any other matter which is likely to prove objectionable.[9]

By November, Breen had given his approval to Hellman's new script, with a few minor dialogue changes.[10]

When Wyler came onboard, Selznick had already cast Miriam Hopkins as Martha and Merle Oberon as Karen, but Wyler's master stroke of casting was Bonita Granville as Mary Tilford. By casting Granville, Wyler hoped to shift the dramatic focus from the shock of the "big lie" to its instigator. Granville's Mary is a complete terror, and a massive emotional manipulator. Her ability to change from crying-innocent to conniving anger in seconds is chilling, and her determined cruelty is frightening to watch. Compared to the other girls, such as Rosalie (Marcia Mae Jones), Mary comes across as eerily psychotic. After the confrontation between Martha and her aunt, Mary and the other girls are sent to prepare to switch rooms, in order to separate the girls from Mary's influence. It is here we learn that Mary has not only a past of pressuring her peers for money but is willing to get violent to get what she wants. Learning that Rosalie knows something about Martha, Mary physically attacks the girl. While the Mary in Hellman's original play was largely the same textually, Granville's performance, as guided by Wyler, stands out as the film's most notable element. For her role, Granville was nominated for best supporting actress.

Granville's outstanding performance cleverly covers the film's adaptation bumps, particularly in the downplaying Martha's role in the story. Either Wyler or Hellman, or both, seem to have reversed some of the earlier decisions in Hellman's first screen treatment as submitted to the PCA. Gone are Martha's and Karen's English backstory, and instead the film adds a new first act before the events of the Broadway play. This preamble largely focuses on foreshadowing and setting up the relationship of Karen and Dr. Cardin (Joel McCrea). Now, instead of Mrs. Mortar's Shakespeare class, the story opens on Karen's and Martha's graduation, establishing Mrs. Mortar's flaky and strained relationship with Martha, before the women move to a rural town to take over an inherited house in ruin. There they meet Dr. Cardin, who immediately becomes a dividing figure, in cinematic framing. Prior to meeting Dr. Cardin, both Martha and Karen are kept in close proximity with two-person, medium shots. In their first meeting with Dr. Cardin (who has been harvesting honey from a hive in the roof of their inherited home), Martha clutches Karen's arm as both women try to identify his intentions. As soon as he properly introduces himself and offers to share his lunch, Wyler immediately begins to separate the women. Karen standing close to Cardin, with Martha facing away from the camera sitting a few feet away. When they finish, Cardin forcefully separates the women by grabbing each by the arm and pulling them roughly apart to allow him room to give them a tour of the property. Throughout the film there is a marked attempt to separate the women in both space and proximity. Often Cardin will be staged between them, or Martha will be separated by several feet. When the trio confront Mrs. Tilford, Martha is staged several feet to the right and behind the couple. While certainly some of the motivation must be to keep the romantic leads close together, it seems a deliberate choice on Wyler's part to emphasize Martha's loneliness. Intentional or not, Martha's "love" for Cardin seems to lack chemistry, and aside from a plot-specific love scene (to replace a Martha/Karen scene in the stage play), Martha's romantic feelings seem opaquer. By 1936, "loneliness" had become tied to lesbianism due primarily to the popular, but equally scandalous, 1928 lesbian novel, *The Well of Loneliness* by Radclyffe Hall. This attitude became so widespread that a now-lost, exploitation film about homosexuals, released in 1935, was even entitled *Children of Loneliness*.[11] Hollywood, too, had taken notice: *Big City Blues* (Mervyn LeRoy, 1932) features a chorus girl who avoids socializing at a party by reading Hall's novel before she is killed in a brawl.

Early in the preamble of *These Three*, during the ladies refurbishing of the house, we are presented an odd sequence between Martha and Cardin. Martha is peeling off the worn wallpaper in the foyer, revealing an even older wallpaper—an old newspaper which relates the opening of the Brooklyn Bridge. Martha becomes lost in a lonely fantasy of the past—"of bows and belles and their finery." It is an odd scene, and seems to undermine its purpose of establishing Martha's own "feelings" toward Cardin. Martha wants to escape, but not Cardin. The moment between Martha and Cardin is broken when he is called away by Karen, who is off-screen. Wyler then cuts to Martha in close-up, her voice trailing off as Cardin walks away and her face reads of wistful sadness. Wyler has created visual "loneliness."

Martha's loneliness comes up again when Cardin visits the school late at night. Karen is out, but Martha asks him to join her in painting a table. Martha, doing work traditionally associated with men, begins to tell her life story to Cardin.

I was so alone, and so sad I didn't have what other kids had, but I think that's really the reason I decided to teach. Being young is awfully hard, and I wanted to make it easier for other kids when I grew up.

By this point Cardin has fallen asleep. The film score suggests this is a romantic moment, with Martha sitting and watching him all night. Indeed, this is the only moment that heterosexuality seems to be the intent, but its introduction is odd. Wyler emphasizes Martha's loneliness rather than any suppressed affection, forgoing any cute moments of dialogue, or even physical closeness. When he awakes, Mrs. Mortar sees him out, and she emphasizes to Martha that she will see more of Cardin when Karen and he marry. This causes Martha to weep, though the film leaves her reaction opaque—is her reaction due to her affections for Cardin, or because Cardin will separate her and Karen? Naturally this is overseen by Mary. In emphasizing Martha's loneliness both in her bedroom speech to Dr. Cardin, as he is falling asleep, and in her physical isolation from Karen in several shots, Wyler seems to suggest that Martha may have more upsetting her than just her past or her unrequited love for Dr. Cardin. Indeed, her continued emphasis on "the three of us" suggests that Martha may want both Cardin and Karen, rather than Cardin alone. The bowdlerizing of the play's content also leads to Martha surviving the events of the story. While Martha does remain isolated from Karen and Cardin, a much tamer ending than suicide, the biggest departure from Hellman may well be the Hollywood happy ending of Karen and Cardin reunited in Vienna.

Despite the surgery Hellman performed on her script, at the request of Goldwyn and the insistence of the PCA, Wyler's film continued to meet some controversy. The PCA could bar Goldwyn and their distributor United Artists from referencing the play and its lesbian content, but they could not prevent film critics from acknowledging the film's source. Likewise, the play's reputation gave the film a difficult international release, with it facing bans in several places and the PCA having to visit the Vatican to meet with Church officials about their concerns with the film.[12] Despite these obstacles, the film did not vanish, but remained in the popular consciousness. In 1937, Barbara Stanwyck and Errol Flynn starred in an adaptation of the Wyler film for *Lux Radio Theatre*, but it is the film's influence on Oscar Micheaux that is truly striking.

While a low budget, independent "race film," Micheaux repurposes Wyler's strongest elements of *These Three* in *God's Step Children* (1938). Pioneer black filmmaker, Micheaux, had struck his mark during the silent era, making popular political films that cast African Americans in consciously middle-class roles, in stark contrast to mainstream American cinema's limited, offensive, and patronizing roles. Other Micheaux films such as *Within Our Gates* (1920), a response to *The Birth of a Nation* (D. W. Griffith, 1915), and *The Symbol of the Unconquered* (1920) addressed the complicated nature of race and racism from a black perspective. *God's Step Children* attempts to address internalized racism. The film was met with controversy and protests from African Americans, and was recut shortly after its release; however, it is the film's familiar plot that deserves clearer attention. The trailer bills the film as "A combination of the events that shocked, but gripped and held you in *Imitation of Life* and *These Three*." While reportedly based on a short story, *Naomi Negress!*, the film combines Wyler's psychotic Mary-centered plot, with themes of racial passing, which is central to *Imitation of Life* (John M. Stahl, 1934).[13]

By focusing on the child-accuser, Micheaux is clearly following the Wyler film over Hellman's play, where Mary is less a menace than a spoiled child who is unaware of the consequences of her actions. Micheaux's "Mary" is Naomi (Jacqueline Lewis), a light-skinned African American girl, who has been adopted by a darker-skinned mother. Naomi, like Wyler's direction of Mary, is an explosive, angry, and conniving manipulator. Unhappy with being made to go to the segregated black school, Naomi sneaks away and manipulates white children to lead her to their school. When confronted, she lies, and then lashes out. Her behavior worsens when sent back to her segregated school, where she lashes out at her teacher, Mrs. Cushinberry (Ethel Moses), making her the focus of her racial fury. When Mrs. Cushinberry says, "We're all God's children," Naomi responds, "[God] didn't make the black ones." When challenged, Naomi responds by spitting in Mrs. Cushinberry's face.[14] Mrs. Cushinberry reacts by bending Naomi over her desk and spanking her. That evening, Mrs. Cushinberry visits Naomi's mother but leaves when she realizes Naomi has not said anything about being punished. Micheaux intercuts this with shots of Naomi eavesdropping from the stairs, echoing a similar sequence with Granville in *These Three*. In revenge, Naomi invents a lie about catching Mrs. Cushinberry with a married professor, which she shares with two classmates, clearly echoing the narrative events in *These Three*. The rumor swells and, like *These Three*, stony-faced parents pull their children from Mrs. Cushinberry's class. The crowd becomes a mob, bringing both Cushinberry and her supposed lover to the superintendent's office. Only Naomi's mother's intervention prevents disaster. While the film's remaining plot shifts forward to Naomi's adulthood, it is clear that it is Wyler's direction of Granville's performance that inspired the film's first half. Micheaux's Naomi is Wyler's Mary, expanded from a supporting character to leading role.

By the 1960s, however, things had changed both for Wyler and for lesbian representation in films as Wyler's star rose and the PCA's powers waned. The 1950s had seen a wide-scale erosion of the PCA's power to control content, and the influx of foreign films, which were not subject to the PCA, empowered filmmakers like Wyler to push the PCA. Foreign films with strong homosexual themes such as *The Trials of Oscar Wilde* (Ken Hughes, 1960, UK) and *Olivia* (Jacqueline Audry, 1951, France; released as *The Pit of Loneliness* in the USA) faced limited action by the PCA, though they were often subject to local censors. Hollywood films dabbled with queer subjects but were met with dour enthusiasm from the PCA. *Tea and Sympathy* (Vincente Minnelli, 1956), a Broadway adaptation that, like *The Children's Hour*, focused on an accusation of homosexuality, was greeted as coldly by the PCA as Hellman's play. The 1953 play features a teenage boy, accused of homosexuality, who is driven to a whorehouse and then to the bed of his mentor's wife in order to prove his masculinity. All three plot points violated the code, making the film unfilmable. Columbia, Warner Bros., Paramount, MGM, 20th Century-Fox, and Samuel Goldwyn all expressed interest in adapting the play, but the PCA was adamant concerning the unacceptability of homosexuality, which playwright Robert Anderson refused to have neutered. 20th Century-Fox was strongly interested and inquired about use of the play's title. According to internal PCA correspondence, the PCA was using the decisions related to Wyler's *These Three* as their defense template.[15] Pressure from MGM led to a compromised film, which runs high on emotion, but can't seem to escape from flowery, lavender language, or to clarify the source of the main character's social problem. Despite this, the film's completion led to press attention, with *The New York Times* stating that "[the] Production Code—is slowly and quietly being loosened to accord with what is obviously a change in social attitudes."[16] While the PCA would continue to battle queer themes in Hollywood films, most notably and publicly *Suddenly, Last Summer* (Joseph L. Mankiewicz, 1959), the stonewall that had greeted *These Three* was crumbling.

Wyler was no stranger to queer content, as screenwriter Gore Vidal and actor Stephen Boyd expressed interest in including queer subtext to the relationship of Judah Ben-Hur and Messala in *Ben-Hur* (1959). The two wanted to insinuate that Messala's interest in Judah was deeper than friendship, which would add a layer of pathos to the turning of two young men from friends into enemies.[17] After *Ben-Hur*, Wyler became interested in revisiting *The Children's Hour*. *These Three* had "blunted the theme of the play to such an extent that Wyler afterward maintained . . . Miss Hellman's play had not yet been filmed."[18] Thus, Wyler approached Hellman about remounting a new production. Hellman agreed and worked on early story treatments while Wyler found a home for the film via the Mirisch organization. Mirisch and United Artists were met with reproach from the PCA, who cited the 1934 decision about the play's content being unfilmable. United Artists immediately pushed back, citing the number of foreign films (particularly *The Trials of Oscar Wilde*) and American films, currently in production or development, with homosexual themes such as *The Best Man* (Franklin Schaffner, 1964) and *Advise and Consent* (Otto Preminger, 1962).[19] The PCA was meeting public pressure to change and, in October 1961, they relented stating, "In keeping with the culture, the mores and the values of our time, homosexuality and other sexual aberrations may now be treated with care, discretion and restraint."[20] The PCA would pass the film in November 1961, five months after United Artists pressured them to do so.

Wyler's new adaptation represents a marked departure from the original not only in its contents but in its framing and handling of characters. Like the original, there is a preamble, but it avoids the 1930s' Hollywood romance set-up of *These Three*. Instead, the focus is spent on establishing the relationship between Martha (Shirley MacLaine) and Karen (Audrey Hepburn), Martha and Mrs. Mortar (Miriam Hopkins, a sly connection to *These Three*), and Martha and Dr. "Joe" Cardin (James Garner). Set a week or so before the events of the play, the preamble establishes the hard-earned success of Martha and Karen. Both women are exhausted, but Martha seems particularly bothered. Her characterization by Shirley MacLaine suggests a woman who uses humor and a deadpan delivery to unsuccessfully paper over the emotional storms beneath her surface. Martha is particularly concerned with preserving what she and Karen built, accounting for every penny and staying up late to see to every last detail. Karen has been dating Dr. Cardin, and, now that she and Martha are financially secure, she decides to finally accept Joe's offer of marriage. Martha greets Cardin with cold ambivalence, and is annoyed at his appetite for their food, which she sees as draining their meager funds. When Cardin confronts Martha, she seems taken aback. Unlike the Martha of *These Three*, who seems to be wallowing in a dream, MacLaine's Martha seems to have suppressed her emotions out of a sense of survival. Cardin's mild confrontation seems to jolt Martha back into awareness of her emotions. Later, when Karen announces her engagement to Cardin, Martha verbally snaps, and shatters some dishware. Martha's temper explodes as she expresses her anger (and fears) at possibly losing all that they had worked for together. A sense of exhaustion, loneliness, and confusion washes over Martha, and she retires to her room. The noise has awoken Mary, who peeks out of her room. Karen goes to comfort Martha and gives her a platonic kiss on the forehead when she leaves her. The intercutting between Mary and the two women suggests that Mary may have seen the kiss.

Mary, as played by Karen Balkin, is a muted force in Wyler's new vision. Unlike Granville, who had previously worked in vaudeville and in film, Balkin had never before performed before the camera. Although Balkin's Mary commits the same acts as Granville's, her performance lacks much of the hysterics that Granville exhibits. In doing this, Wyler resets the story's focus away from the accuser to the victims. Wyler wisely avoids one weakness in Hellman's play, and the original film—the believability of Mary's lie. In the play and original script, Mrs. Tilford comes across as extremely naïve not to notice her granddaughter's constructed story, and in Granville's case, Mary's chilling, adaptive mood swings should make her construction obvious. In Balkin's performance, Mary's lie is accompanied by an eerie score, and we only see the reaction of Mrs.

Tilford through the windshield, and the privacy window of Mrs. Tilford's Rolls Royce, thus pulling the audience away to view this reaction from afar. Balkin's Mary is less a menace, than an unwitting pawn to fate, making the accusation painfully random in its success. Balkin's performance is less a hysterical and evil child than a spoiled innocent unaware of the consequences of her actions.

Wyler's attempts to soften the visual marginalization of Martha, which occurs in his original film, by having the camera, and thus the audience, adopt her position. In both versions, when the school is being quickly emptied of its students, the women try to confront the parents and wards and find out why. In the original film and in the play, a man tells them to their face what the scandal is. In the new version, Wyler separates Karen and Martha, with Karen following a father outside, creating an exterior, two-person shot. We cut several times between a close-up of Martha, and a point-of-view shot through the screen door, where we see, but do not hear, the conversation between Karen and the parent. This puts us in Martha's place, and the complete silence of the scene adds to our anticipation along with Martha's. Martha then steps into the point-of-view shot to approach Karen, leaving the audience "standing" in her former place, again witnessing the lie from a distance. In addition, the confrontation scene with Mrs. Tilford no longer favors staging Karen and Cardin together, as the original film does. Instead, the positioning of the three principles is constantly shifting. Wyler's staging suggests multiple relationships at work in the new film, and favors grouping Karen and Martha whenever possible. As in the previous film, Martha is the most outspoken, yet, in the new version, MacLaine's performance is more layered. Her temper is clearly on display, as in the original, but MacLaine's performance includes a fragility, a fear, that foreshadows Martha's later realization that there is truth in this nightmare, that she does indeed love Karen romantically.

The 1961 film's final act shows a marked change from both the previous filmed version and the original play. When Martha confesses her confused feelings in a gripping and very empathic sequence, an emotionally exhausted Karen reacts with exasperation, and soft denial. Unlike the stage play, Mrs. Tilford arrives early. She offers amends and is rejected by Karen. Martha begins to laugh hysterically at the insufficiency of Mrs. Tilford's apology and runs upstairs. Karen follows her. Wyler then cuts to Martha's room where Martha sits quietly in the window seat, seemingly at peace. Karen tells Martha that she plans on leaving the town and, in a sign of continued friendship, despite Martha's confession, invites her to come with her. Martha does not give her an answer and says she wants only to sleep now. Karen decides to go for a walk, but soon realizes that Martha should not be left alone. Returning to the house, Mrs. Mortar is raising a fuss. Martha is in her room, door locked, and not responding to Mrs. Mortar. Panicked, Karen breaks the door down, only to find Karen dead, a victim of suicide by hanging. While the stage play also ends in Martha's suicide, the play does not follow Martha offstage; we only hear a gunshot. Wyler, however, allows his audience to see Martha, in her room, apparently quite tranquil, just before committing suicide. This is where, unfortunately, Wyler's empathic treatment of Martha makes a problematic statement. Whether intentional or not, the film seems to suggest that the only peace that Martha can be granted as a lesbian is that of death.

The Children's Hour, being the first major Hollywood film, under the PCA's revised standards, to openly include homosexuality as the primary theme, would naturally become an important historical film for LGBT history, but Wyler's choices as director led to an unfortunate extension of harmful stereotypes of queer existence. In the documentary adaptation of Vito Russo's book, *The Celluloid Closet: Homosexuality in the Movies*, Shirley MacLaine states that several scenes of Martha coming to terms with her sexuality were cut from the film by Wyler. Another sequence, the trial before the judge, was filmed but also cut by Wyler. This explains why MacLaine's performance clearly hints at Martha's internal realization of her sexuality but robs the film of context of Martha's suicide. In Hellman's play, the suicide is just one of several ironic turns in the play's final minutes—Karen leaving Cardin and Mrs. Tilford's last-minute appearance to clear her conscious. Wyler purposefully has structured his film around an empathic positioning of Martha at the forefront of many of the film's scenes. Yet he does not allow us to understand her post-coming-out self, instead favoring Karen's perspective. Did Martha commit suicide because she saw no future for herself? Because of her lesbianism? Or because she felt that she somehow had "wronged" her friend? The film seems uninterested in exploring this. The film's prominence, as the first Hollywood studio film to center on homosexuality, its prestige as a Wyler film, and its A-list casting had unintentional consequences of furthering a popular literary narrative that gays and lesbians are ultimately doomed to suicide. Major studio releases dealing with homosexuality, such as *Advise and Consent*, *Reflections in a Golden Eye* (John Huston, 1967), and *The Fox* (Mark Rydell, 1967), all continued the trend of *The Children's Hour* by having their queer characters die, often by suicide.

While far from perfect, however, Wyler's two adaptations of *The Children's Hour* bookmark two historical realities in both Hollywood and queer cinema history. With *These Three*, Wyler's film became the case example of purging queer content in adaptation. *The Children's Hour* marked the death of the PCA's strong stance against queer content and the problematic standard set for future studio films. Furthermore, Wyler's handling of Martha, and his empathy toward her in his camera work, direction of performance, and characterization should be emphasized even if its execution was flawed.

NOTES

1. Mirisch Company memo to PCA "Facts about The Children's Hour," undated [c.1961], MS, Hollywood, Censorship, and the Motion Picture Production Code, 1927–1968: History of Cinema, Series 1, Hollywood and Production Code Administration. Margaret Herrick Library. *Archives Unbound.*
2. Parts of this summary were taken from the PCA's summary of the play: Breen, Joseph, Untitled Overview and Comments of *The Children's Hour*, November 21, 1934. William Wyler, *These Three* (United Artists, 1936). MS, Hollywood, Censorship, and the Motion Picture Production Code, 1927–1968: History of Cinema, Series 1, Hollywood and Production Code Administration. Margaret Herrick Library. *Archives Unbound*; Lillian Hellman, *The Children's Hour* (1934), in *Six Plays by Lillian Hellman* (New York: Vintage Books, 1979), 1–78.
3. Ibid.
4. James Zeruk, Jr., *Peg Entwistle and the Hollywood Sign Suicide* (Jefferson, NC: McFarland and Company, 2014), 158–82.
5. McKenzie, [first name unknown], to William Hays, Interoffice Memo, Feb. 6, 1935. William Wyler, *These Three* (United Artists, 1936). MS, Hollywood, Censorship, and the Motion Picture Production Code, 1927–1968: History of Cinema, Series 1, Hollywood and Production Code Administration. Margaret Herrick Library. *Archives Unbound.*
6. Gabriel Miller, *William Wyler: The Life and Films of Hollywood's Most Celebrated Director* (Lexington: University of Kentucky Press, 2013), 63.
7. *Directed by William Wyler*, directed by Aviva Slesin (Topgallant Prod., 1986).
8. Hullbert, Merritt to Geoffrey Shurlock, July 24, 1935. William Wyler, *These Three* (United Artists, 1936). MS, Hollywood, Censorship, and the Motion Picture Production Code, 1927–1968: History of Cinema, Series 1, Hollywood and Production Code Administration. Margaret Herrick Library. *Archives Unbound.*
9. Breen, Joseph to Samuel Goldwyn, July 31, 1935. William Wyler, *These Three* (United Artists, 1936). MS, Hollywood, Censorship, and the Motion Picture Production Code, 1927–1968: History of Cinema, Series 1, Hollywood and Production Code Administration. Margaret Herrick Library. *Archives Unbound.*
10. Breen, Joseph to Samuel Goldwyn, November 12, 1935. William Wyler, *These Three* (United Artists, 1936). MS, Hollywood, Censorship, and the Motion Picture Production Code, 1927–1968: History of Cinema, Series 1, Hollywood and Production Code Administration. Margaret Herrick Library. *Archives Unbound.*
11. Cary O'Neil, "Gay Cinema/Lost Cinema: 'Children of Loneliness' (1935)," *Now See Hear!:* The National Audio-Visual Conservation Center Blog, November 17, 2015, <https://blogs.loc.gov/now-see-hear/2015/11/a-movie-missing-in-action-children-of-loneliness-1935/> (last accessed August 23, 2022).
12. Archibald, G. to Harold Smith, April 15, 1937; and Luporini, Mario to G. Archibald, undated. William Wyler, *These Three* (United Artists, 1936). MS, Hollywood, Censorship, and the Motion Picture Production Code, 1927–1968: History of Cinema, Series 1, Hollywood and Production Code Administration. Margaret Herrick Library. *Archives Unbound.*
13. *God's Step Children*, AFI Catalog of Feature Films, <https://catalog.afi.com/Film/2255-GODS-STEPCHILDREN> (last accessed August 23, 2022).
14. Ibid.
15. Geoffrey Shurlock, "Memo for the File," *Tea and Sympathy* (Metro-Goldwyn-Mayer, 1956). MS, Hollywood, Censorship, and the Motion Picture Production Code, 1927–1968:

History of Cinema, Series 1, Hollywood and Production Code Administration. Margaret Herrick Library. *Archives Unbound*.
16. Bosley Crowther, "Loosening the Code, Understanding Shown in *Tea and Sympathy*," *The New York Times*, October 7, 1956, A125.
17. William Fitzgerald, "Oppositions, Anxieties, and Ambiguities in the Toga Movie," in eds. Sandra R. Joshel, Margaret Malamud, and Donald T. McGuire, Jr., *Imperial Projections: Ancient Rome in Modern Popular Culture* (Baltimore: John Hopkins University Press, 2001), 38.
18. Mirisch Company memo to PCA "Facts about The Children's Hour", undated [*c.*1961], William Wyler, *The Children's Hour* (United Artists, 1961). May 3, 1961 – October 1962. MS, Hollywood, Censorship, and the Motion Picture Production Code, 1927–1968: History of Cinema, Series 1, Hollywood and Production Code Administration. Margaret Herrick Library. *Archives Unbound*.
19. [Illegible addressee] to Eric Johnston, May 10, 1961. William Wyler, *The Children's Hour* (United Artists, 1961). May 3, 1961 – October 1962. MS, Hollywood, Censorship, and the Motion Picture Production Code, 1927–1968: History of Cinema, Series 1, Hollywood and Production Code Administration. Margaret Herrick Library. *Archives Unbound*.
20. Vito Russo, *The Celluloid Closet: Homosexuality in the Movies*, revised edition (New York: Harper and Row, 1987), 121–2.

PART IV
War and Peace

CHAPTER 10

A War of the People: Destruction, Community, and Hope in William Wyler's Wartime Films

Robert Ribera

During WWI, the young Willy Wyler watched as the Great War raged through his hometown of Mulhouse[1], in Alsace, which for generations before, and years to come, would change hands between France and Germany. Mulhouse was the site of continuous fighting during the war, and the teenager had a front row seat. He witnessed a dogfight, running up to the downed plane to find a dead French soldier, keeping a piece of the plane as a souvenir.[2] He saw as the French and German flags were raised on the flagpole of city hall depending on which army held the town. He spent hours in an air raid shelter, watching the battles through a small window, once pushing a dead soldier away so he and his friends could see what was happening on the streets outside.[3] In the mornings his family would emerge, he wryly noted later, to see "whether we were French or German."[4] Thirty years later, in the midst of WWII, Wyler would find himself in another air raid shelter—this time on a Hollywood backlot with Greer Garson and Walter Pigeon, directing them in scenes where they too wondered if their home would be destroyed in the night. And Wyler would witness more fighting in the skies, himself crouched down in the B-17 bombers of the Army Air Force, or filming the Thunderbolts of the 57th Fighter Group as they crisscrossed the Italian countryside.

When war finally came to the United States in December of 1941, the German Jewish émigré was an experienced Hollywood director at the height of his career and powers, with a streak of Best Picture and Best Director Academy Award nominations unrivaled by his peers. On the morning of December 7, Wyler was hosting John Huston at his home in Bel Air. They were playing tennis when they heard the news about Pearl Harbor.[5] Both were immediately drawn to the fight, itching to get themselves and their cameras to the battlefront. As Talli, Wyler's wife noted, "He couldn't stand the thought of sitting on the sidelines."[6] After news of the bombing interrupted their game and their lives, they would both race to finish their current productions, then go off to make documentaries for the US government, turning their attention to wartime work.

The entire film industry faced challenges during the war years, while attendance reached heights never again seen, and the tone of many films embraced the timely influence of war. As film historian Thomas Schatz notes, the nature of cinema changed, but such changes were vital to both the morale of the country and the survival of the industry:

> Never before had the interests of the nation and the industry been so closely aligned, and never had its status as a national cinema been so vital. The industry's "conversion to war production" from 1942 to 1945 was eminently successful, as Hollywood enjoyed what may have been its finest hour as a social institution and a cultural force.[7]

Wyler's output during these years was no exception. His features, *Mrs. Miniver* (1942) and *The Best Years of Our Lives* (1946), were two of the most successful Hollywood films of the era, held up as examples of the fulfillment of Hollywood's powers to both entertain and boost morale. One is set in the early years of war, the other is about its aftermath and demobilization. And in between, there are two about the actual combat, *The Memphis Belle: A Story of a Flying Fortress* (1944) and *Thunderbolt* (1947), each focusing on air power and the communities of pilots, bombardiers, gunners, and navigators who risked their lives flying over enemy territory. As Sarah Kolzoff succinctly notes, Wyler put his life and career on the line during the war, making films that revealed his ideals and reflected his politics:

> The films made by William Wyler before, during, and after World War II offer a first-rate guide to his celluloid politics, but they also bear the marks of the wars he fought in real life and the political engagement underlying his art.[8]

For Wyler, the war was a chance for him to create engaging personal pictures that also entertained the audience.

It is no coincidence that the characters in *Miniver* and *Best Years* are profoundly affected by the threat of death from above, and ultimately concerned with how life will continue on the very ground they survey from the skies. Captain Fred Derry (Dana Andrews) and RAF pilot Vin Miniver (Richard Ney) are easy stand-ins as one of the bombers from the Memphis Belle or fighter pilots from *Thunderbolt*. Wyler's four films made during the war years tell stories about suffering and loss, with nearly every moment of these films devoted to trauma and healing, but they are connected by his focus on process, community, and cooperation. Not only do similar themes bind these films, familiar narrative beats and even lines of narration or dialogue reinforce the themes of unity and community. In their totality, they could be understood as following the same set of characters, leading up to war, fighting in it, and returning home. This chapter will argue that the overall thrust of Wyler's wartime films is a call to action and unity—something must be done, and it must be done *together*. The films are about breaking down social barriers, self-sacrifice, and finding common ground to first defeat an enemy and then to heal the wounds, both seen and unseen.

WE ARE THE FIGHTERS: *MRS. MINIVER*

For a message to reach an audience, Wyler explained, propaganda must "not look like propaganda." Instead, a successful film will reach an audience. "The most satisfaction I get out of a film," he remarked in an interview, "is its contribution to the thinking of people, socially or politically." *Mrs. Miniver* "was perfect as propaganda for the British," Wyler later claimed, "because it was a story about a family, about the kind of people audiences would care about."[9] He might have added that it was perfect for Americans as well.

Mrs. Miniver, loosely based on the book of vignettes about the early years of the war by Jan Struther, sets the stage for the call to unity and individual action that will dominate Wyler's wartime films. Wyler takes pains to show the "average English middle-class" Minivers as just another family blissfully separated from the conflict brewing in Europe. The generalities presented as the nuclear family are so broad, with an idyllic small town with white picket fences that looks just like any corresponding place in America. Indeed, remove the accents, specific connections to the British class system, and the battle of Dunkirk, and they might as well be middle-class Americans struggling to come to terms with the impending war. As the opening title reads:

> This story of an average English middle-class family begins with the summer of 1939; when the sun shone down on a happy, careless people, who worked and played, reared their children and tended their gardens in that happy, easy-going England that was so soon to be fighting desperately for her way of life and for life itself.

The "happy, careless people" are shown economically through the opening sequence, where Mr. Miniver, Clem, and Mrs. Miniver, Kay (Walter Pidgeon and Greer Garson), both hide an overindulgence from each other—in her case, a hat, and in his, a fancy car. But the frivolity of these purchases seems trivial in short order, as the family's carefree lives quickly give way to the fears of war, and what it will do to their community.

When their young son, Vin, arrives for a break from university, he warns them of his new ideals in the face of the class structure. But he is met by bemused parents early on after exclaiming, "I think I've developed a social consciousness." His philosophy on the exploitation of the lower classes is quickly challenged by someone who actually helps out. When Carol Beldon (Teresa Wright), granddaughter of the local Lady Beldon (Dame May Whitty), visits to ask that the station master's rose be withdrawn from the upcoming flower competition, Vin berates her for making such a request and criticizes the family for imposing their rule over the village. But she coolly takes him to task for the ease of rhetoric rather than work. It's "just talk," she claims. Books filled with big words are nothing. "A bit of action is required now and then." With this indignity heaped upon him by an upper-class neighbor, Wyler is able to both criticize the class structure and show how individual action can ease tensions and unify the community. It is in fact the melding of the two families, the Minivers and the Beldons, which showcases such unification.

Lady Beldon's own softening toward the people in the village, bit by bit, aided by the love of Vin for her granddaughter, the respectability of Mrs. Miniver, and the eventual confrontation with Mr. Ballard (Henry Travers) over his rose, collapses the structures which separate them. "We can take care of ourselves. We've been doing it for the last 800 years," Lady Beldon scoffs when Vin runs over to help with an air raid early on in the film. She rejects Vin as a suitor due to his social standing and his name—including the name of the mother and rose he represents. When warned about a possible air strike and the orders to shelter, she cries out, "We don't take orders, we give them! Worst thing about this war is the chance it gives these dreadful little persons to make themselves important." An air raid siren cuts her off just as she ridicules the idea of the Germans bombing the town. "They wouldn't dare!"

At this moment, Wyler lays the groundwork for his later wartime films. In *The Memphis Belle*, the narration in the opening moments talks of a British people defending their land for 1000 years. The vicar's speech at the end of *Mrs. Miniver* also alludes to the 1000 years of history behind the country as it defends itself. Likewise, in *The Best Years of Our Lives*, the man at the soda counter says, "Every soda jerk in this country's got an idea he's somebody." In this climactic scene, Fred Derry knocks the man to the floor and Homer Parrish (Harold Russell) picks up the American flag pin that he's ripped off his lapel. Whereas the unnamed man at the lunch counter is never seen again, Lady Beldon shows her humility with her acceptance of Vin, and her "loss" to Mr. Ballard's rose, the third Mrs. Miniver of the film.

Over the course of the narrative, the Minivers show their willingness to step up in light of total war, from Clem Miniver going off to Dunkirk while Vin flies overhead, to the standout sequence of Kay Miniver's confrontation with a German pilot. While Vin and Clem are away at Dunkirk, Kay finds a German pilot hiding in the bushes around their home. Held at gunpoint, she is accosted with the intentions of the Nazis. "We will come. We will bomb your cities," he screams at her, sneering as he acknowledges that women and children will die. Here, the battlefront dramatically invades the home front, and the pilot's vicious words highlight the consequences of total war while showcasing Kay's steadfastness and courage in the face of a fight.

The celebrated final sequence of *Mrs. Miniver* combines grief and hope. It is a call for resilience. As the community gathers to honor the dead—Mr. Ballard, Carol, the newlywed Mrs. Miniver, a young boy from the church choir—social standing has been erased. They are all simply Christian soldiers now; the bombed-out church a center of refuge, the busted roofbeams of the church revealing a dangerous sky. But the people sing on, and the vicar (Henry Wilcoxon) delivers his unifying message:

> Because this is not only a war of soldiers in uniform. It is a war of the people, of all the people, and it must be fought not only on the battlefield but in the cities and in the villages, in the factories and on the farms, in the home, and in the heart of every man, woman, and child who loves freedom. Well, we have buried our dead, but we shall not forget them. Instead they will inspire us with an unbreakable determination to free ourselves and those who come after us from the tyranny and terror that threaten to strike us down. This is the people's war! It is our war! We are the fighters! Fight it, then! Fight it with all that is in us! And may God defend the right.

Like the "They're listening in America" radio address from the end of Hitchcock's *Foreign Correspondent* (1940), or Chaplin's "Look up, Hannah," plea from *The Great Dictator* (1941), the vicar's homily remains one of the most stirring of the war. Like the rest of the film, it was an acceptance of total war, and a call for unity.

Acknowledging that his work has something to say, Wyler spoke of the value of propaganda along with the desire for audiences to be moved and entertained. He called *Miniver* "a pure propaganda film. It was absolute propaganda for England and against Germany. It was a propaganda film for the war and was tremendously successful. It had a message."[10] While his immediate wartime experiences changed his opinions that the film reflected the realities of war, at a screening in London, Wyler, the reluctant audience member for his own film, cried along with the rest of the audience, exclaiming, "Christ, what a tearjerker!"[11] Churchill asked that prints of the film be sent out right away, calling it "propaganda worth a hundred battleships."[12] Roosevelt asked for the vicar's speech to be played over the air by Voice of America, and dropped as leaflets over Germany.[13]

Bosley Crowther, applauding *Mrs. Miniver* as "the finest film yet made about the present war, and a most exalting tribute to the British, who have taken it gallantly," highlights the effects of focusing on the shifting battlefronts of the conflict. War has invaded the home front, and so "This is a film of modern warfare in which civilians become the front-line fighters and the ingrained courage of the people becomes the nation's most vital strength."[14] As the critic notes, there is the absence of battlefields and bloody battles. Total war envelopes everyone, from the Lady of the village to the kindly station master. None are left unaffected, and although the film is set in the opening months of the Battle of Britain, it is a call to action for audiences around the world. In a second review, he writes of the power of the film to engender sympathy in the American audience. "Let a man's sympathy be enjoined and he is definitely on your side. Make him identify his own life with your sorrow or suffering and the set of his mind is as rigid as though he had experienced it himself."[15] Experience would remain a key part of Wyler's wartime films, and in the coming years, Wyler would turn his attention to another new battlefront, where the audience would experience the danger and excitement of battle firsthand: the air.

JUST ONE PLANE: *THE MEMPHIS BELLE: A STORY OF A FLYING FORTRESS* AND *THUNDERBOLT*

Hollywood was drafted into the documentary and propaganda effort immediately after the attack on Pearl Harbor. Thousands of individuals in the filmmaking community went into military service, including established directors of some of Hollywood's most popular feature films of the previous decade. John Ford would soon ship off to the Pacific Ocean with the Navy to capture the Battle of Midway; Frank Capra, a major in the Signal Corps, would apply his patriotic fervor to the *Why We Fight Series*, and John Huston would travel the Aleutians in Alaska and the Italian countryside with the Army. Films were seen not just as morale boosters, but as educational tools for soldiers and a valid new source for training in various industrial fields. As Roger Manvell has argued, all sides were quick to understand the power of film and its possible uses during the war:

> Military and civilian strategists on both sides of the conflict realized, from the beginning, the important role which motion pictures could play in modern warfare. Films could train soldiers and industrial workers; they could build opinion, strengthen attitudes, and stimulate emotions; they could be invaluable in reconnaissance and later in combat.[16]

With the advent of war, the United States government was eager to tap into the power of fiction and non-fiction films to boost morale and help explain the war to the masses. At the 14th Annual Academy Awards banquet in 1942, John Grierson praised those gathered for their continued work in wartime production. "At this time we are all, in one way or another, concerned in the high duty of creating and maintaining the morale which is necessary for a hard and absolute war." Grierson called these efforts to come "humble" and "deeply ordinary"— the tasks of providing both information and morale to the American people in the face of such adversity.[17] Only a few months after the United States entered the war, it was not only a recognition of the work already done, but a cinematic call to arms for all that was left to accomplish. Hollywood filmmakers obliged, with producers and directors adjusting the rhetoric of each film to fit the targeted audience. The resulting differences, combined with the personal style of the directors involved, made for a vast variety of approaches to documentary and propaganda production.

Saverio Giovacchini sees the WWII documentaries as evidence of the 1930s progressives in Hollywood finding their voice in war, as just one way that filmmakers were able to "fight fascism with their real bodies, or, at the very least, through their films."[18] Putting their bodies on the line to capture footage was, for many of the filmmakers and cameramen, a reality. John Ford memorably captured the Battle of Midway as planes flew overhead. Huston encountered shelling in the Liri Valley and was horrified by the death he saw on the battlefield. Wyler received permanent hearing loss during his flights filming the Thunderbolts. Giovacchini argues that the documentaries of the Hollywood directors became not just personal statements, but self-portraits of them as soldiers.[19] And although they did not directly insert themselves into the documentaries, these men did relish the opportunity to experience war and consider themselves an active part of the war effort as they lent their personal touch to each film.

What's more, according to Jeanine Basinger, Wyler's documentaries were part of a group of films which helped to solidify the genre of wartime documentaries.

> The filmmakers begin to use the conventions as if they believe them to be recognizable to audiences. They begin to use an image—presumably familiar from first wave combat films—as a kind of visual shorthand for viewers. The power of the purely visual is that it demonstrates the belief that an audience can look at a group, a hero, or an objective and supply dialogue and meaning it knows from prior films.[20]

According to Basinger this move from "the verbal/visual toward the visual/verbal,"[21] is solidified in the shorthand filmmakers were able to use after the establishment of the genre.

A similar setup links both Wyler's wartime documentaries. We first are grounded in the landscape, which frames our perspective of the air front. Then we meet the men, from each corner of the United States. We are given the details of their mission and then watch it unfold in the sky and on the ground below. Finally, we have the catharsis of the safe return of the crew. Key to the power of both *Belle* and *Thunderbolt* is their interiority. As Wyler would explain when describing his work on *The Best Years of Our Lives*, he was interested in "the inner workings of the people the scene is about,"[22] and in the documentaries, this is no different. As Basinger argues, *The Memphis Belle* was a transformative film because of the way Wyler shifted the audience's perspective from the exterior of the plane to the pilot seat. The film

> makes the experience of being inside a bomber during combat vivid and real. It influenced the look of air films which followed, because the point of view of the combat experience is from inside the plane. This is an important consideration because it changes the role of the viewer from observer to participant.[23]

In the same way that the experience of total war in *Mrs. Miniver* invited the audience to empathize, to see themselves as part of the fight against total war, Wyler's documentaries place the audience directly in the action. We see the war through streaked plexiglass, the shadows of the fighter planes crisscrossing the landscape. In *Thunderbolt* the camera is so close to the pilots we oftentimes see them from the chin down, their hands shifting the gears of war. In one of the most arresting images of *Memphis Belle*, the camera is trained on the shadow of the B-17 bomber as it descends from the sky, getting closer and closer until touchdown. In these films we experience the thrills and traumas of battle from the sky above. The immediacy is striking and all-encompassing. We are right there with the fighting men.

Memphis Belle begins with images of an English village. We see homes, a church. The narrator intones: "This is a battlefront. A battlefront like no other in the long history of mankind's wars. This is an air front." Wyler lingers on the crew in charge of preparing the ship for its flight, and notes that this crew is as important a part of the plane as the wings. In the promotional pamphlet that went along with their war bond tour after they returned home, Captain Morgan's sentiments about the necessity of community are in line with the images we see in the film:

> If you want in just one word how we were able to go through the hell of Europe 25 times and get back home without a casualty, I'll give it to you. TEAMWORK. Until you have been over there, you can't know how essential that is. We had 10 men working together, each ready and able to help out anybody else who might need him.[24]

As the community in *Mrs. Miniver* learns over the course of the film, community will be the key to confronting total war. But in battle, cooperation is necessary for survival. Both documentaries begin by embracing the selfless acts of the crews, while making sure the audience knows that they are just one of many. "This is the crew of the Memphis Belle," we hear in the opening minutes of the first film. Wyler isolates their place in the Army Air Force—the 324th Squadron, heavy bombardment group. But, they are "just one plane and one crew, in one squadron, in one group, of one wing, of one Air Force, out of 15 United States Army Air Forces." The same language is used in the opening message from General Carl Spaatz in *Thunderbolt*, and read by James Stewart. Though we focus on the missions of the 57th Fighter Group, stationed on the island of Corsica off the coast of Italy, "[t]his story belongs to all men who fought for freedom, and did it a long way from home."

The homes that Stewart mentions in his prologue are just as important. In *The Memphis Belle* the men are from New Jersey and Connecticut, Spokane and Green Bay. They were students, carpenters, and stevedores. Now they crew the Belle as the captain, navigator, or gunner. The film documents the radical changes in their lives, noting this through a simple juxtaposition of their former jobs. Sergeant Tony Nastal, for example, "used to repair washing machines in Detroit when he was a kid. Now he's 19 and has two Nazi fighters confirmed." In *Thunderbolt*, because the P-47 planes were single seat fighters, we do not focus on a communal effort of the ten-person crew as Wyler did in *Memphis Belle*. We do not follow "Hun Hunter XIV," for example. But the embrace of community is the same. The pilots were together through fifty-eight maneuvers in two years. Egypt and Sicily, now Corsica. One hails from New Mexico, once had a desk job, and is young at age twenty-two. One young pilot is from Ames, Iowa. Another, from Louisville, Kentucky. In this way, Wyler again makes their sacrifices individual and communal. Sacrifice is spread across the United States, war collapsing differences as they fight for freedom. Even a soldier who receives a blood transfusion after the mission provides an opportunity for Wyler to make a nod to the community: "The new, life giving blood flowing through his veins might be from a high school girl in Des Moines, a miner in Alabama, a movie star in Hollywood. Or it might be your blood. Whoever it is, thanks." Here, Wyler not only erases the lines between the soldiers, he calls out to the audience, linking the glamour of Hollywood to the lives of the working class and children.

In *Thunderbolt*, not only are we inside the planes with the pilots, we are inside their heads. When presented with their mission, the narrator explains that the pilots don't have time to think of themselves. The voice-over flows like an internal monologue. Later the pilots narrate the bombs dropped, they wonder aloud whether munitions are hidden in a house, comment on the relations between the French and American forces. And they think of home. Although a community has been built up around the base, they long to return, as they feel time "slipping by" and leaving them "standing still" as they wait and kill time. As they wait for their chance to head home, they lament the time lost in a stream of consciousness. "These are your years. Years to get started. Find yourself your job, profession. Get married. Kids. Home of your own. These are the years that count." Of course, this will echo later in *The Best Years of Our Lives*: "I gave up the best years of my life," Marie Derry (Virginia Mayo) laments to her husband Fred as their marriage falls apart. Her complaint, however, moves her to "live for myself," the selfish response to Wyler's continued call for empathy and community.

The framing of *Belle* and *Thunderbolt* may engender empathy for the pilots, and give American audiences a direct look at how battles are fought, seemingly at a distance, but this perspective also guides our understanding of total war, and the implications for those on the ground. As Jeffrey Geiger notes, perspective is no less political than Wyler's choices in *Mrs. Miniver* or *The Best Years of Our Lives*:

> The *Memphis Belle* is, in short, an idea-weapon: its ideological messages are constituted as much by what the film suppresses as what it chooses to show. Indeed, its impact is grounded in this "less is more" strategy, which constructs a highly restricted point of view.[25]

As Daniel Marcus has argued, Wyler's documentaries changed the way audiences viewed air warfare as they

> sought to allay anxieties about the morality of the new strategies and tactics accompanying the development of air forces ... to discursively trace the increasing acceptance of large-scale civilian casualties by means of aerial bombardment as a consequence of the imperatives of war in the modern age.[26]

Though the landscape looks like any other, it is, the narration warns, filled with danger and destruction. Among the usual military targets, the depots and ports, the hidden caches of ammunition, there are civilians, but they are in the "houses and fields of those who invade and oppress." These words both prepare the audience for the destruction ahead, and temper the moral justifications for the bombing:

> They are the factories and roads of the people who twice in one generation have flooded the world with suffering, suffering in such quantity as the history of the human race has never known, brought torment and anguish into countless American homes, gold stars and telegrams from the war department.

The film, Geiger argues, explains the necessity of total war, "while offering hope that highly professionalized, technically sophisticated, precision attacks can minimize civilian casualties, and defining bombing runs as part of the people's war."[27] As presented in both films, air war was a key element to the Allied victory.

Belle ends with the men ready to return home, their release granted after twenty-five missions over the European battlefields. *Thunderbolt*'s finale shows an end title card splashed with a giant red question mark, a reminder that wars may end, but the fear of their return lingers. In fact, by the time Wyler was back in the United States and *Thunderbolt* was ready for distribution, the war was over. When the film was finally released by Monogram Pictures in 1947, James Stewart jokingly referred to 1945 as "ancient history."

When *Memphis Belle* was screened for President Roosevelt at the White House, however, the results of the war were still uncertain. Wyler, sitting next to FDR, noticed the president's emotional response. It may not have been a surprise that he told the assembled audience, "This has to be shown right away, everywhere."[28] In James Agee's approving review of *The Memphis Belle* for *The Nation*, published in the spring of 1944, he concludes, "Postwar planners should work out a better fate for him [Wyler] than going back to Hollywood."[29]

NOT TOO MUCH TO ASK: *THE BEST YEARS OF OUR LIVES*

Staring out from the hull of a B-17 bomber, three returning veterans take in the landscape of their hometown. In their years of absence, the ground below them has changed dramatically, and they can only hope they can ease back into life. Homer has lost his hands, and fears he'll never be able to reconnect with his fiancé; Captain Fred Derry, once a soda jerk in the local pharmacy, fears he'll never make ends meet; Sergeant Al Stephenson (Fredric March), a banker, isn't so eager to return to the rat race and materialism his salary affords him. Sitting back, Stephenson remarks that he hopes no one will try to rehabilitate him, to which Fred replies, "All I want's a good job, a mild future and a little house big enough for me and my wife. Gimme that, and I'm rehabilitated like that." As Fred snaps his fingers, Al looks upward, saying, "Well I'd say that's not too much to ask."

This scene from William Wyler's *The Best Years of Our Lives* reflects the anxiety not only of the returning veterans, but of the country awaiting their return. With an overwhelming number of men returning, two issues became immediately pressing—their housing and their readjustment. Like millions of other servicemen and women, Wyler would also need to readjust to life stateside. Wyler famously suffered permanent hearing loss documenting the flights of the P-47 Thunderbolts in their flights over Italy. He returned to the United States in the spring of 1945, and spent his first few weeks back shuffled around different military hospitals, where doctors attempted to restore his hearing.[30] It would never fully return. In the introduction to Harold Russell's autobiography, *The Best Years of My Life*, Wyler explained that, just like Russell did not need to "act" like a man who lost his hands, his work "required no research on my part, no wondering and sweating about how a man would act and react to a given situation."[31]

Wyler, recognizing the vitality of the issues facing returning veterans, himself included, wanted a project to tackle the issue. After Samuel Goldwyn read an article, "The Way Home," an account of returning soldiers in *Time* magazine in the summer of 1944, he gave MacKinlay Kantor the job of turning it into a treatment for a film. The resulting blank verse novel, *Glory for Me*, became the blueprint for Robert E. Sherwood's screenplay for *The Best Years of Our Lives*.

In the article, as the veterans get closer to their homes, they turn to thoughts of the future, and their fears.

> The heroes peeled off their natty field greens and settled down in their khakis on the scratchy green seats, scared and lonely, wondering how home would be now that it was suddenly so close. "I'm a little worried about how I'll look to them, about how much I've changed . . ."[32]

The promise of a bright future, and a return to normalcy, provided hope for the returning soldier. Historian John Morton Blum writes, "the Germans and the Japanese, the targets of heroic striving, were dragons to be slain, after which the hero could return to his fair lady in her fair land."[33] The images of home would vary from soldier to soldier: one reminisced about blueberry pie, one of a beautiful girl, but all these remained simple "badges of home." Dolores Hayden points out, the "triple dream" of house, land, and community drove investors to advertise newly planned communities as such. An advertisement for General Electric's "Victory Homes" displays these hopeful sketches: "That little home sketched there in the sand is a symbol of faith and hope and courage. It's a promise, too. A promise of gloriously happy days to come . . . when Victory is won."[34]

Wyler understood the hopes of the returning vets all too well, and went about examining the three intersecting lives of these men and their families, the hardship of readjustment, all without the candy coating. As Kolzoff argues, "the film faces social problems, particularly the fissures caused by class identity, alcoholism, and unemployment, with a steady gaze."[35] The situations are clear as the men take the cab ride back home. Homer is first dropped off in front of his home, where his parents, a kid sister, and the girl next door, Wilma, his fiancé (Cathy O'Donnell), all greet him. Sergeant Stephenson is let off in front of a fancy apartment building, shyly admitting he's a banker as he steps out. Captain Derry, though outranking both, is dropped off on the bad side of town, the image not so subtly completed as a train can be seen to amble by in the distance through the Derry family shack's window.

Both Homer's and Fred's fears of worthlessness take the form of the fear of an unstable future. Homer is unable to see the loving family as able to take him in, and creeps into a depression. Fred returns to a wife that apparently married him for the image of his uniform and the promise of stability. Al Stephenson finds himself back at the bank rather quickly, while Fred Derry has to settle for a job at the drugstore. Homer tries to create a new life, believing his fiancé will never stand to take care of him. It becomes clear that Fred is falling in love with Al's daughter Peggy (Teresa Wright), though he is already married. When he realizes his wife has been unfaithful, he plans to divorce and get out of the town as quickly as possible.

The role of community is heightened in their readjustment, and their livelihood is tied to the banks and the opportunities they afford. Stephenson falls quickly into the realm of comfort, though he has doubts about his return to the rat race, exclaiming, "Last year it's kill Japs, this year it's make money!" Because of his war experiences, he is promoted to the office of GI loans upon his return by the board. Now in charge of securing a promising future for his fellow veterans, he takes every step he can to ensure just that, with or without proper collateral. At a dinner in his honor, Al accepts his new responsibility humbly, while making comments that are clearly about the community and the struggles ahead. While speaking about the future of the country, he makes an impassioned speech about veterans and farmers all seeking "and getting!" small loans. In fact, he stakes his own reputation, and the reputation of the bank, on his desire to help out his fellow veterans.

For Captain Fred Derry, reintegration is not so simple. Though he muses about his dreams in the B-17, these dreams are not so easily attained when he cannot find a suitable job to meet such ends. By the end of the film, he has lost his job, his wife, and the woman he truly loves. He winds up in a plane graveyard, reliving the trauma of the war in the shell of a bomber. *Round Trip?* painted on the side of one of the planes, reminds us that, yes, the ship made it through the war, but the hopes and fears of the men inside are ever present. As his father, miles away in the rundown family shack sits down and reads his citation for the Distinguished Flying Cross, given to his son for accomplishing a mission despite "complete disregard of his personal safety," Derry makes his way through the graveyard. Filmed at an army scrapheap for planes in Ontario, California, here reality and Hollywood narrative collide. Total war, the fight for air supremacy, the victories and the losses, and the trauma the war left in its wake all descend upon Fred Derry's face, as he relives the nightmare one last time before intending to leave Boone City for good.

In Abraham Polonsky's original review of the film, he criticizes Wyler and screenwriter Sherwood for their lack of emotional consciousness with characters like Fred Derry, allowing the "southern California mist" to create a Hollywood happy ending. But Wyler saw it otherwise:

> We wanted to say to millions of men like Fred Derry, that if they were being realistic, they could expect no special favors because they were veterans, and they would not get good jobs unless they were qualified to hold them. Therefore it was up to Fred to pick a trade or profession, and learn it, as thoroughly as he learned the trade of a bombardier.[36]

As Wyler notes about Derry standing in front of hundreds of scrapped planes, "At once the parallel was apparent: for four years Fred was trained, disciplined, and formed into a precise human instrument for destruction. Now his work is done, and he too has been thrown to the junk pile." Like the other veterans in the film and those adjusting to life back home in America, the future would take courage to face. Like the bombed roof of the chapel, the twisted metal husks of the B-17s will be transformed, renewed through a recognition of trauma, but with the hope for a better future.

The final moments of *The Best Years of Our Lives* echo those of *Mrs. Miniver*. A community comes together, not to reflect on death and the resolve needed for the sacrifices yet to come, but in celebration of a marriage and the hope for the future. André Bazin's famous analysis of Wyler's "ethical reverence for reality," through his *mise en scène* and Gregg Toland's cinematography, leads him to exclaim,

> Thank God, Wyler was not satisfied merely to be faithful to the psychological and social truth of the action (which truths, by the way, did not come off so well). He tried to find aesthetic equivalents for psychological and social truth in the *mise en scène*.[37]

Wyler needs no church this time. Instead, we are in the heart of the postwar American home, with our main characters all moving together toward the rehabilitation they so longed for in the opening scenes. As Homer and Wilma finally exchange their vows, we are free to scan the room for Fred and Peggy's reactions. After the ceremony, Fred walks over to Peggy and delivers a promise of struggle. "You know what it'll be, don't you Peggy? It may take us years to get anywhere. We'll have no money, no decent place to live. We'll have to work, get kicked around . . ." All through Fred's speech, Peggy just smiles. They are ready for the best years to come.

Although he expressed hesitancy for Wyler's return to Hollywood after the war, James Agee hailed the film as a triumph, within the confines of what Hollywood could achieve:

William Wyler has always seemed to me an exceedingly sincere and good director; he now seems one of the few great ones. He has come back from the war with a style of great purity, directness, and warmth, about as cleanly devoid of mannerism, haste, superfluous motion, aesthetic or emotional overreaching, as any I know; and I felt complete confidence, as I watched this work, that he could have handled any degree to which this material might have been matured as well as or even better than the job he was given to do.[38]

The Best Years of Our Lives won seven Academy Awards, including Best Actress, Supporting Actor, and Screenplay. Harold Russell won a special award for "bringing aid and comfort to disabled veterans through the medium of motion pictures." And William Wyler bookended the war years with his own statues. *Mrs. Miniver* and *The Best Years of Our Lives* both won Best Picture and earned Wyler Best Director awards.

POSTSCRIPT

In the years after the war, the specter of the Blacklist and loyalty oaths continued to tear through Hollywood. The conservative members of The Motion Picture Alliance for the Preservation of American Ideals' *Screen Guide for Americans*, published in 1947, outlined films to avoid, including ones that "deified" the common man. In the same year, Wyler became a founding member of the Committee for the First Amendment, which made a public showing against the blacklist but could not accomplish much in the face of the famous Waldorf Statement by the studio heads and the continued threat of the blacklist.

In a statement for the book *Hollywood on Trial*, Wyler claimed that he would never be able to make a film like *The Best Years of Our Lives* ever again, and warned about the political censorship then paralyzing film production. "In the last analysis," he writes, speaking directly to the audience, "you will suffer. You will be deprived of entertainment which stimulates you, and you will be given a diet of pictures which conform to arbitrary standards of Americanism."[39] Wyler would continue to fight in both his films and in Hollywood. At a meeting of the Screen Directors Guild in the fall of 1950, the director would not stand for anyone questioning his loyalty to the United States. During the tense meeting, which exposed the divisions at the heart of the guild and threatened its very existence, conservative members of the group led by Cecil B. DeMille suggested that perhaps a loyalty oath should be taken by the members. Wyler stood up and defended his past work, his service in the war, and his politics in a forceful speech:

I have signed other oaths too, long before any of these, and just as important. I have signed and sworn to . . . [uphold] and defend the Constitution of the United States of America against all enemies. That is what I am doing now . . . I am sick and tired of . . . having people question my loyalty to my country. The next time I hear somebody do it, I am going to kick the Hell out of him. I don't care how old he is or how big . . . I have seen some of these super-patriots from this room and in other rooms, and I have also seen as many real patriots, and they don't act like that or talk like that or wave the flag or pound their chests.[40]

Perhaps Wyler had a bit of Fred Derry still in him. Having directed two films celebrating the contributions of American and British citizens to the war effort, outlining their victories and struggles, and suffering nearly total hearing loss after flying missions across Germany and Italy to do the same for the Army Air Force, perhaps it should have been clear where his loyalties lay.

NOTES

1. Mulhouse was also the hometown of Captain Alfred Dreyfus, who had been exonerated for the false accusations of treason only a few years after Wyler was born.
2. Jan Herman, *A Talent for Trouble* (New York: Putnam, 1995), 14.
3. Herman, 13.
4. Ibid.
5. Mark Harris, *Five Came Back: A Story of Hollywood and the Second World War* (New York: Penguin Books, 2015), 4. Harris's book provides a full account of the transitions of Wyler, Ford, Capra, Huston, and Stevens from Hollywood to their time in WWII, and is an essential volume on the history of the era.
6. Herman, 238.
7. Thomas Schatz, *Boom and Bust: The American Cinema in the 1940s* (New York: Scribner, 1997), 1.
8. Sarah Kozloff, "Wyler's Wars," *Film History (New York, N.Y.)* 20, no. 4 (2008): 456. I am indebted to Kolzoff's work on Wyler during the war years, both the essay noted here and her BFI Companion to *The Best Years of Our Lives*. Both are invaluable sources for any Wyler scholar, and my work here runs parallel to her own.
9. Axel Madsen, *William Wyler: The Authorized Biography* (New York: Crowell, 1973), 214.
10. Bernard R. Kantor, Irwin R. Blacker, and Anne Kramer, *Directors at Work* (New York: Funk & Wagnalls, 1970), 418.
11. Herman, 253.
12. Herman, 235.
13. Ibid.
14. Bosley Crowther, "*Mrs. Miniver*, Excellent Picture of England at War, Opens at the Music Hall," *The New York Times*, June 5, 1942.
15. Bosley Crowther, "'Mrs. Miniver' Expresses the Inspiring Strength and Dignity of Ordinary Civilians under Total War," *The New York Times*, June 14, 1942.
16. Roger Manvell, *Films and the Second World War* (South Brunswick: A. S. Barnes, 1974), 161.

17. Markus Nornes and Fukushima Yukio, *The Japan/America Film Wars: World War II Propaganda and its Cultural Contexts* (Chur: Harwood Academic Publishers, 1944), 3.
18. Saverio Giovacchini, *Hollywood Modernism: Film and Politics in the Age of the New Deal* (Philadelphia: Temple University Press, 2001), 139.
19. Ibid.
20. Jeanine Basinger, *The World War II Combat Film: Anatomy of a Genre* (Middletown, CT: Wesleyan University Press, 2003), 112.
21. Ibid.
22. William Wyler, "No Magic Wand," *The Screen Writer* 2, no. 9 (February 1947): 112, <https://archive.org/details/screenwriterjun102scre/page/n457/mode/2up> (last accessed August 29, 2022).
23. Basinger, 114.
24. Army Air Forces, *25 Missions, The Story of the Memphis Belle* (Memphis: Memphis Belle Memorial Association, 1977).
25. Jeffrey Geiger, *American Documentary Film: Projecting the Nation* (Edinburgh: Edinburgh University Press, 2011), 149.
26. Daniel Marcus, "William Wyler's World War II Films and the Bombing of Civilian Populations," *Historical Journal of Film, Radio and Television* 29, no. 1 (March 2009): 79.
27. Geiger, 85.
28. Herman, 265.
29. James Agee, *Agee on Film* (Boston: Beacon Press, 1966), 89.
30. Herman, 275.
31. Harold Russell and Dan Ferullo, *The Best Years of My Life* (Middlebury, VT: Paul S. Eriksson Publisher, 1981), ix.
32. MacKinlay Kantor, "The Way Home," *Time* 44.6 (August 7, 1944): 15.
33. John Morton Blum, *V was for Victory: Politics and American Culture During World War II* (New York and London: Harcourt Brace Jovanovich, 1977), 70.
34. Dolores Hayden, *Building American Suburbia: Green Fields and Urban Growth, 1820-2000* (New York: Pantheon Books, 2003), 8.
35. Kozloff, 462.
36. Wyler, "No Magic Wand," 110.
37. André Bazin, "William Wyler, or the Jansenist of Directing," in *Bazin at Work: Major Essays and Reviews from the Forties and Fifties*, trans. Alain Piette and Bert Cardullo, ed. Bert Cardullo (New York: Routledge, 1997), 6. (Originally published as "William Wyler ou le janséniste de la mise en scene," *Revue du Cinéma* no. 10 (February 1948)).
38. Agee, 232.
39. Gordon Kahn, *Hollywood on Trial: The Story of the Ten Who Were Indicted* (New York: Boni & Gaer, 1948), 221.
40. Kevin Brianton, *Hollywood Divided: The 1950 Screen Directors Guild Meeting and the Impact of the Blacklist* (Lexington: University Press of Kentucky, 2016), 65.

CHAPTER II

Turning the Other Cheek: Wyler's Pacifism Trilogy—*Friendly Persuasion* (1956), *The Big Country* (1958), and *Ben-Hur* (1959)

John M. Price

The representation and evaluation of *Friendly Persuasion* (1956), *The Big Country* (1858), and *Ben-Hur* (1959) as William Wyler's pacifist trilogy should in no way be taken to suggest a premeditated plan, on the part of Wyler, to create a three-pronged project unified by a common issue. The connecting of these three films as a trilogy is, of course, a subsequent projection by film analysts and is not a uniform analysis. In 1979, Michael Anderegg lumped all three films into one chapter of his book and entitled it "Pacifism and Violence,"[1] but although Anderegg does discuss pacifism in connection with the first two films, he never once mentions pacifism in connection with *Ben-Hur*. Jan Herman's 1995 *A Talent for Trouble* has a chapter entitled "Pacifist's Dilemma" that deals only with *Friendly Persuasion*. The other two films each have their own chapters.[2] Needless to say, Herman never uses the term "trilogy." Similarly, in 2013, Gabriel Miller also uses the title "Pacifist's Dilemma" for a chapter in his book.[3] Although this one chapter is dedicated to all three films, he does not refer to them as a pacifist trilogy either. Despite the lack of authors employing the term *trilogy*, the thematic link between these three entries into the Wyler canon is clear. Less clear is deciphering Wyler's view towards pacifism, a difficulty particularly on view in Miller's analysis.

Wyler once opined that a motion picture should say something,[4] and while this seems slightly disingenuous when one thinks of Wyler's more frivolous fare, there is no mistaking that there is more gravitas in Wyler's postwar films. Even *Roman Holiday* (1953) is not the lighthearted escapism one would expect of a romantic comedy. It is understandable that Wyler's military experience in the Second World War would lead him to create films that were weightier than much of his earlier work, and that, as a disabled veteran, he would want to tackle a story like *The Best Years of Our Lives* (1946), which deals intensely with the struggles of returning serviceman to assimilate back into society. However, in *Friendly Persuasion*, *The Big Country*, and *Ben-Hur*, Wyler examines the more universal topic of war in general, and even more broadly, the very nature of violence. In his pacifism trilogy, Wyler is undoubtedly wrestling with his own participation in war and is evolving an ethos toward the question of "when to fight."

To summarize the thematic and narrative aspects that these three films have in common, also reveals the ways in which they differ. *Friendly Persuasion* is the story of a man of religious principle, a Quaker, and a man of peace. He is tested by the assault of a violent world on his family. When pressed, he is ready to hold his beliefs in abeyance, but he does not. Conversely, his son, who is much more afraid to not fight than to fight, does in fact go against his creed. The thematic roadmap of this story begins with religious principles which are tested and fail in one case and barely succeed in another. In *The Big Country*, we also have a seemingly peace-loving protagonist, but his principles are not religiously based. In his case, he will not fight when provoked because he sets the agenda in his life—he only fights on his terms. He condemns his father's death in a duel as unnecessary, but he is willing to fight one in the end. As in *Friendly Persuasion*, here is a hero tempted to violence by a threat to someone he cares about, but in this film, he gives into the provocation. This story starts from non-religious conviction which the main character cannot hold onto. Lastly, in *Ben-Hur*, we also have a man of principle. In this case, his convictions are more racial and ethnic than religious, although for this character, religion and ethnicity are closely interwoven. This character is also tested by a violent world's assault on his family, but he eventually turns from his secular allegiances to a presumably transcendent one.

Wyler seems ambivalent toward the role that religion plays in pacifism. On one hand, in *The Big Country*, the would-be pacifist, who is not based in religious conviction whatsoever, is the one who most easily jettisons his peaceful ways. However, in *Friendly Persuasion*, when we have two characters, in the same family, that have strong religious convictions against fighting, one fights, albeit with great difficulty, and the other restrains this urge. Perhaps the last example is Wyler's final evaluation of the significance of religion in the issue of to fight or not fight. In *Ben-Hur*, the main character, like Wyler's ethos, seems conflicted toward religion. One moment he professes that God has helped him survive in the galleys, but later, when told that his enemies will be punished by God, he avows that he does not believe in miracles. While the hero is Jewish, such comments lead one to believe that it is more important to him as an element of his nationality than as religious fervor. Of all Wyler's pacifists, he is the most filled with violent desire, until he is forestalled from his anger by a whole new religion. Despite what this seems to suggest, it is highly unlikely that Wyler, himself Jewish, meant to advocate Christianity as the answer to his pacifism dilemma.

Also, the two characters from *Friendly Persuasion* are Christian and they have mixed success at adhering to their beliefs.

What affirmations then, if any, does Wyler make in this trilogy? Wyler's youth certainly influenced his attitude toward violence; he spent the First World War watching combat up close. No doubt it created in him, to some degree, a revulsion for war, and perhaps, for violence in general. If such an aversion to violence did exist early in Wyler, it did not prevent him from launching his film career on the violence integral to the Western genre, albeit an early-screen, sanitized violence. Whatever his view on violence was early in his career, the futility of war would, late in his career, as demonstrated by this trilogy, come to be of personal significance and consternation.

If Wyler did have a youthful revulsion of warfare, it would have mirrored the attitude of most Americans toward war in the 1930s. At that time, a vast majority of Americans had come to view their nation's involvement in the First World War as a mistake. This sentiment is the underlining cause of the isolationism which was so prevalent in the US between the wars. However, Wyler had become convinced that Nazi aggression must be repulsed. This attitude is best demonstrated by a certain scene in *Mrs. Miniver* (1942) and, perhaps even more so, by Wyler's later defense of his handling of that scene. Mrs. Miniver (Greer Garson) comes upon a shot-down German pilot. The soldier avers in a rant to Miniver how the German Reich will triumph over the people of England. Wyler was criticized for not treating the German people in a more even-handed manner. Wyler responded, "If I had several Germans in the film, I wouldn't mind having one decent young fellow, but I've only got one German and if I make this picture, this one German is going to be a typical little Nazi son-of-a-bitch."[5] Whatever hesitation Wyler may have once had toward war, *Mrs. Miniver* clearly displays Wyler's belief in the need to fight back, and if the film does not demonstrate it, his joining the US Army Air Corps, and personal participation in the War, certainly did. When Wyler returned from war, however, his ardor was somewhat dampened by the horrors of war and his own personal injury. His first film, *The Best Years of Our Lives*, while saluting those who had fought, did not gloss over the horrendous price tag of that fight. This homage to the sacrifice of servicemen, even if the violence was justified, would lead Wyler to go far beyond the parameters of this film and delve into the very essence of violence itself.

Wyler's first descent into this inscrutable topic, *Friendly Persuasion*, was the story of a family of Quakers who attempt to adhere to the nonviolent core of their faith despite the fact that the ravages of the American Civil War creep ever closer to their family farm. Wyler's attitude towards Quakerism was presented, at least in a superficial analysis, when he stated, "The trouble with Quakers is that there aren't enough of them."[6] He also made his view of pacifism known in an interview with *Picture Show and Film Pictorial*:

I have never seen any great virtue in the American tradition of punching a guy in the nose if he said something you didn't like. It only proves who can punch the quickest or the hardest, nothing else. The problem that intrigues me is whether people can have faith in a man who doesn't punch.[7]

While such a statement displays a tacit admiration for pacifism, it falls far short of a ringing endorsement, as these three films show. Wyler did make it clear that despite any admiration he might have for pacifism, he could not go along with it completely:

I have always been sort of a pacifist . . . But I am not an all-out pacifist of the Quaker style. That's why in *Friendly Persuasion* we lay out the problem, but we couldn't really answer it. It was not our job to resolve it. How far can a pacifist go? . . . In *The Big Country*, we had a man who also had pacifist notions and didn't believe in fighting. Even at the risk of being thought a coward.[8]

It is the seemingly contradictory nature of certain comments by Wyler on the subject of pacifism that has led some critics to see his position as ambivalent.

Friendly Persuasion was to be an adaptation of a novel by Jessamyn West—a second cousin of Richard Nixon. Her original work was a loose collection of previously published stories, but she never saw her book as advocating pacifism. The rights were initially bought by Frank Capra for his new Liberty Films, and although screenwriter Michael Wilson finished a second draft of a script in 1947, the project never got off the ground. When Paramount bought Liberty, the script, among all other Liberty properties, became theirs and it was from Paramount that Wyler eventually bought the rights. He was, however, unhappy with the original script by Wilson, which he felt, like the book, did not focus enough on the pacifist dilemma. Back in the late 1930s, the writer, Wilson, had joined the Communist Party, and despite serving in the United States Marine Corps during the Second World War, he was subpoenaed by the House Committee on Un-American Activities (HUAC). When he refused to cooperate with HUAC, he was blacklisted by Hollywood. Wilson became a member of the infamous "Hollywood Ten." Surprisingly, shortly after being deemed an "unfriendly" witness, Wilson received the screenwriting Oscar for *A Place in the Sun* (George Stevens, 1951). Wyler's dissatisfaction with the original script meant rewrites and whether it was the danger in using a blacklisted writer or just his lack of enthusiasm for Wilson's initial efforts, the job of revising went to West and Wyler's brother, Robert. The question as to just how major these revisions were would lead to a feud about screen credit, and would ultimately lead to *Friendly Persuasion* being the first and only Hollywood film to be released without any screenwriting credit in the opening titles. Wyler would later claim that he had suggested all three be given screen credit, but the studio knew the political backlash that Wilson's name could bring about, and so no one was given credit.[9] Furthermore, Wyler would considerably alter West and his brother's version during the actual shooting. Wyler's main concern was that this film must be the story of a man who is tempted to reject his faith and act with violence, and yet, at the crucial moment, does not. As a man who had personally answered the call and participated in war, why was this perspective so important to Wyler? There must have been something in Wyler that was not completely at ease with his personal decision to fight.

The main character in *Friendly Persuasion* is the father of the Quaker family, Jess Birdwell. Both Wyler and West wanted Gary Cooper to play Birdwell, but prior to the film, Cooper expressed his displeasure at Wyler's interpretation of the character.

> Cooper: "There comes a time in a picture of mine when the people watching me expect me to do something."
> West: "I know it. You'll do something."
> Cooper: "What?"
> West: "Refrain. You will furnish your public with the refreshing picture of a strong man refraining."[10]

West had been converted to Wyler's view that Jess had to be tempted to violence. Cooper, of course, was not totally unfamiliar with the role of a reluctant warrior, as both *Sergeant York* (Howard Hawks, 1941) and *High Noon* (Fred Zinnemann, 1952) attest, but he was correct concerning audience expectations for violent resolutions. Guy Westwell sees this aspect of film as part of an indictment of society in general: "There is an entrenched preconception that war is necessary and positive and . . . this view is held in place by popular culture, including the cinema."[11] Indeed, it could be argued that any film that even tacitly advocated pacifism would be going against the very nature of movies. As Thorold Dickinson says, "warfare is cinegenic and goes with the grain of cinema."[12]

Hollywood does, indeed, have a long tradition of supporting the notion that the good guy overcomes the bad guy only through violence. Even in a lighthearted picture like John Ford's *The Quiet Man* (1952), despite Sean Thornton's (John Wayne) vow, after having killed a man in a boxing match, to never fight again, there is no doubt that a Ford–Wayne movie, even a comedy, will, or rather must, end in a fist fight between the hero and the bully. It is little wonder, therefore, that Dickinson would proclaim that "Every film that uses a stand-up fight as a solution accepts the idea of violence and wraps the audience yet more cosily in all its preconceptions."[13] For Wyler to present a hero who does not hit back thrusts him into conflict with a Hollywood maxim, expressed by film critic Bosley Crowther as, "Peace is a pious precept but fightin' is more excitin'."[4] Anderegg gives us an even more cynical description of Hollywood's treatment of characters who profess an adherence to nonviolence:

> In Hollywood's traditional depiction a pacifist is someone who refuses to fight or kill as long as he is not faced with any reason to do so, but who gives up his principles whenever a good, compelling, immediate, and personal motive presents itself. A pacifist will watch your children die but not his own.[5]

An example of this is in *High Noon*. Will Kane's bride (Grace Kelly), a Quaker, must shoot and kill the bad guy. As Anderegg states, "Quakerism . . . ends up seeming like little more than a quaint veneer, one of the ingredients of which happens to be nonviolence . . . it comes perilously close to making nonsense of the very virtues the film tries to exalt."[6] Hollywood presents Quakerism as charming but impractical and even foolish. In *The Angel and the Badman* (James Edward Grant, 1947), a wounded gunfighter (John Wayne) is convalescing with a family of Quakers. When he is told by his later-love-interest (Gail Russell) that Quakers believe that an act of violence can only hurt the perpetrator, he responds, "Well supposing somebody whacks you over the head with a branding iron, won't that hurt?" She replies only physically, and that only the doer can be hurt by a mean or evil act. Wayne's character asks, "Are there very many of your Quakers?" She answers, "Very few." He comments, "Sort of figured that." Many believe that, despite its claim to seriously handle the issue of pacifism, *Friendly Persuasion* presents us with Quakers that renown film critic Pauline Kael says, "are there only to violate their convictions,"[17] or as Anderegg accuses the film, "none of these pacific Quakers really holds fast against an immediate challenge to his or her faith."[18]

Regardless of such analysis, Wyler's equivocacy toward nonviolence can clearly be seen in the way he presents all three of the major characters in *Friendly Persuasion*. The mother, Eliza Birdwell (Dorothy McGuire), is not only the religious cornerstone of her family, she is also one of the elders of her church. She appears to be the most unrelenting of the three main characters. Due to her strong religious conviction, she is appalled that her son, Josh Birdwell (Anthony Perkins), is strongly considering fighting in the war. Eliza seems the most ardent, but she never faces actual combat as her son does, or a moment of truth like her husband resists. Nonetheless, Eliza does have her own moment of weakness. A goose, which Eliza considers a pet, is about to be eaten by a Confederate soldier. Eliza grabs a broom, begins striking the soldier repeatedly, yelling that the goose is a pet. Later, to Jess's amusement and Eliza's chagrin, her "violent" outburst is related to the entire family as

"Momma wacked a Reb." While this is obviously being played for humor, it reveals a serious component to the issue Wyler is examining. Wyler seems to be agreeing with others as to the impracticality of total nonviolence, since everyone, including Eliza, has something for which they will fight. However, this is equally problematic for Wyler's fluctuating conviction. If you concede that in certain circumstances, it is okay to strike back, then each person will see different circumstances as qualifying. In such a world, would fighting against Hitler be as justifiable as fighting for him?

Miller believes that "much of the film . . . is too lighthearted to be taken seriously as an examination of the moral issue it raises."[19] The specific incidents of humor that Miller points out are the Sunday ritual of Jess racing his neighbor Sam Jordan (Robert Middleton) to church services, the strife between the youngest boy and the goose, and Jess's purchase of an organ despite Eliza's religious objection. The assessment that such moments diminish the seriousness of the film's issue is not valid, and sometimes even contradicted by Miller himself. The Sunday races demonstrate that even a man of peace can have a competitive nature, which one could determine to be the ultimate source of all violence. It also shows that, unlike Eliza, Jess is not unrelenting in his beliefs, which makes his later picking up of the gun not completely out of character for him. When the youngest Birdwell, Little Jess (Richard Eyer), threatens to kill the goose, the mother admonishes him for "talk of killing." The ongoing feud between Little Jess and the goose, as Miller even points out, "immediately introduce[s] the subject of . . . the human tendency toward violence."[20] Jess's purchase of an organ, when he knows his wife will not want it in the house, and even more his defiance of her in keeping it, once again demonstrates that Jess is a man of conviction but also of adaptability in his faith, and again foreshadows more crucial junctures in the narrative.

Eliza's problem with her son's decision to fight is not just one of a protective mother who does not want to see her son killed, but also that of any parent who feels their child is rejecting the tenets upon which they had raised them. What she fails to appreciate is that Josh is decidedly a reluctant warrior. "Mother, I hate fighting. I don't want to die. I don't know if I could kill anyone if I tried. But I have to try as long as other people do." Indeed, when Josh does get eventually into a battle, he fires his first shot with his eyes closed and his second shot with tears in his eyes. Wyler had some concern that the story was becoming Josh's and not Jess's. If this were so, it might be due to the fact that, subconsciously, Wyler saw his personal decisions best personified by the son, Josh. Yet, Wyler's struggle with the issue of nonviolence and his participation in the War is what actually makes the father the main character (being played by a big-name star like Gary Cooper solidifies the point). Jess, after all, is at the center of this crisis of conscience. If the son represented Wyler's real-life actions, but the father held Wyler's admiration, it plainly shows Wyler's own uncertainty towards his personal decision to fight. While Wyler takes great pains to present Eliza and Josh with earnest understanding, it is Jess Birdwell that Wyler holds aloft as the man of peace, who picks up the gun in readiness, but does not use it, even when it would certainly be justified to do so. Miller believes that the fact that Wyler has Josh not only fight, but even kill, as well as the fact that the runaway slave Enoch (Joel Fluellen) also wants to fight, demonstrates "Wyler's belief that pacifism is no defense against hatred and racism."[21] Yet how would Miller explain his analysis of Wyler's view on pacifism in light of Jess's ultimate decision to not kill.

Wyler's eagerness to fairly display all three characters' views on the question of whether to fight or not makes it difficult to pronounce a clear Wyler viewpoint on pacifism. In fact, Miller credits Wyler with "avoiding the impression of prioritizing one position over the other" as typified by the staged-in-depth shot (Figure 11.1) when Josh comes downstairs, rifle in hand.[22] However, if Wyler is truly presenting all sides equally, then it should be difficult to sum up his view on this issue. West said that in Wyler's view, "evil . . . had to be resisted with violence."[23] This does not sound like ambivalence.

> Although Wyler's film has sometimes been described as an homage to pacifism, it is hardly that; his dramatic framings and editing invariably undercut its value as a viable philosophy in today's world. The film's idyllic mood reflects Wyler's fondness for the Birdwell's way of life . . . these scenes function more as a wish fulfillment dream than a realistic portrait of life.[24]

Figure 11.1 Staging-in-depth to demonstrate dissimilar views toward violence simultaneously (*Friendly Persuasion*, 1956)

Here, Miller too claims to see through to Wyler's true feeling about pacifism. However, Miller also says that Wyler's staging of certain scenes and certain dialogue "points to the director's ambivalence toward the Quakers' philosophy."[25] It seems that the ambivalence lies in the ability of analysts to characterize Wyler's attitude on the subject. Miller also points out that the West and Robert Wyler script included praise from Abraham Lincoln for the Quakers' faith, but Miller feels that director Wyler cut it because it "lent more credence to the Quaker position than he wanted to show."[26] If this assessment is correct, then this action is not ambivalent toward pacifism either. However, Lincoln's praise could not carry more credibility for the pacifist cause than does Sam Jordan's utterance that he would "like to see someone hold out for a better way of settling things," as does Jess's ultimate refusal to shoot when he has the opportunity. Wyler may just have seen the inclusion of Lincoln's words as too didactic and, given the above examples, redundant to a lofty evaluation of pacifism.

Those who see *Friendly Persuasion* as a rejection of Quakerism, and an indictment of pacifism's feasibility, do, however, have plenty to support their appraisal. As many have correctly noted, Josh completely jettisons his family's religious values, although the Quakerism gainsayers would be forced to admit that this is far from an easy decision for Josh. Jess is also ready to abandon his beliefs when he picks up a gun and seems ready to use it. Even Eliza resorts to "violence" when her "pet" is threatened. So, it would seem that, as the detractors point out, Hollywood, and Wyler specifically, create pacifists "only to violate their convictions." However, those who opine that the extreme pacifism of Quakers "may be laudatory, [but] their ideals are seemingly out of sync with the world they live in,"[27] must still account for Jess's abstention from violence at the crucial moment of its justified implementation. Ultimately, determining Wyler's opinion on pacifism in *Friendly Persuasion* is elusive, as evidenced by analysts who claim that Wyler's position is both clear and ambivalent.

Miller also asserts that in *The Big Country*, Wyler "would explore similar issues with the same muddled results."[28] Again Miller assesses Wyler's view of pacifism as vacillating, and specifically when describing the last scene of this film. Miller points out that after seemingly distancing his audience from violence throughout the film, Wyler has the Terrill's foreman, Steve Leech (Charlton Heston) and the other ranch hands join their boss for a final gunfight, complete with music swelling. This does, as Miller suggests, appear to applaud the *esprit de corps* of violent men. In Miller's view, "Wyler's shot of the two riding side by side, followed by the rest of the men, undercuts whatever power the pacifist message might have had."[29] However, there are at least a couple of other ways to see this final scene. In the first place, the sight of the men joining their boss with soaring music could be seen as sardonic. The Terrill–Hannassey feud, epitomized by the heads of each clan, Rufus Hannassey (Burl Ives) and

Major Henry Terrill (Charles Bickford), has been depicted as foolish throughout the film. Thus, these men riding to their meaningless deaths, cloaked in glory, certainly can be seen as an anti-violence message. Secondly, although they are very different, both the hero of *The Big Country*, James McKay (Gregory Peck), and Leech have their codes (as does Jess Birdwell). Yet, as Wyler shows with Jess Birdwell, one must sometimes be at least ready to alter his beliefs if the situation calls for it. McKay's earlier statements concerning non-violence are not forfeited, by McKay or the film, when Julie (Jean Simmons) is attacked, and McKay becomes ready to fight. As with Birdwell, Wyler seems to display the belief that conviction is not necessarily antithetical to adaptability. Leech, at first, professes that he will no longer do the Major's biding, specifically in terms of perpetrating violence, and yet in the end, joins his boss in the last futile endeavor. Ultimately, Leech cannot go against his code; he cannot change. McKay, the man of reason, has core beliefs but they are not adamantine. Therefore, there are several ways to see the film as not undercutting any pacifist message it might have made.

It is interesting that this foray by Wyler into the theme of violence versus nonviolence would be a Western. Indeed, *The Big Country* has been characterized as an anti-Western, since in it, Wyler deconstructs many myths of masculinity that he himself helped to create within the genre. Herman quotes Gregory Peck as describing *The Big Country* as "an anti-macho Western."[30] Anti-Western sentiments within the film can be most attributed to the central character who will not accept the Western code of behavior. Miller says of *The Big Country* that it "posit[s] that pacifism is antithetical to human nature or, at least, that it violates masculine codes of conduct."[31] First, to lump these two conditions as similar in any way, or even that one is a subset of the other, is to totally mischaracterize both. It can be argued, rather convincingly, that both *The Big Country* and *Friendly Persuasion* suggest that it is masculine codes of conduct that are in fact antithetical to human nature. McKay may eventually give into violence, but it is precisely his seemingly anti-violent ways that separate him from the masculine codes of the Terrills and the Hannasseys, and indeed from the Western genre specifically and Hollywood in general.

The Big Country is the story of James McKay, a man who comes out west to marry his fiancée, Patricia Terrill (Carroll Baker). As an ex-sea captain, McKay must have been a man of action, but he seems reticent to stand up to local bullies like Buck Hannassey (Chuck Connors). The Hannasseys are the great enemies of his fiancée's father, the Major. This apparent lack of courage loses McKay both respect and, eventually, his fiancée. Like Jess Birdwell, McKay is unwilling to fight, but there is an important difference. Birdwell is adamantly opposed to fighting and even though he has prepared himself to use a gun, he does not. McKay's reluctance, on the other hand, is only because, as an erstwhile captain, he will decide when and where he will fight. This is really not pacifism at all. McKay rejects fighting when circumstances attempt to force him to, and he refuses to fight to prove anything to others. He believes a man only has to prove his courage to himself. When Leech tries to get him to ride an unbroken horse, McKay says, "some other time," and then goes back and rides the horse when no one is around. More significant is when Leech attempts to provoke McKay into a fist fight, again in front of everyone, but McKay again refuses. Instead, McKay goes to Leech's quarters later, in the middle of the night, and agrees to fight him in the middle of nowhere with no one around. So, despite Wyler's admiration for Jess Birdwell's readiness but restraint, perhaps the director feels more akin to McKay.

The fact that McKay is more than willing to fight for the right reason, just like Wyler, is stressed in the climax of the film. Buck Hannassey strikes the friend of McKay's ex-fiancée, Julie Maragon, the woman to whom McKay's love interest has now been transferred. When this happens, McKay does not hesitate to attack Buck. Despite having said, earlier in the film, that his father was killed in a senseless duel, the instigation of which no one could remember, McKay is now ready, on his terms, to face Buck with a gun. Like Birdwell, however, McKay does not take violent advantage of his enemy when the opportunity presents itself.

Although Wyler may have felt more kinship to McKay than Jess Birdwell, he still demonstrates his idealistic preference for Jess Birdwell's inactive brand of courage when, after the McKay–Leech fight scene, a fight which Wyler shoots in an extremely wide shot (Figure 11.2), in which Leech and McKay are minute figures lost in the landscape, Wyler visually suggests the futility of violence and the insignificance of their actions. When they have beaten each other soundly without any clear winner, McKay says, "Now tell me Leech, what did we prove?" Both Birdwell and McKay feel that they are men who cannot be provoked into violence by others, but they clearly can—at least to the brink of violence.

Figure 11.2 Fight scene shot with extremely long lens to express the futility of violence (*The Big Country*, 1958)

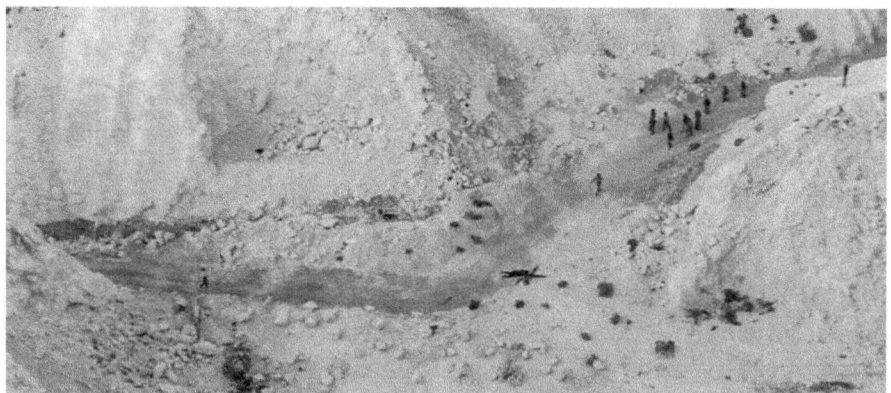

Figure 11.3 God's-eye expressing detachment from or disapproval of human violence (*The Big Country*, 1958)

Wyler, due to his propensity in *The Big Country* for extremely high wide shots at moments of violence (Figure 11.3), is described by Anderegg as being "a cool, dispassionate observer."[32] These shots do not necessarily suggest that Wyler is dispassionate on this theme. On the contrary, these shots observe the senselessness of violence through a god's-eye view, and this sentiment is hardly dispassionate. Anderegg also accuses *The Big Country* of a kind of moral relativism. He states that "the designation of hero and villain . . . becomes less important than the simple inevitability of conflict."[33] This again seems strained. While there is an underlining suggestion that violence is inevitable in the film, there is no mystery as to who is hero and who is villain. There is no moral relativism between McKay and Buck Hannassey in Wyler's perspective. The only real dichotomy between good guy and bad guy, in this film, comes within the character of Leech—the man who comes to see what is right, but cannot find his way through "the code" to do it. Wyler seems to be suggesting that milieu can subjugate one's inclination to a loftier goal.

Miller sees McKay and Eliza Birdwell, and he even mentions Grace Kelly in *High Noon*, as examples of the pacifist tenets being undercut. "When faced with an implacable and irreconcilable enemy, the nonviolent position proves untenable."[34] Not only does this view seem backed up by Wyler's real-life experience, certainly he would have described Hitler as "an implacable and irreconcilable enemy," but there are also many instances in *Friendly Persuasion* and *The Big Country* that uphold this interpretation. Still, there are also those moments that deny it—such as Jess's refusal to use violence. Furthermore, even those moments that Miller believes show pacifism to be unsustainable are often accompanied by Wyler's unwillingness to completely reject pacifism as a viable, or at least explorable, alternative. The notion that pacifism might actually be attainable is conspicuously embraced in the last entry in the trilogy, *Ben-Hur*.

Miller concludes that "what links the three films is Wyler's rejection, in each case, of the pacifist, nonviolent philosophy."[35] Not only does this contradict Miller's own characterization of Wyler's view as ambivalent, it clearly does not apply to *Ben-Hur* at all. The other two films may, due to Wyler's even-handling of a complex issue, invite such analysis, but *Ben-Hur* presents a denouement that is blanketed in a peace-loving solution to all hate. Miller describes Judah Ben-Hur (Charlton Heston) as eventually converting to Jesus's doctrine of forgiveness, but also says that Wyler pays little attention to this aspect of the plot.[36] It is extremely unobservant to say that little attention is paid to this when it is the means by which the entire conflict within Judah and between him and his world are resolved.

Miller is correct when he says that Wyler's film has altered the original novel by General Lew Wallace in significant ways, such as making the relationship between Judah and his childhood friend Messala (Stephen Boyd) central to the plot and not merely cursory as Wallace had.[37] Anderegg concurs. He describes the original novel as dense and pretentious and that the friendship between Judah and Messala "lacks conviction," and the rupture of their friendship "happens abruptly and with little motivation."[38] A reemphasis is, of course, to be expected as deep examination of complex emotions, and friendships particularly, is Wyler's forte. Wyler certainly makes the story of a friendship gone wrong the central catalyst for the narrative, but it is only, despite its plot significance, a springboard from which to launch the themes of hatred, revenge, and pacifism. Conflicts that are resolved ultimately in the adopting of a new faith.

Ben-Hur, which many unfortunately dismiss as another toga-and-sandal spectacle, despite a script that was worked on by Maxwell Anderson, Gore Vidal, and Christopher Fry, among others, in many ways explores the dilemma of fighting back at greater depth than either of the first two films in this trilogy. In this film, the Roman Messala, childhood friend of the Jewish prince, Judah Ben-Hur, returns to Judea as a grown man and a Roman tribune. He wishes to use Judah to squash out any resistance to Rome and Judah refuses, thus ending their friendship. When the chance comes to strike back at his erstwhile friend and companion, Messala sends Judah to the galleys for a crime he did not commit, and Judah's mother and sister (Martha Scott and Cathy O'Donnell, respectively) into prison. In some ways, the film represents a very simple action and reaction narrative—revenge tales being a very common storyline in the movies. Messala destroys Judah and his family and thus Judah seeks retaliation. Yet both the story and Wyler do not seem to be okay with what many would see as justified violence. Normally, an action sequence, such as the famous chariot race, would be the climax of the film. Instead, we see how Judah's obsession with revenge produces a hollow victory. Judah also learns that his mother and sister have not died in prison, but have contracted leprosy and live outside the city in isolation. What is most striking though is when Judah professes that he does not feel that this evil done to his family was Messala's fault. Rather, Judah sees the responsibility as lying with the evil that is Rome. For Judah, Rome, not Messala, is the true villain, and needs to be resisted with violence. Certainly Wyler, who stood up to the evil of Hitler, and saw it as a necessity, would understand Judah's resolve to fight back against Roman occupation and oppression. This defiance is expressed when Judah rejects his adopted Roman identity of Young Arrius and instead insists defiantly, "I am Judah Ben-Hur!"

Wyler once joked that it took a Jew to make a good movie about Jesus, and indeed the subtitle of both this film and the original written text is *A Tale of the Christ*. Despite this alternate denotation, the central character of the New Testament is only tangential to Judah's story and serves as basically a foil to Judah's struggles. It is this backdrop, however, that may well offer a final insight into Wyler's assessment of pacifism. Although the teachings of Christ strike at the heart of Judah's obsession with revenge, Wyler still does not completely abandon, to the messianic message, the idea that some evil must be opposed. Sheik Ilderim (Hugh Griffith), who wants Judah to drive his horses to victory in the great chariot race, reacts to the peace-loving words of forgiveness that his guest, Balthasar (Finlay Currie) expresses. The Sheik says, "Balthasar is a good man, but until all men are like him, we must keep our swords bright." Wyler is definitely still defending the need for violence in a world full of evil men.

In contrast to the philosophy of the Sheik and Judah's vengeful obsession stands Judah's love interest, Esther (Haya Harareet). "Esther functions as the link between the secular story and the more religious one, since she is the person who leads Judah to Christ."[39] As such a link, she performs a similar function as Eliza Birdwell. It is Judah's viewing of the crucifixion, however, and not Esther's admonishments, that completes Judah's conversion. He relates to Esther the effect of this experience, "I felt his voice take the sword out of my hand." Miller sees Judah's conversion as embracing "a unity with his people and a vision of brotherhood that is seemingly divorced from hatred."[40] Unfortunately, it is impossible to interpret Judah's conversion as a sign of these two "embracings." In fact, these two outcomes are incompatible. The unity with his people, which Judah's renunciation of his Roman name and affirmation of his Jewish identity, is the "embracing" that has set his feet on the path of violent resistance to the oppressors of his people. The vision of brotherhood is an outcome that transcends ethnicity and tribalism.

Wyler is famous for saying that cinematic techniques should never call attention to themselves; they should not overpower the story or performances. However, a certain shot in *Ben-Hur* seems to violate this. Early in the story, when Judah is being dragged to the galleys, he is given a restorative drink of water by the Christ. Then when Christ is on his way to crucifixion, and Judah attempts to

Figure 11.4 Staging-in-depth and deep focus expressing the futility of kindness when faced with extreme violence . . . or perhaps the exploitation of violence for good (*Ben-Hur*, 1959)

reciprocate the kindness, a Roman soldier kicks away the gourd filled with water before the condemned Messiah can drink any. The shot that follows (Figure 11.4) is such a striking staging-in-depth (and width) that it certainly draws attention to itself, despite Wyler's code of unintrusive filmmaking. In terms of thematic evaluation, however, it may provide insight into Wyler's ultimate opinion of pacifism. Interpreting this scene could lead one to resolve that the kindness, which a "divine" being can disseminate, is thwarted when attempted by mere humans. If this is the case, Wyler would not be the first individual to observe the infeasibility, if not impossibility, of following the tenets of Christianity.

Nonetheless, at a pivotal moment, Esther summarizes the destructive nature of Judah's path of violence: "You seem to be now the very thing you set out to destroy. Giving evil for evil. Hatred is turning you to stone. It's as though you had become Messala." Esther espouses what must be seen as the film's (and perhaps Wyler's final word on the subject) rejection of violence—the idea that violence is never a solution. This is an embracing of pacifism at a level far beyond both *Friendly Persuasion* and *The Big Country*. If there is one voice in all three films that is nearly simpatico with Wyler, it is no doubt Sam Jordan's wish, in *Friendly Persuasion*, that a better way could somehow be found. This is not to suggest that Wyler regretted his personal decision to fight in the War, only that he undeniably created a trilogy that, at least in the abstract, advocates "turning the other cheek," even if he himself was personally unable to do so.

NOTES

1. Michael A. Anderegg, *William Wyler* (Boston: Twayne, 1979), 187–203.
2. Jan Herman, *A Talent for Trouble: The Life of Hollywood's Most Acclaimed Director, William Wyler* (New York: G. P. Putnam's Sons, 1995): "Pacifist's Dilemma," 366–79; "The Big Muddy," 380–92; and "*Ben-Hur*," 393–410.

3. Gabriel Miller, "The Pacifist Dilemma," in *William Wyler: The Life and Films of Hollywood's Most Celebrated Director* (Lexington, KY: University Press of Kentucky, 2013), 335–65.
4. "Don't Play 'Safe' on Pix-Wyler," *Variety* 176, no. 5 (October 12, 1949): 20.
5. *Directed by William Wyler*, directed by Aviva Slesin (American Masters, 1986).
6. Ibid.
7. *Picture Show and Film Pictorial* 69, no. 1809 (November 30, 1957).
8. Curtis Hanson, "William Wyler, Pt. 1. An Interview," *Cinema* 3, no. 5 (Summer 1967): 23.
9. A very detailed account of the entire political and legal battles over the screenwriting credit for *Friendly Persuasion* can be found in Joseph Dmohowski's "The *Friendly Persuasion* (1956) Screenplay Controversy: Michael Wilson, Jessamyn West, and the Hollywood Blacklist," *Historical Journal of Film, Radio and Television* 22, no. 4 (2002): 491–512.
10. Jessamyn West, *To See the Dream* (New York: Harcourt, Brace, 1957), 193–4.
11. Guy Westwell, "Peace Cinema: Religious Pacifism and Anti-War Sensibility in *Friendly Persuasion* (1956)," *Open Screens* 2, no. 1 (May 23, 2019): 2, <https://doi.org/10.16995/os.11> (last accessed August 24, 2022).
12. Thorold Dickinson, "Films to Unite the Nations," in *Film: Book 2 – Films of Peace and War*, ed. Robert Hughes (New York: Grove Press, 1962), 149.
13. Dickinson, 150.
14. Bosley Crowther, "War and Peace on Range in 'Big Country,'" *The New York Times*, October 2, 1958, 44.
15. Anderegg, 190.
16. Anderegg, 191.
17. Pauline Kael, "Marlon Brando: An American Hero," *Atlantic* 217, no. 3 (March 1966): 75.
18. Anderegg, 191.
19. Miller, 342.
20. Miller, 341.
21. Miller, 344.
22. Ibid
23. West, 94.
24. Miller, 341.
25. Miller, 342.
26. Miller, 448 (in "Notes").
27. Miller, 342
28. Miller, 349
29. Miller, 357.
30. Herman, 382.
31. Miller, 362.
32. Anderegg, 194.
33. Anderegg, 195.
34. Miller, 358.
35. Miller, 365.
36. Miller, 359
37. Miller, 360–1.
38. Anderegg, 198.
39. Miller, 363.
40. Miller, 364.

PART V
Global Wyler

CHAPTER 12

William Wyler's Voyage to Italy: *Roman Holiday* (1953), Progressive Hollywood, and the Cold War

Anthony Smith

In early September 1953, Hollywood's newest star Audrey Hepburn graced the cover of *Time* magazine.[1] A sketch of her youthful face stood out against a background of Rome's Trevi Fountain and a cone of gelato, Italy's version of American ice cream. The occasion was her movie debut in William Wyler's *Roman Holiday* (1953). The film offered a light, but also subtle, even sad, romance involving Hepburn's character, an innocent princess visiting Rome who escapes from her uptight guardians to explore the city. Out on her own, she meets an American newspaper man played by Gregory Peck. Together they spend a day and night wandering the sites of Rome and falling in love, only to realize the princess–commoner romance can never last.

Critics and audiences embraced the film. *The New York Times* called *Roman Holiday* a "delightfully romantic and wistful comedy." *Newsweek* called it one of "the most original, and endearing comedies to be credited to Hollywood in recent years." *Variety* approvingly wrote, "William Wyler makes his first venture into comedy since 1935 and the switch from heavy drama is all to the good." Al Hine, writing in *Holiday*, noted the movie was "a return to an older tradition of light comedy . . . that will stick in your memory for a long time." The *Hollywood Reporter* remarked on the film's box office success enjoying crowds both in the US and particularly overseas. Referencing an executive from Paramount, the studio responsible for the film, the trade paper stated, "Besides its boxoffice [*sic*] performance 'Roman Holiday' is doing more than any film in years to advance the general prestige of Hollywood films abroad."[2]

Paramount Pictures emphasized the film as completely made in the Eternal City. *Life* magazine, in fact, described *Roman Holiday* as a "first-rate travelogue."[3] The film was the latest, and most successful, instance of American moviemakers decamping to Italy after the war.[4] Taking advantage of low labor costs, restricted money from profits that could not be sent back to the US, and the allure of a city in the midst of revival, Hollywood producers found Rome an attractive city to make movies. Rome had, surprisingly, become the most exciting place in the world of cinema by the early 1950s. Italian filmmakers such as Roberto Rossellini and Vittorio De Sica had captured the attention of critics and audiences on both sides of the Atlantic for their movies of ordinary, working-class people and their everyday struggles. It was not only this new movement in movies, known as neorealism,[5] however, that made Rome special. The refurbished film production center at Cinecittà also signaled to the world that Italy was back in business after the disruptions of the Second World War and ready for film production. From the studios just south of the city to the bohemian Via Margutta to the Spanish Steps, people from all over flocked to Rome, if not to participate, then bask, in the excitement of the city's latest and most modern incarnation.[6]

But amidst all the glamour, new money, and old desires that circulated around movie-made Rome, lay another reality, one where Italian filmmaking, Cold War politics, and Hollywood blacklists entwined in the production of *Roman Holiday*. For the film's highly regarded director William Wyler found himself, amidst the charms of the city, drawn into the Red Scare that was waging its war against the American film community. Dalton Trumbo's work as a blacklisted writer on the story and script has overshadowed this broader anti-communism that informed the backstory of the movie.[7] In Wyler's case, no place, including Rome, remained safe from the accusations and paranoia of the anti-communists seeking to cleanse the United States of every hint of leftist cultural influence.

Roman Holiday fits awkwardly in Wyler's body of work. It exists as a romantic idyll in a long career that included critically acclaimed dramas such *The Best Years of Our Lives* (1946) and commercial epics like *Ben-Hur* (1959). Indeed, as many reviewers commented at the time, the film represented a break from his previous serious social dramas. It is a film both easy to enjoy and to overlook. Gregory Peck's star power and Audrey Hepburn's freshness combined with Wyler's rendering of Rome give the movie a pleasing, effervescent character. Yet attending to the film and its production helps locate Wyler as a film director intimately bound up with the cultural politics of Hollywood cinema of the early Cold War.[8] Whereas the politics of directors such as John Ford and Elia Kazan are noticeable in their films, Wyler's progressivism was just as often evident off the screen as it was on. His interest in widening the horizons of Hollywood beyond its parochial concerns and American self-absorptions demonstrates his capacious and cosmopolitan approach to cinema. Even when he turned to less explicitly social issues, as in *Roman Holiday*, his politics were never far removed as an examination into the production record of the film demonstrates. Exploring Wyler's work and experience while making *Roman Holiday* therefore contributes to broadening an understanding of Wyler as a transnational filmmaker in the early Cold War with all the perils that project entailed.

By the time Wyler made *Roman Holiday* he already had a long distinguished and successful career as a director in Hollywood.[9] Notable successes included *Mrs. Miniver* (1942) and *Jezebel* (1938), the latter winning Bette Davis an Academy Award for best actress. In addition, many of his films before and during the war evidenced his progressive politics. *Dead End* (1937) offered a trenchant social portrait of class hierarchy and poverty in Depression-era America. *The Letter* (1940), though steeped in Hollywood's Orientalism, nevertheless also implied a critique of English colonialism. When the US entered the war, Wyler enlisted and channeled his energies into making two documentaries for the Army, the acclaimed *The Memphis Belle* (1944) about the famous bomber plane and *Thunderbolt* (1947) about the fighter planes used in operations over Italy.

After the war, Wyler's films continued exploring social concerns. *The Best Years of Our Lives* offered a powerful depiction of the struggles returning soldiers faced in peacetime America. That film proved enormously successful both at the box office and among critics. It earned seven Academy Awards including Best Director for Wyler.

Carrie, made six years later, fared much less well among movie-goers. Yet it too offered a critical portrait of America in its rendering of the Theodore Dreiser novel upon which it was based. Perhaps a movie about downward social mobility was too jarring for a postwar culture that increasingly embraced the material abundance and class consensus of a consumer's republic. Indeed, the film is more of an extension of 1930s culture that produced such films as *Dead End* in its preoccupations and sensibilities, than it is of the postwar era.

Wyler felt the compromises he made to *Carrie* in order to get it released ruined the movie, declaring, "I am deeply sorry that I gave my consent to the cuts made because their effect was more far-reaching than any of us guessed at the time." Among the cuts were a scene where Laurence Olivier's character, George Hurstwood a prominent middle-class businessman who descends the American social ladder, winds up living destitute and alone in a flophouse. Wyler regretted cuts that diminished the social inequalities that lay at the heart of the movie:

> What it amounts to is that we started to tell the Dreiser story and then didn't have the courage to tell it. Without the despair and utter degradation contained in these scenes . . . it was not the picture that was ever intended.[10]

Wyler's comments are notable not only for expressing his frustration with the final version of his film but also as a reflection of his social preoccupations with class, greed, and inequality in America even at a time when he had turned to making *Roman Holiday*. They suggest that even while he was in the middle of making a romantic comedy, he had not lost his interest in movies as a vehicle for social commentary.

In addition to his film projects in the late 1940s, Wyler became politically active in liberal causes. In 1947, along with John Huston and Philip Dunne, Wyler formed the Committee for the First Amendment (CFA) to protest the treatment of a number of Hollywood artists at the hands of the House Un-American Activities Committee (HUAC). In its efforts to ferret out what it believed was a communist threat within the American film industry, HUAC issued subpoenas to a number of people. The group divided into "friendly" and "unfriendly" witnesses, those willing to testify before HUAC and identify communists in Hollywood, and those who refused. Eventually ten unfriendly witnesses, mostly screenwriters including Dalton Trumbo, John Howard Lawson, and Lester Cole, but also producer Adrian Scott, and director Edward Dmytryk, were called before the committee.[11] Wyler and CFA organized a letter campaign and a trip to Washington during the hearings in October 1947 to oppose the efforts of HUAC to force individuals to divulge their political beliefs.

The Hollywood Ten, as the group of unfriendly witnesses came to be known, were held in contempt of Congress and sentenced to a year in federal jail. After lengthy court battles, they were sent to prison. Wyler supported their efforts against imprisonment, including letters of support for their parole.[12]

Wyler's advocacy for the Hollywood Ten, and his opposition to HUAC's tactics led to a very public conflict with W. W. Wilkerson, the publisher of the *Hollywood Reporter*. In the July 1950 front page column, Wilkerson spewed xenophobic invective against Wyler, as well as Billy Wilder and Paul Henreid, as disloyal Americans. Singling out their naturalized citizenship, Wilkerson wrote,

> Wilder, Wyler, and Henreid are foreigners, came to this country, applied for and were given citizenships ... All have lived off the many great things this country has to offer. So—as thanks for what they have been given, they want to take to the air and criticize the acts of our courts, the laws of our government.

Then suggesting that as immigrants, they had no right to express their own beliefs, Wilkerson asserted,

> for a naturalized citizen, particularly one who has been given such elevation in our country, as have the above three, to go out and virtually bite the hand that's been feeding them so well, is something we can't take, nor will anyone else in this business or our country.

Wilkerson concluded his column by insisting "something should be done to muzzle them in the future."[13]

Two days later, Wyler responded in a letter to the *Hollywood Reporter*, stating, "In America we make no distinction, legally or otherwise, between naturalized and native born citizens. This has been a fundamental principle of our democratic way of life." Taking aim at the threat with which Wilkerson ended his column, Wyler wrote:

> in this country we do not "muzzle" people . . . On the contrary, one of the basic principles on which our republic is founded is that dissension of opinion and open criticism of government by the citizens is not only permitted but encouraged.

Then noting that "in the course of obtaining American citizenship," immigrants are schooled in democratic values, he concluded "[m]any native citizens would be more enlightened as to the meaning of their democratic heritage and would be better Americans had they been born abroad and obtained their citizenship with the benefit of such schooling."[14]

Wyler's opposition to both the Red Scare and anti-immigrant sentiment in Hollywood is also evident in his role during an effort by conservatives in the Screen Directors Guild to impose a loyalty oath on members. In the fall of 1950, Cecil B. DeMille attempted to orchestrate such an oath while the president of the guild, Joseph Mankiewicz, was out of the country. When Mankiewicz returned, he called a meeting of the guild. De Mille sought to recall Mankiewicz as president. A heated confrontation at a gathering of the guild between the supporters and opponents of De Mille's efforts ensued. Wyler was among those who opposed De Mille. At the meeting, De Mille impugned the Americanism of foreign-born directors such as Wyler, which led to a full-throated condemnation of De Mille's xenophobia.[15]

Wyler was not a radical nor was he a communist. He supported the Hollywood Ten because he saw their plight and the wider Red Scare as threats to civil liberties. But his liberalism also made him part of a dynamic, progressive Hollywood circle that included numerous creative and talented figures working in the postwar film industry.

For instance, in early May 1948, Wyler and his wife Talli hosted a small "meet and greet" gathering for Henry Wallace, the former vice-president under Franklin Roosevelt, who ran for president on a Progressive Party ticket that year. The list of invitees suggests something of Wyler's political network in Hollywood at the time or at the very least those he felt comfortable including in a social event for a leading progressive politician such as Wallace. They included Fritz Lang, Jules Dassin, Robert Siodmak, Alexander Knox, William Dieterle, Walter Wanger, Edward G. Robinson,

Burt Lancaster, Thomas Mann, Ida Lupino, Gregory Peck, Lucille Ball, and Otto Preminger.[16]

In addition to Wyler's political activities, his views about the purpose and role of movies in society indicate his progressive commitments. In an essay he penned for *The Screen Writer*, the journal of the Screen Writers' Guild, in 1947, Wyler hoped the American film industry would mature. The war had made clear the demands and opportunities facing filmmakers. "Hollywood," he lamented, "seems a long way from the world at times." He claimed,

> [A]t the moment, the motion picture in Hollywood is divorced from the main currents of our time. It does not reflect the world in which we live. It often has very little meaning for audiences at home, and even less for audiences abroad.

He insisted, "It is time that we in Hollywood realized the world doesn't revolve about us."

Wyler concluded his essay by hoping American filmmakers would learn from developments overseas. "In Europe," he noted, "I believe great prospects for films are in sight." There, some filmmakers

> approach their work with a simplicity and directness which eludes many of us in Hollywood. The European motion picture people have gone through the war in a very real sense, and I think they are closer to what is going on in the world than we are. The competition from Europe will force us to meet the challenge.

Though Wyler had French and English filmmakers particularly in mind and did not mention Italians, his comments could have been describing films like Rossellini's *Roma città aperta* and the burgeoning neorealist movement in Italy.[17] Wyler, therefore, entered the postwar era sensitive to wider currents in cinema and eager to see American movies become both more socially conscious and responsive to the new cinemas of Europe.

But Wyler realized the Red Scare posed a major threat to such prospects. Writing to Bosley Crowther, *The New York Times* film critic shortly after the HUAC hearings in October 1947, Wyler shared his fears of the consequences of the anti-communist attacks upon Hollywood. "If the censors, through fear and through government regulation have their way," he wrote, "the American people will have to see stereotyped films, further than ever removed from reality and current problems." He noted,

> if in future films we color, retouch and conceal the problems of American life so that we are always appearing in our Sunday best, audiences both

here and abroad soon would cease to accept our films as an accurate reflection of life in America.

Wyler also recognized how the environment for the kinds of movies he had admired was quickly eroding:

> In going over in my mind the great films of the past twenty years, it shocks me to realize how many of them couldn't be made today in the same way. This is due directly to the fear and apprehension which such groups as the Thomas Committee [HUAC] have created in Hollywood.[18]

So, during the late 1940s, Wyler experienced both commercial and critical success and failure for movies that explored the inequalities and injustices of American society. *The Best Years of Our Lives* in particular cast dramatic light on the plight of returning vets and their struggles. *Carrie*, though set at the turn of century, also commented on the cruel disparities that informed American life. Off-screen, Wyler used his voice to oppose the anti-communist hysteria rippling through postwar society. In addition, Wyler became a champion of a more internationalist and open American film industry, encouraging filmmakers to broaden their horizons and pursue movies that reflected greater realism and engage the wider world after the Second World War.

It was this constellation of concerns, associations, and experiences that Wyler took with him when he went to Rome to make *Roman Holiday* in 1952. It may seem a strange choice for a man who had a long history of making socially conscious movies to opt for a lightweight romantic comedy. But given both Wyler's cosmopolitan sensibilities and the increasingly restrictive environment in Hollywood, the chance to make a movie in Italy may have been quite attractive. To a degree, making *Roman Holiday* did provide Wyler with an escape from the growing paranoia that engulfed both the American film industry and the US more broadly. But if he had imagined his troubles with the Red Scare were over by leaving the country, developments while he was in Rome proved him mistaken.

Paramount Pictures billed *Roman Holiday* as a film completely made on location in Italy. A number of films had been partially filmed in Italy, such as *Prince of Foxes* (Henry King, 1949) and *September Affair* (William Dieterle, 1950), but those had entailed a mix of shooting in Italy and post-production in Hollywood. Wyler himself a year after the film premiered noted too that his movie was entirely made in Rome. He prided himself on making it on location and doing the post-production work in Rome as well. He also suggested, in echoes of the neorealist films such as Vittorio De Sica's *Ladri di biciclette* (1948) and Roberto Rossellini's *Paisà* (1946), this story, if it had been made in Hollywood, as was considered at one time, would not be the same picture by a long shot. If we had to build some of the sets, first of all, you couldn't afford to build some of the sets that you have seen, and if the background didn't look real, the whole story would appear to be less real.[19]

Yet if in retrospect, Wyler could later boast about making *Roman Holiday* in Rome, the actual production of the film proved more complicated than his public comments implied.[20] For filming in Italy was no easy task. Henry Henigson the production manager for the film told Wyler as much even before the film went into production. Henigson had lengthy experience working for American film studios in Europe, including working for MGM on its ancient Roman epic *Quo Vadis* (Mervyn LeRoy, 1951), an earlier and immense American production in Rome that preceded *Roman Holiday*. He recognized the challenges that Wyler would face. In a letter to Wyler after he had been to Rome to arrange details of the production two months before shooting was to commence, Henigson warned him, "Italy is not an easy place to work in any sense of the word." The main problems stemmed from the lack of a suitable filmmaking infrastructure to meet Hollywood expectations, what Henigson described as "large organizations thoroughly competent with vast resources at their immediate command." He claimed the "Italian or European motion picture producing industry is not so constituted." Instead "local production is a 'relatively hit-and-miss' affair."[21]

And indeed, while Wyler claimed working on *Roman Holiday* in Rome a satisfying experience, he found making a Hollywood film in a foreign environment posed significant challenges, technical adjustments, and logistical complications. A month into production, Wyler wrote a lengthy letter to Don Hartman, Paramount's production supervisor for the film. Part of the challenge, Wyler admitted to Hartman was "not having a complete final script before we started." Italian authorities wanted changes regarding the "adventure in Rome" and depictions of "the Roman people," made to the original script which were addressed after Wyler got to Italy. Wyler also commented on the difficulties of filming inside the Palazzo Brancaccio which was the setting for the introduction of Audrey Hepburn's character Princess Ann. Problems with lighting, sound, and rigging in a Renaissance palace coupled with "the middle of Rome's worst heat wave in some time" made for challenging filming. But according to Wyler the most serious challenge lay in the raw stock that was used. "Apparently, our negative is not of the top quality," he told Hartman. "We have several scenes ruined with scratches and damaged emulsion." The problem had to be solved by importing new Eastman stock from the US. Further, "several days [*sic*] work" of shooting Wyler reported were "ruined" by complications at the Luce lab processing the film, though he hoped to be able to "salvage what we can." Even for all those challenges, however, he noted he and his crew "have adjusted themselves very well to operating in a foreign country.²² Wyler's foray to Italy therefore entailed real frustrations and misunderstandings. But it also became a creative exercise in learning through adaptation as he and the entire production surmounted the adversities that they continually faced.

In addition to the challenges Wyler faced, however, he also drew upon contributions from important figures in the Italian film industry burgeoning under both the acclaim of neorealism and the renovated movie studies of Cinecittà. Indeed, as much as *Roman Holiday* was a product of Hollywood, it also represented an encounter with and creative labor of Italian film workers. The involvement of people such as Cesare Zavattini, Suso Cecchi D'Amico, Ennio Flaiano, and Luciano Emmer indicates the film existed at the crossroads of both American and Italian film cultures. The film thus embodied a new bridge between Hollywood and Italian moviemakers in the early 1950s.

For instance, during the scripting of the film, Wyler and Pilade Levi, a Paramount executive in Italy, solicited reactions from Cesare Zavattini, the noted neorealist screenwriter best known for his work with Vittorio De Sica on *Ladri di Biciclette*. Zavattini responded with two letters to Wyler. Among the suggestions from Zavattini was to shift a scene in an early version of the script that called for Princess Ann and Joe Bradley to wade barefoot into a fountain from the Piazza di Spagna to the Trevi Fountain. He also concluded his first letter by noting, perhaps informed by his neorealist sensibilities, his evaluation of the story:

> What embarrassed me a great deal was the violent clash found in the contrast between the operetta-like treatment of the story, let us say, and the environment in which the work develops, an environment which has its real streets, its real inhabitants, and its own real and immediate problems.²³

In addition to Zavattini, Suso Cecchi D'Amico and Ennio Flaiano, two noted screenwriters who worked with many of the key Italian directors of the 1940s and 1950s, contributed to the film script. Their involvement was, in fact, more substantial than Zavattini's. Whereas he had offered suggestions in his letters to Wyler, D'Amico and Flaiano were actually hired to help develop the script.

Their involvement with *Roman Holiday* also reflected wider realities about making the movie in Italy. Wyler told Don Hartman that hiring the two Italians, "showed our good will and made the Italian government happy and we were able to get the frozen money and proceed." Yet, he also told Hartman, the two "did valuable work in reconstructing the scenes of Joe and the Princess, from the time she leaves his apartment, and gave us a good situation for the ending."²⁴ It is striking that the early scenes, to which Wyler refers, do take the film into the daily lives and routines of Romans.

But Wyler did not simply draw upon the expertise of D'Amico and Flaiano for the script, he also employed Italian talent in the actual filming of parts of his movie. He hired Italian film director Luciano Emmer who had just made *Le Raggaze di Piazza di Spagna* (1952), to lead what he described as "an excellent second unit." In an update to Hartman in early August, he informed the Paramount executive that Emmer's second unit had been "useful," and he was able to "get some good footage out of them."[25]

Finally, *Roman Holiday* benefited from the labor of Italian film craftsmen and workers both while shooting in the streets of Rome and in Cinecittà. As Wyler indicated to Freeman the actual production of the film could often be frustrating because of film stock and camera problems. But he also credited the dedication and hard work of the Italians on the film crew.

This may have been in part due to an article by Hollywood columnist Louella Parsons that implied Wyler was dissatisfied with his Italian workers. The director publicly challenged Parsons' charge, stating, "[o]ur Italian co-workers are 'all first rate craftsmen'" and requested a retraction.[26]

But Wyler also expressed his respect directly to the Italian crew in October 1952 at the luncheon held at the high-end Grotte del piccione (Caves of the pigeon) to celebrate the completion of primary shooting. His address was both diplomatic and heartfelt. Giving his remarks in Italian, Wyler thanked the film workers for the efforts. He apologized for the difficulties on the set and for his impatience. But he also stated to the Italian film workers that, "I could not expect in Hollywood or anywhere else to get a more hard-working, willing, cooperative and skilled all-around crew as I've had on this picture." He told those assembled,

> I shall miss all of you here. In any case, I know I can speak for all of us who came from Hollywood when I say that this has been a wonderful experience. I think Rome is without a doubt the greatest location in the world.[27]

Wyler would, in fact, return to Rome six years later to film *Ben-Hur*.

While he may have been exaggerating in his estimation of Rome, the city and its film culture did imprint itself upon his movie. Indeed, there are more than a few echoes or indirect refractions of neorealism in *Roman Holiday* and its production. This is not to claim the film as neorealist. Rather, it is to suggest that neorealism hovers around and at the edges of the movie made at a moment when neorealism itself was in transition within Italy. Given how the film existed at the intersection of numerous transatlantic currents including Hollywood's effort to transplant itself to Rome, the increasing restrictions placed upon liberal progressive cinema in the US, and Italian neorealism's own eclipse in the 1950s, one might describe *Roman Holiday* as Wyler's decidedly

American version of *neorealismo rosa*, expatriate Americans in Rome substituting for the working class.

With principal shooting completed, Wyler turned his attention to editing *Roman Holiday* and overseeing secondary shooting. He also hired Georges Auric, the French composer, for the music soundtrack. But in late 1952 and early 1953, while Wyler worked to finish the film in Rome, the Cold War politics at home pulled Wyler back into the anti-communist fears and paranoia that had wracked Hollywood. He quickly became ensnarled in the red hunting that destroyed numerous peoples' careers in the film industry.[28]

The occasion that sparked renewed attack on Wyler was a party celebrating the end of filming he and his wife hosted at their temporary home in the Parioli district in Rome in November 1952. The attendees included Wyler's acquaintances in the city and constituted an extended circle of film people and artists in Rome including Roberto Rossellini and Ingrid Bergman, Kirk Douglas, Pier Angeli, Montgomery Clift, and Truman Capote. But the guests that would cause Wyler problems in the eyes of the anti-communists were Leonardo Bercovici and Bernard Vorhaus. Bercovici had been a successful screenwriter and communist in Hollywood, working on such films as *The Bishop's Wife* (Henry Koster, 1947) and *Kiss the Blood off My Hands* (Norman Foster, 1948). He had been called before HUAC in 1951 but refused to inform on his colleagues. He fled the US and wound up in Rome in 1952. Bernard Vorhaus was a director and also a communist. He too had gone to Europe.[29]

Wyler's party and its guests suggest a broad transatlantic film world that he participated in and encouraged in the early 1950s.[30] Like the production of *Roman Holiday* itself, Wyler moved between Hollywood and Italian filmmakers, where political and creative borders were porous and Rome served as an open artistic, exile community, where neorealists and Hollywood people, and those escaping the ideological and moral guardians of the US, could mingle.

It was precisely this liminal space that conservative crusaders could not stand. The right-wing, anti-communist newsletter, *Counterattack* picked up the story of Wyler's party and in late December ran its own account, questioning Wyler's loyalties. "You wonder," it stated, "just how strongly anti-CP people like WM WYLER are." It mentioned Wyler's party and the attendance of Bercovici and Vorhaus, "both of whom were named as CP members in the film investigations." It wondered, "How many real anti-Communists welcome identified CP members into their homes on such occasions."[31]

The attack on Wyler indicates the anti-communist crusade in America wasn't merely content to focus on activities within the US. Their project extended beyond national boundaries, tracking anyone it deemed suspicious regardless of where they were. Though Rome may have been in Italy, for the red hunters like *Counterattack* it existed as one more site of communist danger.

Wyler must have already been getting worrisome signals from the studio in Hollywood by the end of December given a letter he wrote to Frank Freeman, vice-president of Paramount, in which he stated, "I have decided to keep you informed of anything political concerning me. My last act of a political nature was voting the straight democratic [*sic*] ticket by absentee ballot."[32]

But matters quickly worsened. Freeman wrote to Wyler in early January about the *Counterattack* article and, referencing Bercovici and Vorhaus, chastised Wyler. "[T]hey certainly would not have been guests at any occasion I would have sponsored," he stated:

> It is hard for me to understand how you would have these two men as your guests, knowing their record . . . if you continue to invite identified Communists to visit you or to be part of any affair that you give, then you will have charges leveled at you.[33]

Two weeks later, Wyler's agent Paul Kohner warned the director he would be expected to make amends for his perceived political mistakes. He encouraged Wyler to "think very hard, and as quickly as possible, of something very constructive and strongly anti-communist in which you can participate or do to justify your anti-communist attitude." He told Wyler that in the meantime he would obtain "the dossier on your activities which are being kept on record." He also informed him that "you will need to give an explanation for every one of the points mentioned in this dossier." Kohner concluded his letter by stating, "I urge you not to take this matter lightly."[34]

A week later, Kohner wrote to Wyler, informing him, "there is apparently a very careful check being made on all of your activities and associations in Europe." He repeated his warning, "May I urge you again, Willy, not to take this thing lightly." Kohner also sought to arrange Wyler to work with men who had experience helping John Huston and Jose Ferrer clear their names. He mentioned Arthur Jacobs in particular as an "ideal man to go to work for you on clearing up your situation." Faced with the threat to both his reputation and his career, in other words, Kohner encouraged Wyler to utilize the services of essentially Cold War fixers who could quietly make ideological problems go away. He also suggested Wyler contact Huston himself, who had also been targeted by anti-communists and was also in Italy at the time.[35]

In mid-February Kohner wrote Wyler again attempting to impress upon him the danger the red hunters posed. He told him that his concerns lay with Wyler's own welfare and not simply the bad publicity that it might pose for *Roman Holiday*:

> It is not at all the idea of doing "something for the picture" or "just in time before the picture is released." <u>It has to do with your own personal standing</u>

and the sooner you start to get yourself cleared like all the others are doing, the better it will be for you.

The lawyer also sent Wyler a list of "some of the items on the calendar regarding some of your past activities."[36]

Wyler's mounting troubles with the Red Scare continued into the spring as evidenced by an early April 1953 letter from Art Arthur regarding his statement in response to the accusations. Any personal accounting of activities and associations on Wyler's part posed enormous difficulties since any mistakes regarding his knowledge of other people's political affiliations could be used by suspicious anti-communists to indicate deceit or subterfuge.

With allusions to Bercovici and Vorhaus, Arthur addressed the "problems . . . of fugitives from the House Committee who seek to associate themselves with others in Europe." He acknowledged the difficult situation Wyler had been placed in to account for his acquaintances and activities. He therefore sent the 1952 annual report from HUAC with a list of people identified as communists as an aid for Wyler to use as a guide.[37]

It would take Wyler over a year to complete his account of his political activities and clean his record. In February 1954, he drafted a lengthy explanation to Frank Freeman, vice-president of Paramount, responding to specific items and events in the dossier that Kohner had mentioned in his letters to Wyler in early 1953. He began by asserting that his political activities "have been extremely limited and small." In the 1930s and during the war, he claimed, his politics focused on opposition to fascism. After the war, his primary concern was the defense of civil liberties. Thus, he explained, the reason for his co-founding with John Huston and Philip Dunne the Committee for the First Amendment was to oppose what he believed were the unfair tactics of HUAC in regard to the Hollywood Ten. But Wyler also admitted to "gullibility" and poor judgment regarding some of his decisions. For instance, he claimed he believed a number of the Ten were not communists, only to learn later they all had been at one time. Regarding the Committee, he admitted, in retrospect it "was undoubtedly just what the Communists wanted," and he "often regretted the whole thing." In addition, he confessed that his endorsement of the Cultural and Scientific Congress for World Peace in 1949 "was a big mistake" and "done without much thought." He concluded with a chastised acknowledgement, "in light of events of the last few years, particularly the Korean war, many liberal eyes—including my own—have been opened to many things." He ended by stating, a "clearer course of action and better judgement would have been advisable in the past and will, you can be assured, be applied in the future."[38]

Even then, Wyler would need to revise his account before he finished work on the final version which was completed in early May 1954. For instance, he wrote of the social gathering at his home, hosting Henry Wallace in 1948:

As to the Wallace meeting at my home: I had been told that Wallace was unable to secure a meeting place. After the meeting that was held at my home I learned that I had been misinformed. I did not regard Wallace representing the Communists. Later I became convinced that Wallace had been fooled and used by them.[39]

The implication in his description that his actions were the result of deception allowed Wyler to present himself as victim as much as actor in his entanglements with the left in Hollywood. But they also rendered him politically incompetent. The price of his accounting for himself entailed the need to cast his own commitments and actions as less than his own and more the manipulations of others.

So, what began in late 1952 in Rome while Wyler worked to complete his romantic comedy culminated almost a year and a half later in a forced statement of political submission to the forces of political reaction. His effort to protect his name and reputation and avoid the blacklist proved successful. For Wyler would continue to make movies in Hollywood, most spectacularly with the commercial blockbuster and Academy Award winning *Ben-Hur*, also made in Rome six years later. By then the worst of the anti-communist purges in the American film industry were over and the blacklist would soon crumble.

Yet Wyler's experience of needing to account for his political activities and qualify his commitments, to demonstrate his mistakes and admit his naïvety, amounted to an exercise in enforced self-cleansing. What he had done and supported out of his political and social commitments had to be reinterpreted, under the threat of the red hunters and out of professional fear, as episodes of poor judgment. In this regard, the revisions Wyler wrote upon his own life and politics, paralleled that of other Americans who had embraced progressive causes in the 1930s and 1940s but found themselves under interrogation from anti-communist watchdogs. Wyler's experience, in fact, echoes those of many committed non-communist leftists who had to edit their own lives before HUAC and the reactionary guardians of American culture. As Landon R. Y. Storrs has demonstrated, the result was an enormous narrowing of progressive liberal imagination and politics after the Second World War.[40] Indeed, Wyler's encounter with the threat of the blacklist while in Rome places not only his own postwar career but also *Roman Holiday* and Hollywood on the Tiber[41] in a wider political and cultural context. While the movie may have offered a beguiling romance set in tourist-ready Rome, the Cold War culture of anti-communism asserted itself into Wyler's journey to Italy. Wyler in Rome and his experience making *Roman Holiday* reveal the extent to which Cold War culture in Hollywood reached beyond the shores of the US and ensnared people like Wyler who had gone to Europe to escape constraints and repressions in America.

Many people for numerous reasons—some to work, some to play, some forced into exile and fleeing the United States—wound up in Rome in the late 1940s and 1950s. Wyler's experience making *Roman Holiday* on location revealed Rome to be seen not simply as a tourist destination, but a vital and dynamic city that fostered numerous, intersecting trajectories of transatlantic art and culture. But Wyler's need to respond to the Red Scare while working on the film also reveals how the very opportunities to freely associate and intermingle that postwar Rome made possible also meant that for American anti-communists it was a place in need of policing.

The British psychoanalysis Adam Philips notes for Freud "modern people were as much the survivors of their history as they were makers of it."[42] One need not psychoanalyze Wyler's film to consider the interplay between the foreground of *Roman Holiday*'s attractive surfaces and the backstory of Wyler's encounter with the Red Scare while making the movie. For Rome became the site not only for a bright romantic comedy and a successful production of Hollywood on the Tiber, it also served as the setting where Wyler was forced to attend to the demands of the blacklist, the place where he confronted the aggressive, punishing forces in postwar America that could and did bring many people in Hollywood to their ruin. If *Roman Holiday* represented a moment of triumph for Wyler, it also occasioned his time of survival.

NOTES

1. "Princess Apparent," *Time*, September 7, 1953, 60–5.
2. See *The New York Times* review, September 6, 1953; *Newsweek* review, September 7, 1953; *Daily Variety* review, June 30, 1953; Al Hine, "The Princess Plays Hooky," *Holiday*, September 1953; "Wyler's 'Holiday' Sights $10 Million Worldwide Gross," *Hollywood Reporter* n.d. All in *Roman Holiday*, Production Files, Digital Core Collection, Margaret Herrick Center for Motion Picture Research, Academy of Motion Pictures Arts and Sciences (AMPAS).
3. "A Princess Goes on a Spree," *Life* August 24, 1953, *Roman Holiday*, Production Files, Digital Core Collection, Margaret Herrick Center for Motion Picture Research, AMPAS.
4. "Wyler's 'Holiday' May Snap Jinx on Rome-Made Movies," *Rome Daily American*, April 19, 1953, 5, Folder 355 Roman Holiday—publicity—clippings (foreign), William Wyler Papers, Margaret Herrick Center for Motion Picture Research, AMPAS; see also "Hollywood on the Tiber," *Time* June 26, 1950, 92.
5. The literature on neorealism is extensive. For a brief account, see Mark Shiel, *Italian Neorealism: Rebuilding the Cinematic City* (New York: Wallflower Books, 2006); for more extended studies, see Peter Bondanella, *A History of Italian Cinema* (New York: Continuum, 2011), 61–156; Christopher Wagstaff, *Italian Neorealist Cinema: An Aesthetic Approach* (Toronto: University of Toronto Press, 2007); Millicent Marcus, *Italian Film in Light of Neorealism* (Princeton: Princeton University Press, 1986).
6. For one account of Rome in the late 1940s and 1950s, see Shawn Levy, *Dolce Vita Confidential: Fellini, Loren, Pucci, Paparazzi, and the Swinging High Life of 1950s Rome* (New York: W. W. Norton & Company, 2016).
7. See for instance, Frank Krutnik, Steve Neale, Brian Neve, and Peter Stanfield, eds. *"Un-American" Hollywood: Politics and Film in the Blacklist Era* (New Brunswick: Rutgers University Press, 2007), 200, 216.

8. For an excellent collection of essays on Cold War politics in Hollywood and its consequences for postwar American filmmakers and cinema, see *"Un-American" Hollywood*.
9. Two useful biographies of Wyler's life and career are Gabriel Miller, *William Wyler: The Life and Films of Hollywood's Most Celebrated Director* (Lexington: University Press of Kansas, 2013); Jan Herman, *A Talent for Trouble: The Life of Hollywood's Most Acclaimed Director* (New York: G. P. Putnam's Sons, 1995).
10. Wyler to Don Hartman, July 26, 1952, Folder 349 Roman Holiday Paramount, Wyler Papers, AMPAS.
11. On HUAC, see Larry Ceplair and Steven Englund, *The Inquisition in Hollywood, Politics in the Film Community* (Urbana: University of Illinois Press, 2003); a more recent study is Thomas Doherty, *Show Trial: Hollywood, HUAC, and the Birth of the Blacklist* (New York: Columbia University Press, 2018).
12. Wyler to Federal Parole Board, December 6, 1950, Folder 394 Political, Wyler Papers, AMPAS.
13. W. W. Wilkerson, "Trade Views," *Hollywood Reporter*, July 25, 1950, 1, Folder 695 Political—Clippings, Wyler Papers, AMPAS.
14. Wyler to Hollywood Reporter, *Hollywood Reporter*, July 27, 1950, Folder 695 Political—Clippings, Wyler Papers, AMPAS.
15. On the efforts of loyalty oaths in the Screen Directors Guild and Wyler's opposition to De Mille, see Miller, *William Wyler*, 313–14; Joseph McBride, *Searching for John Ford: A Life* (New York: St. Martin's Press, 2001), 279–84.
16. Mrs. William Wyler to Mr. Mankiewitz [sic] and attachments, May 6, 1948, Folder 694 Political, Wyler Papers, AMPAS.
17. William Wyler, "No Magic Wand," *The Screen Writer* 2, no. 9 (February 1947): 14.
18. Wyler to Crowther, November 6, 1947, Folder 694 Political, Wyler Papers, AMPAS.
19. Wyler speech, Proceedings at Warner Bros Beverly Hills Theater, February 24, 1954, Folder 118 Roman Holiday Speeches, Wyler Papers, AMPAS.
20. On the production of *Roman Holiday*, see also Daniel Steinhart's discussion in his *Runaway Production: Internationalizing Postwar Production and Location Shooting* (Oakland: University of California Press, 2019), 127–40.
21. Henry Henigson to Wyler, April 12, 1952, Folder 343 Roman Holiday—Henigson, Henry, Wyler Papers, AMPAS.
22. Wyler to Don Hartman, July 26, 1952, Folder 349 Roman Holiday Paramount, Wyler Papers, AMPAS.
23. See Pilade Levi to Wyler, October 19, 1951, Folder 340 Roman Holiday—correspondence, Wyler Papers, AMPAS; Zavattini to Wyler, January 15, 1952, and Zavattini to Wyler, January 23, 1952, in English translation, Folder 337 Roman Holiday—Script Notes, Wyler Papers, AMPAS.
24. Wyler to Hartman, July 26, 1952, Folder 349 Roman Holiday Paramount, Wyler Papers, AMPAS.
25. Ibid. See also, Jack Karp to Henry Henigson, July 14, 1952, Folder 343 Roman Holiday—Henigson, Henry, Wyler Papers, AMPAS.
26. "Louella Told of Italians' Siestas Irk Paramount," *Rome Daily American*, September 27, 1952; Louella O. Parsons, *Los Angeles Examiner*, October 1, 1952, Folder 353 Roman Holiday, Wyler Papers, AMPAS.
27. For Wyler's speech and the invitation to the restaurant, see Folder 352, Roman Holiday Production, Wyler Papers, AMPAS.
28. Miller also discusses Wyler's experience with the Red Scare while making *Roman Holiday* in his *William Wyler*, 314–19.

29. On Wyler's party and guests, see "It's Cocktails for Two—Hundred," *Rome Daily American*, November 15, 1952, Folder 355—Roman Holiday, Publications (Foreign), Wyler Papers, AMPAS; on Bercovici and Vorhaus, see Patrick McGilligan and Paul Buhle, *Tender Comrades: A Backstory of the Hollywood Blacklist* (New York: St. Martin's Press, 1997), 29–42, 657–81.
30. While Wyler never became an exile, an important study that explores American filmmakers forced to leave the US because of the blacklist and continue their film careers in Europe can be found in Rebecca Prime's *Hollywood Exiles in Europe: The Blacklist and Cold War Film Culture* (New Brunswick: Rutgers University Press, 2014). Prime also briefly mentions the concerns of anti-communists about Wyler's production of *Roman Holiday*, 69.
31. A typed document quoting the Counterattack article was part of a letter from Frank Freeman to Wyler dated January 2, 1953, Folder 697 Political—Personal, Wyler Papers, AMPAS.
32. Wyler to Y. Frank Freeman, December 29, 1952, Folder 349 Roman Holiday Paramount, Wyler Papers, AMPAS.
33. Frank Freeman to Wyler dated January 2, 1953, Folder 697 Political—Personal, Wyler Papers, AMPAS.
34. Paul Kohner to Wyler, January 15, 1953, Folder 697 Political—Personal, Wyler Papers, AMPAS.
35. Paul Kohner to Wyler, January 22, 1953, Folder 397 Political—Personal, Wyler Papers, AMPAS.
36. Kohner to Wyler, February 14, 1953, Folder 697 Political—Personal, Wyler Papers, AMPAS. Emphasis in the original.
37. Art Arthur to Wyler, April 8, 1953, Folder 697 Political—Personal, Wyler Papers, AMPAS.
38. Wyler to Y. Frank Freeman, February 24, 1954, and a timeline of Wyler's political activities labeled, "William Wyler—Film Director," no date, both Folder 697 Political—Personal, Wyler Papers, AMPAS.
39. Wyler to Y. Frank Freeman May 3, 1954, Folder 697 Political—Personal, Wyler Papers, AMPAS.
40. Landon R. Y. Storrs, *The Second Red Scare and the Unmaking of the New Deal Left* (Princeton: Princeton University Press, 2013).
41. Hollywood on the Tiber was a term which was coined to describe the trend of American films shooting in Rome.
42. Adam Philips, *Becoming Freud: The Making of a Psychoanalysis* (New Haven: Yale University Press, 2014), 7.

CHAPTER 13

"Down Eros, Up Mars!": Post-Colonialism, Imperial Violence, and the Corrupting Influence of Hate in William Wyler's *Ben-Hur* (1959)

Kaitlin Pontzer

In a gripping scene from *Ben-Hur* (1959), a Jewish prince, Judah of the house of Hur (Charlton Heston), clings to the desk of the Roman tribune, Messala (Stephen Boyd). Messala stands over Judah, unaffected. Soldiers rip Judah away to take him to an unjust punishment, a colonial subject condemned at the hands of a corrupt and ambitious Roman official. Judah looks up into his oppressor's face, praying that Messala lives until he returns to confront him. Messala, a former friend of Judah's, coldly replies, "Return?" This single word captures the Roman figure's callousness at the violence he perpetuates, as well as his comfortable certainty in the structures that support his power and protect him from Judah's revenge. As an audience, we cheer this revenge and empathize with the just anger at Rome's oppressive power. This scene vividly captures the film's post-colonial sentiment, stirring empathy with the plight of the tyrannized and their yearning for justice. The scene also carries a shadow of the danger of this revenge, as Judah first manifests the hatred that will lead him to participate in the very structures of power and hatred that motivate and sustain Messala.

Judah's anger in this scene demands the sympathy of the audience. We applaud the strong and valiant resolve in his voice, the struggle against the overwhelming power that is represented by a Roman tribune ruining innocent lives, and the anger that sustains Judah in his struggle against this power. More troubling for us as an audience, however, are the ramifications of Judah's struggle on his own character and his own loved ones. His hate sustains him, but it also cuts him off from all that he seeks to protect and preserve. The empathy induced by the film for Judah's struggle against unjust imperial power should be understood in the context of the historical period of decolonization in which the film was made. Behind this post-colonial struggle, however, we can also detect a warning, as Judah's character threatens to become the very thing he sets out to destroy. In this chapter, I argue that William Wyler's *Ben-Hur* articulates the anti-imperial sentiment of a post-colonial historical period, but also raises questions about how to oppose unjust force without dangerously embracing the violence of exploitative structures of power.

The first section of this chapter situates Wyler's 1959 film adaptation of *Ben-Hur* within the post-colonial sentiment of the post-World War period, emphasizing the anti-imperial themes at the heart of the story of ruined friendship, unequal power, and violent exploitation. I demonstrate the ways in which the 1959 *Ben-Hur* exhibits the post-colonial ideas of its mid-twentieth-century filming, with a strong emphasis on the injustice of oppressive Roman imperialism and the patriotic impulses of subjugated characters in the colonial setting of first century Roman-occupied Judea.

I further argue that Wyler's film goes beyond the critique of imperial power to warn of the fluid nature of corrupting imperial cruelty. The second section will draw out the subtle warning behind this post-colonial sentiment. In addition to the twentieth-century post-colonial setting, Wyler is attentive to the dangers of nationalism that can shade into impulses as corrupted as imperial power. Wyler's presentation of *Ben-Hur* alerts us to the dangers of an anti-imperial patriotism that takes on the worst impulses of imperial aggression. In the post-World War II period, situated in the context of post-colonialism as well as in the aftermath of World War II's nationalistic fury, Wyler is attentive to the unstable divisions between imperial and national constructs, as well as the fluid nature of power structures. Wyler's *Ben-Hur* warns that the struggle against oppression can reproduce the corruption it sets out to defeat.

"THE DAY ROME FALLS": POST-COLONIALISM AND WYLER'S *BEN-HUR*

Wyler's *Ben-Hur* was filmed in the late 1950s. It participates in a period of post-colonial sentiment that was inspired by the ongoing breakup of the major historical empires. Based on an 1880 novel by the Civil War general Lew Wallace, *Ben-Hur* had earlier been adapted to screen in the silent film epic of 1925. While the book and the silent film focus on the subtitled theme, "A Tale of the Christ," the mid-century adaptation places Judah's confrontation with Rome's power centerstage. The struggle with imperial force depicted in the film draws on the cultural impetus of post-colonialism, a movement in which "the decolonizations of the post-war era extinguished the category of colonial empire from the repertoire of polities that were legitimate and viable in international politics."[1] This mid-twentieth century era of the disintegration and delegitimization of empires was characterized by cultural, political, and literary articulations of liberation from colonial rule and by critiques of imperial power.[2] Wyler's *Ben-Hur* participates extensively in these articulations. For much of the film, Judah confronts injustice in a struggle that joins in the purest impulses of anti-imperial discontent.

The story of Judah begins before the film starts with a deep and important friendship with the same Roman tribune who would later condemn him. In fact, the story can in many ways be thought of as the story of both men, Judah and Messala. In Messala's own words, they "were close as boys . . . were like brothers." When the film opens, Messala is returning to Judea, the land of his boyhood, after many years in Rome. Reunited with his boyhood friend, the two men are immediately confronted with the insurmountable imperial divide that now separates them. Messala is a Roman, and Judah is a Jew. When Messala pressures Judah to inform on other Jews, they quarrel, culminating in Messala's unjust and deeply cruel sentencing of Judah, his mother, and his sister to slavery and imprisonment. Miriam (Martha Scott) and Tirzah (Cathy O'Donnell), the mother and sister, are imprisoned and contract leprosy. Judah is made a galley slave but vows to return. Against all odds, he does return. Saving the life of a Roman consul, Judah is made an adopted son and, effectively, a Roman. When he returns to confront Messala, the divide between them has deepened into an irreconcilable animosity. Ultimately, he defeats Messala in a violent chariot race that destroys his former friend. Once like brothers, the two men have become pitted against each other in an experience that perpetuates oppression, hatred, and violence.

Anti-Roman sentiment is voiced strongly throughout the movie and speaks powerfully with the voice of post-colonialism. From the very opening of the film, the voice-over narration tells us that this story is fraught with great political and religious tension. The narrator begins by clearly mapping the city of Jerusalem under Roman power. He describes the fortress of Antonia that "dominated" the city, and contrasts it with the Jewish temple, a sign of the lasting and "imperishable" Jewish faith. The narrator reminds us of the ancient traditions of the people of Judea, but also that, at this time in history, they are subjugated by Rome. In these descriptions, a clear imperial geography is mapped out, with the sympathetic sentiments clearly aligned with the colonized inhabitants of the city. The narrator even aligns conceptions of transcendent religious morality on the side of the colonized.

Soon after, the biblical character of Joseph makes a brief appearance as Roman soldiers march through the town of Nazareth. When his neighbor comments that he is not watching the soldiers, Joseph replies wearily, "We've seen Romans before," to which his neighbor replies with added misery, "Yes. And we will see them again." Again, post-colonial sentiments are voiced, this time depicting images from the Christian tradition in contrast to Roman power. Like the image of the Jewish temple in the opening, a dichotomy is set up between oppressive, Roman, imperial power and colonized subjects aligned with a transcendent morality.

Other hints of colonial tensions are voiced when we encounter individual Romans. When Messala arrives and relieves the previous commander, he is told that the command is his. He responds with thanks. The previous commander wearily and ominously *thanks Messala* for relieving him. It is the same subtle but significant weariness expressed by Joseph's neighbor in the previous scene. It alerts us not only to the divisiveness of the colonial structure, but to the destructive nature of the colonial encounter on both sides of the divide.

The remarks on the colonial encounter continue as Messala discusses the situation in Judea in his quarters. He is informed by a follow Roman named Sextus (André Morell) that in "this godforsaken land" people don't pay their taxes, that there is "an irrational resentment of Rome," and even that Roman statues are being smashed. Messala demands mercilessly, "Punish them!" Sextus's response echoes the weariness with the colonial encounter that we heard previously: "We do, when we can find them."

The critique of Rome's power and the demonstration of deep-seated colonial tensions continues in Messala's personal encounters. At his first reunion with Judah, he comments that the local wine is terrible. Judah jokes that it is fermented specifically for the Romans. Both men laugh, then Messala attempts his own humor: "You're very cruel to your conquerors." The laughter dies. Similarly, at a family dinner with Judah, Miriam, and Tirzah, the mood is disrupted by Messala's soldierly description of the destruction of conquered people. He brings Tirzah a gift from Libya, which turns out to be a spoil of war. He tells how marvelous the Libyan capital was before the Romans utterly destroyed it. The same silent tension ensues that Messala and Judah experienced over the wine. Throughout these personal encounters, the aggression of Rome, the tensions between Rome and Judea, and the division and oppression of colonial experiences pervade conversations and undermine the characters' persistent attempts at harmonious interaction.

Much later in the story, after Judah has journeyed to Rome, we encounter Pontius Pilate (Frank Thring). Pilate embodies Roman power and demand for control of the "rebellious" land of Judea. When he first meets Judah, he tells him he has been appointed governor to Judea, inquiring worriedly, "I hear the climate is difficult to live in." Judah's response is witty, concise, and distinctly post-colonial in its sentiment: "Not for Judeans." The sentiment that Romans simply do not belong in Judea, governing over a suppressed people, is reiterated when Pilate presides over the chariot race in Jerusalem toward the end of the movie. When he calls out the names and countries of the participating charioteers, the crowd is noticeably quiet when Messala, the Roman charioteer, is announced. This quiet is particularly pronounced in comparison to the announcement of Judah's name, who rides for Judea.

A moment later, Pilate calls for the crowd to shout, "Hail Caesar!" The call falls dangerously flat.

Perhaps one of the keenest voices of anti-imperial sentiment in the film is the Arab Sheik Ilderim (Hugh Griffith). After Judah has returned to Judea, he determines to confront Messala in a dangerous chariot race. He will drive a team of horses owned by Sheik Ilderim, who encourages Judah to race, partly for the sake of victory, and partly to confront Roman might. In a scene just before the famous chariot race, we witness Sheik Ilderim's interaction with several Roman officers: he attempts to engage them in a bet on who will win the upcoming chariot race, Tribune Messala or the Jewish Prince of Hur. He greets them grandly as the "defenders of great Rome's imperium." As he attempts to take bets on the race, he quietly taunts their lack of courage and their meager wagers. He finally openly derides them, saying, "Noble Romans, men of the Tiber, masters of the earth. Where is the courage, the daring that made Rome master of the world?" When a Roman soldier, surrounded by the sumptuous imperial setting and the support of his compatriots, insults the Arab and his absent Jewish friend, Sheik Ilderim calmly and ironically states, "bravely spoken." Amusingly, he goes on to undermine Roman claims to superiority by cleverly deploying his own extensive personal wealth in a bet that disadvantages the Roman gamblers.

This taunting confrontation between Sheik Ilderim and the Romans is followed by a scene in which he gives one of the clearest articulations of anti-colonial sentiments yet. While the conflict between Judah and Messala is personal for Judah, it is also important for Sheik Ilderim. The Sheik exults over the prospect of Judah winning the race at Messala's expense. He declares that such a Roman humiliation will show what kind of men inhabit this land. The political implications of the sentiment are driven home when the Sheik predicts that Judah's victory would "scorch the streets of the whole Roman world." His animosity to the new Roman governor is voiced in decidedly anti-imperial tones, as he suggests that Pilate will grind his heel into them. Later, immediately before the race, he gives Judah a Star of David, saying that it will "shine out for your people and my people together, and blind the eyes of Rome!" As with the Jewish temple at the beginning of the film, religious symbolism is placed in direct contrast to the oppressive immorality of the Roman imperium.

The indictment of the Roman Empire is most prominent, most painful, and most tragic in the story of the two men, former friends and near brothers, whose love for each other is destroyed by the desire for imperial power and the subsequent experience of colonial violence. We hear that Messala and Judah were like brothers, and that Messala even saved Judah's life. All this had changed, though, when Messala went to Rome. He comes back filled with ambition and a devotion to the power represented by Rome. In his ambition, he destroys his old friendship with Judah, as well as Judah's life, wealth, and family. In Judah's suffering at the hands of irresistible power, his anger and revenge turn him irrevocably against Messala as well. Once the nearest of friends, the men are now fundamentally divided. This friendship and the divide between colonizer and colonized draws out the painful tragedy of colonial division and oppression.

In the scene in which we first see Judah and Messala reunited at the beginning of the film, they encounter one another in an empty hall. One scene before, the hall was filled with Roman soldiers, a visible representation of Roman power. Now it is empty, except for the two friends. Embracing, they laugh about old times. At one point, Messala goes to a row of spears in a gesture clearly understood by both, indicating old pastimes and familiar ways. Taking a spear for each of them, they cry in sequence, "Down Eros! Up Mars!" Throwing the spears at a place where two beams cross, both men hit their mark, laugh, and proclaim that, after so many years, they are still close in every way. The assertion of closeness, however, is overshadowed by the exaltation of Mars over Eros. The militant sound of the cry is reminiscent of boyhood games, but darkly portends the turn that their relationship will take in the grip of imperial forces. These forces will indeed suppress love and nurse a war-like aggression.

The ensuing conversations between the two men carry the same tensions regarding the colonial relationship that we have seen in images of the colonial geography of Jerusalem, in the weariness of the imperial forces and colonial subjects, and in the many characters who articulate the deep antagonism between the colonizer and the colonized. Messala and Judah try to brush past this tension, but it repeatedly reasserts itself. Messala admits to Judah that his job will be difficult and asks for Judah's advice. The only advice Judah can give is to have Rome withdraw from Judea. Messala says that will be difficult since the emperor, devoted to his empire, is especially fond of Judea. Judah responds that Judea is not fond of the emperor. After this exchange, Messala laughs but Judah does not. Messala concludes by asking lightly whether there is anything as sad as unrequited love.

The exploitative nature of an imperial presence is emphasized by Messala's words of friendship. This pseudo-friendship is expressed in the emperor's love for the province, a love which, in the colonial relationship, is an ironic cover for exploitation. The painful similarity between this pretense of love for an imperial possession is reflected in Messala's own ongoing gestures of friendship throughout his scenes with Judah. Wyler skillfully directs a nuanced performance that leaves us unsure of the actual affection that remains in Messala's words to Judah, riddled as they clearly are with the same exploitative claims of the imperial conqueror. It is certainly clear that, however genuine Messala's gestures of affection, he believes that he has a right to the cooperation of Judah in the governance of the province.

The tension between Messala's gestures of friendship and his opportunistic goal of exploitation is matched by the tension between the two characters as they constantly flirt with disaster. The politics of the two men emerge dangerously in their conversation in Messala's quarters. Judah describes the room as "grim," while Messala characterizes it as austere, even virtuous, and ultimately, Roman. Judah stops and turns to him, but Messala changes tack, talking of his new responsibilities, which turns to talk of imperial power and the emperor's displeasure. He warns Judah that rebellion in Judea will be crushed. He then reassures Judah that *he* is not in danger, but the ensuing conversation brings out the full tension of the colonial divide between the two men. When Judah reminds Messala that he is a Jew, Messala counters with the ethnically insensitive, elitist, and backhanded praise that Judah is more like a Roman. Messala further reminds Judah that it is a Roman world and that to live in it requires becoming a part of it. Messala does not stop at pragmatism. He states the chauvinistic mantra which is at the core of all colonialism: "it is no accident that one small village on the Tiber was chosen to rule the world . . . no, it was fate that chose us to civilize the world."

Messala goes on to praise the achievements of Rome that, in his view, are the height of human achievement. In response, Judah reminds his "friend" that he believes in his own people. Messala latches onto this sentiment, exhorting Judah to do the best for his people: he insists that Judah speak against resistance to Rome, which Messala claims will end in the annihilation of the Jewish people. In this exchange, we see an explicit confrontation between a universalizing imperial mentality that claims the right and an almost divine mandate to "civilize the world," pitted directly against the particularity of a post-colonial patriotism, seen in Judah's statement, "I believe in the future of my people." The confrontation is fittingly summed up by an expression of imperial violence uttered by Messala as the inevitable triumph of a universalizing imperial destiny.

The final scene in which Judah and Messala attempt to be friends culminates in their feud. In it the political tensions illustrated in the previous conversation divide the former friends irreconcilably. Messala says that it is going to be like old times, but then immediately questions Judah on the names of rebels who threaten the Roman state. When he continues to press Judah, he refers to them as criminals, to which Judah responds by referring to them as patriots. Judah again tries to express to Messala how he believes in the future of his people, but Messala insinuates that conquered people have no future. At this point, Judah's friendliness disappears, and he displays openly a full sympathy with the anti-Roman sentiment that motivates the rebellious Jewish patriots: "You may conquer the land. You may slaughter the people. But that is not the end. We will rise again!" The fight concludes with Judah asserting that "the day Rome falls there will be a shout of freedom such as the world has never heard before." The division is complete and the two erstwhile friends now part as enemies.

In this analysis of the theme of imperial power in the 1959 adaptation of *Ben-Hur*, we see elements of anti-imperialism expressed in the tension between former friends, a Roman and a Jew. Their positions in the imperial structures of Roman power divide them in a battle between oppressed and oppressor that leaves no room for mutual survival and destroys much that they once held dear. In the destroyed friendship of Messala and Judah, we see the hideous power of empire and a patriotic cry for freedom from the tyranny that imperial power exercises. Wyler's direction of Heston's and Boyd's performances as Judah and Messala is one of the most powerful elements of the film. The performances display with painful tension the post-colonial politics that inform the narrative throughout the movie, as well as the deeply personal pain of two men whose political circumstances in a colonial structure pit them so disastrously against one another. In the end, both actors perform the ghost of a former friendship that exquisitely heightens the tragedy of this divide, as they are pulled apart not only by imperial structures, but by the characters' own ambitions, affections, loyalties, and desires. However, there is an even more painful closeness between these two characters, whose paths through the colonial spaces of ancient Rome lead them through analogous experiences of hatred and violence. It is to this painful similarity between Judah's and Messala's stories that we will now turn.

"THE VULTURE BREEDS THE VULTURE": THE CORRUPTING CRUELTY OF ROME

Having established the post-colonial critique that develops throughout the film, we can now uncover an added element: the fluidity between the colonial and colonizing individuals that links Messala's and Judah's narratives, even as they are divided. Casting Roman roles with British actors and the colonial subject with the American Heston, Wyler's adaptation plays off the cultural memory of the expansive British Empire to explore the theme of imperial power and colonial resistance.[3] Certainly, given the historical memory of British imperialism and the unprecedented expanse of the British Empire in its heyday, the association between Britain and Rome is an easy and convenient one. Thus, it is useful to explore themes in British historical scholarship that give further insight into the film. Certain aspects of this historiography suggest an important fluidity, a destabilization of the dichotomy between colonizer and colonized. This destabilization is discernable in Wyler's film, side by side with the staunch critique of imperial power. I argue in this section that, in addition to articulating a strong sense of anti-imperial sentiment, the film also warns about the very instability and fluidity of colonial structures, in which movement across imperial spaces can impact colonizer and colonized in comparable ways. If in the previous section we witnessed how Messala and Judah were divided by the imperial power structures, in this section we will see their closeness. Despite their antagonism, Messala and Judah are linked by the corrupting power of colonial violence.

The traditional image of empire relies on a rigid structure of dominance and subjugation that is as divided as the feuding Messala and Judah. However, historiographies of empire alert us to the important fact that historical empires were in many ways messy constructs. Imperial bureaucracy and legal systems, brute force, and economic control are dreadfully concrete. However, individual identities, cultural influences, and movement across contested boundaries destabilize the dichotomy between colonizer and colonized that we saw so painfully dramatized in the divide between Messala and Judah.

Historians of empire in the last several decades have provided a variety of images of empire that complicate the stark dichotomy between dominant and subjugated entities. One way in which this dichotomy breaks down is on the individual level. Kathleen Wilson points to the eighteenth-century British Empire, noting that, "Britons from London to Calcutta recognized (that) British power abroad was a precarious entity," noting the "cultural *mélange* of English, Scots, Irish, European, Native Americans, Indians, and Africans that jostled, often violently, for authority, wealth, and freedom."[4] While Wilson notes the diverse empire of messily integrated individuals "jostling" for power, others emphasize figures in the in-between spaces of empire. For example, the image of slave-holding colonial subjects is one instance in which structures of dominance and subjection are multidirectional.[5] Another example of colonial in-betweenness is depicted in John Demos's narrative of a daughter of colonial settlers who is abducted by Mohawks at an early age, resulting in a culture gap between herself and her English family, a tie to her Native American family, and an upending of traditional structures of colonial power.[6] Yet another compelling model for such colonial in-betweenness can be found in Richard White's concept of the imperial "middle ground," a space of cultural encounter and creative misunderstandings that emphasizes creative mutual production over colonial erasure or imperial conflicts.[7] This model also leaves room to attend to assertiveness on the part of colonized people. In various instances, then, individuals exercise power or are subject to it in ways that complicate dichotomous depictions of imperial power.

As with individuals, so with nations. Attention to colonial powers in history reveals transient positions of power and liminal colonial spaces. The above-mentioned jostling of myriad individuals can also be seen in the transient nature of empires, and some historians have explored former colonial identities behind what came to be colonizing powers. This point is apparent if we note that England itself was a colony of Rome and in the early modern period retained a long cultural memory of linguistic and legal insecurity as a "colonial backwater."[8] Similar shifts in power might be noted with regard to American patriotism and the tension between cultural memories of colonial identities and growing globalized power in the twentieth century. Finally, an intriguing instance in which the traditional imperial power dichotomy does not hold up is in reference to liminal colonial spaces, which can simultaneously operate on both sides of the dominance/subjugation dichotomy. For instance, Scotland stands out historically as a region that is alternatively viewed as a colonized space and as a colonizing entity.[9] The historical transience of empires and the colonial memories of colonizers, as well as the hybrid and "jostling" nature of the populations of empires, all push back on any simplistic conception of empire as a stable, unidirectional power structure.

This historiographical awareness of the liminal spaces of empire, in which regions and individuals do not always fit neatly into a dichotomy between colonizer and colonized, is fascinatingly reflected in the twin journeys of Messala and Judah. Throughout the interaction between these characters and the power of Rome, we see many instances that upend traditional conceptions of unidirectional imperial power. Power is exerted subversively within a power structure, particularly as Judah takes on a Roman identity, and then as he seeks revenge against Messala and later Rome itself. Importantly for this film, Judah's participation in this exercise of power and his embrace of an empowering hatred lead him on a path that resembles that of his former friend and sworn enemy.

One reflection of fluid colonial structures in the film is the way in which we see colonized forces working on colonizers in instances of subversion and cultural counter-imperialism. When Messala first returns to Judea, for example, as he speaks to Sextus about the state of the province, Sextus demonstrates that he is being influenced by the Jewish cultural narratives of a messiah. He speaks of a carpenter from Nazareth and comments thoughtfully, almost wistfully, that some of his teachings are quite profound. Messala is taken aback by his tone and immediately suggests that Sextus has been away from Rome for too long, and that he should return to the imperial metropole and "forget that God is in every man," as the Nazarene teaches. This clearly exhibits not only the potential for colonial cultural impact on the imperial center, but also the anxiety it provokes on the part of colonizers.[10]

In keeping with the theme of the fluid individual interaction in an imperial structure of dominance, it is important to note the changing character of Messala himself. Although we only encounter him as a villain, the ghost of his friendship with Judah speaks volumes about his former self and the goodness of a boy uncorrupted by the power of empire. We hear that he saved Judah's life and that Judah's sister has always been in love with him. Judah's mother recalls that they were both good boys. The closeness of the family, the descriptions of the former friendship, and the periodic references to Messala's former character attest to the dramatic shift in his character, after "the cruelty of Rome spread in his veins," as Judah puts it.

Judah makes this statement about the change in Messala at the hands of Rome to Pilate in an important scene about empire. In this scene, Pilate is informing Judah that he has been made a Roman citizen. Judah refuses the honor, saying that the "stamp" of Rome has made lepers of his family and he wants no part of it. He counters Pilate's claim that Messala has been punished for his deeds and he rejects Pilate's attempt to exculpate the imperial structures at fault. Judah insists that it was Rome that destroyed both Messala and his family. Messala has moved about in empire to his own destruction, changed and ruined by the power of Rome.

The most significant way in which the film explores the idea of fluid colonial structures, however, is in the changes undergone by Judah, and the parallels between his transformations and Messala's. Like Messala, Judah also moves through the fluid paths of an unstable colonial structure. This is most poignantly illustrated by a pair of shots after he has saved the life of the consul of Rome. After saving Quintus Arrius (Jack Hawkins) during a sea battle, Judah is following him across the deck of a Roman ship. We hear the music previously associated with the rowing of galley slaves. The camera cuts to a shot from below deck, looking up at Judah from the depths of the slave section of the ship, with the pounding music and the sounds of rowing. Immediately after this shot, we cut to a rousing scene of the triumphant march through the streets of Rome, where Judah stands in glory beside Arrius. This stark visual shift emphasizes Judah's movement from one side of the hierarchy of empire to the other, a movement which culminates when Judah is adopted by Arrius. Judah, the Jewish Prince of Hur, becomes first a condemned slave and then becomes young Arrius and, eventually, is granted Roman citizenship.

Like Messala, Judah moves through the unstable spaces of empire, and it changes him. The similarity between Judah and Messala in this regard complicates the stark dichotomy between the oppressed and the oppressor in a system that is mutually corrupting. For although Judah observes this destructive influence of Rome and rejects Roman citizenship, he does not initially reject the destructive influences of empire. On the contrary, it could be argued that he further embraces them, going ever more deeply down a path of hatred. When he rejects Roman citizenship, he also abandons Arrius, his adopted Roman father, and all of the love that that relationship implies. The path of destructive hatred that he walks during much of the film resembles strikingly the path by which the cruelty of Rome destroyed Messala.

Judah's destructive path begins when he pledges revenge. This pledge and the hatred that animates it keeps him alive in the galleys for years. This hatred brings him back to Judea, mingled with the desire to see his family again. It is only after he believes his family to be dead that he fully embraces revenge. However, the seeds are growing long before, as observed by a character named Balthazar (Finlay Currie). Well before learning anything about his mother and sister, on his journey back from Rome, Judah says that he will deal with Messala in his own way. Balthazar observes that Judah's "way" is to kill Messala. Balthazar warns that, no matter what Judah has suffered, he has no right to take life. Judah rejects the warning, as well as Balthazar's messages of faith and forgiveness.

The darkness of Judah's transformation and his embrace of Rome's cruelty is most powerfully captured in his scenes with his love interest, Esther (Haya Harareet). When Judah returns to find his former servants, Esther and her father, Simonides (Sam Jaffe), hiding out in his ruined home with no word from Miriam or Tirzah, he and Esther struggle with their many losses and with fundamental differences on what the future can hold. While Judah holds onto the past, the pain, and the loss, Esther asserts that hatred has completely destroyed her father and that Judah must stay away from Messala in order to stay alive. In a dramatic moment in which Judah believes he has finally lost his mother and sister, she cries desperately that Judah's search has come to an end and that he must go back to Rome. Fearful for the violence she sees in his intentions, she is anxious to remove him from the scene of his tragedy, from the proximity of the object of his hate, and from the cycle of violence in which he is caught.

Another important scene between Judah and Esther makes explicit the parallel between Judah and Messala. When Judah returns to the house late at night, he tells Esther that he has business with her father. Simonides is a gentle and elderly man who was imprisoned by the Romans for his association with Judah. In prison, he is tortured and broken, released only after being made a cripple. When it becomes clear that Judah might not find his mother and sister alive, Simonides tells him, "If one purpose fails it is good to have another." Describing to Judah how he managed to hide some of Judah's riches from the Romans, he tells him that the money is still hidden, waiting "to put power into our hands and buy death for the Romans." Esther is concerned that they are meeting, being aware of the violent intentions of Judah and her father in their growing plans for resistance. Judah vehemently tells Esther that the only way to clean his land of tyranny is with blood. Esther responds that blood will only bring more blood and that "death generates death as the vulture breeds the vulture." She also tries to tell Judah of the message she has heard from a Nazarene who preaches love of one's enemy. Judah dismisses such talk as only bringing more suffering. Esther realizes that she has lost Judah to hate. She asserts: "You seem to be now the very thing you set out to destroy, giving evil for evil. Hatred is turning you to stone. It's as though you had become Messala." In the beginning of this conversation, we heard themes of the anti-colonialism and the division that we encountered in the first section of this chapter. In the dramatic moment in which Esther makes this declaration, it becomes clear that, in his attempts to counter tyranny, Judah has become indistinguishable from Messala.

The strength of Judah's hatred and the path he sets for himself is openly proclaimed before the chariot race, the scene of his final confrontation with Messala. In his prayer, he whispers, "God forgive me for seeking vengeance, but my path is set." It is important to note that there is more at stake than the race itself in this revenge. Although Sheik Ilderim describes the goal as a delightful disgracing of Messala, his "defeat and humiliation at the hands of a Jew," there is a strong suggestion that Judah hopes for more than a racing victory, however symbolic and significant. As Sheik Ilderim puts it when convincing Judah to race against Messala, "There are no laws in the arena. Many are killed." Judah will go on to defeat Messala, and to see him broken and dying after the race. His anger does not die with Messala. It continues until he witnesses Jesus's crucifixion, which produces a conversion experience and takes "the sword out of [his] hands." But in the action leading up to and propelling him through the crucial chariot race, Judah embraces the politics of power that destroyed his former friend, subjugated his land, and set him on a path of resolved hatred.

CONCLUSION

The politics of aggression and violence attached to Roman imperialism throughout *Ben-Hur* are summed up in the problematic statement that Quintus Arrius makes to Judah when he first meets him in the slave galleys of a Roman warship: "Your eyes are full of hate . . . That's good. Hate keeps a man alive." This is the same hate that Judah would later draw on when he confronts Messala after returning to Judea, animating the revenge that he "vowed with every stroke of that oar [Messala] chained him to." The politics of violence is learned through the unimaginable suffering of a conquered person, condemned by cruel imperial injustice to a painful and uncertain existence. It is a hatred that keeps Judah alive to confront the cruelty of his oppressor and makes him successful in his revenge. But it is also a hatred that leaves him incapable of the love that Esther asks of him, incapable of returning to the early days his mother references when she wistfully says of Messala and Judah together, "You were good boys. I would have those days again." Ultimately, the film does offer a spiritual solution convincingly, miraculously, and movingly. The narrative does not, however, resolve the political problem that the film brings up in the post-colonial setting: how to oppose tyranny without embracing the violence it practices. In a telling conversation between Judah and Sheik Ilderim, both men agree that Balthazar, with his philosophy of forgiveness, is a good and peaceful man, but that, until all men are like him, "we must keep our swords bright." The film leaves this political problem of power and violence unresolved. It does, however, leave us with an important warning: in the context of post-colonial sentiment, Wyler emphasizes not only the violence and evil of colonial power, but the dangers that come with opposing that power. It is, simply, the warning not to become the very thing one sets out to destroy.

NOTES

1. Frederick Cooper, *Colonialism in Question: Theory, Knowledge, History* (Berkeley: University of California Press, 2005), 19.
2. For one of the most famous expressions of this post-colonial literature, see Franz Fanon, *The Wretched of the Earth*, trans. Richard Philcox (New York: Grove Press, 2004).
3. The same trend is repeated in other film presentations of the Roman Empire from the period, such as Stanley Kubrick's *Spartacus* (1960). Romans are played by British actors and oppressed peoples are portrayed by American actors.
4. Kathleen Wilson, "Introduction," in *New Imperial History: Culture, Identity and Modernity in Britain and the Empire, 1660-1840*, ed. Kathleen Wilson (Cambridge: Cambridge University Press, 2004), 12–13.
5. Christopher Brown gives a representation of economic and political aspects of slavery in eighteenth-century British West Indies from the perspective of plantation owners, not to privilege their view, but because they were "men in between, at once the elite in the colonies where they lived and the subjects of an imperial state over which they had little control." See Christopher Brown, "The Politics of Slavery," in *The British Atlantic World: 1500-1800*, eds David Armitage and Michael Braddick (London: Palgrave Macmillan, 2002), 232.
6. See John Demos, *The Unredeemed Captive: A Family Story from Early America* (New York: Alfred A. Knopf, 1994).
7. See Richard White, *The Middle Ground: Indians, Empires, and Republics in the Great Lakes Region, 1650-1815* (Cambridge: Cambridge University Press, 1991). See also Susan Sleeper-Smith, "The Middle Ground Revisited: Introduction," *The William and Mary Quarterly*, 63, no.1 (January, 2006): 3–8 and White, "Creative Understandings and New Understandings," *The William and Mary Quarterly*, 63, no.1 (January, 2006): 9–14.
8. For studies of the colonial identity as it persisted in English literature and rhetoric into the early modern period, particularly as a vernacular insecurity against the legacy of Roman rule and cultural dominance, see Paula Blank, *Broken English: Dialects and the Politics of Language in Renaissance Writing* (London: Routledge, 1996) and Jenny Mann, *Outlaw Rhetoric: Figuring Vernacular Eloquence in Shakespeare's England* (Ithaca and London: Cornell University Press, 2012).
9. For Scotland as a colonized space, see Michael Hechter, *Internal Colonialism: The Celtic Fringe in British National Development, 1536-1966* (Berkeley: University of California Press, 1975). For an alternative presentation of Scotland as an imperial force, see T. M. Devine, *Scotland's Empire and the Shaping of the Americas, 1600-1815* (Washington, DC: Smithsonian Books, 2003). For an image of Scotland in a project of nation building that overlaps with empire building, see Linda Colley, *Britons: Forging the Nation 1707-1832* (New Haven: Yale University Press, 1992).
10. For a post-colonial discussion of the multidirectional exchange of cultural material that refocuses attention on the agency and production of colonized people, see Dipesh Chakrabarty, *Provincializing Europe* (Princeton: Princeton University Press, 2000).

CHAPTER 14

"Life Isn't Always What One Likes": The Unbearable Lightness of Royalty, and Other Stereotypes in *Roman Holiday* (1953)

Etienne Boumans

Rome. I will cherish my visit here in memory as long as I live.[1]

Toward the end of William Wyler's *Roman Holiday*, the runaway Princess Ann (Audrey Hepburn) offers to cook for her "holiday" companion, American reporter Joe Bradley (Gregory Peck). He informs her that he has no kitchen, and so, he always eats out. She is intrigued and asks if he likes that. He responds, "Life isn't always what one likes." This conflict between necessity and enjoyment is a major theme of Wyler's film and raises the romantic comedy to a higher echelon of meaning than most instances of the genre.

The intimate relationship between international relations—or, if you prefer, high politics—and popular culture has been extensively researched and commented on. This was certainly the case for the era of the Cold War, when two world powers were opposing each other and made use of cultural signifiers, inter alia, to convince audiences of the superiority of "their" world view. Less researched is the period immediately after World War II, when Europe was licking its war wounds and the first seeds of the ensuing Cold War were planted.

In the early years of the Cold War—also called the "Age of Anxiety" after W. H. Auden's 1948 dramatic poem—US President Harry Truman and his successor Dwight Eisenhower worried a lot. They were convinced that if a democratic and pro-Western Italy was lost, the consequences for NATO, European integration, and the evolution of the Cold War in Europe could be immense.[2] The presidential worries were not entirely unjustified. In the aftermath of World War II, American presence in Italy in the military, political, and economic field was massive, and not universally endorsed across the local political spectrum. Hence, the US government officially recognized psychological activities—alongside military, economics, and diplomacy—as one of the basic means of influencing foreign affairs.[3] In the 1951–2 local elections in Italy, center parties suffered a general loss of popular vote and, following national elections in June 1953, the CIA judged the political situation still as "highly unstable."[4] A 1953 memorandum established that the US had aided materially—perhaps decisively—the government to "remain in power of a broadly representative, moderate, anti-Communist government friendly to the United States . . . Despite Communist influence, there exists among the Italian people, a large reservoir of good will for the United States and for Americans."[5]

It is against this troublesome background that *Roman Holiday* was filmed during summer of 1952. Rome was noisy, hot, and crowded. The script was written by the blacklisted screenwriter Dalton Trumbo, whose fronted work[6]—obtaining an Academy Award in 1954—passed uncredited for nearly forty years. The story is well known: an American reporter falls in love with a princess who is bored with the constraints that her regal status places on her. It was the first so-called "runaway production" whereby a major Hollywood film studio organized location shooting, studio work, and post-production on the spot.[7] Productions in which the actors were filmed on location outside Hollywood were called runaway productions. The illegitimate sound of the term, implying a flight from home, stems from the trade union leaders of the filmmaking branch, who criticized the loss of jobs for their members.

There were several reasons for William Wyler to make *Roman Holiday* in Italy, one of them the use of "frozen funds." European countries, suffering from severe balance-of-payments inequities with the US, had been compelled to tighten exchange regulations and freeze box-office revenues, which could not be repatriated to the home front.[8] Reinvesting these frozen funds in the local economy made great business sense.[9] First, permission had to be sought from the Italian Ministry of Enlightenment and Tourism. This would not be easy following complaints that the original script for *Roman Holiday* was a clichéd storyline involving the kidnapping of Princess Ann by the Mafia. Deemed inappropriate because of stereotypical material, this version was abandoned.[10] Another justification for a major studio to exploit the runaway production model was to take advantage of the "eighteen months tax exemption,"[11] which allowed motion picture professionals to avoid income tax on their foreign earnings when they resided abroad for long, uninterrupted periods.[12] Consequently, in spite of fierce opposition from Hollywood unions, runaway productions were an extremely attractive opportunity for the studios.

Yet another advantage of the runaway model was an aesthetic one. By filming *Roman Holiday* on location in the Eternal City, the authenticity of scenes and the credibility of the narrative could be greatly enhanced. In fact, *Roman Holiday*, epitomized as the cinematic incarnation of postwar chic, was one of the first films to introduce real and recognizable landmarks to delight audiences, even if their representation—in the words of Tom Carson—came close to that of a magical theme park, a "playground for Americans."[13] It was surely impossible to have the same impact if the movie were filmed in Hollywood—or any other make-believe location. Thus, Paramount initiated a stereotypical travelogue romance format, picked up by other studios who turned it into an, admittedly, short-lived cycle in the romantic comedy genre in the 1950s and 1960s.

As demonstrated by Trieu, the major US film studios were weakened by a 1948 Supreme Court Decision (*US v. Paramount Pictures Inc.*) dismantling the money-spinning studio system, and suffered inquiries run by the Congressional Subcommittee on Un-American Activities.[14] Moreover, due to the rapidly declining American market in terms of admissions, the European markets were becoming increasingly important.[15] Inspired by the relative success of Italian neorealism, the majors hoped to be able to reconnect with the masses through location shooting.[16] After all, neorealism, dealing with subject matter corresponding more closely with people's daily lives, "was able to speak to a global audience by visually conveying information about Italy, which was embedded in local reality but implied a universal appeal."[17] Of course, Paramount's "local reality" was different from the one in neorealist filmmaking. For one thing, Italian neorealism rejected the star system, while Hollywood was built on it. This chapter will closely examine US foreign policies which attempted to control the portrayal of America abroad in the Cold War era, and the efforts of US agencies to expel negative stereotypes from movie projects.

"SOFT" PROPAGANDA

In view of the political situation in Italy, US state agencies like the CIA, the Economic Cooperation Administration (ECA), the US Information Services (USIS), and the United States Information Agency (USIA) played a role likely to be labelled as "propaganda" in promoting national security through entertainment media. Millions of US dollars were invested into propaganda campaigns combating communism in Western Europe.[18] In March 1953, Senator Hickenlooper complained to the Motion Picture Association of America (MPAA) about the negative impact of US films on foreign audiences, as they "counteracted the efforts of American information experts."[19] While we have not been able to identify an unmistakable CIA—or any other government agency—involvement in the making of *Roman Holiday*, national security interests were never at a great distance from the filmmaking process, even if the overall purpose was to sell the American Dream by portraying capitalism in lifestyle terms.[20] With *Roman Holiday*, the US promoted world understanding and celebrated individual freedom and material affluence.[21]

In the 1950s, for political, economic, and diplomatic reasons, runaway productions exhibited a form of "soft" propaganda fortifying existing beliefs and sentiments, so much more effective than trying to convince through proselytizing, and *Roman Holiday* was no exception to the rule.[22] At first sight being a gentle romantic comedy, it was also a vehicle to disseminate the classic American ideal: the right to have a good time, which is well exemplified by the Romanian poster for *Vacanţă la Roma*, showing the image of Audrey Hepburn holding on happily to Gregory Peck during the scooter ride.[23]

Another foreign policy-related objective of shooting a postcard-like version of *Roman Holiday* was to lure the American middle class to Rome—the city being a principal character in the film. Paramount did little to hide this: "Although in no sense a travelogue, the film will give moviegoers a full picture of Rome."[24] As a matter of fact, the studio accompanied film screenings with tie-ins to win a "Free All-Expense Paid Round Trip to Rome for Two!" because "You'll want to see Rome after you see *Roman Holiday*."[25] It worked out exactly this way.

It has been alleged that Luigi Luraschi, head of censorship at Paramount, worked for the CIA. He believed Hollywood had a vital role in exporting "positive American values"—including the elimination of historical negative stereotypes—and put that in practice by checking the studio's pictures to eliminate possibly offensive material.[26] Other researchers consider him "a Hollywood insider," acting out of his personal idea of patriotic dedication to liaise with the CIA; thus, they advocate the watering down of the perception of the CIA as "puppet master" of cinematic censorship.[27] In the words of American diplomat and historian George F. Kennan: "This country [US] has no Ministry of Culture, and CIA was obliged to do what it could do to try to fill the gap."[28]

In 1953, US Ambassador Clare Boothe Luce sensed that "Italians are beginning to think more about pasta than guns, and more about national prosperity than European integration," fearful that "no amount of American propaganda couched in ideological terms will greatly alter this situation."[29] In a reaction, President Eisenhower suspected that this "increasing resentment against us . . . comes about because in the average mind the American is rich, pampered, spoiled, and, in spite of all his advantages, is socially and culturally little better than a barbarian."[30] With this remark, he affirmed that the elimination of negative stereotyping is a two-way street.

Convinced of the subversive potential of *Roman Holiday*, the US propaganda machine was particularly eager to sell the Western way of life—modern, glamorous, full of opportunity, and fun—to the Soviets. In 1958, an agreement was reached between governments to exchange seven movies produced in the USSR, for ten Hollywood feature films, including *Roman Holiday*.[31]

ROYALTY AND SOCIAL BOUNDARIES

Whereas Wyler initially thought of Liz Taylor or Jean Simmons as his heroine, he changed his mind after seeing Hepburn's screen test. He preferred a European flavor rather than a Hollywoodian one for the incarnation of a credible royal character: "I wanted someone you could believe was brought up as a princess: that was the main requisite . . . besides acting, looks, and personality."[32] Thus, he did not resort to typecasting, since his chosen actress had no acting record of any renown. In casting the film's protagonist, Wyler departed from common stereotypical perceptions of royalty. In so doing, he made a deliberate, and unique, choice to please his audience and lure them to the movie theatres. In retrospect, the choice was a good one.

At the time of casting, Hepburn was the perfect would-be princess: irreproachable, young, beautiful, fashionable, and white, and belonging linguistically and culturally to the higher social class, close enough to create a realistic portrayal of a regal education. Hepburn also had a British upper-class accent, generally known as "received pronunciation" (RP), without regional flavor and traditionally associated with high social prestige, power, and money. Due to her international upbringing in Belgium, England, and the Netherlands—her mother was a Dutch baroness—the accent was not flawless: she spoke it more slowly than native, upper-class British people.[33]

Joanne B. Freeman, American History Professor at Yale, asserts that Americans always had a double-edged attitude toward (British) royalty: "Even during the American Revolution we were revolting against Britain—and its monarchy—and yet we were awe-struck by all things royal."[34] Americans, deprived of the reassuring concept of a constitutional monarchy, seem to embrace royalty and nobility and this fascination has affected even non-royals like the Kennedys, the Jacksons, and, more recently, the Kardashians. The awe for Hepburn, incarnating Princess Ann in *Roman Holiday*, is part of this obsession.

Before the start of filming, Paramount had to make a deal with the UK censor that Hepburn's character should not be presented as a member of the British royal family to avoid any association with Princess Margaret. Hence, Princess Ann becomes a member of the royal family of an unnamed European country.[35] The British monarchy being ruled out, the establishing newsreel asserts that she is "a gracious young member of one of Europe's oldest ruling families." She is addressed as "Your Royal Highness" no less than eleven times. During her fugue, the ambassador reminds staff that "the Princess is the direct heir to the throne" while both "Their Majesties" are alive and well.

Peter Krämer rightly stresses that "a strong effort is made here to blur the boundary between the fictional princess and real-life royalty, to link her story to the political realities of post-war Europe, and also to show her appeal to the people across Europe."[36] The permeability of reality and fiction was successful enough to confuse, occasionally, even the media: the caption underneath a picture taken at a 1953 trade screening of *Roman Holiday* in London, mistook actress Margaret Rawlings, impersonating Countess Vereberg in the movie, as "Lady-in-Waiting to Queen Elizabeth."[37]

Roman Holiday offers the epitome of regal illusions. Princess Ann is the honorary guest at a sumptuous ball, and wears an opulent gown and jewelry, while welcoming the "fine fleur" of diplomacy and nobility. Her immediate staff (the ambassador, the countess, and the general) displays not only a striking age difference with the princess, but they are also heavily stereotyped as the usual human furniture of a royal household.

The princess is on a "much publicized goodwill tour of European capitals." She is a royal with a mission. However, she is also bored to death (Figure 14.1). Rebelling against her royal obligations, the princess goes out on a spree in Rome, and falls in love with an American newspaperman, Joe Bradley. He is a cultured, kind, honest, handsome, and tall man with some money worries, and is not very materialistic, exactly how the US government wanted Americans to be represented. Bradley finds the fugitive princess sleeping on a low city wall. This is reminiscent of the Sleeping Beauty

Figure 14.1 Life isn't always what one likes (*Roman Holiday*, 1953)

narrative—an innocent, pretty heroine, persecuted by an "evil" royal household, waiting to be saved by a would-be prince. Though, in this instance, the princess is not searching for a definitive love interest, but for herself and the meaning of life. This fairy tale transformation shows that stereotypes are not always fixed and are subject to change to make them suitable for new audiences in a different timeframe and media. It also demonstrates Wyler's talent for taking formulaic narratives and giving them a slight twist.

By focusing on the relationship between a princess and a commoner, Wyler succeeded in transcending social boundaries.[38] However, "after the first embrace, she pulls herself away and regains her royal composure; after the second, she pulls away to fulfil her royal duty."[39] When she returns to her embassy, she (ab)uses her regal prerogatives to subdue her staff. Her fugue and encounter with commoners may have liberated her and given her perspective on "the good life" of ordinary people, but it has not rendered her conduct more democratic or empathic towards her servants.

Far from it. When being reminded of "her duty" by the ambassador, she replies with a commanding presence:

> Your Excellency: I trust you will not find it necessary to use that word again. Were I not completely aware of my duty to my family and my country, I would not have come tonight. [They look at her, in silence; after a pause, grimly.] Or indeed ever again. [Ann walks across the room.] Now, since I understand we have a very full schedule today, you have my permission to withdraw.[40]

In fact, in her newly found self-confidence, Princess Ann appears resentful towards her staff, who she seems to hold—at least partly—responsible for her puzzled state of mind. This characterization is very different from a 1960 theatrical movie pressbook's catchphrase: "the princess who yearned for a common touch!"[41]

The final scene, the meeting of the international press at the embassy, takes place in a far too majestic place for a fuzzy monarchy. Princess Ann, "a true-blue blood right down to her royal fingertips,"[42] falls back into a stately stereotype, acting high and mighty though in breach of protocol. Joe Bradley and his photographer stand in awe of Her Royal Highness; intimacy and equality have faded away. While displaying a kind attitude regarding her former partners-in-crime and without being able to hide her emotions, Ann cannot but abide to regal standards, treating both men as the commoners they are. And thus, the initial social disparity, a favorite theme of Wyler's, is reconducted. Not a pretty, nor hopeful sight.

The marketing tools (posters, pressbooks) in Japan had only eyes for the royal pose of Princess Ann, wearing her tiara, leaving little space for other movie shots. In other regions, the (ambiguous) movie title was modified focusing on a trope to please local audiences: Latin America, *La princesa que quería vivir* (*The Princess Who Wanted to Live*); Germany, *Ein Herz und eine Krone* (*A Heart and a Crown*); Switzerland, *Römische Nächte* (*Roman Nights*); or Brazil, *A Princesa e o Plebeu* (*The Princess and the Pauper*).

Stanley Cavell postulated that "advanced popular cinema narration is based more on types than on stereotypes,"[43] and these types were there to stay. With the character of Princess Ann, however, Wyler created not an *individual*, but an *individuality*: more original than "stereotype" figures and, through an emphasis on difference, a "striking separateness from other actors, but also from the people in the audience's everyday surroundings."[44] In fact, the *separateness* was so stunning in *Roman Holiday* that it was also *exclusive*, at least until other movies picked up the image and turned it into a type.

This is where Hollywood and royalty meet: authenticity, the glamour of stardom, the embodiment of integrity and influence—if not power—and the yearning for escapism. In the eye of biographer Martin Gitlin:

> Viewers felt as if she [Hepburn] were Princess Ann, from the moment she escaped from her confining royal existence to the point at which she was discovered dancing on a barge with the man with whom she had fallen in love and was forced to return to her life of sheltered misery.[45]

This would seem divergent from the widely expected "happy ending," and is replaced by a resolution of "doing what is right for one's country."[46] It may be true that, at this time, audiences expected a royal heir(ess) to take up their duties, which is what Princess Ann does in the end (Figure 14.2). In this sense, Ann's choice of duty over personal emancipation could be seen as a happy ending, despite the fact that it leaves Joe Bradley lonely and pensive.

BEAUTY AND MEASUREMENTS

At the time of her first American-backed movie, there was some controversy over the looks and physique of Hepburn. The fan magazines, abiding by the female stereotypes popularized during the Studio Era, described her in terms slightly new to the Hollywood vocabulary: "coquettish, saint-like, tom-boy, hoydenish, disarming, sensitive, captivating."[47] Under the suggestive title "Who needs Beauty!," *Photoplay* columnist Mike Connolly reminded readers of what was of importance in stardom in those days: "By Hollywood standards—and one must never, *never* minimize Hollywood standards!—Audrey Hepburn is flat-chested, slim-hipped and altogether un-Marilyn Monroe-ish.

Figure 14.2 Duty comes before pleasure (*Roman Holiday*, 1953)

Her measurements are: bust, 32"; waist, 20½"; hips, 34. Nothing sensational there, is there?"[48] Pauline Swanson made a similar judgement:

> For modelling . . . her figure would be an asset. But the films, traditionally, have required more voluptuous contours. She is string-bean-like by Hollywood's standards, too tall, too thin, and virtually, as she herself candidly admits, flat-chested. And she will have no truck with "falsies" either.[49]

Likewise, Carl Clement compares Hepburn to "the rounded blondes in the shape of a Marilyn or a Jayne," and concludes: "Audrey never fitted any of these clichés nor did any of these clichés fit her."[50] Such comments would not be accepted today and would be highly criticized for objectifying women. Not so in the 1950s. Such negative assessments were confuted when, upon her arrival on the set, Hepburn was handed over to multiple Academy Awards winning costume designer Edith Head, who turned the actress's "waif-like physique into assets, making her stylish and elegant"—unlike in her earlier movie *Monte Carlo Baby* (Jean Boyer and Lester Fuller, 1951).[51]

Whatever some fan and film magazines' columnists and commentators wrote about her looks and physique, the public and critics instantly adored Hepburn. Wyler was a great director, who succeeded through clever camera work and cutting in organizing the moviegoers' sympathy for and even identification with Princess Ann. It was the beginning of a successful film career for a new kind of actress who overturned the stereotypical "femme fatale" or the voluptuous tart-like image of yesteryear's moviemaking. Hepburn became a highly accomplished performer sufficiently versatile "to rise above both type and stereotype."[52]

Wyler made sure that his heroine was neither sexually objectified, nor a trophy girlfriend, a disposable woman or femme fatale, nor an awkward virgin, a gold digger, or an asexual career woman, and not even a bridezilla (we're in the midst of a fairy tale, are we not?). In other words: Princess Ann was authentic, genuine, and credible and her femininity not stereotyped according to the narrative.

If Hepburn was not attractive according to the standards of the day, then how does one account for her immediate popularity? The answer is that Hepburn's screen persona was not created for the "male gaze," but for a feminine audience. Her story of the little girl who suffered hardship and helped out the resistance during the German occupation of Holland, later to become a fragile film star, personifying beauty, romance, fashion and taste, and social mobility, fascinated female filmgoers.[53] She was precursor of a democratization of beauty standards, offering a combination of boyish-ness and feminine chic, "potentially available to and achievable by any young woman."[54]

The cross-cultural consumption of stars involves a complex negotiation between similarity and difference, says Yaeri Kim, but records and research on how local audiences perceive these differences are rare. What we do know is that, up to 2018, Hepburn ranked first among the "most beautiful foreign actresses" loved by South Koreans. Nowadays, Hepburn still has a considerable influence on South Korean culture, as illustrated by the 2014 film *Miss Granny* reminiscing about *Roman Holiday*.[55] The actress recreating Hepburn's look in *Roman Holiday* fails to attain the same level of sophistication due to her unmistakable (and thus stereotypical) Korean features. However, she achieves her goal in life by striving towards "inner beauty."[56]

FLANERIE AND THE GAZE

It was Charles Baudelaire, the French romantic poet and art critic, who portrayed the stereotypical concept of the *flâneur* in his essay *"Le peintre de la vie moderne"* (*The Painter of Modern Life*, 1863); the German philosopher and literary critic Walter Benjamin analyzed this concept in urban sociological terms.[57] *Flânerie* is associated with idleness and the act of strolling without purpose, and is "resisting the logic of straight lines."[58] A recurrent feature of the *flâneur* is also their disappearance in the anonymous crowd.

Amy Murphy explained that in romantic comedies, "the narratives convey the idea that urban experience is not universal but is, in fact, highly contingent upon gender, age, race, and/or class."[59] In the nineteenth century—and well into the twentieth—the *flâneur* was a prototypical male social type, as only men, often well off, enjoyed the liberty to stroll the contemporary city street and relate to it. As late as 1985, Janet Wolff repudiated the existence of the female *flâneur*.[60] Subject to spatial classification, women on the street were of dubious virtue and the proper kind of lady was often confined to a secluded, private space. In order not to be seen as a "street walker," French romantic, female writer George Sand dressed as a man to gain access to urban public spaces—in breach of the law, which in the 1830s prohibited women to dress like men; thus, Sand applied Baudelaire's mandatory prerequisite of *flânerie*: its invisibility.[61] Princess Ann does something similar by dressing down on her spree.

Several authors, among them Jane Rendell, suggested that the "uncontrollability" of *flâneuses* in the city causes confusion with their male narrative counterparts.[62] This is what happens in *Roman Holiday* to Peck's character, who, at first, unaware of Ann's royal status, perceives her as a drunken girl and exhibits so-called "stranger wariness." This disruption, emanating from a female protagonist, is omnipresent in *Roman Holiday*, as Hepburn's character successively shatters the protocol by her fugue from the embassy, perturbs an American journalist's everyday behavior, causes turmoil by the motorcycle ride in the city center, and joins in the dance bar riot. At the same time, we recognize these events not only as emancipatory for Hepburn's persona, but also as liberating in the larger sense.

Users of public spaces like tourists, street workers, shoppers, commuters, and *flâneurs* all function alongside each other in an urban environment. Most of them are unaware of or indifferent to the presence of others, reducing urban others to ultimate invisibility (Figure 14.3). In *Roman Holiday*, Joe and Ann do not behave like tourists (no pictures taken, no travel guide) or like shoppers (apart from an ice cone); they connect with the urban public space and its enticements, while they only have eyes for each other. In his movie, Wyler did his best to integrate his female actor into the urban environment, without ever suggesting that she was an object of the "male gaze".[63] In reality, the film crew had a lot of trouble clearing the streets of onlooking film buffs, eager to watch Peck in particular, since his female partner was just starting her career and therefore more of an anonymous figure.

Figure 14.3 *Flâneurs* are invisible to others (*Roman Holiday*, 1953)

ITALIANS AND PERFORMATIVE MASCULINITY

Mass media, and Hollywood in particular, have a tradition of negatively depicting Italians living in the US as impulsive, passionate, family protective, aggressive (if not violent), religious, and displaying peculiar eating habits and exaggerated gestures. These stereotypical representations were recurring from the early silent films onwards and changed only slowly over time.[64] Elisabeth Hart revealed that these essentialist stereotypes "satisfy an aesthetic need, partly fueled by a sense of exotic difference."[65] While these on-screen portrayals are deeply influential of spectators' perceptions, often precursory of prejudices, discrimination and injustices, audiences can accept or challenge these long-lasting representations and organize their own deconstruction or re-construction process.[66] It led to the humiliation of Italian immigrants rejecting their own backgrounds to "become an American."[67] The participation of thousands of Italian Americans in World War II on the side of the "good guys" led to greater social acceptance and a paradigmatic change in their depiction in the media, including movies.[68]

Wyler, who originated from the Alsace region, then German, currently French, was sensitive to stereotypical imagery and put every effort into

Figure 14.4 "Positive" stereotypes of Italian locals (*Roman Holiday*, 1953)

avoiding these characteristic pitfalls. He did, however, employ stereotypes with regards to the local Italians (both actors and hundreds of extras), but through what might be seen as positive stereotypes – cheerful, honest, simple, kind, poor but confident about the future[69] (Figure 14.4). He avoided portraying the performative masculinity, generally attributed to Mediterranean males. Hence, *Roman Holiday* depicts an American-friendly vision of Rome, without any reference to the fascist period, and in line with the US government's expectations.

Stereotyping also occurs in the film's soundscape. In this case, the cameras have captured the (diegetic) noises and music—waltzes at the embassy ball, jazz at the dancing barge—of a lively, everyday Rome, of sidewalk cafes, the Pantheon, the Forum; and of such landmarks as the Castel Sant'Angelo and the mirrored grandeur of the Colonna, Brancaccio, and Barberini Palazzi.[70]

The *Roman Holiday* production itself was not immune from bad press reviving these stereotypes. Gossip writer Louella Parsons wrote: "From Rome comes word that Willie Wyler is having troubles getting *Roman Holiday* on the screen. Italians no likee [*sic*] to work in the hot weather and take siestas every afternoon."[71]

SCOOTERS AND SHOOTING

Perhaps the most iconic scene of this film—and a milestone in cinematic history—is the ride of the two protagonists on the famous Piaggio *ur*-scooter, the Vespa (Italian for "wasp") (Figure 14.5). Designed in 1946, it is one of the most seminal creations of Italian craftsmanship, inspiring media, advertisers, and creatives alike. Originally meant to offer cheap mobility to Italians having survived World War II and without means to buy a car, the Vespa turned into a must-have for generations of young users.[72]

One should think that the company management should have been utterly pleased to be able to showcase its finest piece of engineering. Alas, product placement in Italy was illegal, and the Piaggio company management had no idea that the Vespa's "organic inclusion" in a crucial scene would engender considerable commercial benefit. In this context, it should be noted that American-style publicity campaigns and marketing clashed with an obvious European preoccupation with aesthetics and taste.[73] As was to be expected, sales of the scooter soared sky-high once the movie was screened globally and brought the Vespa worldwide visibility. Yet, the Piaggio people requested that Paramount return both vehicles, which had been put at the studio's disposal,

Figure 14.5 The iconic Vespa ride from *Roman Holiday* (1953) lives on

when shooting was complete. This, however, did not prevent Wyler from requesting a brand-new Vespa after his return to Hollywood.[74]

According to Paramount's pressbook, the Vespa ride was one of the most difficult scenes to shoot: "Each time Wyler tried to film the scene, fun loving Italians drove their own scooters into the camera view to wave to the stars and to join in the frolic."[75] Though this story might have been a marketing invention, it did take Wyler five days to finish the scene.

The Vespa scene, which summarized the youthful, mischievous spirit of the film, was extensively exploited by the publicity people at Paramount through movie posters, lobby cards, and pressbooks. Images of the scooter ride adorned the front page of a Danish pressbook (*Prinsessen holder Fridag*; The princess takes a day off), an Italian movie poster, and an English-language series of lobby cards, which had a drawing of the Vespa ride in the baseline. A 1962 re-release pressbook contained small impressions and a still of the Vespa ride.[76] On the whole, this can be considered a rather meagre harvest for this archetypal scene. It may be concluded, therefore, that the use of the Vespa ride as an extensive marketing tool is more myth than reality.

Indeed, the Piaggio company's archives list some 800 films showcasing the Vespa between its first appearance in *Roman Holiday* and the present era.[77] The prop also had earlier appearances in *Roma città aperta* (Roberto Rossellini, 1945) and *Ladri di biciclette* (Vittorio De Sica, 1948), as well as later appearances in *La Dolce Vita* (Federico Fellini, 1960) and *Caro diario* (Nanni Moretti, 1993). In *The Talented Mr. Ripley* (Anthony Minghella, 1999), a story which takes place in 1958–9, Tom Ripley (Matt Damon) takes Marge Sherwood (Gwyneth Paltrow) on a Vespa ride around Rome—a scene which one could easily see as a homage to *Roman Holiday*. One of the most awkward replicas of the original ride takes place in the made-for-TV *Rome in Love* (Eric Bross, 2019) by Hallmark. The story involves the making of a remake of *Roman Holiday*. Amelia (Italia Ricci), hoping to be casted as Princess Ann, takes a Vespa driving lesson. The ensuing scene is too strained to even be characterized as derivative. Thus, over the years, the once iconic Vespa ride evolved (or more appropriately, devolved) into one of the most painful clichés in the history of film.

CONCLUSION

Over the years, as Daniel Steinhart remarks, *Roman Holiday* has become an exemplar of Hollywood's postwar international productions: it has received attention for its continental charm, the Roman backdrops, and its stars.[78] It was also "a film that showed the promise of rebirth, recovery and optimism and represented a new beginning for Rome in the 1950s."[79]

Well ahead of his time, Wyler eliminated a great deal of overt expressions of prejudice and negative stereotyping from his inverted fairy-tale movie, even if he may have been pressurized by a US government (or censor) watching over his shoulder. Cooper and Meeuf insist that "the link between [the travelogue romance] cycle and US foreign policy is functional, not causal."[80] The movie inspired other directors through its subject matter, camera work, style, genre, and methodology for years to come. Multiple later movies paid homage to *Roman Holiday*, and scenes are replicated or diegetically introduced into many narratives.[81]

Some seventy years after its inception, *Roman Holiday* still stands, not only as another example of Wyler's ability to deftly handle different genres, but also a highly successful foreign investment, not only in economic terms, but perhaps even more in cultural terms. By introducing standards of political correctness well before they became widespread, *Roman Holiday* could be termed "wokeness *avant la lettre*." For both the US and Italian governments, *Roman Holiday*, filmed on location in Rome and Cinécitta, remains a major US contribution to democracy and prosperity in Italy. So much so that on October 18, 2016, to celebrate the centenary of the birth of Gregory Peck, the US Embassy in Rome organized a public screening of *Roman Holiday* at the Piazza di Spagna, where it all began.[82]

NOTES

1. Princess Ann (Audrey Hepburn).
2. CIA, Confidential-Security Information, 30jul1953, approved for release 2003/03/28, CIA-RDP80-01065A000200120002-1.
3. Nicholas J. Cull, *The Cold War and the United States Information Agency: American Propaganda and Public Diplomacy, 1945-1989* (New York: Cambridge University Press, 2008), 54; Kenneth Osgood, *Total Cold War: Eisenhower's Secret Propaganda Battle at Home and Abroad* (Lawrence: University Press of Kansas, 2006), 7–9.
4. CIA, SECRET. Approved for release 2005/06/23: CIA-RDP79R00904A000100030045-1; CIA, Memorandum for the Intelligence Advisory Committee, Dec 28, 1953, approved for release 2000/08/29: CIA-RDP79R00890A000020042-7.
5. CIA, An Evaluation of Psychological Effect of U.S. Efforts in Italy. SECRET-Security Information. Approved for release 2006/03/17: CIA-RDP80R01731R003300190049-7.
6. Fronted work refers to the practice by blacklisted writers of having another individual, or "front," present the work as theirs.
7. Robert R. Shandley, *Runaway Romances: Hollywood's Postwar Tour of Europe* (Philadelphia: Temple University Press, 2009), 20.
8. Paul Thomas, "Runaways," *Film Quarterly* 63, no. 2 (December 1, 2009): 86, <https://doi.org/10.1525/FQ.2009.63.2.86> (last accessed August 24, 2022).
9. Zennie Trieu, "Domestic Troubles Take a 'Holiday': William Wyler's Pro-American Adventure Overseas in the Early Cold War Era," *Medium* 13 (December 2016), <https://medium.com/@zennietrieu/domestic-troubles-take-a-holiday-14296a6cb559> (last accessed August 24, 2022).

10. Tony Shaw and Denise J. Youngblood, *Cinematic Cold War: The American and Soviet Struggle for Hearts and Minds* (Lawrence: University Press of Kansas, 2010), 106, <https://www.amazon.com/Cinematic-Cold-War-American-Struggle/dp/0700620206> (last accessed August 24, 2022).
11. Eric Hoyt, "Hollywood and the Income Tax, 1929–1955," *Film History* 22, no. 1 (2010): 5–21, <https://doi.org/10.2979/fil.2010.22.1.5> (last accessed August 24, 2022).
12. Daniel Steinhart, *Runaway Hollywood: Internationalizing Postwar Production and Location Shooting* (Berkeley: University of California Press, 2019), 130.
13. Tom Carson, "True Fakes on Location: World-Building, Hollywood-Style," *The Baffler*, no. 31 (2016): 36, <www.jstor.org/stable/43958933> (last accessed August 24, 2022).
14. Trieu, "Domestic Troubles Take a 'Holiday'".
15. Peter Krämer, "'Faith in Relations between People': Audrey Hepburn, Roman Holiday and European Integration," in 100 *Years of European Cinema: Entertainment or Ideology?*, eds. Diana Holmes and Allison Smith (Manchester and New York: Manchester University Press, 2000) 199.
16. Shandley, 23.
17. Francesco Pitassio, *Neorealist Film Culture 1945-1954: Rome, Open Cinema* (Amsterdam: Amsterdam University Press, 2019), 101.
18. Shaw and Youngblood, 107; John Dean, "The Diffusion of American Culture in Western Europe Since World War Two: A Crosscultural Survey," *Journal of American Culture*, 20 (1997): 11–24, <https://doi.org/10.1111/j.1542-734X.1997.t01-1-00011.x> (last accessed August 24, 2022).
19. Laura A. Belmonte, *Selling the American Way: U.S. Propaganda and the Cold War* (Philadelphia: University of Pennsylvania Press, 2008), 168.
20. Shaw and Youngblood, 98–9.
21. Hiroshi Kitamura, review, "Cinematic Cold War: The American and Soviet Struggle for Hearts and Minds, Tony Shaw and Youngblood, Denise J.. Lawrence: University Press Kansas, 2010," *Journal of American Culture*, 38 (2015): 157–8, <https://doi.org/10.1111/jacc.12313> (last accessed August 24, 2022); Stephen Gundle, "'We Have Everything to Learn from the Americans': Film Promotion, Product Placement and Consumer Culture in Italy, 1945-1965," *Historical Journal of Film, Radio and Television* 40, no. 1 (2020): 59, <https://doi.org/10.1080/01439685.2020.1715596> (last accessed August 24, 2022).
22. Shaw and Youngblood, 218.
23. Sam Sarowitz, *Translating Hollywood: The World of Movie Posters* (New York: Mark Batty Publisher, 2007), 26. The author mistook the poster's language for Italian instead of Romanian; Shaw and Youngblood, 100.
24. *Roman Holiday Paramount Merchandising manual and press book*, Paramount Pictures Corp. 1962, 2.
25. *Roman Holiday press book*, 5.
26. Shaw and Youngblood, 108; John S. Bowman, *Pergolesi in the Pentagon: Life at the Front Lines of the Cultural Cold War* (Bloomington: Xlibris LLC, 2014), 130; David Eldridge, "'Dear Owen': The CIA, Luigi Luraschi and Hollywood, 1953," *Historical Journal of Film, Radio and Television*, 20 (2000): 149–96, is an important corrective to Saunders' account of the CIA's activities in the US film industry, in particular her misidentification of Carleton Alsop as the Agency's "man in Hollywood." (See Frances Stonor Saunders, *The Cultural Cold War: The CIA and the World of Arts and Letters* (New York and London: The New Press, 2013), 244–7.)
27. Simon Willmetts, "Quiet Americans: The CIA and Early Cold War Hollywood Cinema," *Journal of American Studies* 47, no. 1 (2013): 127–47, <https://doi.org/10.1017/S0021875812000060> (last accessed August 24, 2022).

28. Josef Joffe, "America's Secret Weapon," *The New York Times*, April 23, 2000, 15.
29. Dispatch (labelled "secret") by Ms. Clare Boothe Luce, US Ambassador, Aug 7, 1953, <https://history.state.gov/historicaldocuments/frus1952-54v06p2/d751> (last accessed August 24, 2022).
30. Letter (labelled "top secret") from Dwight D. Eisenhower to Ambassador Luce, Nov 7, 1953, <https://history.state.gov/historicaldocuments/frus1952-54v06p2/d754> (last accessed August 24, 2022).
31. Shaw and Youngblood, 100, 110.
32. Neil Sinyard, *A Wonderful Heart: The Films of William Wyler* (Jefferson: McFarland & Company, 2013), 148.
33. Audrey Hepburn repeatedly said that "she had no mother tongue." Kirtley Baskette, "Dutch Treat", *Modern Screen* (April 1954): 91, <https://archive.org/stream/modernscreen48unse#page/n415/mode/2up> (last accessed August 24, 2022).
34. Linton Weeks, "Royalty, Schmoyalty: Revolting against the Wedding," aired April 28, 2011, on *National Public Radio*, <https://text.npr.org/135733972> (last accessed August 24, 2022).
35. Though Shaw and Youngblood think she's from Coravia (Shaw and Youngblood, 101, 104). To avoid associations with existing countries, directors have invented fictional countries like Krakozhia (*The Terminal*, Steven Spielberg, 2004), Freedonia (*Duck Soup*, Leo McCarey, 1933), or Bacteria (*The Great Dictator*, Charlie Chaplin, 1940).
36. Krämer, 202.
37. *Motion Picture Herald*, August 8, 1953, 11.
38. Dom Holdaway and Filippo Trentin, "Roman Fever: Anarchiving Eternal Rome, from Roman Holiday to Petrolio," *Journal of Romance Studies* 14, no. 3 (2014): 9, <https://doi.org/10.3828/jrs.14.3.5> (last accessed August 24, 2022).
39. Radie Harris, "Audrey Hepburn: The Girl, the Gamin and the Star," *Photoplay* (March 1955): 112.
40. <http://www.script-o-rama.com/movie_scripts/r/roman-holiday-script-transcript.html> (last accessed August 24, 2022).
41. Paramount Press Book, *Detective Story/Roman Holiday*, 1960, 6. <https://www.worthpoint.com/worthopedia/roman-holiday-detective-story-1839142113> (last accessed August 30, 2022).
42. Philip Hamburger, "The Current Cinema: Holiday," *New Yorker*, August 29, 1953, 52.
43. Stanley Cavell, *The World Viewed: Reflections on the Ontology of Film* (Cambridge, MA: Harvard University Press, 1979), 33. Quoted in Jörg Schweinitz, *Film and Stereotype: A Challenge for Cinema and Theory* (New York: Columbia University Press, 2011), 47.
44. Schweinitz, 48; Stanley Cavell, *The World Viewed: Reflections on the Ontology of Film* (Cambridge, MA: Harvard University Press, 1979), 33.
45. Martin Gitlin, *Audrey Hepburn: A Biography* (Westport: Greenwood, 2009), 44.
46. Trieu, "Domestic Troubles Take a 'Holiday'".
47. Jane Wilkie, "Audrey Hepburn," *Modern Screen* (November 1953): 92.
48. Mike Connolly, "Who Needs Beauty!," *Photoplay* (January 1954): 48.
49. Pauline Swanson, "Knee-deep in Stardust," *Photoplay* (April 1954): 102; Donald Spoto, *Enchantment: The Life of Audrey Hepburn* (London: Arrow Books, 2006), 60.
50. Carl Clement, "You're Going, Audrey!," *Photoplay* (June 1957): 47.
51. Shaw and Youngblood, 103; Réka Buckley, "Elsa Martinelli: Italy's Audrey Hepburn," *Historical Journal of Film, Radio and Television* 26, no. 3 (2006): 328.
52. Arthur Knight, "Types, Stereotypes, and Acting in Films," *College English* 15, no. 1 (October 1953): 5.
53. Rachel Moseley, "Trousers and Tiaras: Audrey Hepburn, a Woman's Star," *Feminist Review* 71 (2002): 40, <https://doi.org/10.1057/palgrave.fr.9400025> (last accessed August 24, 2022).

54. Moseley, 44–5.
55. Yaeri Kim, "Like Audrey: Adoring, Imitating, and Localizing Hepburn in *Miss Granny* (2014)," *Journal of Popular Culture* 53, no. 3 (2020): 626–7.
56. Kim, 634–5.
57. Walter Benjamin, *Charles Baudelaire: A Lyric Poet in the Era of High Capitalism*, trans. Harry Zohn, second ed. (London and New York: Verso, 1997), 37; Arina Cirstea, "A Space of One's Own: Reading Michèle Roberts' Urban Imaginary," *Peer English* 9 (2014): 44.
58. "Found in Translation: The Restless 'Flâneur'", <https://www.lomography.com/magazine/337024-found-in-translation-the-restless-flaneur> (last accessed August 24, 2022); Mark W. Turner, "Zigzagging," in *Restless Cities*, eds. Matthew Beaumont and Gregory Dart (London and New York: Verso, 2010), 307.
59. Amy Murphy, "Traces of the Flâneuse," *Journal of Architectural Education* 60, no. 1 (2006): 33, <https://www.tandfonline.com/doi/abs/10.1111/j.1531-314X.2006.00058.x> (last accessed August 24, 2022).
60. Janet Wolff, "The Invisible Flâneuse: Women and the Literature of Modernity," *Theory, Culture and Society* 2, no. 3 (1985): 37–48; Elfriede Dreyer and Estelle McDowall, "Imagining the Flaneur as a Woman," *Communicatio: South African Journal for Communication Theory and Research* 38, no.1 (2012): 33; Elizabeth Wilson, *The Contradictions of Culture: Cities, Culture, Women* (London: Sage Publications, 2001), 84.
61. Philippa Stockley, review, "Flâneuse: Women Walk the City in Paris, New York, Tokyo, Venice and London, by Lauren Elkin—review," *Evening Standard* (July 28, 2016).
62. Jane Rendell, "Ramblers and Cyprians: Mobility, Visuality and the Gendering of Architectural Space," in *Gender and Architecture*, eds. M. L. Durning and Richard Wrigley (Chichester: John Wiley & Sons, 2000), 143.
63. Unlike Ruth Orkin's photograph, "American Girl in Italy," taken in Florence in 1951, showing sixteen mesmerized Italian men all gazing at an American girl passing by. Published above Emily Jay's article "When you travel alone . . ." in the September 1952 issue of *Cosmopolitan*.
64. Karen A. Szczepanski, "The Scalding Pot: Stereotyping of Italian-American Males in Hollywood Films," *Italian Americana* 5, no. 2 (Spring/summer 1979): 202, <https://www.jstor.org/stable/29775974> (last accessed August 24, 2022).
65. Elizabeth Hart, "Destabilising Paradise: Men, Women and Mafiosi: Sicilian Stereotypes," *Journal of Intercultural Studies* 28, no. 2 (2007): 213, 225, <https://doi.org/10.1080/07256860701236625> (last accessed August 24, 2022).
66. Frank P. Tomasulo, "Italian Americans in the Hollywood Cinema: Filmmakers, Characters, Audiences," *VIA: Voices in Italian Americana* 7, no. 1 (1996).
67. Rosanne De Luca Braun, "Made in Hollywood: Italian Stereotypes in the Movies," March 2006, <https://www.slideshare.net/mattheworegan/made-in-hollywood-italian-americans-in-film> (last accessed August 24, 2022).
68. Jonathan J. Cavallero, "Written Out of the Story: Issues of Television Authorship, Reception, and Ethnicity in NBC's 'Marty,'" *Cinema Journal* 56, no. 3 (2017): 67, <www.jstor.org/stable/44867820> (last accessed August 24, 2022); Matteo Pretelli, "Hollywood's Depiction of Italian American Servicemen During the Italian Campaign of World War II," *European Journal of American Studies* 15, no. 2 (2020), <http://journals.openedition.org/ejas/15758> (last accessed August 24, 2022).
69. Gundle, 70.
70. A. W. Weiler, "Roman Holiday at Music Hall is Modern Fairy Tale Starring Peck and Audrey Hepburn," *The New York Times*, August 28, 1953, 13.
71. Steinhart, 130.

72. Following "a criminal attack" by a cyclist in December 1943, the German occupying forces prohibited "the use of bicycles in the territory of the Open City of Rome," "transgressors will be shot [without prior notice]" and "the bicycle will be requisitioned with no right of compensation" (Robert Katz, *Fatal Silence: The Pope, the Resistance and the German Occupation of Rome* (London: Cassell, 2003), 128). This is one of the reasons why Vittorio De Sica's 1948 neorealist film *Bicycle Thieves*, highlighting a crime committed out of necessity, is so historically relevant. In this movie, made three years after World War II, Rome is being depicted as far from welcoming or friendly towards its users, in great contrast with *Roman Holiday*, produced merely five years later.
73. Gundle, 58.
74. Gundle, 70–1.
75. *Roman Holiday press book*, 2.
76. Still #10059-15, *Roman Holiday press book*, 5.
77. <http://vesposofia.altervista.org/filmografia-della-vespa/?doing_wp_cron=1638470236.4653038978576660156250> (last accessed August 24, 2022).
78. Steinhart, 128.
79. Caroline Young, *Roman Holiday: The Secret Life of Hollywood in Rome* (Cheltenham: The History Press, 2020), 80.
80. Anna Cooper and Russell Meeuf, eds. *Projecting the World: Representing the "Foreign" in Classical Hollywood* (Detroit: Wayne State University Press, 2017), 119.
81. Recent examples are *Notting Hill* (Michell, 1999), the tale of a bookseller falling in love with a movie star; *The Talented Mr. Ripley* (Minghella, 1999), *infra*; *Elisabethtown* (C. Crowe, 2005) with Orlando Bloom and Kirsten Dunst watching a scene from *Roman Holiday* on TV; and in *To Rome With Love* (Allen, 2012), Alec Baldwin walks through the Via Margutta where Gregory Peck's character lived.
82. <https://it.usembassy.gov/tribute-gregory-peck/> (last accessed August 24, 2022).

Filmography

SILENT FILMS SERIES

Universal – Mustang series of Westerns

Two reels – 24 minutes $2,000 budget; produced 1 per week.

1925	*The Crook Buster*
1926	*The Gunless Bad Man, Ridin' for Love, The Fire Barrier, Don't Shoot, The Pinnacle Rider, Martin of the Mounted*
1927	*Two Fister, Kelcy Gets His Man, Tenderfoot Courage, The Silent Partner, Galloping Justice, The Haunted Homestead, The Lone Star, The Ore Riders, The Home Trail, Gun Justice, The Phantom Outlaw, The Square Shooter, The Horse Trader, Daze of the West.*

Universal – Blue Streak series of Westerns

Five reels – approximately 1 hour

1926	*Lazy Lightning, The Stolen Ranch*
1927	*Blazing Days, Hard Fists, The Border Cavalier, Straight Shootin'*

SILENT FILMS

1927	*Desert Dust*	Universal	Western
1928	*Thunder Riders*	Universal	Western

1928	*Anybody Here Seen Kelly?*	Universal	Comedy	First non-Western
1929	*The Shakedown*	Universal	Drama	
1929	*The Love Trap*	Universal	Comedy	

SOUND FILMS

1929	*Hell's Heroes*	Universal	Western	
1930	*The Storm*	Universal	Drama	
1931	*A House Divided*	Universal	Drama	
1932	*Tom Brown of Culver*	Universal	Drama	
1933	*Her First Mate*	Universal	Comedy	
1933	*Counsellor at Law*	Universal	Drama	
1934	*Glamour*	Universal	Drama	
1935	*The Good Fairy*	Universal	Comedy	
1935	*The Gay Deception*	Fox Film	Comedy	
1936	*These Three*	Goldwyn/UA	Drama	
1936	*Dodsworth*	Goldwyn/UA	Drama	Nominated Best Picture and Director
1936	*Come and Get It*	Goldwyn/UA	Drama	Co-directed with Hawks
1937	*Dead End*	Goldwyn/UA	Crime	Nominated Best Picture
1938	*Jezebel*	Warner Bros.	Romance	Nominated Best Picture
1939	*Wuthering Heights*	Goldwyn/UA	Romance	Nominated Best Picture and Director
1940	*The Westerner*	Goldwyn/UA	Western	
1940	*The Letter*	Warner Bros.	Drama	Nominated Best Picture and Director
1941	*The Little Foxes*	Goldwyn/RKO	Drama	Nominated Best Picture and Director

Year	Title	Studio	Genre	Awards
1942	Mrs. Miniver	MGM	Drama	Won Best Picture and Director
1944	The Memphis Belle	US War Dept.	Documentary	
1946	The Best Years of Our Lives	Goldwyn/RKO	Drama	Won Best Picture and Director
1947	Thunderbolt	US War Dept.	Documentary	
1949	The Heiress	Paramount	Drama	Nominated Best Picture and Director
1951	Detective Story	Paramount	Film noir	Nominated Best Director
1952	Carrie	Paramount	Drama	
1953	Roman Holiday	Paramount	Romance	Nominated Best Picture and Director
1955	The Desperate Hours	Paramount	Film noir	
1956	Friendly Persuasion	Allied Artists	Drama	Nominated Best Picture and Director
1958	The Big Country	Anthony/UA	Western	
1959	Ben-Hur	MGM	Drama	Won Best Picture and Director
1961	The Children's Hour	Mirsch/UA	Drama	
1965	The Collector	Columbia	Thriller	Nominated Best Director
1966	How to Steal a Million	20th Century Fox	Comedy	
1968	Funny Girl	Columbia	Musical	Nominated Best Picture
1970	The Liberation of L.B. Jones	Columbia	Drama	

Academy Awards for Acting under Wyler

1936	Best Supporting Actor	Won	Walter Brennan	*Come and Get It*
1936	Best Actor	Nominated	Walter Huston	*Dodsworth*
1936	Best Supporting Actress	Nominated	Maria Ouspenskaya	*Dodsworth*
1936	Best Supporting Actress	Nominated	Bonita Granville	*These Three*
1937	Best Supporting Actress	Nominated	Claire Trevor	*Dead End*
1938	Best Supporting Actress	Won	Fay Bainter	*Jezebel*
1938	Best Actress	Won	Bette Davis	*Jezebel*
1939	Best Actor	Nominated	Laurence Olivier	*Wuthering Heights*
1939	Best Supporting Actress	Nominated	Geraldine Fitzgerald	*Wuthering Heights*
1940	Best Supporting Actor	Nominated	James Stephenson	*The Letter*
1940	Best Actress	Nominated	Bette Davis	*The Letter*
1940	Best Supporting Actor	Won	Walter Brennan	*The Westerner*

Year	Category	Result	Nominee	Film
1941	Best Supporting Actress	Nominated	Patricia Collinge	*The Little Foxes*
1941	Best Supporting Actress	Nominated	Teresa Wright	*The Little Foxes*
1941	Best Actress	Nominated	Bette Davis	*The Little Foxes*
1942	Best Supporting Actress	Nominated	Dame May Whitty	*Mrs. Miniver*
1942	Best Supporting Actor	Nominated	Henry Travers	*Mrs. Miniver*
1942	Best Actor	Nominated	Walter Pidgeon	*Mrs. Miniver*
1942	Best Supporting Actress	Won	Teresa Wright	*Mrs. Miniver*
1942	Best Actress	Won	Greer Garson	*Mrs. Miniver*
1946	Best Supporting Actor	Won	Harold Russell	*The Best Years of Our Lives*
1946	Best Actor	Won	Fredric March	*The Best Years of Our Lives*
1949	Best Supporting Actor	Nominated	Ralph Richardson	*The Heiress*
1949	Best Actress	Won	Olivia de Havilland	*The Heiress*
1951	Best Actress	Nominated	Eleanor Parker	*Detective Story*
1951	Best Supporting Actress	Nominated	Lee Grant	*Detective Story*
1953	Best Supporting Actor	Nominated	Eddie Albert	*Roman Holiday*
1953	Best Actress	Won	Audrey Hepburn	*Roman Holiday*
1956	Best Supporting Actor	Nominated	Anthony Perkins	*Friendly Persuasion*
1958	Best Supporting Actor	Won	Burl Ives	*The Big Country*
1959	Best Supporting Actor	Won	Hugh Griffith	*Ben-Hur*

1959	Best Actor	Won	Charlton Heston	*Ben-Hur*
1961	Best Supporting Actress	Nominated	Fay Bainter	*The Children's Hour*
1965	Best Actress	Nominated	Samantha Eggar	*The Collector*
1968	Best Supporting Actress	Nominated	Kay Medford	*Funny Girl*
1968	Best Actress	Won	Barbara Streisand	*Funny Girl*

Index

Academy Awards, 3, 15, 20n15 and n19, 104n19, 111, 112, 197, 205, 229, 266, 279–80, 281–3
adaptation, 89, 103n1, 122, 183; *see also* Victorian novel, Wyler and, and individual movie titles
aesthetics
    European, 271
    Wyler and, 55–7, 66n16
Agee, James, 51, 204
Alsace-Lorraine, 3, 14, 110, 191, 269
Altman, Rick, 70
American Film Institute (AFI), 10, 16
American Madness, 19
Americanism, 4, 16, 205, 231
Andrews, Dana, 58, 68, 83, 100, 192
anti-communism, 228, 240, 260
anti-imperialism, 245, 251, 253, 256
antisemitism, 3, 44
anti-western, 217
Anybody Here Seen Kelly?, 5, 27
architectural space (*espace architecturale*), 93–4
art cinema, 70, 85
aspect ratio 2.35:1, widescreen, 15, 58
auteur (theory), 1, 16, 26, 54–5, 62–4
auteurist(s), 1, 57, 62–3, 65, 146
author-based criticism, 55–6, 65n2
authorship, 6, 54–5, 62, 65n2

Bainter, Fay, 58
Baker, Carroll, 217
Balkin, Karen, 58, 184–5
Barnes, George, 119–20
Barrymore, John, 6, 44, 111
Bazin, André, 2, 16, 25–6, 55–60, 62, 64, 65n6, 66n14, 68–70, 73–4, 77–8, 85, 86n3, 204
Ben-Hur (1925), 4, 245
Ben-Hur (1959), 1, 3, 10, 15, 19n6, 20n16, 27, 40–2, 57, 88, 99, 103, 124, 183, 208–9, 220–2, 228, 236, 240, 245, 248, 250–2, 255–7
    chariot race in, 19, 220–1, 246–8, 256
    Christianity in, 209, 220, 221–2, 253, 255
    imperialism in, 244–54, 255–6
    post-colonialism in, 244–7, 250–1, 252, 256
Bercovici, Leonardo, 237–9
Bergman, Ingmar, 55, 56
Bergman, Ingrid, 111–14, 161, 237
Best Years of Our Lives, The, 3, 6, 14, 21n56, 56–64, 66n17, 71, 74–9, 83–9, 86n14, 87n30, 89, 99–103, 109, 111, 192, 194, 198, 200, 208, 210, 228–9
    deep focus in, 59, 75, 77, 101
    liminal space in, 101

INDEX

myth (and demythologizing) in, 68–70, 79–80, 82, 84–5
    narrative path in, 69–70, 79
    rehabilitation in, 68–74, 77–8, 80–1, 84–5, 204
    stylistic path in, 69–70, 73–4, 86n3
Bickford, Charles, 38, 58, 217
Big Country, The, 15, 20n16, 58, 63, 94, 124, 217
Bishop's Wife, The, 80, 237
blacklist(-ing)(-ed), 16, 104n4, 122, 205, 211, 223n9, 228, 240–1, 243n30, 259, 273n6
Blue Streak series, 5, 27
Bogart, Humphrey, 20n29, 103, 116, 138, 140
Boyd, Stephen, 99, 183, 220, 244, 251
Breen, Joseph, 178–9
Brontë, Emily, 12, 143, 145–7, 153–4

camera movement, 3; see also Wyler and
Capra, Frank, 4, 14, 88, 92–3, 97, 99, 104–5n19, 196, 206n5, 211
Carmichael, Hoagy, 77
Carrie, 11, 21n57, 109–10, 112–24, 229, 233
    as tragic romance, 121, 123
Cavell, Stanley, 54, 161–3, 166, 173, 265
Chandler, Helen, 40
Chaplin, Charlie, 90, 92, 195, 275n35
chiaroscuro lighting, 83
Children's Hour, The (film), 12, 58, 182, 184, 186
Children's Hour, The (play), 11, 176–9, 181
Cinecittà, 122, 228, 235–6, 273
Citizen Kane, 7, 26, 44, 47, 50, 77, 89–90
classic(al) Hollywood, 2–4, 26, 32, 34, 54–5, 69–71, 73–4, 77, 82, 85
classical gangster cycle see gangsters, gangster films
Clift, Montgomery, 123, 163, 237
Cold War, 122, 128, 228–9, 237–8, 240, 258, 260
Collector, The, 15
Collinge, Patricia, 64, 66n17
Come and Get It, 6–7, 86n14

Committee for the First Amendment, 16, 205, 230, 239
Connors, Chuck, 94, 217
Cooper, Gary, 12, 64, 97, 212, 214
Counsellor at Law, 5–6, 15, 40, 42–8, 53n25, 56, 111
Crook Buster, The, 4–5
Currie, Finlay, 221, 254

Davis, Bette, 5, 10–11, 13, 37, 52, 52n20, 56, 58, 64, 94, 112, 145, 162, 164–5, 229
Dead End, 6, 11, 15, 20n29, 20n30, 56, 63, 86n14, 89–92, 103, 111, 127–8, 131–41, 145, 229
deep focus, 3, 7, 8–10, 13, 20n34, 26, 28, 36, 37, 42, 55, 59, 73, 75, 77, 88–90, 101
de Havilland, Olivia, 14, 161
DeMille, Cecil B., 1, 120, 122–3, 205, 231
De Sica, Vittorio, 86n3, 116, 124, 228, 233, 235, 272, 277n72
Desert Dust, 5
Desperate Hours, The, 15, 21n57, 124, 127–8, 131, 134, 136–41
Detective Story, 15, 20n16, 21n57, 56–7, 63, 88, 93, 95–96, 99, 122, 129
dialogue, 97, 166, 179, 197
    Preston Sturges and, 47, 49
    Wyler and, 6–9, 14, 30–2, 34, 36, 38, 40, 42, 47, 49, 67n17, 83, 88–9, 101, 118, 149, 151, 153–4, 181, 193, 216
Diary of a Sergeant, 80–1
Dieterle, William, 89, 112, 115, 231, 233
Dingle, Charles, 64
Directors Guild of America (DGA), 3, 20n16; see also Screen Directors Guild
Dmytryk, Edward, 87n30, 230
Dodsworth, 4, 6, 12, 40, 89, 90–1, 99, 103, 111
Douglas, Kirk, 15, 57, 95, 122, 237
Dreiser, Theodore, 109, 112, 114, 118–19, 121–2, 229
dual-focus, 69–72

Dunkirk, 193–5
Duryea, Dan, 67n17

Ellis, Robert, 32
Epictetus, 162, 165, 172
ethics of criticism, 62–3
European immigration to Hollywood, 3–4
expressionism, 83; *see also* German Expressionism

film noir, 15, 42, 48, 83, 85, 88, 129, 138
filmic space (*éspace filmique*), 93–4, 96
five-reelers, 5, 27
Fonda, Henry, 52n20, 94, 112
Ford, John, 2, 14, 53n24, 54–5, 65n6, 89–90, 196–7, 212, 228
Foreign Correspondent, 195
formalism, 25
Fox Films, later Twentieth Century Fox, 6, 51, 178, 183
frame within a frame, 32, 35, 38, 39
framing, 94; *see also* Wyler and
Freeman, Frank, 122, 236, 238–9
Friendly Persuasion, 15–16, 20n16, 40, 64, 104n4, 105n19, 208–12, 215–17, 219, 222, 223n9
Funny Girl, 15, 20n16, 88

gangsters, gangster films
  amplified failure in, 130–4, 136–8, 140–1
  civilian-hero in, 130, 136, 139–40
  classical gangster cycle, 127–30, 132–4, 136–7, 140
  dual protagonist in, 127–8, 130, 132, 135, 138–9
  gangster-loser, 133–4, 141
  gangster-villain, 134, 136, 138–41
  and the modern city, 128, 132
  prolonged fall in, 137–9
Garner, James, 184
Garson, Greer, 11, 191, 193, 210
Gay Deception, The, 6, 15, 51, 102, 178
generational trauma, 144–6
"genius of the system," 62

genre, 62, 70, 88, 127, 129–30, 132, 134, 147, 155, 161–3, 197, 260; *see also* Wyler and
German Expressionism, 4; *see also* expressionism
Glory for Me, 80, 202
God's Step Children, 181–2
Goldwyn, Samuel, 2, 6–7, 10–11, 14, 20n32, 52, 80, 89–90, 111, 113, 144–6, 151–3, 155, 176, 178, 181, 183, 202
Gone with the Wind, 111–12, 124
Good Fairy, The, 6, 11, 13, 44, 47, 49, 88
Gothic(ism), 111, 143, 145, 147–53, 155
Great Dictator, The, 195
Greed, 26
Griffith, Hugh, 221, 248

Hamilton, Neil, 32
Hanlon, Jack, 30
Harareet, Haya, 221, 255
Hawkins, Jack, 254
Hawks, Howard, 6, 14, 54–5, 89, 97, 127, 212
Hays Code, 154–5
hearing loss *see* Wyler and
Hegelian, 163, 166–7, 169, 170
Heiress, The, 14, 40–1, 90, 98–9, 111, 115, 122, 161–74
  freedom in, 161–9, 171–2
  humiliation in, 163–5, 171–3
  repetition in, 163, 172–3
  self-reliance in, 163, 165, 168
Hellman, Lillian, 11–13, 20n30, 176, 178–9, 181–4, 186
Hell's Heroes, 5, 12, 38–9, 53n24, 88
Hepburn, Audrey, 11, 15, 98, 184, 227–8, 234, 258, 261–2, 265–8, 275n33
Her First Mate, 39–40
Herman, Jan, 1, 12, 16, 208, 217
Heston, Charlton, 10, 57, 94, 99, 216, 220, 244, 251
High Noon, 97, 212–13, 219
Hitchcock, Alfred, 2, 54, 56, 88, 93, 97, 111–12, 195
Hitler, Adolph, 214, 219, 221

Hollywood on the Tiber, 240–1
Hollywood Ten, 211, 230–1, 239
Hopkins, Miriam, 163, 179, 184
House Committee on Un-American Activities or House Un-American Activities Committee (HUAC), 16, 122, 211, 230, 232–3, 237, 239–40
House Divided, A, 12, 20n17, 39–40
How to Steal a Million, 15, 102
human condition, 86n7; *see also* Wyler and the
humor, 143, 184, 247; *see also* Wyler and
Huston, John, 3, 14, 16, 20n17, 39–40, 84–5, 115, 124, 129, 133, 145–6, 186, 191, 196–7, 230, 238–9
Huston, Walter, 12, 40, 99

image facts, 69–70, 74
imperialism *see* in *Ben-Hur* (1959)
Intermezzo, 113–14
intertitles, 34, 38
invisible style, 2, 25–6, 73
isolationism, 13, 210
It Happened One Night, 97
Italian film industry, 228, 232, 235–7, 273
Italy, 79, 199, 201, 206 227–9, 232–8, 240, 258–60, 271, 273
Ives, Burl, 58, 94, 216

Jaffe, Sam, 255
James, Henry, 115, 163, 167
Jewish (people and culture), 14, 44, 209, 220–1, 244, 246, 248, 250, 253–4
  Wyler, 3, 14, 110, 191, 209
Jezebel, 10, 20n17, 52n20, 56, 63, 94, 103, 112, 229
Jones, Jennifer, 109–11, 115–21, 123–4

Kantor, MacKinlay, 80, 87n24, 202
Kelly, Grace, 213, 219
Kent, Barbara, 30
Kingsley, Sidney, 20n30, 145
Klein, Amanda Ann, 127, 130–2, 135
Kohner, Paul, 238–9
Kotsonaros, George, 28
Kubrick, Stanley, 62, 257n3

Kuleshovian, 94
Kurosawa, Akira, 55
Kyne, Peter B., 53n24

La Plante, Laura, 30
Laemmle, Carl, 4, 110
Laemmle Jr., Carl, 7
Lazy Lightning, 5
Lee, Jocelyn, 32
LeRoy, Mervyn, 123, 127, 180, 234
lesbianism, 178, 180, 186; *see also The Children's Hour* (play) and (film), and *These Three*
Letter from an Unknown Woman, 161–3
Letter, The, 13, 56, 111, 229
Liberation of L. B. Jones, 15
Liberty Films, 14, 21n57, 104–5n19, 211
liminal spaces, 101, 237, 252–3
Little Caesar, 127–8, 131, 134
Little Foxes, The, 6–7, 9–10, 13, 37, 40, 58, 64, 66n17, 86n14, 109, 111, 164–5
Long Voyage Home, The, 90
Love Trap, The, 5, 27, 30, 33–7, 93
Loy, Myrna, 71, 101

McCrea, Joel, 179
McGuire, Dorothy, 111, 213
MacLaine, Shirley, 184–6
Mädchen in Uniform, 178
Mamoulian, Rouben, 89
March, Fredric, 68, 139, 201
Marshall, Herbert, 58
masculinity, 75, 183, 270; *see also* in *The Big Country*, and in gangster films
master and slave dialectics, 163, 166–7, 169
Maté, Rudolph, 90
Mayo, Virginia, 71, 100, 200
Meet McGonegal, 81
melodrama(tic), 26–30, 32, 40, 47, 69–71, 81, 130–2, 135–6, 152, 173–4
  and moral identity, 86n9
  and the unknown woman, 161–2, 173
  mute, 82
myth, 73, 80, 82
redemption plot, 131, 135

288 INDEX

Memphis Belle, 102, 192, 199
Memphis Belle, The, 14, 79, 102, 192, 194, 198–9, 200–1, 229
meta-filmic, 88, 98–9
Metro-Goldwyn-Mayer (MGM), 15, 90, 110, 115, 183, 234
Micheaux, Oscar, 181–2
Miller, Gabriel, 146, 154–5, 208, 214–17, 219–21
Mirisch (Corporation), 183
mise-en-abyme, 170
mise en scène, 3, 13, 25–6, 57, 59, 74, 77–8, 204
montage, 3, 25, 29, 38
Morgan, Frank, 49
motifs, 2, 32, 40, 58–9, 86n8, 103, 118
MPAA, 176, 260
Mrs. Miniver, 3, 11, 13–14, 19, 88, 90, 98, 109, 111, 192–6, 198–200, 204–5, 210, 229
  as propaganda, 14, 104n16, 104n18, 193, 195
Mulhouse (Mülhausen), 3, 110, 191, 206n1
multiple-focus, 70–1, 74–5, 77–8
multiple planes *see* Wyler and
Murray, James, 27
Mustang series, 4, 27
myth, 85n2, 162, 217, 272; *see also* in *Best Years of Our Lives*, and melodramatic myth

National Socialism (Nazi), 3, 14, 98, 199, 210
neorealism, 62, 74, 228, 235–7, 260
Neutrality Act (U.S. neutrality), 14, 21n54
neutrality and transparency of style, 26, 57
Nye-Clark Senate Committee, 21n54

O'Donnell, Cathy, 72, 202, 220, 246
Oberon, Merle, 66n16, 145, 152–5, 179
Olivier, Laurence, 11, 66n16, 103n1, 109, 116–17, 120–1, 153–5, 229
"opening up" a play, 6, 20n26
Othello, 94
Owen, Reginald, 47

pacifism, 208–13, 215–22
Paramount Pictures, 21n57, 105n19, 109–22, 124, 183, 211, 227, 233–6, 238–9, 260–2, 271–2
Parker, Eleanor, 57, 96
part-talkie, 5, 27
Peck, Gregory, 4, 64, 94, 98, 112, 217, 227–8, 232, 258, 261, 268, 273
Perkins, Anthony, 213
Perkins, V. F., 55–64, 66n14
pictorial space (*espace picturale*), 93–6
Place in the Sun, A, 122, 211
post-colonialism *see* in *Ben-Hur*
Preminger, Otto, 54, 183, 232
primordial scene, 163–7, 172
Production Code administration (PCA), 110, 129, 177–9, 181–4
propaganda, 14, 21n54, 100, 193, 196–7, 260–1; *see also* Mrs. Miniver as
Public Enemy, The, 129–31, 135

Quaker(-ism), 209–13, 216

Ray, Nicholas, 54
realism, 6, 25–6, 40, 52n18
  reborn realism, 68–70, 72–4, 82, 85, 86n3 and n9; *see also* Wyler's sense of realism
Rebecca, 111, 119
Red Scare, 100, 228, 231–3, 239, 241
Reid, Carl Benton, 64, 67n17
Rice, Elmer, 42
Richardson, Ralph, 98, 163
RKO, 77, 110
Rohmer, Eric, 93–4, 96–7
Roman Holiday, 15, 88, 93, 98, 105n19, 122, 124, 208, 227–30, 233–8, 240–1, 258–63, 265–73
romance, 110–11, 121, 123, 146–8, 151–5, 168, 184, 227, 240, 260, 267, 273
Rome in Love, 272
Rossellini, Roberto, 70, 86n3, 228, 232–3, 237, 272
Russell, Harold, 21n56, 56, 68, 80–2, 100, 194, 202, 205
Ruttenberg, Joseph, 90

Sarris, Andrew, 55, 63, 66n14
Scarface, 127–8, 131, 134
Schatz, Thomas, 127–30, 132, 134–5, 192
Scott, Martha, 220, 246
Screen Directors Guild, 205, 231; *see also* Directors Guild of America (DGA)
Selznick, David O., 178–9, 110–24
  collaborations, 112, 124; *see also* Wyler collaborations with Selznick
sentimentality, 39, 69, 80, 123, 147–8
Shakedown, The, 5, 7, 8, 27–31, 56
Sherwood, Robert, 80, 84, 202–3
silent films, 34, 132, 144, 181, 245, 269; *see also* Wyler and
single-focus, 69–72, 77
Simmons, Jean, 94, 217, 262
Sister Carrie (novel), 109–10, 112, 114, 117
Sound of Music, The, 20n14
sound 5, 34, 36, 38, 40, 72; *see also* Wyler and
staging-in-depth, 2–3, 8, 13, 25–39, 42, 49–51, 52n18, 90, 215, 222
Stevens, George, 14, 66n14, 104n19, 122, 211
stoicism, 162–3, 166, 172, 174
Storm, The, 15, 39
Streisand, Barbara, 10, 17
Sturges, Preston, 88, 93; *see also* dialogue
"styleless style," 2–3, 26, 57, 73
Sullavan, Margaret, 11–12, 47

tableau composition, 34, 37
Tallichet, Margaret "Talli," 12, 112–13
temporality, 29, 34, 98, 153, 173–4
temporal duration, 69, 73–4
temporal reality, 30
These Three, 6–7, 11, 40–1, 111, 176, 179–84, 186
Three Godfathers, The, 53n24
Thring, Frank, 247
Thunder Riders, 5
Thunderbolt, 14, 79, 192, 198–201, 229
Thunderbolts, 191, 192, 197, 201
Till the End of Time, 87n30

Toland, Gregg, 2, 7, 10, 13–14, 20n34, 26, 47, 52, 77, 86n14, 89–90, 92–3, 100–1, 114
Tom Brown of Culver, 39–40
Tover, Leo, 90
transnational(-ism), 143, 146, 153, 155, 229
Trevor, Norman, 36
tropes, 5, 26, 88
Trumbo, Dalton, 228, 230, 259
two-reelers, 4–5, 27, 88, 110

United Artists, 183–4
Universal Pictures, 4–7, 12, 27, 44, 51, 52, 89–90, 93, 110, 178

verisimilitude, 6, 25, 68–70, 72–4, 77, 83–4
veterans, 14, 68–9, 72, 74, 79–80, 83–4, 100, 111, 201–5, 233
Victorian novel, 143, 143–4, 146–7, 153, 155
Vidor, King, 110–11, 124, 161
violence, 82, 128–9, 131, 137, 139–40, 149, 151, 208–10, 212–22, 244–6, 248, 250–2, 255–7
von Sternberg, Josef, 4, 93
von Stroheim, Erich, 4, 26
Vorhaus, Bernard, 237–9

Waldorf Statement, 205
Wallace, Gen. Lew, 220, 245
Wallace, Henry, 231, 239–40
Warner Bros., 10, 112, 140, 145, 183
Washington Square, 115, 163, 167
Washington Square, 169–71
Wayne, John, 116, 212–13
Well of Loneliness, The, 180
Welles, Orson, 7, 26, 44, 77, 86n3, 89–90, 93–4, 103
Wellman, William, 105n19, 111, 130
West, Jessamyn, 104n4, 211–12, 215–16
Westerner, The, 6, 12, 27, 86n14, 111
Westerns, 3–6, 12, 26–7, 58, 86n7, 88–9, 94 110–11, 124, 210, 217
Wilder, Billy, 4, 17, 230
Wilson, Michael, 104n4, 211–12
Wise, Robert, 20n14

Wizard of Oz, The, 51
World War I, 3–4, 81, 210
World War II, 68, 85, 99–100, 140, 192, 208, 211, 228, 233, 240, 245, 258, 269, 271
Wright, Teresa, 58, 67n17, 71, 98, 100, 194, 203
Wuthering Heights, 6–8, 11–13, 66n16, 89, 99, 109, 111, 113–14, 143–8, 152–5
Wyler, Robert, 16, 104n4, 211, 216
Wyler, William; *see also individual film titles*
  and abstraction, 57–8, 60
  and adaptation, 5–6, 12–14, 42, 47, 103 n1, 163, 167, 176, 184, 186, 211, 245, 251
  and anger, 103, 244
  and camera angles, 7, 42, 89, 90–1, 96, 164
  and camera movement, 2, 6, 26–8, 30, 38, 42, 52n20, 72, 83; dolly moves, 30, 94, 95; tracking shots, 26, 29–30, 32, 38
  and close-ups, 28–30, 34, 40, 60, 74, 77, 83, 94
  collaborations, 2, 110, 112; with Toland, 7, 10, 26, 52, 89, 90, 92, 100; with actors, 5–6, 40, 52; with Goldwyn, 6–7, 52; with John Huston, 39; with Selznick, 110–24
  and documentary look, 5, 39, 85
  and framing, 32, 38, 57, 74, 83, 93–5, 120, 171, 180, 215
  and genre(s), 1–3, 12, 15, 26–7, 85, 88, 124, 127, 130, 132–3, 162, 197, 210, 217, 258, 273
  and hearing loss, 14, 79–80, 197, 201–2, 206
  and the human condition, 4, 11, 40, 63
  and human relationships, 2, 13, 27, 63
  and humor, 16, 30, 32, 34, 49, 214
  and immigrant experience, 3–4
  and long shots, 32, 60, 94
  and multiple planes, 28, 73, 75, 92, 101
  perfectionist, 1, 7, 11
  realism, sense of, 2, 5–7, 11–12, 26–7, 30–4, 38–42, 83, 152, 233; *see also* reborn realism
  and silent films, 4–5, 7, 27, 30, 32, 37
  and simultaneous action, 77–8
  and sound, 5, 12, 27, 30, 34, 37–40, 61, 72, 83, 144, 149, 234, 237, 270
  and stairs, 13, 40–2, 163, 165, 172, 182
  storytelling, 16, 64, 89
  visual style, 4, 44, 52, 77

Zimbalist, Sam, 1–2
Zinnemann, Fred, 97, 212